Between the Sheets,
In the Streets

VISIBLE EVIDENCE

Edited by Michael Renov, Faye Ginsburg, and Jane Gaines

Public confidence in the "real" is everywhere in decline. This series will offer a forum for the in-depth consideration of the representation of the real, with books that will engage issues that bear upon questions of cultural and historical representation, and that forward the work of challenging prevailing notions of the "documentary tradition" and of nonfiction culture more generally.

Between the Sheets, In the Streets

Queer, Lesbian, Gay Documentary

Chris Holmlund and Cynthia Fuchs, *editors*

University of Minnesota Press

Minneapolis

London

Published by the University of Minnesota Press
111 Third Avenue South, Suite 290, Minneapolis, MN 55401-2520
Printed in the United States of America on acid-free paper

Series design by Will H. Powers
Typeset in Sabon and Memphis by Stanton Publication Services, Inc.

Library of Congress Cataloging-in-Publication Data

Between the sheets, in the streets : queer, lesbian, gay documentary /
  Chris Holmlund and Cynthia Fuchs, editors.
      p.   cm.—(Visible evidence ; v. 1)
   Includes bibliographical references and index.
   Filmography: p.
   ISBN 0-8166-2774-6 (hardcover : alk. paper).—ISBN 0-8166-2775-4
(pbk. : alk. paper)
   1. Documentary mass media—United States.   2. Gays in popular
culture—United States.   I. Holmlund, Chris.   II. Fuchs, Cynthia.
III. Series.
P96.D622U63   1997
306.76′6—dc21   96-47751

The University of Minnesota is an equal-opportunity educator and employer.

To Roxanne Ellis and Michelle Abdill, longtime partners known for their tireless work against anti-gay ballot measures in rural Oregon. In December 1995 they were murdered by a California man who said that the fact that they were gay "made it easier." We value their courage, their lives, and their love.

Contents

Acknowledgments

When she is asked who influences her work, video artist Sadie Benning sometimes replies that people she hates influence her a lot—people who are, in her words, "just total assholes." Many people we despise have motivated our editing of this book, though like Benning we will do the right (as opposed to the New Right) thing and avoid mentioning them by name . . .

We do have a lot of people we would like to thank, first and foremost all of the contributors to this volume: their love, support, ideas, and criticism have stimulated and sustained us during the three years we have worked on *Between the Sheets, In the Streets,* as have all of the films and videos they, and we, have written about. The warmest of thanks to Diane Waldman and Chon Noriega for commenting on the original manuscript and, later, the introduction, and for sharing their takes on the process of editing. Sincere thanks, too, to Chuck Kleinhans for his suggestions regarding the proposal. The responses of the participants at the second Visible Evidence Film and Documentary Conference organized by Jane Gaines, José Muñoz, Tom Whiteside, and Michael Renov and held at Duke University were energizing; this book grew out of that conference—during panel presentations and discussions, over dinners, on shopping expeditions. We are grateful that Jane and Michael have supported this enterprise from the start. The keen interest and steady encouragement that our first editor at Minnesota, Janaki Bakhle, showed in the project made a difference in how we felt and thought about editing a book; fortunately, our current editor, Micah Kleit, is as committed as Janaki and we are to social (broadly defined) documentary. As women who have, respectively, taught French grammar and English composition in past lives, we have also truly appreciated Lynn Marasco's careful copyediting and Mary Byers's managing.

Our "families," in the expansive sense the word has among queers, lesbians, and gays, have made and make a difference: Chris thanks her dad, brother, Knoxville buddies, and friends around the United States and Europe; Cindy thanks her sister, Ellise, and her queer theory students. We are also indebted to all those real and fictional "characters," including but not limited to writers, artists, actors, activists, and secretaries, who have helped us with and through this project.

Last but not least we would like to acknowledge each other and to recall how much fun we have managed to have as we have worked on this manuscript, reading drafts, exchanging ideas, watching movies, even eating cold pizza.

CHRIS HOLMLUND
CYNTHIA FUCHS

Introduction

> As I've gone along, it seems more important to . . . look out
> both the front and back doors as well as windows; to still
> assume that there are infinite possibilities in how a film can
> be made, and what it can say. . . . If someone feels deeply
> moved by the plight of an oppressed group, and thinks their
> message should be delivered in a rational, linear, accessible
> voice, then so be it. If someone else is a gifted storyteller and
> believes in the efficacy of narrative devices for presenting
> that story, more power to her or him. And if someone else
> wants to make a film about walls and floors and sunlight,
> then I hope he or she does it so that I see those floors as I've
> never seen them before.
> ::   Su Friedrich

▶━━

Seeing and Speaking "Differently"

We begin with this statement by lesbian experimental filmmaker Su
Friedrich because we find it exemplary in two senses, typical and paradig-
matic.[1] Noteworthy, we feel, is Friedrich's catholic appreciation of both
documenting and storytelling. Significant too is her uncoupling, in 1989, of
identity (and not just lesbian or gay identity) from any particular aesthetic.
As we and other contributors to *Between the Sheets, In the Streets* will argue, the desire to acknowledge, challenge, and expand conventional ways
of seeing that Friedrich expresses here characterizes many contemporary
queer/lesbian/gay films and videos, much recent criticism, and some earlier
homosexual work as well.[2] That this should be so is not surprising: after
all, to see and be seen is a matter not only of visual representation but also
of social acceptance and political clout. Increasingly, queer media makers

and queer critics also take up questions of communication and translation, reconsidering how speaking and naming, silence and suggestion, are expressed and experienced.[3]

In this volume on queer/lesbian/gay documentary we continue to explore the implications of grounding art and activism in metaphors of seeing and speaking "differently," complementing, questioning, and, we hope, extending work begun by others. This is not to imply, of course, that we, as contributors, always agreed about this project. After all, for those who identify or are identified as gay, lesbian, bisexual, transgendered, or queer, identities, identifications, and hence politics are inevitably complicated, often contradictory. Nevertheless, all fourteen of us would concur with Su Friedrich that openness to "the infinite possibilities of how a film can be made" is vital, especially since firm distinctions among documentary, fiction, and avant-garde films and videos are increasingly untenable.

Because generic distinctions do still shape the reception, distribution, and exhibition of documentaries on both individual and institutional levels,[4] however, these essays focus squarely—yet perversely—on documentary, charting some of the overlaps and disjunctures that emerge from what Bill Nichols calls the "status of documentary film as *evidence from* the world" and the "status of documentary as *discourse about* the world."[5] Several articles in this anthology discuss texts and viewing experiences that exceed familiar equations of documentary with the historical, material world in order to examine diverse documentaries' changing relations to truth, trust, emotion, reason, and belief.

That this anthology, with its dual emphasis on queer/lesbian/gay identities and documentary representations, should appear at this time is no coincidence. Recent book-length works on documentary addressed to academic audiences make a point of acknowledging the presence, proliferation, and importance of queer documentary, though usually only in individual essays or chapters.[6] Many queer studies collections examine queer documentaries, but typically without overt concern for documentary as such.[7] Queer popular and activist publications often review queer documentaries and are widely read by gays and lesbians, but they remain largely unknown by other communities of readers.[8]

Our primary goal in editing and contributing to this book is not, however, to legitimate queer documentary as either an academic or a popular subfield. As queer media critics and activists, we are keenly aware that for lesbian, gay, bisexual, and transgendered people, sexuality (the sheets) and activism (the streets) are closely connected. We have only to turn on the television, open a magazine, or walk down the street to be reminded of the central role accorded queer representations in New Right attacks on funding for the arts; to witness the deadly repercussions of mass media portrayals of AIDS as a "gay disease" (with all HIV-positive people marginalized as "nominally queer");[9] to encounter stereotypical or homophobic portrayals of queers in popular fiction, films, and television shows.

The extent to which such concerns and experiences are recognized, known, or shared by nonqueers is, however, less clear. We link textual analyses to our own and others' lived experiences in our essays because we want to make the conditions and effects of queer cultures more broadly accessible. At the same time, because we believe it is important to study the effects that documentary representations have had, can have, in charged ideological contexts, we examine the impact that different contexts and intertextual knowledge have on production and reception.

Like the works we analyze, we aim, in short, simultaneously to document queers and to queer documentary. We seek, in addition, to increase the visibility of queer documentaries beyond the venues of lesbian and gay media festivals. We wish, further, to resist the heterosexist, racist, sexist, and classist restrictions that have relegated such important and far-reaching work to "social margins." And we want, finally, to salute the courage and creativity of makers, programmers, distributors, and audiences.

To these ends, all of the essays here work the boundaries of familiar categories of genre and identity, reality and representation. By delineating some of the problems and possibilities that attend definitions, and by reformulating differences so that they might also, at times, be understood as connections, the book as a whole aims to trouble all four terms following the main title—queer, lesbian, gay, and documentary.

▶ ─────────────────────────────────────

Queering Documentary

Most documentary theorists and many makers point to the difficulty of deciding what is and what is not documentary, particularly when textual characteristics are at stake. Trinh T. Minh-ha, for example, has famously asserted that "there is no such thing as a documentary, whether the term designates a category of material, a genre, or a set of techniques."[10] Following Georges Franju, she insists that "reality runs away" in, by, and throughout representation, an assessment that, while it may seem obvious, also provokes another, perhaps preliminary, question: what can this "reality" be?[11]

Even as we take Trinh's argument seriously and are conscious that "reality" is never translatable to a fixed "document" to be possessed or perused, that multiple, unstable "realities" are present as profilmic events and experiences, we realize that documentaries do exist, in rhetorical and political dimensions. Definitions are necessary, we recognize, for communication and exchange, yet we would emphasize the extent to which they are effects, of policy and history. What constitutes "reality" and "documentary" changes over time, in response to technological and institutional shifts. New forms of media (video, film, and transfers from one media to another) affect how we conceptualize documentary. Nevertheless, the belief persists that documentary is a medium that, in Julianne Burton's words, "simply packages and transmits information to passive viewers."[12] And this belief determines not only which works are regarded as documentaries but also which works are funded, exhibited, and broadcast as documentaries.

Some of the films and videos we discuss in this volume will be readily recognizable as documentaries, because they employ voice-of-God narration, long takes and sync sound, talking heads, archival photographs and footage, interviews, and so on. The majority of films and videos analyzed here are not, however, usually categorized as documentaries, and therefore fall outside the institutional and discursive networks established for documentary. Most have been previously classified, funded, and exhibited as "experimental" or "avant-garde" works. Many—a prime example is *Silverlake Life*—self-consciously assert their distance from and debts to documentary traditions in order to reinscribe, expose, and contest familiar techniques around what many straight and more than a few queer viewers will consider to be unfamiliar content.

That so many spectators, when (if) they see these films, find them "queer" in the sense of weird, odd, or perverse necessarily speaks to the representational regime that queer/lesbian/gay documentaries must negotiate, where reality, truth, and valued representations are always a priori, and usually implicitly, heterosexual. While some of the works we analyze date from the 1960s, 1970s, and early 1980s, it is not coincidental that most have been made since 1985, as by-products of and contributors to the gay, lesbian, and, most recently, queer political movements that have redefined identity and politics in relation to public spaces, community, and the nation. Because the situations and subjects that these works seek to document and (re)imagine are fluid, at risk, and in flux, most of them mix documentary modes; a few also mix media, and many consciously blur distinctions between documentary and fiction. Each text is nonetheless "a fiction unlike any other,"[13] speaking to and about worlds that exist "outside" and "inside" of ourselves, assuming the efficacy of social actors and groups, and, crucially, providing a source of counterinformation to hegemonic news media.

Overtly or implicitly concerned with representing subjects in cultures as well as subjects "out" in cultures, many of these queer documentaries also link ethnography and autobiography. That they do so is not, however, an exclusive feature of queer/lesbian/gay documentary: as Nichols points out in "The Ethnographer's Tale," many documentarists are currently engaged in studies of their own cultures. Instead of assuming a classic ethnographic paradigm in which "We speak about Them to Us," "We" must now assume responsibility for framing and shaping what "We" see and represent. This "We" is, as a result, more likely than ever before to be somehow framed through autobiography, as "I speak about myself for myself and others like me," "I speak about Us for Us," "We speak about Ourselves to Them," or "We speak about Them speaking about Us."[14]

As ethnography and autobiography become more recognizable as constructed processes of representation, the places of the first-person narrator and the singular subject are thrown open to a variety of questions, many revolving around issues of representativeness. In our essays about these queer/lesbian/gay documentaries we generally agree that no longer does "being representative" equal being a "positive image," that no longer can we assume a transparent correspondence between sign and meaning. For us, seeing and speaking "differently" requires challenging cultural assumptions about what constitute "positive images" and volitional speech, especially since binary models of difference so often restrict how gender, race, sexuality, and age can be thought, lived, and represented.

Moreover, as we see it, autobiographical and ethnographic studies of "our own cultures" compel studies of "our own audiences." Throughout these essays, we acknowledge the impact that specific contexts, interpretive communities, and sexual and emotional desires have on reception. As Bruce Brasell notes elsewhere of John Greyson's *The Making of "Monsters,"* "Queer audiences and queer filmmakers collaborate to produce a queer discourse, one which exists not only during the film viewing process but which also circulates outside in the streets of the lesbian and gay community."[15]

Yet how this queer discourse arises and circulates, what form it takes, what effect it has, are not obvious, predictable, or guaranteed. To begin an exploration of the paths that this collaborative, constitutional process follows, several contributors look at how the films and videos they study are contextualized on television (PBS or MTV), as part of queer media festivals, through direct-mail campaigns, even in wide theatrical release and then on to video, available for rental at some video stores or through certain mail-order outfits. Other authors analyze the impact of extratextual and intertextual materials. All survey ways in which identities and identifications are framed, negotiated, and interpreted. We therefore, again like the queer/lesbian/gay documentaries we write about, aim not only to analyze the present and study the past, but also to envision the future.

Our discussions of reception necessarily exceed problems of documentary definition in that they also hinge on the elasticity of lesbian, gay, bisexual, and transgendered identities. In our essays we explore the various meanings "queer," "lesbian," and "gay" can have in diverse contexts, and we necessarily ask how viable, desirable, or effective, for whom and for what reasons, definitions of identity can be.

As editors, we list three terms evocative of identity in the after-the-colon title of this book because we recognize that for many individuals and communities, "identity" is a critical concern, a matter of lived relations, a jumping-off point for political involvement. We include three terms to call attention to the diversity of audiences and artists; there could, perhaps should, have been more, for identities are increasingly mixed and multiple in (post)modern societies. We intend the slashes between these terms to be awkward, distracting, performative, to point to how language can never quite keep up with developing cultural and political realities.

We choose *queer* as a fighting word, designating resistance to ongoing social and physical abuses, and suggesting generational allegiances and differences. Like Alexander Doty and bell hooks, we see the term *queer* "as both . . . a consciously chosen 'site of resistance' and a 'location of radical openness and possibility'" for the expression of erotically "marginal" perspectives.[16] *Queer* is also, for now, the most inclusive term available, in many instances used also to address bisexual and transgendered concerns as well as those considered gay and lesbian. Finally, and precisely because we are aware that *queer* can be reduced to opposition, marginality, and/or lesbian and gay, we intend the word *queer* to question and exceed binary distinctions based on physical boundaries, to point to the ways in which, as Doty puts it, "the queer . . . operates within the nonqueer, as the nonqueer does within the queer."[17]

We include *lesbian* and *gay* in our title, however, because we do not want gender or sexual orientation to be lost to view, and because the majority of the essays collected here do focus on lesbian and gay images. As women, we know that women in particular tend to get lost under the expansive weight of *queer*. We would therefore stress, with the Bad Object-Choices group, that "access to power and resources and consequent visibility continue to be unequal across gender, maintaining a comparatively greater marginalization of lesbians than of gay men."[18]

The problem, of course, with each of the three terms we use is that they are not mutually exclusive, but instead are, in Michael Warner's words, "defined by multiple boundaries that make the question of who is and who is not 'one of them' not merely ambiguous but rather a perpetually and necessarily contested issue."[19] Such multiplicities can be at once liberatory and dangerous. As Martha Gever writes, "to *be* a lesbian means engaging in a complex, often treacherous, system of cultural identities, representations and institutions, and a history of sexual regulation."[20] Conceptualizing such identities becomes additionally difficult because what Warner calls "different identity environments" (for instance, race-based and gender-based movements, queer movements, and other "new" social movements, such as those organized around peace and environmental concerns) are "neither parallel—so that the tactics and values of one might be assumed to be appropriate for another—nor separable."[21]

Recognizing that identity politics are premised on shifting grounds—sometimes interwoven, often disjunctive—these essays thus regard "identity" as situational, provisional, and rhetorical rather than essential. Nevertheless, or perhaps consequently, what terms are used and how they might be understood vary from essay to essay, sometimes even within individual essays. Facile analogies to former modes of theorizing and organizing around fixed notions of race, gender, and class are inadequate, because visibility and voicing function differently for lesbians, gays, and queers than they might for more clearly "marked" embodied identities; because homosexual, bisexual, and transgendered identities do not conform to the same logics of inclusion and exclusion dictated by more manifest markers; and because all three terms are also, simultaneously, inflected by race, class, and age. As a result, as Evelynn Hammond argues in "Black (W)holes," the goal cannot be only to be seen or, for that matter, heard: "visibility in and of itself does not erase a history of silence nor does it challenge the structure of power and domination, symbolic and material, that determines what can and cannot be seen."[22] The consequences of Hammond's statement for queer/lesbian/gay documentaries are, we find, profound.

Organizing Strategies

In arranging the essays in this book, we as editors were confronted with exactly these difficulties of definition. Our response has been to establish four divisions that blur distinctions among documentary, avant-garde, and fiction as genres, and lesbian, gay, and queer sexualities as identities. These divisions are designed to function less as a linear mapping than as a set of intersections: each is conceived to fold into and take issue with the others, in ways that question the value of groupings even as they assume their rhetorical efficacy. All suggest new ways of seeing and articulating experiences, ways that privilege instability and nuance, interpretation and expansiveness.

We begin with "Markers" to emphasize the importance of location in perception. Ronald Gregg's essay highlights a situation all too familiar to queers since the late 1970s, when Anita Bryant, John Briggs, and other New Righters began to redefine and defend "family values." Gregg looks at how these attacks were directed and defenses offered in media representations developed around Oregon's Ballot Measure 9, voicing concern about the ways a politics premised on "mainstreaming" fuels both self-censorship and the censorship of marginal groups. Chris Cagle posits that, though it is posed as a "national" movement, "queer" frequently means specifically Northern and/or metropolitan, while Southern queers living in the South are viewed as an amorphous group of "others." Documentary work on Southern queers living in the South is limited, exacerbating the problem, though Marlon Riggs and Ellen Spiro have begun to speak about, show, and listen to Southern queers, albeit as "exiles." Erika Suderburg extends these examinations of location and representation by focusing on the tropes of journey and travel, examining who is addressed and positioned as "young queers" in metropolises and on the road in three television series three decades apart. Because she looks at changes in how "reality" is formulated and marketed over time and according to age, her piece, we feel, serves as a bridge to the second section of the collection, "Memories."

"Memories" brings together essays on broad questions about remembering and representing the past, the better to evaluate the present and prepare for the future. Our understanding of temporality is not fixed: the past is not a singular experience, and it is continually refracted and rewritten. Linda Dittmar focuses on documentaries about and by older lesbians. Although she acknowledges that lesbian audiences enjoy and sometimes even prefer straightforward "feel good" portraits of aging, in large part because our society so thoroughly rejects single, sick, solitary old women, she argues that, to help effect change, documentary investigations of the institutional parameters bounding individual lives are needed. Marc Siegel studies Jack Smith's *Flaming Creatures*, considering its reception as a documentary and linking it to current performance-based documentaries. For Siegel, the controversies and debates occasioned by Smith's film for nearly three decades offer an opportunity to reevaluate the strategies deployed to defend sexually explicit experimental works that, like *Creatures*, challenge the normalization of erotic life. Thomas Waugh reevaluates 1970s and early 1980s gay and lesbian documentaries, also with regard to performance, and suggests that erotic films ("cumming out") and affirmation documentary ("coming out") are involved in similar projects of self-declaration. In conclusion he notes the unavailability of earlier films, the threats of renewed censorship, and the historical amnesia of queer youth living in a now-oriented culture, urging readers to consider the perceived political gains of the present in light of the "famine years" of the past.

Echoing themes raised in "Markers" and "Memories," the section entitled "Marriage and Mourning" comprises essays on how love and loss are inscribed in contemporary queer documentaries that link autobiography and ethnography. Again these articles consider the dangers of censorship and right-wing attacks, now, however, in connection with AIDS and queer reframings of family. Chris Holmlund looks explicitly at how autobiography and ethnography function in the "dyke docs" of Sadie Benning and Su Friedrich, examining the ways their works "lesbianize" and queer marriage and mourning. She ends by investigating how critics and audiences see the "dykes" of these "dyke docs," stressing the importance of social context where definition and distinction are concerned. With different viewing sites in mind (now community theaters and PBS broadcasts), Beverly Seckinger and Janet Jakobsen evaluate *Silverlake Life*'s autobiographical portrait of two gay long-term partners who ultimately die from AIDS. Situating *Silverlake* in relation to 1970s documentary practices, Seckinger and Jakobsen note how seldom death and dying are shown in documentaries, emphasizing however that visibility guarantees neither "truth" nor activism. Justin Wyatt explores the ways that personal and public gay life intersect around family structures and AIDS in three of Derek Jarman's works and traces ways in which Jarman, too, questions cultural reliance on visibility as a gauge for knowledge. How Jarman's experimental documentaries are received, however, Wyatt argues, depends on audience familiarity or lack of familiarity with intertextual sources (Jarman's print diaries) and contextual frames (queer life in 1980s and 1990s England).

Like all of the essays in "Marriage and Mourning" and some in "Memories," those in "Mirrors" chart relationships between audiences and texts and engage with documentaries that are often expressly performative. Here the emphasis is on the impact of performative styles on binary cultural boundaries. Lynda Goldstein discusses whether and how white lesbian spectators "get into" short works by lesbians of color at queer film festivals. Though she suggests several ways that such appreciations might occur, she also questions how much autobiography or ethnography can be understood—or read—by viewers from outside the subject culture. Cynthia Fuchs investigates self-conscious representations of documentary conventions—for example, references to and constructions of "the real," in three (sets of) works: *Paris Is Burning, Without You I'm Nothing,* and Cheryl Dunye's short videos. Her aim is to rethink the ways that narrative structures and visual economies inform documentary aesthetics as well as political and social identities. Each of these texts, she argues, refigures the assumptions, formations, and effects of "knowledge" as these circulate among viewers, makers, and textual subjects. Chris Straayer taps two independent video documentaries, *Juggling Gender* and *OUTLAW*, to "take a queering look" at feminist philosophies of gender. In Straayer's view, performative documentaries like these two function as "counterdominant" discourses, producing "countermeanings" that position gender as interactive and in process. Kathleen McHugh examines the roles deceptive appearances play as source material for both documentary and queer cultural identity. In her discussions of experimental documentaries by Goss, Saunders, and Jones, McHugh is attentive to the limitations of ethnographers' questions and scientific "facts"; she concludes that the most truthful statements are those that document their own limitations.

▶───

Talking Back, Looking Ahead

We begin with the essay by Gregg and end with the article by McHugh to reinforce the political significance of questions of identity and documentary, and to give some sense of the depth and range of material in a field where production so outstrips analysis. We are confident that this collection provides some measure of what McHugh calls the "myriad possibilities of representational tactics available to apprehend very elusive subjectivities." As editors, however, we are conscious not only of what this book does, but also of what it does not do. We have tried throughout to put race forward together with sexuality and gender and not to present it as a ghettoized subject, discussed solely in individual essays, by individual authors, in separate sections. Readers will notice, however, that some racial groups are represented and others are not. We regret that though many essays explore multiple identities, none questions the current, rather comfortable, practice of affixing labels like "queer," "lesbian," or "gay" only to works with explicit "queer" content, made by "out" or "outed" makers. For us, the diversity of works produced by queer artists suggests that "queer" is not always directly related either to visual or verbal content or to a maker's stated or assumed sexual identity. We hope that future programming and discussion of queer documentaries will include such works. Last but not least, we consider it urgent that more, and more sustained, discussions of earlier documentaries, and of work not produced in the United States, be undertaken.

The scores of films and videos not discussed in this collection but described in the film/videography compiled by Lynda McAfee offer alternative routes for study. We expect that this listing (incomplete even as it was typed) will also serve as an additional resource for exhibition and investigation. To be sure, there is no definitive way of knowing to what use these addenda, the analyses offered in this book, or even the media texts themselves will be put by queer, lesbian, gay, or straight readers or audience members. Our project, once again, is one of suggestion, provocation, and encouragement, meant to remind ourselves and our readers how important it is to acknowledge and value the shifting layerings of identity and community, even as we work toward what we feel is the crucial task of coalition building.

We have no doubt that together these essays and their objects make it clear that no "straight" lines can be drawn around documentary. Still, we would argue, the force of these films, television shows, and videos stems from the fact that they remain narratives grounded in some version of actuality and experience, involving social actors, as opposed to characters. Our most immediate hope is that, taken individually and collectively, this introduction and the essays that follow will convey something of the variety and depth of passionate engagement that characterize queer/lesbian/gay documentary, past and present, without fetishizing difference *qua* difference.

None of the contributors to this book would argue that speaking and seeing differently are merely a matter of extending tolerance or facilitating acceptance, even as we can all envision cases in which we would argue and fight for tolerance and acceptance. Our goal in placing the works we analyze within broad cultural, historical, and political contexts is ultimately, of course, not only to provide accessible tools for use in classrooms and communities, but also, necessarily, to provoke ongoing discussion, exhibition, and activism, between the sheets and in the streets.

NOTES

Sincere thanks to Chon Noriega, Diane Waldman, Justin Wyatt, and Tom Waugh for their comments and suggestions.

1. Su Friedrich, "Radical Form, Radical Content," *Millennium Film Journal* 22 (1989): 183.
2. The titles of recent critical work on queer media themselves suggest how important vision and visibility are. Consider, for example, Bad Object-Choices, ed., *How Do I Look? Queer Film and Video* (Seattle: Bay Press, 1991); Richard Dyer, *Now You See It: Studies on Lesbian and Gay Film* (London: Routledge, 1990); Martha Gever, John Greyson, and Pratibha Parmar, eds., *Queer Looks: Perspectives on Lesbian and Gay Film and Video* (New York: Routledge, 1993); Judith Mayne, "A Parallax View of Lesbian Authorship," in *Inside/Out: Lesbian Theories, Gay Theories*, ed. Diana Fuss (New York: Routledge, 1991); and Fabienne Worth, "Of Gayzes and Bodies: A Bibliographical Essay on Queer Theory, Psychoanalysis and Archeology," *Quarterly Review of Film and Video* 15.1 (1993): 1-13.
3. Again, the titles of critical work on repre-

sentation are indicative. Examples include Corey K. Creekmur and Alexander Doty, eds., *Out in Culture: Gay, Lesbian, and Queer Essays on Popular Culture* (Durham, N.C.: Duke University Press, 1995); Russell Ferguson, Martha Gever, Trinh T. Minh-ha, and Cornel West, eds., *Out There: Marginalization and Contemporary Cultures* (New York: New Museum of Contemporary Art, 1990); and Diana Fuss, *Essentially Speaking: Feminism, Nature, and Difference* (New York: Routledge, 1989).

4. For a critical summary of recent works on documentary, see Dirk Eitzen, "What Is a Documentary? Documentary as a Mode of Reception," *Cinema Journal* 35.1 (Fall 1995): 81-102.

5. Bill Nichols, *Representing Reality: Issues and Concepts in Documentary* (Bloomington: Indiana University Press, 1991), ix-x; emphasis in the original.

6. See, for example, Lee Atwell, "Word Is Out and *Gay U.S.A.*," in *New Challenges for Documentary*, ed. Alan Rosenthal (Berkeley: University of California Press, 1987), 571-80; R. Bruce Brasell, "Bullets, Ballots, and Bibles: Documenting the History of the Gay and Lesbian Struggle in America," *Cineaste* 21.4 (1995): 17–21; Bill Horrigan, "Notes on AIDS and Its Combatants: An Appreciation," in *Theorizing Documentary*, ed. Michael Renov (New York: Routledge, 1993), 164–73; Thomas Waugh, "Lesbian and Gay Documentary: Minority Self-Imaging, Oppositional Film Practice, and the Question of Image Ethics," in *Image Ethics*, ed. Larry Gross, John Stuart Katz, and Jay Ruby (New York: Oxford University Press, 1988), 248–72. Though not on documentary and queer representation per se, several of the essays in *Resolutions: Contemporary Video Practices*, ed. Michael Renov and Erika Suderburg (Minneapolis: University of Minnesota Press, 1996), take up these topics.

7. See, for example, John Champagne, *The Ethics of Marginality: A New Approach to Gay Studies* (Minneapolis: University of Minnesota Press, 1995); Richard Dyer, "From and for the Movement," in *Now You See It*, 211–86; Martha Gever, "The Names We Give Ourselves," in *Out There*, 191-202; Judith Mayne, "A Parallax View of Lesbian Authorship," in *Inside/Out*. See also *Queer Looks*, where roughly half of the essays deal with documentary.

8. Such articles can be found in *The Advocate*, *10 Percent*, *Genre*, *Christopher Street*, *Sojourner*, *Deneuve*, *Off Our Backs*, *On Our Backs*, *Fuse*, the defunct *Gay Community News*, *Outweek*, and *OUT/LOOK*, to name a few.

9. On the equation of AIDS and queers, see Cindy Patton, "Tremble, Hetero Swine!" in *Fear of a Queer Planet: Queer Politics and Social Theory*, ed. Michael Warner (Minneapolis: University of Minnesota Press, 1993), 143–77.

10. Trinh T. Minh-ha, "The Totalizing Quest of Meaning," reprinted in *Theorizing Documentary*, ed. Michael Renov (New York: Routledge, 1993), 90.

11. Ibid., 99 and 101. Trinh takes the Franju citation from G. Roy Levin, *Documentary Explorations: Fifteen Interviews with Film-Makers* (Garden City, N.Y.: Doubleday, 1971), 121, 128.

12. Julianne Burton, "Toward a History of Social Documentary in Latin America," in *The Social Documentary in Latin America*, ed. Julianne Burton (Pittsburgh: University of Pittsburgh Press, 1990), 7.

13. Nichols, *Representing Reality*, xv, 105–98.

14. Bill Nichols, *Blurred Boundaries: Questions of Meaning in Contemporary Culture* (Bloomington: Indiana University Press, 1994), 86.

15. R. Bruce Brasell, "The Queer as Producer: Benjamin, Brecht, and *The Making of 'Monsters*,'" *Jump Cut* 40 (1996): 47–54.

16. Alexander Doty, "There's Something Queer Here," in *Making Things Perfectly Queer* (Minneapolis: University of Minnesota Press, 1993), 3, citing bell hooks, "Choosing the Margins as a Space of Radical Openness," *Yearning: Race, Gender, and Cultural Politics* (Boston: South End Press, 1990), 153.

17. Ibid.

18. Bad Object-Choices, introduction to *How Do I Look?*, 28.

19. Michael Warner, introduction to *Fear of a Queer Planet*, xxv.

20. Martha Gever, "The Names We Give Ourselves," in *Out There*, 191.

21. Warner, introduction to *Fear of a Queer Planet*, xviii.

22. Evelynn Hammonds, "Black (W)holes and the Geometry of Black Female Sexuality," *differences* 6.2–3 (1994): 141.

Markers

RONALD GREGG

[1] *Queer Representation and Oregon's 1992 Anti-Gay Ballot Measure: Measuring the Politics of Mainstreaming*

> *Craig Parshall, explaining how to get church leaders involved in the movement against the homosexual agenda (Concerned Women of America Conference, 1992): Use the old list of horribles . . . one day your pastor's going to preach on Romans 13, and as your church leaves there'll be a circle of leather-clad motorcycled lesbians and homosexuals screaming and yelling about the bigotry of your church and that's where it's heading. It's knocking on the doors of our church.*

> *Marshall Kirk and Hunter Madsen, Ph.D., After the Ball: How America Will Conquer Its Fear and Hatred of Gays in the '90s: We're not fighting to eliminate community ethics, to live like selfish brats, narcissistically and meanly. . . . We're not fighting to eradicate Family; we're fighting for the right to be Family. We're fighting to be decent human beings. . . . We're fighting not only for America's love and respect, but to become people unquestionably deserving of America's love and respect . . . and one another's too.*[1]

While I was attending the University of Oregon in the early 1990s, I enjoyed the freedom of a safe, supportive space to study gay and lesbian history and theory and was able to incorporate this queer scholarship along with my own experiences as a gay white male into my film studies teaching and writing. This sense of safety was short-lived.

In 1992 the Oregon Citizens Alliance (OCA), a local conservative Christian political action committee, submitted the anti-gay Ballot Measure 9 to the voters. Measure 9 would have amended the state constitution to prevent state, regional, and local governments from "promoting," "encouraging," or "facilitating" homosexuality. The measure further would have decreed that the state Department of Higher Education and Oregon public schools "assist in setting a standard" for young students by identifying homosexuality as "abnormal, wrong, unnatural, and perverse."[2] Ballot Measure 9 held out the possibility of renewed anti-gay surveillance and state-sanctioned disapproval of my gay-themed dissertation and "queer" perspective in the classroom.

The debate over Measure 9 pervaded Oregon's media, schools, churches, and public meeting places and confronted Oregonians with contradictory, impassioned representations of what it means to be gay or lesbian. You couldn't get away from it. Key to this struggle to represent the practices and beliefs of that ethereal "gay community" were two locally produced, emotionally charged political video documentaries, the OCA's anti-gay *Gay Pride?* (1991) and the pro-gay *Fighting for Our Lives* (1992).

In recent national political struggles, video has increasingly become an important, inexpensive propaganda tool for organizing political campaigns and conveying political agendas, especially conservative causes. By direct-mail video or through organized public showings, conservative activists have targeted sympathetic constituents and have built support among undecided voters.[3] Conservative Christians pioneered this tactic in their successful organizing efforts against gay rights.[4]

In the video *Gay Pride?* the OCA adeptly used emotionally manipulated images, sounds, and stories to arouse their intended audience. *Gay Pride?* begins with an edited sequence of startling images from a gay pride parade—dancing nude men, a leather-clad man with chained "slave," shirtless women—to invoke the "old list of horribles," as Craig Parshall said. Following this eye-catching, shocking opening, the video spotlights descriptions of a promiscuous, perverted, diseased "homosexual lifestyle" and the scary "homosexual militant agenda" of child recruitment and the undoing of the traditional family. The video's closing argument incites the viewer to take action against this homosexual enemy by volunteering for, giving money to, and voting with the anti-gay cause. This video was widely distributed throughout Oregon.

Pro-gay forces have also turned to video in their outreach to constituents and as part of their response to malicious anti-gay imagery and rhetoric. But pro-gay political and cultural producers have been faced with the uneasy task of how to represent gay sexual behavior. In past political struggles, pro-gay strategists have insisted that gays and lesbians hide their sexual behaviors and cultural differences in political discourse in order to avoid arousing the homophobia of mainstream voters.[5] Responding to the OCA's anti-gay representation in 1992, Oregon's pro-gay political strategists also sought to "mainstream" gays and lesbians in the media by depicting them as respectable, nonconfrontational, nonsexualized people with families just like other Oregonians. Many gays and lesbians, however, complained that this "sanitized" strategy "attempted to make gays and lesbians invisible."[6]

According to Chuck Kleinhans, this "mainstreaming" strategy attempts to "assimilate" the documentarist and the marginalized group—gays and lesbians—into dominant culture. In crafting a film or video, the maker uses those "dominant forms and values of conventional media" that offer gays and lesbians a way to "construct a discourse within the already established system of power in order to speak effectively within a larger circle."[7] While this approach can successfully find a wider audience through familiar and conventional narratives, styles, and rhetoric, the strategy raises problems for gays and lesbians since certain behaviors and identities within gay subcultures are purposely hidden or misrepresented. This "closeting" thus limits the portrayal of gay and lesbian individuals, communities, and cultures, implicitly allowing the demonization of elements that are unrepresented and, in the long run, changing the way gays and lesbians see themselves, singly, in groups, and as a group.

I was angered by the mean-spirited, simplistic portrayals of gays and lesbians in the OCA's video. But I also became troubled by the pro-gay response as measured by the political documentary *Fighting for Our Lives*, distributed during the Measure 9 campaign. More recently, I had the same reactions to Heather MacDonald's *Ballot Measure 9* (1994). Both videos embrace an image of respectability, while queer eroticism and sexual behaviors are buried in the "closet," contained by gays and lesbians themselves. In spite of the happiness that came with the defeat of Measure 9, I felt then and feel now a certain curtailment of my own liberation.

Having participated actively in the campaign against Measure 9 and experienced the exhilaration of defeating the OCA's ballot measure, I find it hard to criticize a successful strategy that offered a momentary respite from the OCA's seemingly endless attacks as expressed through 1994's Ballot Measure 13 and the announcement of future anti-gay initiatives. But the experience in Oregon taught me that while the image of mainstream "normality" can win political gains for gays and lesbians, something is lost in the translation. Although they are not groundbreaking documentaries, the videos *Fighting for Our Lives* and *Ballot Measure 9* do offer a recent historical context for measuring "queer" strategies for representing gay and lesbian identities and sexual behaviors in difficult political struggles. There are no easy answers to the question of how to counter the dangers posed by the anti-gay efforts of the religious right, but by analyzing these videos, we may better prepare for future struggles.

▶

Political Documentaries of Oregon's Gays and Lesbians:
Dangerous Perverts or Sanitized Citizens?

The OCA, sponsor of Ballot Measure 9, was founded in 1987 in Klamath Falls, a small community in southern Oregon. Led by Lon Mabon, a Vietnam veteran and former hippie, the conservative Christian organization recruited its early membership among local farmers, home schoolers, and fundamentalist Christians. Since then the group has steadily grown to include more than a hundred thousand Oregonians, still mostly white small-town or rural working-class individuals, many of whom are fundamentalist Christians.

The activities of the OCA demonstrate that its members are certainly not political novices. In 1988 Oregon governor Neil Goldschmidt, by executive order, prohibited discrimination based on sexual orientation in state government. The OCA immediately submitted Ballot Measure 8 to the voters, who overturned the governor's order by a margin of 56 percent to 44 percent. In 1990 the OCA expanded its statewide concerns and in state elections championed an antiabortion initiative that was defeated by a large margin. It also supported a third-party gubernatorial candidate who siphoned off enough votes from the Republican candidate to elect the Democrat, Barbara Roberts. After these defeats in 1990, the OCA returned to the issue with which it had been successful, gay rights.[8]

To convince Oregonians of the need for the draconian Ballot Measure 9, the OCA released an anti-gay video documentary, *Gay Pride?* (1991), which was exhibited across the state in conservative Oregon churches and on cable-access stations. The video's propagandistic strategy is to show a "homosexual lifestyle" defined by promiscuity, pornography, sadomasochism, pedophilia, and AIDS, and to depict a dangerous, militant "gay agenda" seeking child recruitment and the destruction of the traditional heterosexual family and Christian values. Crafty editing of crude, amateurish video footage from the 1987 gay and lesbian march on Washington and the 1990 and 1991 gay pride parades in San Francisco mixes the most "shocking" participants at gay pride events—NAMBLA (the North American Man/Boy Love Association), outspoken sadomasochists, drag queens in sacrilegious garb, naked men and shirtless lesbians—with more conventional-looking participants associated with community-oriented, familial, and educational organizations. Through this juxtaposition, these various elements of the queer community are made to seem united under an umbrella of gay pride and a single, unifying "gay agenda." For example, in one key sequence, the documentary segues from parade images of

NAMBLA to gay and lesbian parents' and teachers' organizations, momentarily pausing on images of male adults, probably gay parents, carrying children. Thanks to the previous images of NAMBLA, these adults are repositioned as "child molesters." This edited sequence and the authoritative male narrator implicitly connect the goals of NAMBLA, gay parents' groups, and gay-friendly school programs, especially Project 10, a California program designed to help troubled gay teens succeed in school. No gay or lesbian spokesperson is allowed to defend Project 10 or to differ with NAMBLA's objectives. *Gay Pride?* thus willfully ignores the complexity and variety of gay and lesbian sexual, moral, and political identities.

In Oregon, gay and lesbian activists united with straight activist allies working in other movements for gender and racial equality. Together they denounced the OCA's anti-gay barrage and developed political strategies for responding to it. The most successful political action committee to evolve from this liberal coalition, the No on 9 campaign, raised two million dollars from the gay and straight political and business communities. Two-thirds of these funds were spent on advertising that blanketed the television, cable, radio, and print media, primarily in the tricounty Portland metropolitan area where more than 40 percent of all Oregonians live.

Sherry Oeser, chair of No on 9, explained that the campaign "decided to focus on the issue of discrimination because that's a message people generally respond to. . . . It would have been risky to solely address the issue of sexual orientation."[9] No on 9's broadcast and cable ads ignored the OCA's condemnation of gay and lesbian sexual behaviors and never asked viewers to reject homophobia or to condone homosexuality. Straight spokespersons instead urged Oregonians to support "human rights" for all Oregonians, guaranteeing freedom from discrimination in employment and housing. One television ad featured the leaders of Oregon's Republican and Democratic Parties uniting to denounce discrimination and the OCA amendment. Other ads hammered home the tag line "It's a danger to us all."

Because No on 9 focused on Portland-area constituents, Elaine Velazquez and Barbara Bernstein produced the video documentary *Fighting for Our Lives* (1992) as a grassroots organizing tool designed to reach rural and small-town communities. Before deciding on their documentary's rhetorical approach, the two women conferred with a number of lesbians and feminists who were working on political strategies for dealing with the OCA tactics. From these discussions, Velazquez and Bernstein designed a narrative that resembled that of No on 9, framing their documentary's argument around antidiscrimination issues and the OCA's hatemongering tactics.

Their approach differed, however, in that they chose a wider range of pro-gay spokespersons, including people speaking from different back-grounds of religion, age, gender, race, and class, thus expanding their possible audience. Moreover, they selected appealing, straight spokespersons from outside the Portland area, particularly individuals who had never met an openly lesbian or gay person and were thus less prone to be sympathetic to gay and lesbian causes.[10] Sympathizing with viewers unacquainted with a gay world, the Reverend John Sandusky from the coastal community of Tillamook, for example, admits to a certain ignorance about homosexuality; he asserts, however, that his lack of understanding does not allow him to miss the point that discrimination against any group is wrong.

Fighting for Our Lives was widely distributed across the state through a number of grassroots, anti-OCA organizations such as Human Dignity Projects, No on 9 in Lane County, People of Faith Against Bigotry, and the Rural Organizing Project. To counter the OCA's distribution of *Gay Pride?* in churches, the video was distributed to and shown in some five hundred churches across Oregon, including a number of evangelical churches. The documentary also was shown on cable-access channels across the state.[11]

By juxtaposing images of militant, hatemongering OCA activists with images of articulate, calm, appealing homosexuals, *Fighting for Our Lives* inverts the rhetorical strategy of *Gay Pride?* Velazquez and Bernstein begin with a clip from *Good Morning America* in which co-host Charles Gibson states that Measure 9 "is being called the strongest antihomosexual measure ever considered by a state." A montage of pro-OCA Oregonians speaking against "the homosexual lifestyle," proclaiming biblical condemnation, and seeking the curtailment of homosexual rights immediately follows Gibson's implicit characterization of Measure 9 as a historically extreme initiative. The documentary later compares the OCA to Nazi Germany and McCarthyism and blames the OCA for, as one speaker asserts, "churning up the dark side" and thereby contributing to a statewide rise of hatred. Verbal and visual abuse against gays recorded by the videomakers during the Measure 9 campaign—including, for instance, a young white man spitting on a composed gay protester—illustrates the charge of fanning hatred. The OCA, in this narrative, appears as the dangerous, reactionary villain.

Besieged by the OCA's malicious rhetoric, homosexuals become peaceful yet determined victims "fighting for their lives." After the opening sequence, the documentary cuts to a march against Measure 9 that is reminiscent of black civil rights marches. The marchers carry a banner that says "For Love and Justice" and sing harmoniously. After the singing, a chant is taken up, but instead of the usual "Hey, hey! Ho, ho! Homophobia has got to go," it is "OCA has got to go," identifying the OCA and not homophobia as the villain. Instead of the gay pink triangle, a symbol associated with gay persecution and protest, the marchers carry rainbow flags, a symbol suggesting both utopian dreaming (as in the gay-appropriated song *Over the Rainbow*) and the harmonious blending of gender, race, ethnicity, and sexual orientation identified with Jesse Jackson's Rainbow Coalition.

The film features two "out" lesbians, Donna Red Wing, identified by her association with Portland's Lesbian Community Project, and Lois Van Leer, a Corvallis United Church of Christ minister, who explains that she is "out" to the children and parents with whom she works. The documentary otherwise uses unidentified and therefore presumably straight spokespersons to discuss the desires and fears of a generalized "lesbian and gay community." The video specifically includes Asian-American, black, and Jewish people who typify traditionally oppressed racial and ethnic groups and relate antigay discrimination and hatemongering to past discrimination and violence. The video also pointedly identifies the people who live outside Oregon's cities, such as Elise Self from Grants Pass and Georgia Wildfang from Independence. This involvement of diverse identities and groups, in a state more multicultural than many, illustrates a broad coalition of pro-gay support and broadens the "our" in *Fighting for Our Lives* to include all Oregonians.

The documentary's conventional, talking-heads format also suggests connection and unity among these speakers, who are similarly centered in the frame, filmed in a medium shot to medium close-up, from a straight-on angle. Each speaker is situated in an environment that typifies her or his area of work—a housewife in the kitchen, a pastor in the sanctuary. Taken together, these environments connote the common concerns of all the documentary's participants, gay or straight, for home, for family, for job, and for religion.

By including and identifying people from rural and small-town Oregon, emphasizing middle- and working-class concerns like job security and family unity, and distributing the video through grassroots organizations, Velazquez and Bernstein reached out to rural and small-town viewers. But this strategy has certain weaknesses. First, by featuring only Red Wing and Van Leer, respectively from the larger cities of Portland and Corvallis, the documentary does not allow small-town and rural lesbians and gays to address their straight neighbors. As Amber Hollibaugh points out, drawing on her own grassroots experiences during the 1978 anti-gay Briggs initiative in California, gays and lesbians who grew up in small towns and rural communities are often particularly effective in turning around anti-gay sentiments because they can connect with those audiences.[12] And, since conservative Christianity is an integral part of many rural communities, the video undoubtedly alienates some of its intended viewers by equating the OCA (and, by implication, its conservative Christian condemnation of homosexuality) with nazism and McCarthyism.

The documentary also "mainstreams" gay and lesbian identities. Red Wing and Van Leer are used for their conventional-seeming appearance and viewpoints, not to address differences of race, class, and culture among gays and lesbians. No gay men appear in this mix—a serious omission, since anti-gay depictions target gay men and portray them as promiscuous, diseased child molesters.[13] Nor are there images of queer "otherness." The rare references to gay and lesbian sexuality are couched in terms of denial—lesbians and gays are *not* pedophiles, *not* promiscuous. Since there is no representation at all of gay sexuality and little discussion of gay identities and concerns, gays and lesbians seem to have no sexual identities, no subcultures, no differences from the dominant culture.

▶ —————————————————————————————————————

Ballot Measure 9: The History of a Hysterical Conflict

In *Ballot Measure 9* (1994), New York–based video documentarist Heather MacDonald chronicles the Oregon struggle and presents a survey of political activism, rhetoric, and personal impressions from activists and everyday citizens on both sides of the conflict. Although it closes with a pro-gay victory, the video offers a warning of future OCA activity and predicts more strife and violence in Oregon's future.

As of this writing, *Ballot Measure 9* has been exhibited only at special screenings and film festivals, tying for the 1995 Sundance Audience Award for Documentary. In the publicity material, MacDonald clearly targets a broader audience than *Fighting for Our Lives* does, framing the video as an organizing tool against the religious right for a variety of pro-gay civic, religious, and political organizations.[14] This conscious choice of audience is characterized by a conventional, objective style dominated by a mix of talking-head and on-the-street interviews and various videotaped segments from television news broadcasts, news conferences, organizational speeches, and state congressional hearings.[15]

The video opens with a set of establishing shots of Oregon's beautiful natural environment accompanied by a mellow acoustic guitar musical track. The guitar music ends when we see Lon Mabon, head of the OCA, traveling by car through this serene environment. Contentiously he asserts that, even in private, homosexuality, lesbianism, sadism, and masochism are "wrong behavior" and explains that this is why he has brought Measure 9 to the voters. From Mabon on the road, the video segues to a short

Ballot Measure 9 (Heather MacDonald 1994). Courtesy Zeitgeist Films

discordant segment of groups of Measure 9 supporters and opponents shouting their opposite views while a nondiegetic, tense, repetitious musical drumming plays. Mabon then returns, now speaking before a gathering, and declares that "this is a war, this is a culture war," throwing down a metaphorical gauntlet to his opponents. Three anti-9 activists, major participants in the campaign, follow Mabon's declaration and pick up on his violent rhetoric. Donna Red Wing, the lesbian activist featured in *Fighting for Our Lives*, contends that because of Measure 9, "people died in Oregon," and she warns that people will die across America because of similar anti-gay efforts. Gay activist Scott Seibert, an ex-marine and former police officer, labels the anti-gay initiatives "the neutron bomb of politics." Finally, Kathleen Saadat, an activist in gay and lesbian and African-American groups, notes that people were "terrified" during this time. A final shot completes this introductory thread: a peaceful candlelight vigil, later identified as a memorial for two victims of an apartment firebombing, is disrupted by a tape-recorded male phone caller who declares, "You guys are dead," plainly a death threat for gays and lesbians; the caller ends his anti-gay harangue by shouting "OCA rules." Through this introductory sequence, the video clearly establishes its thematic and narrative focus on the conflict between the aggressors, Mabon and the OCA, and their gay and lesbian victims and calls attention to the ways that this "war" has disrupted Oregon's serenity and sense of community.

Next, the video cuts to a scrolled text explaining the content of the

1992 anti-gay initiatives in Colorado and Oregon, noting that these states served as "testing grounds" for future initiatives. The video then specifically turns to "the story of what happened in Oregon," shifting to a chronological narrative that starts with the OCA's submission of the initiative and concludes with the final vote on Measure 9. Through its goal-oriented, linear narrative, with two principal opposing sides, *Ballot Measure 9* presents a classical narration that serves to assimilate the story of gays and lesbians in a familiar form. The ending marks the defeat of Measure 9, a clear victory for gay and lesbian activists, but is followed by a brief afterword warning that the "war" is not over: the OCA is continuing its anti-gay activity. Unfortunately but understandably, this emotional focus on the villainous OCA substitutes for a comprehensive analysis of Oregon's gay and lesbian communities and the roots of homophobia.

While *Ballot Measure 9* incorporates interviews with various Oregonians on both sides of the issue, it clearly sides with pro-gay activists. Starting with Mabon's condemnation of gay and lesbian behavior and his declaration of a "culture war," MacDonald vilifies the OCA. The OCA's activities are later compared by gay activists and their supporters to the historical persecution of American Indians and African-Americans and, more specifically, persecution of Catholics in Oregon by the KKK and the internment of Asian-Americans in the United States during World War II. This historical comparison of the OCA's harassment of gays and lesbians with persecution of other groups is similar to the correlation shown in *Fighting for Our Lives* between the rhetoric of the OCA and the Nazis.

MacDonald implicitly rebukes the OCA's rhetoric in one particular segment; while the earlier repetitious drumming, a marker of discord, replays, she rapidly cuts between various white male OCA members first claiming "factual" truth about common gay sexual "perversities," then describing those "factual" "perverse" behaviors. MacDonald takes the most shocking words in the descriptions, such as *feces* and *rectum,* and superimposes them in large print over the speaking men's images. Her manipulation of image and sound suggests—and condemns—a cacophony of frenzied hostility toward gay men.

Unlike *Fighting for Our Lives*, MacDonald's video features a broad cross-section of openly gay and lesbian people involved in anti-9 activism, including experienced and first-time activists, people of color, and activists both from the city and from rural areas and small towns. In addition to recording the activists' accounts of day-to-day political activities, MacDonald accentuates their private lives through home interviews, personal stories and asides, and visual cutaways of home life. Donna Red Wing, for instance, discusses the campaign with a cup of tea or coffee in the intimacy of a din-

Ballot Measure 9 (Heather MacDonald 1994). Kathleen Saadat is on the right.
Courtesy Zeitgeist Films

ing room setting; in another domestic setting, she describes the threats that
she and her partner received during the Measure 9 campaign; and in one
scene she and a woman, presumably her partner, cook together and then
eat with friends.

Even with MacDonald's expanded representation of gay and lesbian
voices, home life, and personal experiences, however, gays and lesbians are
still assimilated into a nonthreatening, nonsexual image. The narrative's
simplistic construction of two opposing camps suggests that gays and lesbians are united, with a single viewpoint and voice. As in *Fighting for Our
Lives*, these well-dressed, well-behaved gay and lesbian activists appear in
familiar middle-class environments and articulate familiar concerns about
financial and personal security at work and at home.

Both *Fighting for Our Lives* and *Ballot Measure 9* thereby fail to
represent the complexity of gay and lesbian identities, communities, and
sexual behaviors. Both fail to represent any specific aspects of the gay subculture that might mark it as different from the mainstream; iconographies,
histories, and literature remain unexplored. Both videos decline to tackle
the complex response among gays and lesbians to the boy-lovers, political
militants, and other politically and sexually charged queer identities demonized so effectively by the OCA in *Gay Pride?* In fact, these pro-gay docu-

mentaries give no voice at all to these demonized "others," although, ironically, even the OCA gets to argue its case in MacDonald's video.

An Afterword:
The Traps of Mainstreaming

Measure 9 was defeated, but the strategy used to defeat it had a price. Those "extreme" queer behaviors and identities marked by the OCA were increasingly silenced and excluded from gay and lesbian spaces in Oregon. For instance, in the spring following the 1992 election, those of us involved in setting the program for the First Annual Queer Film/Video Festival at the University of Oregon reluctantly decided that we could not publicly show Alice B. Brave's well-made, vexing lesbian sadomasochistic video *Bittersweet* as part of the campus program for fear of giving the OCA more fuel for its anti-gay initiatives and damaging the future of the festival. It wasn't just in the months before the election that we felt we had to pretend that lesbian S/M does not exist.

Also after the election, several letters in the gay press enthusiastically applauded the "new" mainstream image of gayness and called for censoring certain queer behaviors, apparently with none of the reluctance that accompanied our censorship decision at the University of Oregon. To deflect future characterizations of Oregon's lesbian and gay community as promiscuous, several letters demanded the self-policing of gay and lesbian sexual behaviors. One gay letter writer criticized those "careless" gay men "who feel it is necessary to cruise for sexual partners" in parks and rest stops. Another unsigned letter to the *Lavender Network* lamented its willingness to publish sex ads and the ads' suggestion that "some gays (none that I know!) like sex toys, leather and S/M!!"[16]

These letters and our exclusion of the Brave video show how the anti-Measure 9 strategy for "mainstreaming" gay and lesbian identities helped establish conservative sexual standards that many gays and lesbians adopted, sometimes reluctantly, sometimes wholeheartedly. Relegated to the closet during the election, queer identities and behaviors that disturbed the "mainstream" found it difficult to come out again. The erasure of such identities in *Fighting for Our Lives* and *Ballot Measure 9* thus documents, however unconsciously, the political closets that gays and lesbians construct for themselves.

It has not taken long, moreover, for this strategy to be challenged by conservative Christians. Their video *The Gay Agenda* (1992) challenges gay activists' claims that the majority of gays and lesbians are "loving, car-ing, and monogamous" by claiming that most gays, especially gay men, are involved in "anonymous sexual encounters" and a variety of "perverse" behaviors, such as oral and anal sex, "fisting," and "golden showers." Straight viewers thus stand forewarned that even though gays and lesbians might appear attractive and friendly, they are not really as "normal" as they appear to be.

Given that the "mainstreaming" of gayness tends to hide gay and lesbian sexuality and to exclude queer "otherness" and that the Christian right has immediately responded to this mainstream gay image, gay and lesbian activists and political documentarists need to reconsider how to discuss and to represent queer differences in future political struggles. Activists and artists clearly need to work with more-complex representational strategies that honestly deal with differences of ideology, class, race, culture, and sexuality within queer communities while at the same time confronting the homophobia and propaganda of the religious right.

Many gay and lesbian film and video artists already offer new styles and narratives for transforming political video from the articulation of "mainstream" assimilation to a particular subcultural viewpoint. Marlon Riggs, for one, in his innovative video *Tongues Untied* (1989), analyzes racism, homophobia, and desire through a complex blend of documentary and experimental styles and poetic, autobiographical, and historical discourses. While Riggs's video opened the "closet" and revealed gay African-American men openly speaking about their sexual identities for the first time to many straight, "mainstream" viewers (and white gay viewers), its history of censorship also unfortunately reveals the difficulties of funding and exhibiting. Yet *Tongues Untied* suggests that by drawing on gay and lesbian iconographies, personal stories, histories, and sexual identities, gays and lesbians can begin to acknowledge, to analyze, to affirm, and to celebrate each subcultural identity for itself, for its allies, and, more importantly, for new constituencies.

In his discussion of "radical political documentary," Chuck Kleinhans suggests that political documentarists "underestimate their audience by soft-pedaling their message and sanitizing its radical content, even when those films take on a supposedly militant subject matter." Kleinhans, who made this assertion in the early 1980s, noted even then how viewers are increasingly reared on complex commercials, MTV, and other less mainstream styles; these same audiences, including a new generation of Oregonians, can surely deal with more complex styles, narratives, and ideas.[17]

Obviously, no one video documentary can deal with all the identities, behaviors, histories, and subcultures that claim a space under the queer umbrella. But gay political documentarists could engage in more complex and fair depictions of controversial queer identities, behaviors, and sub-cultures in addition to challenging homophobic stereotypes (like those that depict gay men as diseased and as child molesters) and demanding gay civil rights. Engagement does not mean that film- and video-makers have to pretend that gays and lesbians are united on all issues. NAMBLA, for instance, is a contentious subject, not only for the religious right but for many gays and lesbians as well. But the near-blanket condemnation of NAMBLA among gay and lesbian groups and the silence about it in gay political documentaries has seemingly closed off any possible public debate over the political and social issues that NAMBLA raises: the relationship of power in child-adult sexual situations, age-of-consent laws, and the sexual rights of youth. Once they are "closeted," these issues have a hard time finding their way back into the public sphere.

The right wing has no intention of allowing us to keep our sexualities hidden and undiscussed. It may be time to put our sexual identities, behaviors, cultures, controversies, and disagreements on the agenda along with the "mainstream" issues of discrimination and civil rights—not to shock, but to begin a dialogue among ourselves and with the voting public that we can no longer avoid and should, in any case, embrace.

◆————————————————————————————————

NOTES

Special thanks to George Chauncey and Chris Holmlund for their comments on this paper.

1. Video of Craig Parshall lecture "Exposing the Homosexual Agenda" (Concerned Women of America, 1992); Marshall Kirk and Hunter Madsen, Ph.D., *After the Ball: How America Will Conquer Its Fear and Hatred of Gays in the '90s* (New York: Doubleday, 1989), 380–81.
2. The complete text of Ballot Measure 9 and the OCA's explanation of intention is published in Oregon's "Official Voter's Pamphlet" for the November 3, 1992, election. The text of Measure 9 also condemned "pedophilia," "sadism," and "masochism." Because of this wording and the arguments for and against the measure discussing homosexuality and these other behaviors, the secretary of state included a warning that sections of the pamphlet "contain language that citizens and parents may find objectionable."
3. In 1994, for instance, Oliver North, in his bid to be the Republican nominee for one of Virginia's seats in the U.S. Senate, sidestepped television commercials and instead used direct-mail video to address the specific con-

cerns of Republican delegates to the state nominating convention. This tactic proved to be fruitful: he consequently won the party's nomination, though he ultimately lost the election. Andy Meisler, "From Your Mailbox to Your VCR: More Ads," *New York Times*, Oct. 16, 1994, 6E.
4. In addition to *The Gay Agenda* (1992), discussed in my conclusion, *Gay Rights, Special Rights* (1993) has also been used by the Christian right in organizing efforts against gays-in-the-military and state and local pro-gay initiatives.
5. In different degrees and forms, gay activists have often embraced a public silence surrounding homosexual behavior while emphasizing mainstream likenesses. This historical strategy of "silence" and "likeness" was utilized in early-1960s homosexual protests in Washington, D.C., as noted in the documentary *Before Stonewall* (1984), and Anita Bryant's 1977 "Save Our Children" campaign. Bryant's campaign successfully overturned a gay rights ordinance in Dade County, Florida. During the Dade County conflict, pro-gay activists discouraged gays from canvassing local neighborhoods so as not to stir up anti-gay sentiment. On the

heels of Bryant's campaign, John Briggs, state senator from Orange County, California, submitted Proposition 6 to a state ballot in 1978. The Briggs Amendment would have denied employment to gays and lesbians in the California public school system. In the campaign waged against "6," David Goodstein, owner of the *Advocate*, suggested that "all gay people could help best by maintaining very low profiles." The initiative was defeated by 58 percent of those voting. The responses to anti-gay activities in Dade County and California are discussed in Michael Ward and Mark Freeman, "Defending Gay Rights: The Campaign against the Briggs Amendment in California," *Radical America* 13.4 (1979): 11-26. For a more complete discussion of the various organized efforts against the Briggs initiative, see both Ward and Freeman, "Defending Gay Rights," 11–26, and Amber Hollibaugh, "Building a Movement beyond Anti-Gay Referenda," *Resist Newsletter*, June 1990, 4–5, 9.

6. These gay and lesbian complaints are discussed in "No on 9 Faces the Music," *Alternative Connection*, Jan. 1993, 1, 11. *Alternative Connection* is a Portland newspaper "serving the community of alternative lifestyles."

7. Chuck Kleinhans, "Mainstreams and Margins: *Ethnic Notions, Tongues Untied*," *Jump Cut* 36 (1991): 109.

8. A brief history of the OCA is included in "Bashers," *New Republic*, Sept. 21, 1992: 9–10. The history of OCA results at the ballot box is taken from "OCA Suffers Legal Setback," *Alternative Connection*, Dec. 1992, 6, and "No on 9 Chair Reveals Winning Strategy," *Alternative Connection*, Jan. 1993, 9.

9. The No on 9 campaign's strategy and finances are reported in "No on 9 Campaign Ponders Future, Calls for Dialogue," *Alternative Connection*, Dec. 1992, 1, 3; "No on 9 Chair Reveals Winning Strategy," *Alternative Connection*, Jan. 1993, 9; and "No on 9 Faces the Music."

10. I interviewed Barbara Bernstein and Elaine Velazquez about the history of *Fighting for Our Lives* in Portland, Oregon, on July 13, 1994. Bernstein is a Pacifica radio talk show host and Velazquez made the video *Moving Mountains: The Story of the Yin Mien*. Both expressed apprehension about the potential for marginalizing segments of the lesbian and gay community through this use of nonthreatening speakers, though both equally felt this was required given the political urgency of the moment and the time constraints.

11. The information on the distribution and exhibition history of *Fighting for Our Lives* is taken from the Velazquez and Bernstein interview.

12. Hollibaugh, "Building a Movement," 4–5, 9.

13. In my interview with the videomakers, Velazquez explained that using lesbians rather than gay men was a conscious choice to give voice to women in a situation in which she felt gay male voices usually dominated.

14. In her release statement for the video, MacDonald asserts that "*Ballot Measure 9* is a powerful tool for change, and a vivid testament to the courage and stamina of lesbians, gay men, bisexuals and their supporters. This video is ideal to share with family and friends, for community and church gatherings, PFLAG [Parents, Families and Friends of Lesbians and Gays] members, students, labor groups, professional associations and lesbian and gay organizations."

15. *Ballot Measure 9* is a well-filmed and -edited video. Given its availability and its skillful construction, it would be useful for classroom discussions on gay and lesbian politics and representation, conservative Christian organizing and rhetoric, and other concerns related to anti-gay ballot measures.

16. Dale C. Sattergren, "Gays Should Police Themselves," *Alternative Connection*, Jan. 1993, 4; unsigned letter, *Lavender Network*, May 1993, 8.

17. See Chuck Kleinhans, "Forms, Politics, Makers, and Contexts: Basic Issues for a Theory of Radical Political Documentary," in "*Show Us Life*": *Toward a History and Aesthetics of the Committed Documentary*, ed. Thomas Waugh (Metuchen, N.J.: Scarecrow, 1984), 323.

CHRIS CAGLE

[2] *Imaging the Queer South:*
Southern Lesbian and
Gay Documentary

"Southern lesbian and gay documentary," like many categories, presents practical difficulties and political hazards. Notably, the term is somewhat of a neologism, christening a new cinematic genre for which there exist very few examples. Part of its difficulty, in fact, lies in the instability of "the South" as an analytic concept: Does the term refer to documentaries by lesbians or gay men currently living in the South, or who have ever lived in the South? To those about the lives, cultures, or experiences of Southern lesbians and gays? Or perhaps to documentaries with a particular inherent aesthetic? Even to imagine these possibilities leaves others unexplored and the contested meanings of "lesbian," "gay," and "documentary" more or less unexamined.

I have chosen an equally perilous phrase — "imaging the queer South" — for the first half of the title not out of a faith in the existence, much less the knowability, of a single queer South. Rather, I wish to emphasize the primary means through which Southern and lesbian and gay filmic representations continue to be understood both popularly and academically: the good (true) image versus the bad (false) image. In this understanding, Hollywood cinema has fabricated the false image, the myths of the idyllic Old South and the backward present-day South, whereas documentaries about or set in the South present a truer image. Images of gays and lesbians in the South have long been present in films. Tennessee Williams's *Suddenly Last Summer* and *Cat on a Hot Tin Roof* and Carson McCullers's *Member of the Wedding* and *Reflections in a Golden Eye* provided material for Hollywood views of Southern gays and lesbians, while seminal and popular gay liberation documentaries like *Gay USA* (Arthur Bressan 1977) and *Word Is Out* (Mariposa Film Group 1977) have included men and women who are queer and from the South. Less forthcoming, however, has been an adequate political or critical vocabulary with which to understand the complex intersections of Southern and lesbian, bisexual, or gay identities. Nor have studies of Southern regionality in film or video found a model sufficiently sophisticated to evade the limitations inherent in "images of" analysis.[1]

Further, very little scholarship to date addresses either the theoretical connections between lesbian and gay identities and Southern regional identity or the cultures and lives of specific groups of lesbian, bisexual, and gay Southerners. In order to begin this project, I will examine the relationship between documentary representations and Benedict Anderson's and Immanuel Wallerstein's theorizations of "imagined community." While the concept originally was used to explain the rise of nationalism, it also allows the cultural critic to think regional and sexual collectivities simultaneously, and to relate them to mass-mediated representations.

The documentaries I consider here are by two Southern "exiles," Marlon Riggs's *Tongues Untied* (1989) and Ellen Spiro's *DiAna's Hair Ego* (1990) and *Greetings from Out Here* (1993). The figure of the regional exile, the individual who leaves her or his home region, represents one instance of conflicting allegiance and thereby underscores the potential disjuncture between regional affiliation and participation in gay and lesbian subcultures. I trace the different and conflicting ways these documentaries imagine regional and sexual community to clarify the intersection of region and sexuality in these films and, at the same time, to address the dearth of historical and critical scholarship on Southern gays and lesbians.

▶

Imagining Regional and Sexual Community

Attempts to describe Southern culture have often relied on a notion of a distinct tradition and history. As romanticized in the media, in histories, and in political rhetoric, "Southern culture" often means Old South "tradition" in the face of "Northernization." Yet as the development of mass media and regional economies allows for some liberalization, lesbian, bisexual, and gay subcultures are finding more breathing room in many Southern communities. As one woman in *Greetings from Out Here* says, "There's this term called the New South, and I think a lot of what is going on is contributing to it. A lot of lesbians and gays want to be a part of that." Nonetheless, evocations of a New South cannot fully explain what that South is, how it relates to an Old South, or how it is specifically Southern.

"What can one mean by Southern culture?" asks Immanuel Wallerstein in the title of an essay in which he argues that the concept of Southern culture is far from self-evident or even coherent.[2] The multiple meanings of his question are instructive because they prod us to think not only of the surface question—what is Southern culture?—but also of how "Southern culture" as a concept serves a particular political project and functions rhetorically. For many writers on the South, Wallerstein notes,

> culture turns out to be less an analytic construct than a rhetorical flag around which one rallies, a weapon in larger political battles. This concept of culture as shorthand for a political program is not about to disappear, in the South or anywhere else. But unless we distance ourselves from it just a bit, our vision of social reality risks being obscured. I should like, therefore, to attempt to see how the rhetoric is created and why it is treated as "culture."[3]

Wallerstein traces in turn three principal rhetorics of "culture" used in describing the South. The first is Southern culture as "a description of a set of traits, culture as 'tradition' . . . some summum of institutions and ideas/values that is thought to be long-existing and highly resistant to change."[4] The second is Southern culture as an ethical stance or as virtue. "In this kind of analysis," Wallerstein notes, "culture does not refer to the traits of a group, but to those of a minority, almost inevitably a beleaguered minority, within some larger whole. This minority could be a regional minority, a class minority, an ethnic minority."[5] The third is Southern culture in binary relation to the North.

Benedict Anderson's formulation of the imagined community helps us begin to distance ourselves from the shorthand of regional culture without ignoring the markings of geographic origin on individuals and cultures. For Anderson, the nation is an imagined community: "*imagined* because the members of even the smallest nation will never know most of their fellow-members, meet them or even hear of them, yet in the minds of each lives the image of their communion" and "*community*, because, regardless of the actual inequality and exploitation that may prevail in each, the nation is always conceived as a deep, horizontal comradeship."[6] Anderson seeks to reconcile contradictions arising when Marxist and leftist historians and theorists discuss the nation—namely, the disparity between the "objective" artificiality of nations and the experienced reality of nations and nationalism.

Anderson's concept of imagined community has been popular with media scholars because it defines the process of nation building as that of mediated identification, whether the mediation is print capitalism (in Anderson's account of the rise of nations) or modern-day mass media. Yet the concept of imagined community also helps to explain the construction of the "South" as a mediated communion of otherwise unconnected people; lateral identification allows for many disparate localities and cultures to see themselves as one region—the South—united by culture or tradition. In this way, the subjective antiquity of the "Old South" tradition continually clashes with the reality of the modern "New South"; supporters of Confederate state flags, for instance, frequently claim that the flags honor a long-running "heritage" or "tradition" but rarely mention that the stars and bars were added to state flags in defiance of integration. This instance is not isolated but points to a central ambivalence about what defines the South, as definitions that rely on one criterion (e.g., the geographic confines of thirteen states) often compete with mediated images of Deep South culture and heritage.

Consequently, assertions of the cultural specificity of Southern lesbians and gays tend to set the modern-day queer Southerner against an all too readable backdrop of "Southern heritage." For instance, James Sears's *Growing Up Gay in the South*, the only extended academic study of lesbians and gays in the South to date, establishes itself as an empirical study of thirteen South Carolina youths, but relies on static backdrops of history to explain Southern lesbian and gay experiences. "As a region of the country, the South is defined by its history and culture," writes Sears, yet he does not define this history or culture and in fact reverts to previously defined Southern history:

> More than anything else, though, *South Carolina is a state of mind*, born of history, bounded by war, defeat, reconstruction, and desegregation. . . . Theirs is a collective memory of an idyllic past captured in its Gothic architecture and romance literature. . . . Theirs is also the less remembered collective history of the contributions of the poor, the black, and women. . . . This is a culture in which the antebellum, patriarchal ethos is rooted in Southern honor, Christian faith, and an extended family.[7]

In defining South Carolina (and here, by extension, the South) by its history, Sears engages in a selective memory at once ambiguous and fully conventional. For this "collective history" requires knowledge of many figures and events of which many South Carolinians are undoubtedly unaware, whereas the contributions of poor, black, and female South Carolinians manage to be "less remembered" yet still "collective history" in *a* (singular) culture whose ethos is antebellum patriarchy. Sears's example suggests how difficult it is to think simultaneously of the particularity of lesbian or gay experience in the South and of the collectivity of Southern culture or history. Never does he consider that collectivity may be (though is not necessarily) imagined differently for sexual communities than for regional communities.

In fact, gay and lesbian American counterpublics do imagine themselves both regionally and geographically, as mainstream national gay culture frequently associates urbanity with the North and backwardness with the South. A relatively recent (1992) *Village Voice* article by Richard Goldstein, for instance, cites several victims of oppression in the South—a fired junior high teacher, a murdered gay man, a closeted National Guard member in North Carolina, and the beleaguered Gay and Lesbian Association at Auburn University in Alabama—as proof that homophobia really is still a material problem.[8] Goldstein evokes an imagined community that excludes the South yet at the same time sets up Southern queers as exemplars of an untheorized but lived queer politics. The Southerners who find themselves included in "our" desire and "our" movement end up isolated on the other side of the "we" of the editorial's address. The problem is not quite Goldstein's indecision over whom to include; on the contrary, the article tries to imagine a horizontal communal identification with a group (Southern lesbians and gay men) understood from the beginning as quite distinct and removed from the group that the writer imagines himself addressing through the *Voice*.

Documentary films and videos, too, have provided images of a reactionary South, usually through the same anecdotal representational strategy. *Word Is Out*, for instance, relies on the testimony of a Texan woman who had difficulty coming to terms with her fundamentalist Baptist upbringing. While shifting the focus from personal testimony to the pride parades of New York, San Francisco, Miami, Chicago, and Houston, *Gay USA* still presents homophobia in the South—the Dade County/Miami civil rights battle and the resulting Anita Bryant crusade—as a structuring element. Like Goldstein's article, these films require a South that is part of the community. In situating these "facts" of oppression in the South, however, such community imagining necessarily demarcates non-Southern queer communities from the political reality and imagination of the South. In emphasizing the homophobia of the South, these representations avoid discussing either the homophobia of the nation outside the South or the very centrality of the South as Other in imagined queer collectivities.

The figure of the Southern exile—who migrates from the South to a Northern or a West Coast city—can thematize the importance of community imagining in defining regional identity. The exile is a Southerner not because of geographic location or daily experience but precisely because of imagined communion with the South as a region and culture. The roots of exile are numerous: aspirations for class mobility, desire for a more homophilic environment, resentment of racial oppression, and a relative lack of economic opportunity in many areas of the South are a few. The concentration of economic and cultural capital for filmmaking in West

Coast and Northern cities has additionally meant that Southern filmmakers must go elsewhere to make their films.[9] Thus the concept of exile is central not only to understanding patterns of lesbian and gay migration, identification, and community imagining but also to addressing the body of Southern media work made by filmmakers no longer residing in the South.

Both Goldstein and gay liberation documentary depict a homophobic South to argue for coming out as a prime political strategy. As Richard Dyer and Tom Waugh have noted, lesbian and gay documentary has often made decisions of form, style, and address analogous to the central act of coming out.[10] A politics of affirmation can also structure Southern exile documentaries, but these works begin to deflect narratives of coming out in order to examine regional and imagined communion more explicitly. Whether expository, testimonial, or experimental in tone, the stylistic choices of Riggs's and Spiro's works reframe the affirmational tradition of lesbian and gay documentaries to address regional particularity.

▶

Performative Documentary: *Tongues Untied*

Though it is not generally distributed, exhibited, or received as a "Southern documentary" per se, Marlon Riggs's *Tongues Untied* explores regional exile in tandem with personal exile. The film's geographic affiliation is largely urban (its citation of Harlem Renaissance figures, its focus on the visibility of black gay men in pride demonstrations), but the personal narrative interrogates the crossings and disjunctures between racial, regional, and sexual identities. Like other performative documentaries, the film "does not draw our attention to the formal qualities or political context of the film directly so much as deflect our attention from the referential quality of documentary altogether."[11] This shift away from documentary referentiality and toward a more poetic expressiveness means that *Tongues Untied* often blurs boundaries between autobiography and history, fiction and documentary, the personal and the collective, at the same time that it depicts conflicting racial, sexual, and regional identities.

One "autobiographical" enactment in the film demonstrates this shift toward the performative documentary mode. One speaker, pictured in straight-on medium close-up, presents the narrative of growing up in Augusta, Georgia. "I heard my calling at age six," the narrator says. "We had a word for boys like me. Punk. Not because I played sex with the other boys. Everybody on the block did that. But because I didn't mind giving it away." The film punctuates the monologue with close-ups of a child's mouth uttering the word *punk*. Alternating epithets continue as the fram-

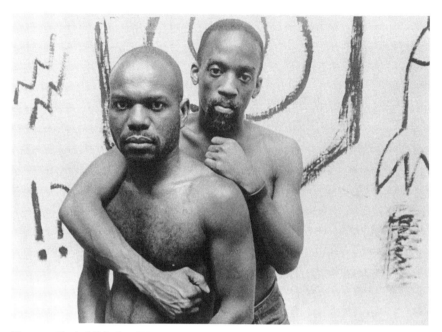

Tongues Untied (Marlon Riggs 1989). Courtesy Frameline, Inc.

ing becomes tighter. The narrator continues to speak about going to secondary school in Augusta, encountering the racism of fellow students. Now, extreme close-ups of the mouths of white men call out the racist taunts "motherfucking coon" and "niggers, go home." "The rednecks hated me," the narrator continues. "Blacks hated me because they assumed my class status made me uppity, assumed my silence as superiority." By this point the speaker's narrative interweaves the spoken narration (grounded in the voice and talking head of the speaker) with the reenacted epithets, which function as autobiographical evidence only on an evocative and performative level.

In works like *Tongues Untied*, Bill Nichols writes, "social actors take on the narrative coherence of a character; they approximate once more those forms of virtual performance that are documentary's answer to professional acting."[12] *Tongues Untied* leaves unclear which words and which performances, if any, are autobiographical, and it fails to identify the man who narrates the story. The film credits Riggs with writing the monologues entitled "Black Chant," "Three Pieces of ID," "Snap Rap," and "The Wages of Silence" and Joseph Beam with another monologue, "Words from the Heart." However, it is difficult to know which words belong to which monologues, and whether the speakers on screen are performing a monologue or recounting their personal histories. The result is deflection from the autobiographical and interactive modes associated with

Tongues Untied (Marlon Riggs 1989). Courtesy Frameline, Inc.

gay-affirmational documentary. Rather than document a black gay man's life through expository or interactive modes, *Tongues Untied* evokes a certain collective autobiography wherein the speakers of the autobiographical narratives are interchangeable precisely because their personal histories are imagined to be congruent. In this light, whether Riggs himself grew up in the South becomes secondary to the meaning of the film, and the South serves mostly to signal the racism and homophobia encountered by the collective black gay subject.

Tongues Untied imagines this collective subject through evocation and ungrounded testimonials. Through aural and visual montage, Riggs links the political work of black gay men today to that of the civil rights movement. One sequence provides a series of obituary photos of black gay men who have died of AIDS, giving way to a voice-over that declares, "Rhythms resonate within me." A shot of Martin Luther King Jr. is intercut with an archive photo of marchers behind a banner that says "March with Selma." The film then intercuts present-day footage of the organization Gay Men of African Descent marching in a New York pride march. The montage cuts back to a sign that says "We Shall Overcome." Riggs's double-edged attack becomes clear: the film condemns the white gay community for its racism and the straight black community for failing to live up to its own political ideals of liberation. If interactive documentary exhibits, in Nichols's words, an "excessive faith in witnesses" and "naive history,"[13] the loss of referential emphasis in performative documentary marks a deflection from historical specificity toward a more evocative history. To the extent that its polemic relies on an iconographic referencing of Southern geography ("March with Selma"), *Tongues Untied* presents the tradition of the civil rights struggle as a static history, a fully known and readable narrative against which the narratives of present-day black gay men can be understood. Further, in its eagerness to evoke a community of black gays, the documentary removes the history of Gay Men of African Descent from its metropolitan locality. To the extent that its referencing of the civil rights struggle evokes an imagined communion across historical eras, the documentary seems unable to imagine geographic specificity.

▶

"A Queer's Eye View": *Greetings from Out Here*

Whereas *Tongues Untied* uses narratives of growing up in the South as a backdrop for its explorations of urban black gay life and identity, Ellen Spiro's *Greetings from Out Here* explicitly seeks to portray lesbians and gay men living in the South and to document a geographic specificity for the lives of the lesbians and gay men she interviews. In one sequence, a man at the Atlanta pride parade says, "This isn't a New York thing, this isn't San Francisco, this is Atlanta, Georgia, and, no, you don't have to pick up and move to San Francisco to be gay." The statement encapsulates some of the optimistic spirit both of Spiro's video and of Atlanta's gay culture, yet Spiro herself did pick up and move from the South to live freely as a dyke. After a credit sequence replete with cows and mock-postcard titling, Spiro's voice-over begins a personal narrative that frames the film. She mentions her childhood and the numerous crushes she had on girls or female celebrities, then adds:

> But it wasn't until I was seventeen that I found the words to describe what I was, and it nearly scared me to death. So I took off from Charlottesville, Virginia, to New York City, where I became a full-fledged gay activist. . . . But there was something funny about this picture: here I was being an out dyke and back home I was still in the closet. I started thinking about those gay people who don't flee but stay home and do the bravest thing of all—be who they are where they are. I was feeling a little homesick and after three years my girlfriend and I were breaking up, so at her suggestion I decided to hit the road.

Retroactive narratives of coming out and personal journeys as political testimony are conventions of lesbian and gay affirmational documentary.[14] But *Greetings* also uses testimonial narratives as foils to Spiro's articulations of her own personal identity. Like Ross McElwee's (straight) Southern exile documentary *Sherman's March* (1979), *Greetings* uses voice-over to situate the events and social actors in an almost diaristic mode of filmmaking.[15] En route to Louisiana, Spiro laments, "I'm feeling some loneliness over my girlfriend who's no longer my girlfriend, but my mind will be on other things soon. I'm going to New Orleans for Mardi Gras." Spiro thereby connects the personal narratives of those she interviews with her own personal narrative; the danger, though, is that she treats these other narratives as foils for her emotional well-being.

The diaristic and autobiographical motifs help authenticate Spiro's videomaking, yet Spiro's own exile position conflicts with an "insider" authenticity. For instance, her voice-over declares, "Once I had the notion that to be free and queer was to be in a big city but here I am in the hills of Tennessee, visiting some Radical Faeries creating their own sanctuary." This voice-over seeks to praise the film's subjects; in no way, though, does Spiro seek to apply her new knowledge to her exile position. The video does not suggest that Spiro herself might move from the big city because it imagines Spiro's New York community and this Southern community as both separate and parallel. As a result, Spiro's exploration of Southern culture becomes double-edged, situated in the same split of imagined community that marks Goldstein's *Village Voice* article and documentaries like *Word Is Out*.

Greetings portrays Southern gay and lesbian collectivity in a lateral fashion, positing an imagined community of otherwise isolated social actors. Toward the beginning of the tape, Spiro's voice-over announces,

> My mission is to explore Southern gay subcultures and to find people who stayed in their small towns instead of joining the anonymous masses of big cities. This is also my attempt to view the Southern world that formed me and to recreate it with my camera, this time with a queer's eye view.

The video narrates Spiro's journey (geographically) through the South and (metaphorically) toward some reconciliation of her Southern background with her current identity as an out lesbian. Nevertheless, while certain scenes do portray some Southern gay subcultures—in particular the gay rodeo in Dallas, the gay krewe in New Orleans, a women's music festival in Cloudland, Georgia, and the Radical Faerie commune in Short Mountain, Tennessee—the video does not offer broader insight into any particular lived community or subculture.

The tape instead proceeds through most of the Southern states, interviewing a "queer" representative in each: DiAna DiAna, an AIDS educator in Columbia, South Carolina; participants in a gay rodeo in Texas; Michael Monk and Isis in rural Arkansas; Alan Gurganus in North Carolina; a gay

Mardi Gras krewe in New Orleans; John Blansett, a person with AIDS in Okolona, Mississippi; members of the Faerie commune; participants at the Cloudland festival; Chance, a sixteen-year-old lesbian in Atlanta; and James Cox, a choir director in Jasper, Alabama. The even distribution of subjects among states and urban and rural locations allows the video to posit a lateral community—lateral because their geographic location "represents" most of the region and community: even though these people do not know each other, they are performing a central act ("being who they are where they are") simultaneously. The tape's image and sound tracks both corroborate this lateral presentation, and the music includes a diverse sampling of queer- and nonqueer-identified Southern music, from openly lesbian bands Two Nice Girls and Girls in the Nose to the obscure classic "I Like Girls" by mid-1960s Louisiana garage band Surrealistic Pillar; from Fats Domino to the Carrboro, North Carolina, band Southern Culture on the Skids.

If the roster of the tape's social actors manages to be both diverse and predictable, a comparison to the promotional blurb for *Word Is Out* reveals a sampling style similar to Spiro's:

> *Word Is Out: "Stories of Some of Our Lives"* is just that: interviews with 26 very diverse people—ranging in age from 18 to 77, in locales from San Francisco to New Mexico to Boston, in type from a beehived housewife to a sultry drag queen—who speak tellingly, funnily, and movingly of their experiences as gay men and women in a way that destroys decades worth of accumulated stereotypes.[16]

Remarkably, this summary participates in the same typing ("beehived housewife," "sultry drag queen") that it berates. Admittedly, *Greetings* does not use stereotype as a shorthand for character as this promotional description does. But much as the video's cartoonish map represents Georgia by an icon of a peach or Mississippi by a boll of cotton, the video ends up resorting to kitschy iconography as an emblem for both Southern culture and the relation of queers to this culture. Like the eclectic panorama of another Southern documentary, *Athens, GA, Inside/Out*, which tries to give a sense of Southern music culture by interweaving excursions into the central Georgia countryside, Spiro's documentary presents anecdotal snippets of Southern culture as backdrop for its subjects' interviews. Brief shots of kitsch street signs ("Camp Street," "Homochitte River"), business establishments (a barbeque restaurant, Wal-Mart) and other Southern "signs" (a *National Enquirer* headline on Garth Brooks's lesbian sister, a Georgia peach stand) fill in the transitions from one vignette to another. Spiro even stops at an Arkansas pet cemetery.

The resulting separation between the tape's Southern communities and the implied audience can be celebratory, but it is also confining. To be queer in the South, *Greetings* seems to say, is to have an abstracted, ironic, even camp-driven distance from the surrounding culture and people. While this type of ironic stance may be shared by many lesbians and gay men in the South—it appears in the interviews with Michael Monk and Alan Gurganis—Spiro is less concerned with documenting how any gay or lesbian individual or subculture has ironized the ambient culture than with positing a necessary cultural difference between the lesbian or gay man and the culture in which she or he lives. Spiro may present queer Southern culture as an imagined horizontal bond, but the presentation continually threatens to slip into the very ironic distance and regional othering it is working against.

Equally problematic is the manner in which *Greetings from Out Here* often subsumes racial difference within its narratives of personal and historical past. In its celebration of Southern lesbian and gay lives, any potential conflicts or disjunctures between African-American and gay or lesbian identities are downplayed. In fact, there seems to be a certain convenience in how the narrative of James Cox, the "gay minister with roots in the civil rights movement," enables the larger political work of the film. "Through James Cox, the openly gay black minister," critic Rob Nixon claims, "Spiro makes a strong connection between racism and homophobia. Cox links his identity as a gay man to his struggles in the civil rights movement."[17] Spiro certainly suggests a connection between racism and homophobia but does not specify what exactly that connection is. The video leaves unstated its own stance on the relation between racial and homophobic oppressions. Does it corroborate Cox's point of view? How might other African-American lesbians or gay men (for instance, Isis, whose "roots" are not specified) conceive of the relation between the two? By leaving these questions unasked, the documentary in fact presents a separation between the very histories it tries to imagine as simultaneous.

▶——————————————————————————————————

Localizing Strategies: *DiAna's Hair Ego*

In contrast to the ironic distance of *Greetings* from its subject matter and from Southern culture in general, an earlier work of Spiro's, *DiAna's Hair Ego*, distinguishes itself by depicting the largely non-gay African-American community of Columbia, South Carolina, in an engaged and respectful manner. *DiAna's Hair Ego* documents the operations of the South Carolina AIDS Education Network (SCAEN), directed by DiAna DiAna from her hair salon. The group's success has largely come from its insistence on reaching out to local communities through grassroots organization and education. Designed to address localized audiences (among them the New York AIDS activists who helped fund, make, and distribute *DiAna's Hair Ego*), Spiro's tape mimics SCAEN's media makers, who strive to be aware of its audience and to communicate with them in their vernacular.

DiAna DiAna founded SCAEN in 1987. The group still runs off tips from DiAna's hair salon and private donations. In articles and in Spiro's video, DiAna discusses several organizing and pedagogical strategies that the group has found effective: speaking to one's community in a way they can hear; training teenagers to educate their peers; talking about sex; redefining "at risk" to include women from different backgrounds and marital status; and drawing churches into the drive for AIDS education.[18] As Dr. Bambi Sumpter, Diana's key collaborator, notes in an interview on the tape, although SCAEN is only one of many grassroots organizations to work on AIDS education, the group has provided one-to-one AIDS information to more than nine thousand individuals in South Carolina.

In contrast to *Greetings*, which uses Spiro's voice-over, and to *Tongues Untied*, which employs narration and voice-over to signal and enact personal narratives, *DiAna's Hair Ego* includes no voice-over narration or extradiegetic music. Instead, the sound track mimics SCAEN's grassroots strategy of letting the participants speak for themselves about political situations. Consequently, the narrative style of *DiAna's Hair Ego* is in part anecdotal. The video starts off with a shot of suds in a sink as a woman gets her hair washed. The only sounds are the water running and the client discussing DiAna's efforts to educate community members about AIDS. The rest of the sound track consists of interviews with DiAna, Bambi, associates of SCAEN, and members of the various communities SCAEN serves. One woman getting her hair done, for instance, describes the firing of a gay man who had AIDS: "I knew he wasn't gonna stay, that they would let him go, I just didn't know how they would go about doing it. I saw how they went about doing it—very quietly and hush-hush." Reginald Morton, SCAEN's twentysomething music director, details the quarantine of a family in Orangeburg County, South Carolina, because of AIDS phobia. But such anecdotes do not simply relate the operation of AIDS phobia, institutional racism, and homophobia in South Carolina. Instead, Spiro's interviews with various members of the Columbia community also recount the grassroots efforts of DiAna and others to educate people about AIDS, through talks at organizations from cosmetology schools to businesswomen's organizations to NAACP fund-raisers. In addition, DiAna, Bambi Sumter, and other members of SCAEN correct what they see as problems in the mass media's depiction of AIDS by making their own AIDS educational media—from informational videos and popular music to low-literacy pamphlets for adults and coloring books for children. The group uses video as a tool for outreach and political persuasion: they have taped around two thousand questions that schoolchildren have about AIDS and show several of them to counter resistance to educating children about AIDS.

DiAna's Hair Ego has been shown to audiences in other areas of the country, through activist video distribution and PBS and other television airings. These screenings do not merely describe AIDS education in South Carolina, but also educate viewers in other areas of the country about AIDS, much in the fashion of DiAna and SCAEN. While the documentary's lack of expository authority may not inform the outside viewer about the current political context of Columbia, South Carolina, it creates a "localness" by aligning the political aspirations of the documentary with those of its subjects. At the same time, thanks to the tape's national distribution and broadcast, it promotes unity and coalition building among blacks and whites, Northerners and Southerners, Easterners and Westerners who organize in the struggle against AIDS.

▶

Conclusion

To return to the question posed earlier—how might collectivity be imagined differently (or the same) for sexual and regional communities?—it seems important to emphasize that an interplay between the concepts of history and geography has often been propped on evocations of a "culture." On the one hand, "a culture" poses the danger of subsuming racial and intra-regional differences under a presumed single voice of "the South." On the other hand, many scholars, including Wallerstein, find references to Southern "culture" necessarily crippling in their particularism, as different states, different counties, different towns and cities, different neighborhoods, different families all have their own "cultures." The challenge is to critique reactionary popular histories of "Southern heritage" while resisting the tendency to discount Southern culture as a more illusory or politically reactionary concept than, say, American culture.

To discuss "Southern lesbian and gay documentary," as I have here, ends up skirting the difficult political ground of particularism. Why designate a lesbian or gay documentary by the region of its origin? Why not categorize its city or its neighborhood of origin? The problem lies in how much meaning we expect categorization itself to give. The three examples here, *Tongues Untied*, *Greetings from Out Here*, and *DiAna's Hair Ego*, hardly demonstrate a unity of aesthetic, reception, or polemic. Furthermore, as I have suggested, to reference a "Southern culture" or "way of life" threatens to fall into a conservative definition of region as an already known entity, be it antebellum glory or, in the New South version, a complete disavowal of Southern accountability for racism or the troubles with industrial-capitalist development. All the same, I insist in my analysis of these documentaries that geographic location is crucial in understanding the histories of Southern gays and lesbians and that region remains a primary and perhaps useful construct in thinking about location.

Geopolitical, "cultural," and historical definitions of regionality may be even more difficult to untangle when one considers the tendency in lesbian and gay politics to value urban geography as a site of political definition and action. Gay and lesbian history, and the queer theoretical work based on it, have often focused on the history of specific places—San Francisco, New York—or understood "community" as the urban queer enclave. Important exceptions to this trend (commune politics, attention to voter referenda in Western states, gay/straight alliances in suburban and non-urban high schools) do suggest alternative ways of conceptualizing the relation between geography and political action. To this end, the recurrence of lesbian and gay "exile" narratives speaks not only to the urban focus of lesbian and gay history, but also to an imagined collectivity that exceeds the particularism of geographic borders.

Each of the three exile documentaries discussed here offers its own strategy for exploring the particularisms of region and sexuality. Through its fusion of political content with interactional, expository, and performative documentary form, *DiAna's Hair Ego* suggests localization of documentary decisions as one possibility for overcoming the problems of regional address in activist video work. *Greetings* ignores the problematic of regional address but is forthright in thematizing and depicting Southern lesbian and gay experiences while trying to adapt various documentary strategies, from interview to filmed spectacle, to suggest the diversity of queer Southern experience. *Tongues Untied* figures the South mostly as a negated past yet suggests that regional and sexual collectivities and personal experiences are closely interrelated, through its final association of black gay pride and civil rights marches. None of these interventions provides *a* formula for representing Southern lesbian and gay experiences, to be sure. Rather, together they show that documenting the lives and cultures of lesbians, bisexuals, and gays in the South requires more than simply adding "region" to an already known narrative of gay and lesbian liberation.

NOTES

1. See in particular Edward D. C. Campbell, *The Celluloid South: Hollywood and the Southern Myth* (Knoxville: University of Tennessee Press, 1981); Warren French, ed., *The South and Film* (Jackson: University Press of Mississippi, 1981); and Karl G. Heider, ed., *Images of the South: Constructing a Regional Culture on Film and Video* (Athens: University of Georgia Press, 1993).

2. Immanuel Wallerstein, "What Can One Mean by Southern Culture?" in *The Evolution of a Southern Culture*, ed. Numan V. Bartley (Athens: University of Georgia Press, 1988), 1-13.

3. Ibid., 7.

4. Ibid., 3.

5. Ibid., 6.

6. Benedict Anderson, *Imagined Communities: Reflections on the Origin and Spread of Nationalism* (London: Verso, 1991), 6.

7. James T. Sears, *Growing Up Gay in the South: Race, Gender, and Journeys of the Spirit* (New York: Haworth, 1991), 72; emphasis in the original.

8. Richard Goldstein, "Welcome to the Safety-drome," *Village Voice* 37.26 (June 30, 1992): 39.

9. This is not to deny the relatively large film industry centered in the South; after California and New York, North Carolina, Florida, and Georgia serve as the most significant sites of film production. See Mike Nielson and Eric Bates, "Bright Lights, Low Wages," *Southern Exposure* 20.4 (Winter 1992): 22–25.

10. Richard Dyer, *Now You See It: Studies on Lesbian and Gay Film* (New York: Routledge, 1992), and Thomas Waugh, "Lesbian and Gay Documentary: Minority Self-Imaging in Oppositional Film Practice," in *Image Ethics: The Moral Rights of Subjects in Photographs, Film and Television*, ed. Larry Gross, John Stuart Katz, and Jay Ruby (New York: Oxford University Press, 1988), 248–74.

11. Bill Nichols, *Blurred Boundaries: Questions of Meaning in Contemporary Culture* (Bloomington: Indiana University Press, 1994), 93.

12. Ibid., 100.

13. Ibid., 95.

14. See Dyer, *Now You See It*, and Waugh, "Lesbian and Gay Documentary."

15. See Tara McPherson, "Both Kinds of Arms," *Velvet Light Trap* 35 (Spring 1995): 3-18, and Sharon R. Roseman, "A Documentary Fiction and Ethnographic Production: An Analysis of *Sherman's March*," *Cultural Anthropology* 6: 505-24. McPherson's essay in particular tackles many of the issues of history and community imagining that are central to this essay, but her analysis slips into a strong regional parochialism that sees any vindication of the South only as a defense of racist history.

16. Videocassette package for *Word Is Out*, New Yorker Films.

17. Rob Nixon, "Film Explores Southern Gays," *Southern Exposure* 21.3 (Fall 1993): 4.

18. DiAna DiAna, "Winning the War against AIDS," *Southern Exposure* 21.4 (Winter 1993): 60–61. See also DiAna DiAna,"Talking that Talk" and Bambi Sumpter, "We Have a Job to Do," in *Women, AIDS, and Activism*, ed. ACT UP/New York Women and AIDS Book Group (Boston: South End Press, 1990), 219–22, 223–26.

ERIKA SUDERBURG

[3] *Real/Young/TV Queer*

Why did I pick reality, out of all the subjects I don't know anything about?

::   Albert Brooks as ersatz documentary maker Albert Brooks in *Real Life : An American Comedy* (1979), a spoof on *An American Family* as refashioned by a Hollywood studio, a generic Human Research Institute, and a hapless comic

Sorry but your lives will not be immortalized this year.

::   Rejection letter sent to "losing families" tested by "research institute" in *Real Life*

I was actually surprised that they brought out the idea of sexuality-homosexuality as something more than just liking to kiss boys on the sly. The way they edited it they made me seem obnoxious. I became harder and harder to take. I did think that I was terribly avant-garde . . . but there I was . . . a big fag.

::   Lance Loud on coming out on the *Dick Cavett Show* in 1973 as recounted in HBO's 1983 follow-up to *An American Family*

Self-identified queer, gay, lesbian, and transgendered youth appear infrequently, if at all, in American "mainstream" television documentary. In the televised nineties repressive parameters are being redrawn slightly, bent a bit to enfold, co-opt or accommodate a previously wallflowered sexual minority. Documentary television is a litmus test of positioning, acceptance, and representation—a charting of how queer images, for so long sewn into the hems of various cultural productions, are revealed. We are in a brief period in which queerness as fashion or queerness as a required demographic core sample occupies heretofore ignored representational space. The straight "teen" market and its televised youth subjects, a market long exploited and seemingly endlessly lucrative, has cracked open the storm door enough to admit, at least temporarily, a queer subset that proves deliciously uncontainable. One can constitute this phenomenon either as a positive step toward the eradication of invisibility or as the selling out of a constituency long associated with defiant marginality. What does "real" queer look like?

Real queer emphatically does not look like its (re)presentations in social-problem documentary. In these scenarios the queer surveyed ends up as the substitute subject, just another "other" to be catalogued and regurgitated within an ossified "you are there" tourist structure. Alternative sexualities are interjected without examination or alteration and grafted onto the social-problem documentary form, which thrives on searching for unrepresented entities in need of description and, more importantly, in need of explanation to a constituted "normative" viewership. This very framing of a difference cast as so unredeemably foreign that a documentary must be constructed to explain it reproduces the alienation of that difference. By definition queerness is cast as "social problem." In American televisual culture this form collapses into dreck, exemplified by 20/20's astonishingly ignorant 1991 neoethnographic cruise "report" on Northampton, Massachusetts, as exotic lesbian enclave. Such is the territory that the group of "real life" documentaries that I will discuss traverses, combats, and bargains with.

Today there is evidence of a kind of "good neighbor policy" at MTV and PBS accompanied by glimmerings of network teases—Sandra Bernhard's shape-shifting character on *Roseanne* or the Cicely town founders story line on *Northern Exposure*, for example. When k.d. lang gets shaved by Cindy Crawford on the cover of *Vanity Fair*, is "it" in effect all over . . . or is "it" just beginning? "It" is amorphously defined here as visibility, desirability, fashionability, any use as decorative motif, naughty window dressing, or generic lip service to any "underground" practices made cute or saleable. How chic can lesbianism be made and will the trickle-down effect alter the launching of queer images in the future? A microcosmic tracing of television documentary programming suggests a way to begin monitoring this mutating representation, starting with the ultimate family documentary *An American Family* and ending with a progressive, neoliberal restating of the documentary ethos in *The Ride*.

It is intriguing, given the media attention to and fashion currency of "alternative" sexualities, to begin examining the representation of gay and lesbian subjects within three important mass media documentary explorations of the American ethos, centered on the construction, disintegration, and definition of "family." Gay, lesbian, transgendered, and bisexual youth are at the epicenter of rightist attacks, forming the most obvious and vulnerable targets for persons trading in various ignorant homophobic clichés. Rabid gay teachers as conversion missionaries and predatory jock gym teachers still populate the propaganda of the "family values" right. The battle, the hate literature screams, is over "our children." The question should be turned around, given that one of the single most wrenching national statistics is the staggering rate of gay teen suicide. The new question is simply, What about "our" children?[1]

This examination will focus on queer identities within *An American Family*, commissioned by PBS and aired in 1971, Music Television Network's (MTV's) *The Real World*, in its New York City, Venice Beach, and San Francisco incarnations (1992–present), and *The Ride*, produced for the Independent Television Service and the Corporation for Public Broadcasting, which aired on selected PBS stations in 1995. This grouping includes a gay-coded but never revealed Lance Loud in *An American Family*. It also includes carefully "cast" and demographically designated Norman, Beth II, and Pedro in the various incarnations of *The Real World*(s). And *The Ride* gives viewers Larry, unsure of his feelings toward men, and Dominic, a preoperative transsexual, and his gay friend Michael. The linkages are specific: all the subjects identified as queer are by necessity (because of the sheer paucity of American representative television options) standing in for all queerness.

The electronically inscribed queers of these three nongay-authored documentaries nevertheless break out of the confines of their demographic niche in a number of surprising and subversive ways. For queer audiences they represent a decisive break from third wheel status; for nonqueer audiences, they cannot help but demystify, enrage, or intrigue. A queer audience in and of itself is essentially impossible to define, encompassing as it does both Queer Nation and Gay Republicans. A deep hunger for any representation at all of identifiably queer images in mass market culture makes each appearance loaded. These images in American television exist tangentially, and the monitoring of them by a diverse queer audience leaves an open debate that underscores the impossibility and undesirability of evolving a coherent queer image despite television's precise demand for a queer formula archetype.[2] By now a portion of a liberal media recognizes that queer representations must be made. Inclusiveness, however, leaves sponsors, networks, and so on open to rabid right-wing attack, often launched over issues of family viewing time and accusations of gay and lesbian advocacy propaganda. Significantly, it is the debate over America's definition of the family in rigid and mythological proportions that connects these documentaries and sets up the possibility for diffusion and identity slippage. A number of questions arise: Who represents a queer "us"? Who makes up

ERIKA SUDERBURG

the demographic queer audience/subject? Who delivers and manipulates queer images via televisual representations? What shapes do these images come in?

▶───

Lance Does the Chelsea, Pat Meets Holly Woodlawn

An American Family was heralded as one of the most important and "shocking" cinema verité examinations of the unraveling of the nuclear family. A camera crew documented the Loud family of Santa Barbara, California, on and off between May 1971 and January 1972. The series introduced into mass media documentary filmmaking discourse a complicated and public moral debate about the responsibilities of documentarians and the rights of their subjects to privacy and control of their own image.[3] These debates took place in a previously unknown climate of mass media attention to the Loud family as a living iconographic American myth.

No one could really be reduced to "type" on *An American Family*, yet Lance, for millions of Americans feeding on standard-issue PBS documentaries, became "the first queer." He was the one who could be wondered aloud at. He hid nothing, and he was literally covered in signifiers if one cared to sift through them. His Super-8 experimental beach movies were of pretty boys kissing and his cultural tastes were defined by Warhol's underground. He arrived hyperreal, alone in television's mainstream, unsupported by the very subcultural avant-garde he floated through, defined by Holly and Andy. Lance becomes, in nostalgic retrospect, a bridge between Santa Barbara and Warhol's Factory. He is the connective tissue between a conception of "normative" America and its urban subculture. All his preparations within the family were for the sole purpose of leaving it.

The filmmaker and crew situated in Santa Barbara were involved daily in the delicate machinations of the imminent disintegration of the Loud family, a disintegration provoked by equal parts marital infidelity, financial problems, general teen hormonal intrigue, divorce, and a growing discomfort with their collective life under the lens. *An American Family* brought to light the very real problems of consent, intimate scrutiny, and the ethical responsibilities of a documentary filmmaker who, in this instance, was privy to information gathered from one family member and withheld from another. Late in the series, Lance Loud almost "comes out" to his mother and is coded as a queer, free spirit, love child, happily adrift in the Chelsea Hotel, with Holly Woodlawn and the marginalia of Warhol's Factory circa the late 1960s. The filmmakers focus on the reading of this boho scene by Lance's mother, who has come for a visit. His queer coding is carefully underscored by the filmmakers, who use the mother as a kind of "everywoman" confronting the confusing definition of her shape-shifting family. The viewer can see her straining to interact calmly with a family moving at lightning speed. Her interactions with Lance are often couched in terms of his outsider status, his desire to define himself but stay close nonetheless. Pat Loud was an agent for this shift; she articulated his positioning at the far reaches of the family. The language used between the two of them is almost entirely about difference. She labels him as the special, creative, unfathomable boy—the one Santa Barbara could not contain.

For American television, a redrawing of societal boundaries began with *An American Family*; it resonates within broadcast history as the tear in the fabric that couldn't be made whole. Lance was part of a family; he was not an isolated specimen. His articulation of his otherness—his removal from the family seat—cast him as a presence whose refusal to play down who he was made it impossible to ignore the life he was fabricating for himself. *An American Family* traded heavily on the legacy of direct cinema/cinema verité.[4] Craig Gilbert, the filmmaker, relied on the tracings of radical American verité masters such as D. A. Pennebaker and Richard Leacock, carefully drawing on their brilliant stylistic patience, lying in wait for the sublime moment of transformation. Gilbert adapted this verité ethos and merged it with a more traditional, "distanced" neoscientific documentary practice, emerging as a kind of hybrid Southern California ethnographic filmmaker. It was a curious hybrid, as Gilbert performed an enthnographic investigation upon his own culture. This position afforded him a sociological screen from which to bracket the proceedings. He formally traversed cinema verité's turf, employing the hovering camera that has now become a cliché signature of the "reality effect," applied like icing to everything from Levi's 501 advertising to *NYPD Blue*. But Gilbert worked in a period right before this technique collapsed completely into advertising signature effect, trading on Pennebaker's and Leacock's penchant for wading through the boredom of real-life subjects to unearth and capture the moment of friction or the intimate space between waiting for something to occur and something to explode.

Lance had a special role in the fishbowl; he was absent from Santa Barbara and present in New York. He was the child absented by his own hand. His presence throughout *An American Family* is constitutively different from that of any other member of the family. Except for one episode devoted exclusively to his mother's visit to New York, his presence is signified only by his voice on the telephone receiver as the family gathers around it. Questions are relayed from parent to parent and parent to siblings. He seeks differentiation from the family and his audio presence is inculcated with an articulation of his otherness, a cultivated but sincere desire to reconstitute himself into another realm, to get out of Santa Barbara alive.

Pat Loud decides to visit Lance in New York. She takes a cab to the Chelsea Hotel from the airport, camera crew in tow, and finds her way to Lance's room. She asks if he told the management that he needed a room for his "very straight mother." His answer is to whisk her off for the evening to a La Mama performance of "Vain Victory" with Jackie Curtis and Ondine, the drag queen lights of off-off-off Broadway. On the way out of the Chelsea, they bump into a wasted Holly Woodlawn, who later unsteadily appears, apparition-like, in the corner of Lance's room. In the same segment Pat and Lance take in an Andy Warhol retrospective, Pat remarking that the Warhols "look good all together." This gay tourist romp is punctuated by some serious mother-son bonding as Lance talks about finally finding a place where he fits in and mom's acknowledgment that this is where he belongs. Lance is articulate about his childhood, saying that "I stood apart from everyone." His frustration is made clear via a nonstop torrent of connective identity language aimed at his mother: he has found his place, he will "make it," these people understand him, he can feel the city's energy, he runs into people in the Chelsea that make the world spin. Walking through Central Park, she wants Lance to point out where Jackie O lives, but Lance is busy recalling dying his hair silver at fourteen. She says that she would like to score some tickets to *No No Nanette*. They are both hungrily feeding on the energy of the city, albeit at different frequencies. Pat is the receiver that allows him to construct himself within the documentary. His economic and emotional life now depends upon convincing the family, via messenger Pat, that this is where he must stay. Mom is on a reconnaissance mission where she comports herself with a certain uneasy ease. Pat's role is partially to negotiate the gulf between Lance and his father (who will later profess his disgust at Lance's sexuality) and partially to make sure Lance is safe. Ultimately she will bring the news home, divorce her husband, and begin reinventing herself.

After *An American Family* was broadcast, the Louds went on a celebrity spree; they did Donahue, Griffin, and Cavett, complaining of humiliation and exploitation. Deliah Loud did *The Dating Game*. Bill Loud, now an ex-husband with mammoth womanizing credentials, appeared in an issue of *Esquire*, part of a photo spread on celebrities in their bedrooms. Lance, ever the last word, posed nude for *Screw* magazine. This was really his family role, co-opting the public site by taking the final shot, choosing the irreverent over the merely tantalizing. Ironically, this high-profile follow-up serves to underscore Gilbert's framing of this crucial visit to New York City, alternately a cultural grazing fest and a collection of awkward repressed pauses, the sensational broken by the banal. At the close of the episode, Pat and Lance wait for her cab to the airport. Little is said; he is fidgeting, she is making herself communicate. The camera seems deeply intrusive in this silence as Gilbert refuses to cut. She is slowly smoking; he is hanging out the window. Please write more often, send Dad a Father's Day card, promise me you'll stop hanging out these windows, and please find something cheaper than the Chelsea to live in, she says. Finally they go downstairs, he puts her in a cab, walks back up endless flights of stairs, trailed by his blinding personal follow spot, enters his room, and turns on the television. He has reentered his adaptive environment, having been briefly observed by a familiar mother and an unfamiliar and unseen audience.

▶──

Real World(s); or, "I'm not gay but my girlfriend is"

> *Interior, Venice Beach house, pool room: Beth II is playing pool wearing an "I'm not gay but my girlfriend is" tee-shirt. The rest of the roommates take this in, wait a bit and ask if the shirt is a joke. Beth replies that yes the shirt is, but then she realizes, as they make small sounds of relief that she needs to clarify: "Yes," she says, "the shirt is a joke, but I AM a lesbian." The roommates sink into their comfy IKEA couch. Cut to next scene.*

> *I AM NOT A STATISTIC. I am a human being. I'll be dead before I am thirty. I believe in God, I believe God will never give me more than I can handle. Until my last dying breath I will be a person living with AIDS.*
> ::   Pedro of *The Real World—San Francisco*

The Real World revolves around the premise that by mixing together a carefully screened and demographically "representative" group of young people and throwing them into a twenty-four-hour video-monitored and controlled living environment for a set period of several months, a hard-hitting, "honest" representation of reality—or at least some fiery television fights—will come to pass.[5] The premise rests on drawing out and capturing a "true" image of the domestic, career and personal aspirations of a group of strangers lodged collectively in a house in New York, Los Angeles, or San Francisco. The premise also relies on a voyeuristic cynicism that trades on conflict and the thrill of an ersatz sociological prime-time entertainment "experiment" pitched roughly to the same age group being surveyed. The first series takes place in a loft in Manhattan, the second in a postmodernish

Beth II in *The Real World—Venice*. Courtesy MTV Network

beach house near Venice Beach, the third in a brightly colored Victorian house in San Francisco. Each series included, among its carefully groomed demographic sample group, an unabashedly queer subject: Norman in New York, Beth II in the Venice house, and Pedro in San Francisco. All of these participants were "out," politicized, vocal, and articulate about their presence as "representatives" of young queerness in the 1990s.

The Real World (TRW) is the amphetamine stepchild of *An American Family*. It also owes much to Craig Gilbert's insistence that the boredom of real life under the myopic television gaze would render indecipherably pleasurable, startling, and frightening the interpersonal collapse and ascension of overtly monitored human subjects left to their own devices. Gilbert's humanistic premise lives on in mutated form in the control room of each *TRW* "set." *The Real World* is one of the last TV-verité projects, and it is also one of the first to position queer images for direct entry into the free flow of MTV.[6] The stylistic and conceptual moves of cinema verité are exhausted by the time *TRW* adopts them. Their reinvention within the confines of the *TRW* house(s) involves stationary surveillance cameras, in-house video confession/complaint booths, and roving camera crews, all plugged into a central control station. Since the place is hardwired, there is no pesky searching for subjects within their own environments. This is a

Pedro in *The Real World—San Francisco*. Courtesy MTV Network

visibility performed and programmed by others, but infiltrated and transgressed by Norman, Beth, Pedro, and assorted housemates. For queer viewers, the power of the antiapologetic stance of all three of these people elicits identificatory glee: there is pleasure in watching Beth II explain her shirt, Pedro define the intricacies of the word *partner*, or Norman wait by the phone for his new love. Queer viewers watch as detectives in possession of the secret decoder ring, members of the new TV family. Within the familiarity of Beth's coming-out scene and Pedro's ongoing struggle with Puck over respect on the basis of sexual orientation lie a wealth of unrepresented narratives that the queer detective grafts onto the representation being played out within *TRW*. These viewers possess a language that speaks of the hidden. The queer detective takes delight in knowing that the MTV multitudes are now also exposed, forming a collective audience (ersatz family) that witnesses the same stories in a multitude of ways. Basic identity politics are outlined within the confines of *TRW*, and in watching them unfold the queer viewer has the potential to rework them, constructing a mobile lexicon of available reference points that can be applied to each new queer image within the television mainstream. It is a pleasure not to be found sitting in the safe audiences of gay film festivals. This is a game of infiltration, assimilation, and disassimilation commingled, for we read these queer youths as token implants and agitative explorers simultaneously. Part of the pleasure here is simply in the power of confrontation and visibility, waiting to see if combat will ensue over the issue of sexuality. The game takes place in a field where heterosexual privilege is dominant and assured, and reruns of both *TRW—NYC* and *TRW—Venice* are comfortable repetitive sites seamlessly slipped in between Beavis, Butt-head, and Cher and the latest MTV-at-the-beach dance party. Norman, Beth, and Pedro are the sole familiar images of queer youth in prime-time commercial television; they use their air time particularly well despite their employment as liberal status flares and incendiary demographic placements.

TRW operates in a new and even more formidable media environment than *An American Family*. It is in such heavy rotation on MTV that each segment loses chronology even though it is initially released in sequence and then slotted in different noncontiguous time slots. We viewers return weekly, much as we would return to a soap opera, to seek catastrophe and resolution. The episodic nature of the series relies on cliffhanger hooks and teasers that promise next week's focal conflict. The producers rely on identificatory narratives, our loyalty in wading through all the other house members' travails to track a favorite subject. We become followers, subscribers to their nascent celebrity. The line between documentary subject and serial character collapses.[7]

One of the most telling moments on the *TRW—NYC* reunion segment comes when house members start recalling encounters with fans who tell them how much they loved the "characters" they "played." One of the participants recounts how she screamed at a fan, "I'm not a character! I am a real person!!!" She is voicing frustration at being mistaken for another interchangeable music video, a spokesmodel, or a veejay. In a final irony, *TRW* alumni are popping up as car saleswomen and MTV-at-the-beach hosts. They are perceived as actors in a giant ongoing soap, no matter their protestations of reality. The Louds' celebrity faded, but maintained a chronology; they are time-coded securely in the past. But *TRW* enters the slipstream seamlessly, lives replayed and telecast daily, favorite episodes rerun into oblivion. They are present as family members at the electronic hearth, potentially more believable or available than their plastic and cardboard brethren around the corner and down the dial on *Melrose Place*.[8]

A midseason replacement for a jettisoned house member in *TRW—Venice*, Beth II had minimal screen time but managed to embody a formidable in-your-face identity that squarely positioned her to do some down and dirty education: about drinking yourself to death, about loving girls, and about the right to exist. *TRW* can be enjoyed from a queer audience position, but it is really fundamentally about a world of boy/girl Sturm und

Drang. Its audiences are MTV-lite, a constituency weaned on Bill Clinton electoral video bytes and sixty-second history nuggets. It is not a queer audience per se, or even queer-positive—but it is an audience that stays tuned while queerness becomes yet another variation and because the neo-liberal, rock and roll–sanctioned slant of MTV programming assures a moderate if token harbor for slight deviations. However, there is a limit to this open door policy. MTV's refusal to air Madonna's "Justify My Love" underscores their discomfort with its pesky is it a boy?/is it a girl? kissing confusion garnished by assorted background leathermen. The increments advance ever so slightly. But we are really talking about a fundamental stream of teen product. *TRW* interrupts Swatch, Fruitopia, and Guess ever so slightly and then gets folded right back in. The IKEA logo rolls with the credits at the end of *TRW—San Francisco*. Both *TRW*'s subversive power and its failure lie in this ability to be folded back in. Is the "normalization" of queerdom either instant death or the only path to power? Are there other options?

Beth II constructs the pivotal queer instant on *TRW—Venice*. She enters the Venice beach house for the first time, announces her AA member-ship, and clears out an errant case of beer from her newly assigned cabinet. The sequence continues with Beth's polite but bristling interchange with Tami, resident self-professed control freak, about a ghetto blaster left on their shared bathroom sink. We immediately are caught in the inevitable explosion of wills. For several episodes Beth II is deeply immersed in ther-apy speak; she establishes intimacy with housemates and reveals the depths of her drinking, her loss of a will to live, and her desire to move away from destructive patterns of the past. Luckily for the producers of the show, the witnesses to this revelation—Jon, a Christian country western singer from Kentucky, and Tami, a street-smart tough girl, disillusioned with her work as an AIDS counselor—are perfect respondents. When Beth comes out to them at the pool table, Tami responds by retreating and attempting to discuss her discomfort with Dominick. She questions her own bigotry with-out directly articulating her own relation to bias; she is the sole African-American woman in the house. This moment inadvertently and inextricably links race and sexuality as targets of oppression and ignorance. And Tami's use of the term bigot to question herself and also label her discomfort makes the interchange between the two of them particularly charged.

Norman, a painter in the New York loft version, situates himself im-mediately as a politicized gay man. He organizes a van pool to the march on Washington for reproductive rights. This segment follows an episode in which he falls in love, and we see him and his new love on a rain-streaked New York street, holding hands and balloons, accompanied by the incessant sound track that fuels *TRW*. His organization of the van ride to Washington mirrors his earlier interest in going to a Jerry Brown rally and his painting of Brown's campaign number on the loft's wall. He is involved in a political process that at the time MTV also had a stake in, with their election-year "Rock the Vote," an intense and successful voter registration drive and electoral information campaign. Norman's campaign activities present the audience with an overt strategy of involvement. His sexuality is presented as another aspect of his progressive politics intrinsically linked to his political actions and to his courtship of Charles. Norman's queerness thus becomes part of his political credentials and vice versa.

The propaganda of assimilationist rhetoric fits nicely with Norman's positioning within *TRW*—*NY*. In *TRW*—*SF*, however, Pedro is a full-time AIDS activist, bringing to the fore a heightened level of political confrontation. Essentially all three *TRW*s can be read together as they exist currently programmed, undifferentiated within the free flow of MTV's scheduling grid. The hypothetical audience is drawn into a giant, user-friendly MTV family, a household essentially made up of people from somewhere else. In retrospect, which is now the only way in which *TRW* can be viewed, the death of Pedro (after *TRW*—*SF* had already been aired in its entirety), lends urgency and poignancy to his image that were to some extent woven into the program at the onset by the revelation that he was HIV-positive.

Pedro's agenda is a minefield. His presence in *TRW*—*SF* is crucial to any articulation of queerness on television. His combativeness with Puck, an "I just want to have fun" bike messenger with astoundingly bad personal habits and limited self-knowledge, sets up a site where issues of identity and political activism and the day-to-day life of a gay man under a TV microscope converge.

The domestic space of *TRW*—*SF* is Pedro's, but early on in the series he is a public blur. He visits a Stanford class and talks about living his life differently. He answers a question posed by a young man who asks if there was ever a day that he didn't think about AIDS. Pedro answers no, it is never absent from his mind. Later, he becomes lovers with a fellow activist, also HIV-positive, and their courtship takes center stage, culminating in a confrontation with Puck, who accuses them behind their backs of making an engagement announcement solely for shock value. But as the series comes to an end, Pedro begins to fully occupy the domestic: housemates converge in the kitchen to hear his T-cell count; his first bout with pneumonia finds him in bed, being visited by a steady stream of exhausting roomies. And toward the end of filming, he and his lover, Shaun, get married in the living room of the house. The everyday is made visible despite *TRW*'s inherently sensationalistic invasive context.

Over the course of just a few episodes, the cameras follow Pedro as he picks up his blood test results, learns that his T-cell count is almost non-existent, goes on television as an AIDS activist, confronts his Republican roommate about her attitude toward his "lifestyle," sets Puck straight when he jokingly refers to Puck and Pedro as the "odd couple" (with Pedro cast in the Felix Unger role), goes to a street demonstration marking the death of Randy Shilts, and accepts his lover's marriage proposal while he is working through the implications of introducing an African-American man to his Cuban family back home in Miami. With this extraordinary narrative progression interjected into the undifferentiated consumer frenzy of MTV and played in heavy rotation, one cannot but hope that Pedro's infiltration will loosen the interchangeable stereotype of AIDS victim/gay man. Pedro refuses this status and is so attuned to others' desires to place him in a neat package that he functions within the televisual flow of *TRW* as a denial of its glib smoothness. The sheer strength of his passion, in terms of his identity as a fierce and angry gay man combating the slowly evolving collapse of his body, positions him within the documentary framework as the focus of both the housemates and the viewers, a rare gay subject who refuses to be isolated solely through his sexual identity.

The tendency within humanist documentary practice has always been to represent lives thought to be outside the experience of the imagined viewer. This mode of operation within cinema verité has been coupled theoretically with a search for the "crisis moment" with which to generate identification, excitement, and a linking of subject to observer. The audience is asked to identify with Pedro's "condition," a dominant and clear crisis trope.[9] His articulation of his own subject position, however, rebuffs a predictable and limited audience inclination to register pity. His refusal of victim status in turn helps to counter one of the foundations of the documentary canon—that through pity or horror the audience can somehow come to understand a subject designated as outside their experience. Puck's accusation that Pedro uses his queerness to block out any other way of "knowing" him functions both to underscore and to complicate the conventional conceptual documentary premise underlying *TRW*. Puck is placed in the position of a spectator trying to comprehend the incomprehensible: he is both repellent and manipulated—the voice of pestering ignorance against which Pedro positions himself as a politicized rather than pathetic individual, fighting for his basic human rights. This classic verité strategy, structuring audience identification predicated upon a neatly polarized situation, is co-opted and remotivated by Pedro. Because of his insistence on queerness and HIV-positive status as defining elements of his character and his position as an activist educator, he was able to navigate the artificial boundaries of the *Real World* house through a series of impassioned and volatile debates that refused both his silencing and his victimization. He remained the focus of the series while he attempted to carry on his private daily life. It is the interaction of these two facets and his refusal to allow them to be rendered as discrete units that make it possible to counter the ubiquitous "I cannot condone your lifestyle" echo that surfaces and resonates through *TRW*'s "family."

▶

The Van Stops Here: Dominic, Michael, and Larry

> *Gays and lesbians are a demon, they are the devil.*
> :: Mother of Larry talking to him after he talks to her about his confused sexual feelings

> *I accept Candy . . . but I do wish that Candy would be, how should I say it? Natural.*
> :: Kathleen Gingrich, mother of House speaker Newt, on her lesbian daughter

The Ride brings together, via a commissioned producer, a group of young people from various ethnic, regional, and class backgrounds. They function as "Travelers," recorders, instigators, and participants on a cross-country road trip. They visit people their own age, live with them for a period of several days, interview them, hang out with them, and camcord their lives. The trip connected a diverse group of people, from Lakota teens on South Dakota's Pine Ridge "Rez" to Cambodian gang members in Dallas. At the close of the road trip the Travelers, in conjunction with the producer, selected and edited a series of thirty-minute episodes from the journey, which traversed seven states and more than thirty lives. As in *The Real World*, a carefully predetermined demographic representation is operative, both in the choice of the Travelers and in their subjects (the Guides). Partial authorship resides with Shauna Garr, the collector of persons taken on the ride, and an important aspect of each section is the assignment of and the briefing on the two parallel stories that will be filmed on each visit. The Travelers and their subjects are on camera and there is no pretense of traditional "documentary objectivity"—that is, the invisibility of those recording the images. There is no "professional" crew, and much of the documentary focuses on the process involved in choosing subjects and selecting which portions of their stories to include. Talk-back is privileged and judgment calls are included on camera, a methodology pointedly aimed at alleviating the omnipotent positioning of maker over subject, or producer

Larry and his mother in *The Ride*. Courtesy ITVS

over maker. These self-reflexive devices, now a staple of documentary work, counter Gilbert's 1970s insistence on the filmmakers' "invisibility" during the filming of *An American Family*. The confessionals within *TRW* are meant to signal a moment of personal "reflection" recorded by the subjects sans crew, but the production meetings and inclusion of the young filmmakers as subjects within *The Ride* employs these devices as a signifier of further "authenticity," removed from both the single-author position of Gilbert in *An American Family* and the in-house production control room(s) of *TRW*. The collision of recorder and recorded, as well as the slippage between the two, ultimately shapes the project.

   The Ride's form is certainly derived from an alternative documentary/activist video context. The commitment to including the producers as subject matter and the attention to at least an appearance of control of authorship by the van riders suggests that a decade of camcorder activist work has inscribed itself in media consciousness. *The Ride* comes out of a specific cultural context defined by its commissioning organization, the Independent Television Service. ITS was mandated into being by a coalition of diverse grassroots film and video makers who lobbied for money (a portion of the Corporation for Public Broadcasting's budget) to place tools and finances in the hands of makers and subjects traditionally bypassed by mainstream media. ITS's very existence extends the liberal documentary

José and Dominic in *The Ride*. Courtesy ITVS

project, the contention that the Corporation for Public Broadcasting has an educational mandate that is rarely fulfilled and often panders to the middle of the road.

The Ride is clear about addressing issues of class and the sexuality of youth, both components of social analysis that American media often overlook. There is no leveling ground of a shared living space and obscured class coding, as there is in *The Real World*. *The Ride* navigates the homes of the Guides, sleeping there, eating there, meeting parents and friends, and touring the neighborhood. At the start of each segment, producer Shauna Garr briefs each team about their subjects or Guides. Each program intertwines two story lines, two sets of Guides' stories that unfold and play off each other. During the briefing, Garr reads from notes that document the focus of the segment as outlined by each Guide through previous interviews. She assigns a Traveler crew to each Guide and asks them to use these initial interviews as a starting point for their segment. What happens after the on-site meeting of Guides and Travelers rarely follows the dictum of the briefing focus, and within this gap the moment is meant to explode.

The Ride banks on these moments, but ironically also spends a great deal of time trying to orchestrate the right catalysts. Within the briefing is the suggestion of control, counteracted in practice by the collapse of the system engendered through consciously self-reflexive moves or sheer happenstance: on-camera crew members, inclusion of exchanges between subject and recorder, crew meetings that rehash the day's events, and, finally, safely in the confines of the van, assessments of the people they have encountered. Activist video of the 1980s, which operated within the art world but also within the documentary film community, followed some of the same strategies earlier advocated by guerrilla video, including ready access to the means of production and attendant skills, the use of cheap technology, and the development of alternative distribution networks. At the conceptual core of these strategic demands lies the utopian beliefs that, given the right tools, the subjects could become makers and that the more makers there were producing images, the less chance for overt manipulation. The filmmakers became the subjects and vice versa. Gradually, the need for an elite trained core of media specialists speaking for "other people," perverting their identity image, and generally running amok over others' lives would be dissipated and media literacy would spread.[10] The complication arising from this stance, implicit in documentary production, arises precisely from this desire to make visible the "underrepresented," the erased or never rendered.

It is this visibility that *The Ride* and to some extent *TRW* work toward, and it is this very representation that provokes a serious challenge to any other work that attempts to represent the margins. This is the fundamental question raised by works of "exposure," and it is a question that has no answer, only more or less successful poseurs.

The current contradiction between "identity politics," with its accent on visibility, and the psychoanalytic/deconstructionist mistrust of visibility as the source of unity or wholeness needs to be refigured, if not resolved. I am not suggesting that continued invisibility is the "proper" political agenda for the disenfranchised, but rather that the binary between the power of visibility and the impotency of invisibility is falsifying. There is real power in remaining unmarked, and there are serious limitations to visual representation as a political goal."[11]

Peggy Phelan lists a series of presumptions that feeds a certain rhetoric of imagemaking the documentary canon has long been based on: reading physical resemblance as a way of constructing and identifying community, and garnering power through this identification. She questions the notion that power is found in visibility and that "if one's mimetic likeness is not represented, one is not addressed." For Phelan the ideology of the visible "erases the power of the unmarked, unspoken, and unseen."[12]

The Ride is inadvertently about this profound quandary because it chose to represent queer youth and because it chose Travelers based on audition tapes of their own personal film and video work. Garr sought people who were already grappling with issues of visual representation in terms of their own production. She chose a constituency that had the street credentials to invade the lives of people who probably would not otherwise have allowed themselves to be surveyed, certainly not in an adult presence. Add to this the desire of the Guides to be recorded, to be witnessed, and to shape the content by indicating which issues they want to present, and you have a situation that begs the question of erasure and revelation.

In two of the episodes, queerness is the focus of the narrative. The Travelers visit a boy, Larry, on a Midwest farm. He wonders aloud if he might be gay and sets off into town to camcord his first gay encounter with a john/pickup in a car in a local city park. In another episode, the Travelers visit a young preoperative transsexual, Dominic, and his/her best friend, Michael, a young gay teen. The Travelers are fascinated with these three subjects' relation to their respective parents and the parents' reaction to their sons' sexuality and gender preference. Queerness is a location "to be visited." The parent-child relationship that is the focus of many of *The Ride*'s other segments is heightened when it is complicated by sexual preference and, most explicitly, by transsexual intent. The Travelers themselves have no self-identified queer members, so they are in a similar position (save for age) as any other documentary crew. They are outside their chosen subject looking in. But they will not be staying. This distanciation is tempered slightly by the experience of living, however briefly, next to the life of another. *The Ride* removes itself from falling into the trap of "this is the way they live" televisual reportage through the placement of Travelers as co-subjects engaged in an on-camera questioning of their own positioning.

The central and probably most controversial segment of *The Ride* involves the actual search for definition, the slippery slope of self-recognition or at least a performance of the question of identity. The Travelers visit Larry in Ohio; because he has made videotapes before, he is soon brought into the production process and suggests an event for their visit. He is grappling with curiosity about men, his comfort with them, his interest in women, but his deeper sexual feelings for men. His method of testing this ground is to suggest to the Travelers that they document him checking out a Dayton cruising area. He mikes himself and gets into a man's car, taking the plan much further than the crew is comfortable with. Left in the van, they audibly argue about whether they should intervene, cut off the shoot and bring Larry back. The editing cuts back and forth between a murky nighttime image of the car and a worried crew on audio wondering whether they have crossed the line and endangered Larry. In the car, Larry asks the man about loving men; they have an extended conversation, and Larry returns to the crew van. This confrontation with himself, emboldened by the presence of the camcorder, is situated in a segment that includes images of him attempting to ask his mother about his confused feelings and having her soundly define sex between men as "against God's law." Larry and Mom stand out back of the farmhouse; he listens, but he doesn't back down and he counters her biblical retort. It's an impasse. Larry says that he has heard that there are "happy gays"; Mom responds by calling homosexuality "the work of the devil." Larry does not pursue the conversation. He has two positions from which to work through his feelings: the gentle, matter-of-fact answers of the man in the car trying to explain why he wants to be with men and the threat of walking with the devil. As the segment closes, this ideological gulf haunts him, the Travelers and the viewers. Where Larry situates himself within it is an open question. Larry and his mother represent the bottom line—the exploration of sexual identity and the chilling conflation of state and religious law evoked to regulate and condemn. The important connection being made throughout this series, at least from the standpoint of queer representation, is that it is impossible to remove queer identity from a family context. Issues of visibility and surviving as a young queer are defined in dangerous contexts. In Larry's situation there are no supportive inner-city rap groups for gay teens, no ACT UP meetings, no next-door grunge queer garage bands. He is not supported by a vocal household, as Pedro is in *TRW*, nor does he have the countercultural underground as an anchor, as Lance did in *An American Family*. The strength and poignancy engendered by *The Ride* is situated precisely within the day-to-day negotiations of Larry and his family. His search for sexual identity is played out in public, his fleetingly mobile support net is the Travelers' van. When the van leaves town, a certain agency for Larry is removed, and his questioning must resonate back within his family, leaving the viewer to wonder how he will enact his next queer exploration.

This placement becomes even more crucial in the Albuquerque section that closes the series. Dominic, seventeen, wants a sex change operation, and when he is questioned about who he would want to be with after the operation, he answers "straight men." His best friend, Michael, fifteen, is an out queer. Dominic battles the school board about needing to be removed from high school because he is constantly harassed. During the sequence he is also shown at a local gay, lesbian, and bisexual support group that does not entirely know where to place him. The group has no members even close to his age and no visible transgendered people. The group personifies Dominic as between worlds. When they hear that Dominic's professed object of desire is "straight men," one member says, "You won't really be in our community once you've had the operation." Between this "support" group and the uncomprehending school officials, Dominic relies on his

mother and on Michael, but in the outside world he must constantly negotiate for acknowledgment and respect.

Dominic's mother, like Pat Loud, is integral to this negotiation. She is
baffled and supportive, but worried that Dominic is too young to make
this decision. She also speaks forcefully about this being his choice, whether
she understands it or not. The segment closes as Dominic cross-dresses in
drag and is escorted to a disco by Traveler José. Dominic rests one hand
lightly on his arm, proud, playful, and beautiful. They are fully on parade.
On the street a man screams at them and hurls a clump of dirt at them. José
is startled, awakening with anger to the danger posed to Dominic every
day. When they are safely in the van, party mood destroyed, José can articulate the danger, become the enunciator of empathy. Later, Dominic speaks
nervously and angrily to a school official about his daily harassment. He
lays out a deeply reasoned argument against being returned to regular
school that holds the inept system responsible for his ostracism. The official listens and turns him down flat, having obviously made up his mind
well before Dominic's arrival. Dominic tearfully calls him irresponsible,
telling him that he cannot know what it is like. This exchange of adult in-
comprehension and the frustrating powerlessness of youth resonates with
an earlier image of Michael telling the Travelers that he thought of killing
himself when he was younger. The power relationships between Larry and
mother, Dominic and school, and Michael and school require that queer
youth shrug off the victim status that would make an emphatic response
knee-jerk and condescending. A profound shift happens when José realizes
the extent to which Dominic walks a dangerous public line. The Travelers,
as interlopers, help to solidify the empathy required of the documentary
spectator, viewing the "invisible." Because the Travelers briefly occupy the
same topography as Dominic, Larry, and Michael, they help to circum-
navigate the pitfall of constructing a neat tour package of the surveyed.
Ultimately, Dominic, Larry, and Michael navigate without the privilege of
a safe space, embodied in the Travelers' receding van and the promise of
closure at the end of a twenty-eight-minute episode.

Within these three works is at least a short routing map of the tactics
American televisual culture employs to represent its queer children. There
is an ambivalence in the methodology and motivation behind these unravel-
ings: exploitation, curiosity, voyeurism or education, visibility and celebration. The project of keeping watch on representations in which a queer
audience has an investment is a tricky one. The amount of time that has
elapsed between the void of nonrepresentation, the repetitive intermediary
stage of tragic gayness, and the recent stage of equal opportunity exposure
is minuscule. *An American Family*, *The Real World*, and *The Ride* sketch

out some of the ways in which young queers are interjected into the matrix of popular culture and how those same people transcend and problematize their compartmentalization. The larger project will have to deal with how these images affect the next wave of commercial narrative producers and what forms are developed to explode traditional documentary's morbid and conceptually limited connection to empathy as knowledge and seeing as living. This expanded project will contend with the very definition of a collective queer culture and its reading of images produced by nonqueer makers, as well as the contradictory impulse to work against the idea of a macrotelevision culture. Sean Cubitt writes,

> I'd argue that the status—ontological, epistemological, political—of television is produced in the individual viewer, in the micro-culture of the living room, in the local, national, and global cultures variously, as a kind of ghost, a frightening, comforting, harmless, powerful, informative, debilitating, enter-taining, boring matrix of contradiction which requires the faith of its viewers in its presence to them as object before it can take on the aspect of producer of meaning. The unstable dialectic of the real and the apparent, the present amid the absent, the visible and the invisible is the condition under which TV enters into the social.[13]

This microculture of the living room contains the microculture of queer identity as well. Lance, Beth, Norman, Pedro, Dominic, Larry, and Michael have all imprinted this transitory broadcast flow with trace visibil-ities in a period in which these images are still deeply marginalized. Queer representation exists as fashion, exotic pause, quick tease, or affirmative action entry. These documentaries raise larger questions of what will tran-spire after queer visibility is no longer an end in itself. What will these new forms of queer imaging look like, and who will author these new distur-bances, interrogations, and celebrations?

◆————————————————————————————————————

NOTES

The author would like to thank Kathleen McHugh, ITVS, Gary Stella, and Lynne Kirby for their kind help, attention, and inspiration. This essay is extracted from a larger, unpub-lished essay.

1. Throughout this essay I use the terms *youth, children, young,* and *teen* in a general way to refer to a group of people defined as still beholden to and under the control of "adults," a legal relationship that labels this group as "under age" with specific legal language and treatment that distinguishes them from older people. In the case of all three of the documentaries, they are defined as extracted from families that they live with and will return to. It is this relationship to the family that aligns them as an age group. Their relationship to the power structures that administer their media image, the panopticon control video room of the *Real World* houses, the day-long tag-along cam-era crew of *An American Family,* and the break from this dynamic in the form of the semiautonomous video crew of *The Ride,* all regulate them to a status distinct from the "adult world" but linked to it via intricate power exchanges between their control over their own image and the machinations of the crew, the network, the family, and the state.

This status of course is precisely why they were chosen as subjects in the first place. For a more in-depth examination in terms of definitions and distinctions, see *Gay and Lesbian Youth*, ed. Gilbert Herdt (New York: Haworth, 1989).

2. A list of gay and lesbian television and Hollywood film stereotypes is not difficult to come up with. Variations include the single killer lesbian, the queen hairdresser next door, the single lesbian parent, the lesbian woman or gay man who is given a lover only to see him or her die horribly in reel one and/or have the aforementioned lover alluded to but never seen.

3. For a discussion of contemporaneous reception and debate, see Craig Gilbert, "Reflections on an American Family Parts I & II," in *New Challenges for Documentary*, ed. Alan Rosenthal (Berkeley: University of California Press, 1988). These reflections outline a climate at WNET (the producing PBS station) and the hard sell of the producers to get the first programs funded. Gilbert also outlines the climate of public and press hostility to the series and the extraordinary amount of media attention, which positioned the series as the final desperate word on the demise of the American family.

4. Cinema verité's legacy, as adopted by Gilbert during this time period, included a commitment to resolving the "truth" of a subject and situation through extended contact; the belief that true moments of human revelation are attained through huge shooting ratios coupled with direct confrontation; and the idealization of the magic moment of revelation, as initialized by the camera's presence.

5. The issue of who inhabits the "real world" in MTV land deserves examination. The producers of *TRW* clearly carefully chose participants who could be read as being "representative." Attention to race, class (especially in terms of educational background), sexuality, and regional point of origin (with special attention to the American South and Western Europe) delineate the parameters.

6. It is important to note that MTV, which grew out of music culture, has patterned itself around the three- to four-minute music video in which the image depends entirely on a preexisting song structure. Only recently, the network began to reinvent itself along the lines of traditional TV formats. MTV now deals in news segments, commissioned "rockumentaries," talk shows, and extended concert broadcasts. Its initial revolutionary televisual format of the short subject has shifted, and in a sense *TRW* contributes to this move toward long play while maintaining the breakneck visual style that initially fueled the format. This speed of intake and output combined with the voyeuristic patience re-

quired of cinema verité proves an intriguing if odd hybrid.

7. When any new "edition" of *TRW* debuts, it is released in a special time slot during prime time in chronological order. After its initial run as "new product" it is put into heavy rotation in the daytime and nighttime MTV schedule. Often the current series in rerun is programmed right before an older *TRW*. So it is possible to begin with an episode of *TRW — SF* filmed within the last year that shows a heated battle between Puck and Pedro, and twenty-two minutes later find yourself watching Norman strolling hand in hand with Charles on a wintry New York City street several years ago. This kind of spatial and temporal distortion in terms of narrative continuity (in a series that relies on viewers tuning in week after week) turns *TRW* into another repeat music video. I suspect that viewers engage with the program in much the same way, tuning in to catch lost or favorite segments repeatedly. Because MTV relies on its audience to leave it on continually, like radio, *TRW* becomes just another bridge into the following program and is probably watched on and off in much the same way as a music video segment. Chronology becomes less and less important as *TRW* enters heavy rotation. *An American Family* also worked with a heightened soap opera sense of viewers' cliff-hanging addiction, but it did this over the space of a few months of programming, not over years.

8. For a discussion of family as television, see Sean Cubitt's rebuttal of Jean Baudrillard's analysis of television as family, as cultural absolute, as living master code/DNA: Sean Cubitt, *Timeshift: On Video Culture* (London: Routledge, 1991).

9. For a discussion of the "crisis moment" as a fundamental stylistic, conceptual, and narrative component of cinema verité, see Stephen Mamber, "The Crisis Moment in Practice," in Stephen Mamber, *Cinema Vérité in America: Studies in Uncontrolled Documentary* (Cambridge, Mass.: MIT Press, 1974).

10. The primer for this kind of video practice remains Michael Shamberg's *Guerrilla Television* (New York: Raindance Corporation and Holt, Rinehart and Winston, 1971). A queer expansion of this strategy can be found in Gregg Bordowitz, "Operative Assumptions Concerning the Community Based Production of Television," in *Resolution(s): Essays on Contemporary Video Practices*, ed. Michael Renov and Erika Suderburg (Minneapolis: University of Minnesota Press, 1996).

11. Peggy Phelan, *Unmarked: The Politics of Performance* (London: Routledge, 1993), 6–7.

12. Ibid.

13. Cubitt, *Timeshift*, 33.

Memories

LINDA DITTMAR

[4] *Of Hags and Crones:*
Reclaiming Lesbian Desire
for the Trouble Zone of Aging

Aging, a biological process readily available to the viewing gaze, has long
functioned as an overdetermined signifier signaling physical and economic
incapacity, social marginality, and impending death. The bodies that inspire
such narratives are seen as ravaged—stiff-jointed, gnarled, and decaying—
rather than changing. Situated at the crossroads of metaphysical and biological crises, aging functions in our culture as a visible register of life's
most terrifying outcome. Yet this very doomsday quality makes the process
of aging a barely acknowledged aspect of ordinary life and accounts for the
marginal place of old people in most media situations, including documentary films. For those whose gender and sexuality place them at the hub of
commodified desires hinging on the allure of youthfulness—notably, reproductive women and in some ways gay men—aging seems especially cruel
because it threatens their very access to well-being. Their power, pleasure,
and income depend on their position as icons of immortality; their aging
will prove so repellent a sight as to make the gaze slide over them, disavow-
ing their visible presence.[1]

It is hardly surprising that even documentary treatments, for all their
"truth" claims, rarely redress this disavowal. Perhaps the most extraordinary instance of the anxieties tangled in such representations occurs in
Maximilian Schell's documentary *Marlene* (1984), where the very notion
of representation devolves on Marlene Dietrich's refusal to be represented
on screen as an old woman. The film includes footage of the crew's preparations for interviewing her and the sound of her voice as they recorded
it. It also includes excerpts of earlier documentaries and uses clips from
her classic films to convey a sense of the visual plenitude associated with
her image. But at no point does Schell's spying camera even glimpse the old
woman who is the present subject of its restless prowling: the "real" person

the film attempts to compile from the detritus of her life and the relics of her representations remains elusive.

Of course, turning to Dietrich as a touchstone for this essay is fraught with difficulties, especially since this legendary phantom woman in no way resembles the flesh and blood lesbians who are my main focus. Still, *Marlene* is helpful both because this documentary's emphasis on the constructed nature of "self"-presentation reminds us of the indeterminacy that besets the supposedly simple notion of "lesbian," and because its phobic recoil from the aging body captures so powerfully women's panic about their decline.[2] In this sense the valorization of the ageless glamour inherent in the Dietrich star persona is widely shared. Like countless others, this *monstre sacré* has become "a woman of a certain age" whose emaciated body, made-up "lifted" face, and firmly permed and sprayed bleached hair invoke the craft of the mortician as much as that of the beautician.[3]

For Dietrich, adhering to the illusion of ageless glamour is just business as usual—a function of her commodified hyperfemininity, now inhabiting the terrain of anxious old age. In contrast, and like the crones and witches of yore, the older and middle-aged lesbians who are the subjects of the documentaries to which I now turn have no use for a mystique of youth. While Hollywood and other mainstream venues produced fiction films that malign or "neuter" such women, these documentaries set out to put forth an anti-ageist agenda that affirms their subjects' vitality and dignity. Primarily addressing lesbian and feminist viewers, they also show their subjects as thriving outside normative heterosexual values.

Coming out of the left and feminist filmmaking tradition discussed in detail by Jan Rosenberg and Julia Lesage, these films evince faith in the documentary genre's reporting of "truth" as a means to political awareness and action.[4] Thus, they claim a much simpler and more direct relation to knowledge than *Marlene* allows. Their emphasis on shoring up commitments and contesting dominant views of gender, age, and sexuality is thematically and formally akin to myriad other treatments of liberation struggles that have found documentary expression in the past three decades. At the same time, their homogenizing defining of "lesbians" as women whose affectional and erotic energy centers on women, their equating of lesbian visibility with political action (as if to see is to know, and to know is to act), and their conveying of all this in ways that often assume a direct relation between representation and reality raise questions and risk oversimplification. Given the increasingly nuanced theorizing regarding gendered, transgendered, transsexual, bisexual, and other destabilized queer identities, and given the postmodern hybridizing of the documentary genre with various avant-garde practices that problematize its claims to "truth," a "documentary" focus on a category of "lesbians" may be naive on both counts.

While these qualifications underlie the following discussion, at issue for activists is the political efficacy of these films' efforts to reclaim older lesbians from invisibility and insert them into a wider queer arena. This political efficacy hinges on how one negotiates the relation between the documentary genre's conventional claims to an indexical access to "truth" and its status as mediated representation.[5] The films' underlying assumption is that representation and activism are linked—an assumption that has been instrumental since the 1960s in left and feminist documentary efforts to reconstruct a "people's history" that affirms the collective nature of historical and political knowledge.[6]

As documentary representations, *Women Like That* (Neild 1991), *Women Like Us* (Neild 1989), *West Coast Crones: A Glimpse into the Lives of Nine Old Lesbians* (Muire 1991), and *It's Not Too Late: A Portrait of Buffy* (Dickoff 1982) are particularly traditional in their unproblematic assumption that the genre has a simple indexical relation to truth. These documentaries focus on middle-aged and older lesbians with an eye to making their histories visible in the activist consciousness-raising tradition. Evincing faith in the epistemological pleasures and political efficacy of visibility and articulation, they let middle-aged and old lesbians speak for themselves and present their aging positively. The point is simple: older lesbians are "here"—visible and viable. They are vibrant participants in a collective history that includes the familiar high and low points—being closeted and coming out, being alone and finding communities, loving and losing mates, and above all feeling empowered by the growth one might risk as well as by the joys and strengths one might discover. The intent here is polemic, affirming, and pragmatic: these films posit a continuum between knowledge and action.

In the British made-for-television *Women Like That* and its sequel a year later, *Women Like Us*, this continuum comes across as axiomatic. A West Indian woman, for example, feels politically compromised because her identity as an antiracist activist necessitated hiding her lesbian identity. The dialogue that emerges between the initial film and its sequel also affirms a reciprocity between identity and politics. Both the women's positive responses to the aftermath of their initial coming out so publicly, on television, to family, neighbors, and friends, and the title shift from "women like *that*" to "women like *us*" treat outing as itself political. *West Coast Crones* is similarly centered on coming out. Though this group of elderly Bay Area lesbians has been meeting regularly in a framework they see as community building and political in the "consciousness-raising" sense, only one of them comments on the group's uniformly white and middle-class composition. "Activism" here, as in the two British documentaries, has more to do with the risks of being "out" and mutual support than with militancy around issues of concern to older lesbians: health care, financial solvency, familial relations, and community as well as intragroup issues such as racism or classism on top of ageism. Presence, it would seem, is itself political. Uncovering histories, affirming self-representation, and making space for erased people's images and voices all assume that visibility generates the political awareness that must precede social change, and that putting one's identity out in the public sphere is therefore itself a political act.

The documentary genre's affinity for personal accounts, "real" subjects, and contextual specificity is crucial to a politics that predicates social amelioration on the relation between visibility, consciousness-raising, and activism. Key to the politics of such filmmaking is, first, the supposedly corroborating and authenticating function of personal testimonials and, second, the informative function of compilation footage as an archaeology of self-definition. Taken together, these films' use of oral histories, testimonials, old photographs, archival materials, verité footage, and staged docudrama sequences stress empathetically that we are viewing previously invisible lesbian subjects whose emerging consciousness is a foundation for political activism. Assertive, straightforward, and clear, these documentaries elicit trust in their treatment of aging as a positive aspect of continuing life and optimism about visibility as an important first step in the larger project of community building, self-help, and rights advocacy. They reassure younger lesbians, buoy older ones, and open up a space for cross-generational understanding.

That lesbian and lesbian-friendly feminist audiences tend to be attracted to such reassurance without questioning the factual or rhetorical status of its "evidence" should not come as a surprise.[7] While these predominantly white and middle-class viewers may acknowledge that these are "feel good" films, they nonetheless enjoy accepting them at face value: the appeal of these representations rests on expository strategies that articulate a utopian project. The satisfaction that they offer lesbian activists and feminists who want to learn more about aging women and lesbian identities devolves on a cinematography that privileges articulation (talking heads, candid address, and filmed conversations) and intercuts compilation footage to organize viewers' expectations with an eye to social transformation. As in the liberation cinemas developed by feminist and third-world activists,[8] such devices validate diverse personal experiences, accord respect to the ordinary folk who are their subjects, and open space for audience identification and insights, creating a community continuous with the informants shown on film.

These important political gains are nonetheless undercut by an acceptance of compilation strategies as factually accurate and of visibility as a political cure-all. Neither assumption stands up to scrutiny. As Martha Gever puts it, "visibility is not a property essential to images, but it is culturally constructed. Thus there is no ideology-free window through which lesbians can be seen."[9] If anything, a politics of identity and visibility, lesbian or otherwise, obscures the material bases of oppression, disregards the fact that awareness may not yield action, and blurs the crucial role of solidarity in bringing about radical social change. In the case of queer politics, for instance, "we're here, we're queer" has come to replace a political strategy of "united we stand, divided we fall," which emphasizes materially based alliances.

Personally as well as politically, the "feel good" effect of *Women Like That*, *Women Like Us*, and *West Coast Crones* depends, then, on uncritical reception where optimism is purchased at the cost of fuller discussion of the difficulties of lesbian old age. We see this, for instance, in the way *Women Like Us* treats the breakup of a couple that was intact in *Women Like That* a year earlier. While the two women probe their feelings movingly on camera, they discuss their breakup mainly in terms of one woman's need for independence and the other's feelings of anger and hurt. They gloss over the fact that the woman who was "left" is seriously disabled and much older than the one who claimed her independence.

In fact, all these documentaries studiously avoid questions of illness, isolation, poverty, the need for elder care, and feelings about impending death, and they generally avoid discussing race, ethnicity, and social class. If anything, the impulse is to resort to positive representations envisioned within a white middle-class norm. An appreciation of life's goodness suffuses both *Women Like That* and *Women Like Us*. When we see one woman strolling with her dog, another arranging flowers on her partner's grave, a third leaving a gym, and the group as a whole ambling across gently rolling hills toward a sparkling sea, lesbian old age looks pretty good. *West Coast Crones* offers a similar reassurance. Starting with an uncontextualized montage of its as yet unidentified subjects engaging in sports, it privileges the physical well-being that flourishes in white and middle-class contexts. Nowhere do we hear about unemployment and poverty; about hysterectomies, cancers, or heart disease; about long-term disabilities, self-insurance, or familial marginality.

Though it is centered on one old woman and not a group, *It's Not Too Late: A Portrait of Buffy* functions in much the same way. It is a heart-warming, uncomplicated account of a white upper-class Yankee, vigorous and likable, who came out late in life and became active in the feminist lesbian community of Cambridge, Massachusetts. Buffy's life is clearly cushioned in ways that are not readily available to most lesbians. Nevertheless, age is more of a problem than the film cares to admit. We always see Buffy with younger women, in a city peopled by younger residents who atypically welcome liberal politics and "alternative" lifestyles. We do not see Buffy with her peers, and we are not asked to consider her situation in relation to older lesbians who have not enjoyed similar privileges. Even the fact that Buffy's former lover is from the working class does not finally lead to useful probing of age and class differentials, and there is no mention of the fact that Buffy's lesbian community is remarkably homogeneous in its whiteness and "alternative" lifestyle.

Designed primarily to affirm an older woman's courage in embarking on a new life, this portrait film succeeds in presenting its subject as an inspiring role model precisely because it skirts such questions. Not coincidentally, it opens with the filmmaker asserting that when she is seventy-five she wants to be like Buffy. Spot interviews with an array of young passersby about what being old means to them follow. "Wrinkled," "sick," "on crutches," they respond with evident distaste. While they are not talking about old lesbians specifically, their blatant ageism constitutes a framework of derogatory expectations that the film counters by celebrating Buffy's resilient engagement in a productive life, concluding with the theme song's insistence that "it is never too late."

This wish to affirm that old age is positively intertwined with life is also the driving force behind *Strangers in Good Company*, though in this case the goal is less didactic and the result is much more subtle and complex. The fictional plot of this semidocumentary concerns a group of seven old women (ranging in age from sixty-five to eighty-eight) and their young bus driver. They find themselves stranded in an abandoned house when their bus breaks down on a remote back road in Ontario, Canada. Within this fictive framework the women play themselves, giving the action an air of documentary authenticity that is further supported by oral histories and photographic documentation. Though this film includes only one lesbian character and though it is not strictly a documentary, it fits into the present discussion both because of its direct ties to lived actuality and because it includes lesbian identity as a formative aspect of women's self-definition coequal with other identity inscriptions such as class and ethnicity (Native American, Jewish, African-Canadian, British Canadian, and unspecified others). Most importantly, this film complements the preceding documentaries by constructing a collective portrait that repositions old women as attention-worthy human beings. The underlying intent here is thus feminist, anti-ageist, antihomophobic, broadly egalitarian, and inclusive.

The film's one lesbian, Mary Meigs, has since published a luminous personal record of the film's making that includes an account of her reluctance to function as the film's token lesbian character. Urged by scriptwriter Gloria Demers to "come out for the team" as a "beautiful, talented, erudite woman [who is] one of the unspeakable ten percent," Meigs balks at the symbolic role. "What team? what corps?" she asks, and "what is the 'part' of a lesbian, anyway?"[10] As her haircut, clothes, and demeanor would have it, she is just an old woman among others. If anything, it is Catherine, the vigorous lanky nun with cropped hair and a dazzling smile, oil-spattered from her efforts to repair the disabled engine, who seems like "the dyke." When Meigs eventually comes out in the film, she does so with minimal self-disclosure, letting her lesbianism remain abstract, unsupported by the kind of anecdotes or snapshots that specify the other women's heterosexual life stories. Most of the screen time goes to exploring the bonds that develop among these strangers within a landscape Meigs describes as "a multiple metaphor for old age, memory, life, and death."[11] Key to her own self-definition in the film, and quite apart from her iconic function as a lesbian, is her awareness of the spiritual resonance of life's endlessly evolving possibilities. Capturing the grace of one woman's dance despite her stiff joints, or the wonder of another's wrinkled lips emitting wonderfully accurate bird calls, or the humor of a third deftly turning her queen-size pantyhose into a fishnet, the film assimilates lesbian identity into a larger whole in keeping with Meigs's own need to mediate her lesbian identity in terms of universals.[12]

Seen from a young queer perspective, the discourse of a lesbian who is not coded as a "lesbian," in a film that is not centrally focused on lesbian issues, stresses the contradictory claims of belonging and separatism, iconic representation and singularity, alienation and acceptance, desire and its closeting. Seen through the lens of old age, this lesbian's position as merely one of seven old women, all (except the nun) known to be heterosexual, subordinates the political implications of her sexual orientation to the film's political intervention in our society's construction of aging as redundancy and decay. Taken together, these two agendas frame the film's attempt to counter the combined assaults of ageism and homophobia through Meigs's lesbian presence.

That spectators of all ages like the film has to do only partly with the acceptance it posits as a norm for human relations. Its claims to documentary authenticity are also crucial to this acceptance. Dwelling on old faces at close range, age spots and all, the film's leisurely takes and unobtrusive editing call for an affectionate reception of its subjects' unadorned person-hood. The photos and snapshots spliced into the footage trace each woman's passage from childhood to adulthood in a nostalgic retrospection that urges loving contemplation of faces we come to know well. Laced with sadness about the death that is presaged in this documented aging, but also overflowing with humor and with pleasure at the persistence of life, the film interweaves melancholia and joy. Indeed, the very setting proclaims as much. The physical beauty of the land, the ceaseless life of its creatures, and the ever-changing effects of mists and lights all suggest that the visible exists in relation to an unknown Beyond.

This evocation and acceptance of aging is further underscored by the film's episodic design. The chronological priorities of causality-driven narratives give way to an expansive randomness that is cumulative and panoramic. In contrast with the archaeological project of many "identity politics" documentaries produced over the past twenty-five years, the appeal of *Strangers in Good Company* is, consequently, more intuitive than factual. Diminishing the importance of compilation reportage as a means to knowledge and eliminating the corroborating function of interviews altogether, it draws audiences into loving intimacy with its protagonists — an intimacy that talking heads, for all their availability, ultimately prevent.

Still, the film's loving gathering of "strangers" in a community it calls "good company" has its political costs. The film recognizes the ethnicity of its Native American woman, for instance, but does not address racism; it tells of poverty in its Jewish woman's past but alludes to her Jewishness only in passing and avoids the subject of anti-Semitism; it mentions dulling assembly-line work in another woman's life but sidesteps questions of class; it acknowledges its lesbian character's sexual orientation but is silent about her history as a lesbian. Absorbed into a company of older women who, at the time of the film's production, were all single or celibate, Meigs's lesbian identity becomes moot even if her coming out makes a strong lesbian-positive statement.

Though *Strangers in Good Company* differs from *Women Like That, Women Like Us, West Coast Crones,* and *It's Not Too Late* in genre and tone, politically it shares with them a shying away from political controversy. Overall, these films' commitment to affirming older lesbians as a category inclines them to blur differences and mute struggles, including, ironically, differences that traverse the erotic arenas of sexual practice. One woman in *Women Like That* does allude to the persistence of desire with evident delight, and Buffy and some others do mention recent love relationships, but in general these films are silent in this regard. Aiming to celebrate sisterhood, not political struggle or sexual specificity, they assimilate their protagonists into a bland, asexual, middle-class, white normativity. As a result, they end up sidestepping both the trouble zones of aging and the intimacies of what it means to be a "lesbian" in the first place—the flow of erotic and affectional libido toward women. Skirting passion, they come across as more ageist than their affirming politics would otherwise suggest.[13]

In contrast, the three films to which I now turn explore the more risky terrain of lesbian sexualities across generational divides. That these films are highly individualized, each heading in its own direction, is hardly surprising. Since longevity is a relatively recent phenomenon for queers as well as for heterosexuals, and since older lesbians are not inclined to display their eroticism, such treatments have been too few to cluster around common thematics, shared politics, or generic practices. *Storme: The Lady of the Jewel Box* (Parkerson 1987) is a compilation portrait film that registers tensions around privacy and visibility. *Nitrate Kisses* (Hammer 1992) is a hybrid experimental piece that mingles fiction and improvised acting with archival and current documentary footage and voice-overs. *Forbidden Love: The Unashamed Stories of Lesbian Lives* (Weissman and Fernie 1992) mingles fiction and documentary in a self-referential dialectic that contrasts with *Strangers in Good Company*'s blending of the two genres.[14] What unites these diverse films is their recognition of female queer desires and their linking of desires, fantasy, and performance as formative aspects of identities situated within specific historical and political contexts. Importantly, the emphasis shifts here from visibility to agency, from health to pleasure, from ease to struggle, and from normalcy to funk.

Though Michelle Parkerson's biographical documentary of Storme DeLarverie is conventional in its compilation of talking-head interviews, verité-style footage, and archival materials, and though its subject clearly shies away from intimate disclosures, it nonetheless differs from the preceding documentaries in that it refuses to offer viewers facile reassurances. *Storme* does, however, subsume its protagonist's age under other considerations; its main concern is to capture the remarkable life of its protagonist and insert it within a queer heritage.

Storme's very presence as a cross-dressing woman from New Orleans raises questions concerning race, region, ethnicity, and class as well as gender and sexuality. First as a dashing tuxedo-clad emcee at the Jewel Box Revue (1959–69), then as a denim-clad bouncer for the Cubbyhole Club, Storme contests the very notion of identity in terms of both class and gender. Whereas the preceding films assume that fixed subject positions exist, Storme's ambiguity destabilizes such assurance. The undecidability that attaches to Storme is most frequently articulated in terms of visibility and its obstruction—not in Hollywood's fetishizing sense, but in terms of documentary access to or blockage of information. At times the film functions as an expository documentary, using straightforward reporting and compilation footage and thereby setting up expectations of informative clarity. At other times Storme becomes a reluctant informant whose efforts to control her image on camera create an enigmatic tension around what is or is not withheld. "I grew up hard in New Orleans, with my mixed blood, so I was my own responsibility," she tells us, without clarifying what "hard" means, why she was her own responsibility, or what being one's "own responsibility" means in her case.

The film consistently stops short of probing the two very different demimondes—that of mixed-race identities in the uniquely French Caribbean atmosphere of New Orleans, and that of sexual inversion in the sophisticated entertainment milieu of Harlem—Storme inhabited. In addition, the film is largely silent about the actual dangers that beset cross-dressing queers, even though Storme's position as a woman inhabiting the danger zones of the entertainment and sex industries certainly places her in the path of violence. Instead, the film focuses on her role as the "overseer" of her "boys," documenting the quasi-familial bonds of their interdependent work. Its record of affection between her and one of these men, and of her grief at the death of another, testifies to a depth of feeling beyond anything articulated on camera. When Storme recalls that death (of an unspecified long illness) in close-up, she says, "I don't even like talking about it now. . . . I think we'd better cut the camera, because I'm going to cry, okay?"

Parkerson cuts the camera, but only after aiming it at her subject's face long enough to make us complicit in its intrusiveness. The drama devolves on a butch's resisting the documentarist's probing. This guarding of privacy does not contradict the apparent plenitude of Storme's self-display as a performer. Rather, it documents the very impenetrability she herself builds into her role as a performer when she says, "All I had to do is be me and let people use their imagination." This notion of a stable self presented as a blank slate is not as simple as it sounds, of course. Whether Storme is sharing the stage with extravagantly turned out male divas or crooning "There will never be another you," her dashing tuxedoed image foregrounds the sexually charged effects of destabilized identities available for contemplation, not probing. Key here is a fierce commitment to the privacy of self-determination. As the film's archival materials suggest, a range of gendered and transgendered fantasies are tangled in this theatricality. The confidence projected by the man-tailored elegance of Storme's cabaret persona taps narratives quite different from her earlier femme persona or her more recent bodyguard persona, pistol on her hip.

To note these distinct personae is to stress the agency that sustains them, in that personae necessarily imply both a spectatorial gaze and willed acts of self-definition and self-presentation. The film conveys this agency when it records Storme's performances, orders (to off-camera passersby to move on), and instructions (to the crew to cut the camera during filming). Although such agency clearly supersedes considerations of aging, in comparison with the other films I have discussed, *Storme*'s most constructive stance is precisely that it does not treat age as a fixed category of being. The film does include representations of Storme at midlife, where her graying hair and thickened body function as registers of strength, not decline, but it does not address as age-related the circumstances affecting her job at the Cubbyhole or explore other aspects of her private affectional life. While both the film's segmented structure and Storme's own stance demarcate such gaps as not open for discussion, the film more than compensates for these silences by relishing the power and vitality that enable its protagonist to transgress gender boundaries. As Joan Nestle notes in an interview included in this film, this woman, whose very presence projects "a kind of nobility," invites us to savor the power of gender and explore the potentials of defining ourselves both within its conventions and in opposition to them.

In so doing, *Storme* foregrounds what the preceding films elide — namely, that erotic fantasies are relished across normative generational divides. It offers us an admiring portrait of a resilient older queer even as it makes it difficult for us to think of its protagonist as either "old" or as specifically "lesbian." Storme's appeal in this film eludes formulation, but has to do with her treating age, gender, and power as available to self-invention. Striding in denim and boots and laughing heartily about a recent scuffle with some men, Storme is a "lady" who works as a bouncer in the heart of an "entertainment" district; a low-caste person whose performing career hinged on simulations of upper-class excess; a woman of mixed parentage whose handsome face at once registers and resists racial definition; and an alto-tenor crossover singer who croons about an unforgettable love for a "you" of an unspecified gender while never confessing to romantic involvements.

Storme is less concerned with making spectators feel good about the prospect of aging than with relishing the eroticized dimensions of gendered performance and fantasy. It may be stoic about loneliness, poverty, disability, and danger, but it accepts responsibility for treating performance as inseparable from living, and it does so with great dignity. Taken in its totality, this documentary's image of a survivor, a woman whose stage name invokes storms and reveries, subsumes aging within a determined commit-

Storme DeLarverie
in *Storme: The
Lady of the Jewel
Box* (Michelle
Parkerson 1987).
Courtesy Storme
DeLarverie

ment to being alive. "The day I'll slow down," Storme tells us, "they'll be
sprinkling my ashes to the four winds."

The refusal to slow down also shapes *Nitrate Kisses'* sexually explicit
treatment of two old lesbians making love. With their wrinkled skins, sag-
ging and emaciated flesh, and white hair, these women are unquestionably
past midlife. They are old enough to come across as archetypal crones and
hags, emblems of the decaying maternal body that in our culture has served
to allegorize sexual excess by embodying it in the imagined grotesquerie of
unruly female lust. The challenge for *Nitrate Kisses* is, precisely, to reclaim
these historically pejorative fantasies and recast them positively. Accord-
ingly, its filming of this couple's intimate embraces exposes the reality of
enduring lesbian sexuality and urges viewers to enter into new relations to
visibility and its taboos. Treating these women as a legitimate subject for
cinematic contemplation and allowing them ample freedom for zestful self-
display, the film challenges whatever prudery and ageism contemporary
queer and straight audiences might bring with them.

Though the impact of this challenge comes partly from the film's portrayal of lesbian lust in old age as a legitimate subject, it is also a function
of the strategic placing of this footage up front, in the first of the film's four
sections. In fact, *Nitrate Kisses* is more thematically wide ranging and for-

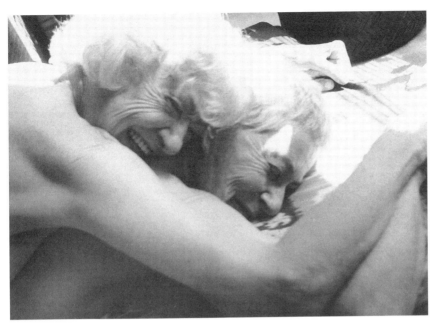

Nitrate Kisses (Barbara Hammer 1992). Courtesy Barbara Hammer

mally heterogeneous than my discussion suggests. The couple's lovemaking takes up only a portion of the first section, and that section is itself barely fifteen minutes long. Nevertheless, the editorial decision to position this footage as a framing device in dialogue with the subsequent three sections' younger queer couples (one male and two female) instructs spectators to adopt an awareness of queer sexualities that is less youth-centered than usual.

The normalization of the older lesbians' sexuality proceeds in many ways via intuitive rather than analytic reception. The editing in *Nitrate Kisses* is impressionistic, often pulverized into brief shots and further mediated through mobile cinematography and overlays of unattributed voice-overs and musical fragments. There are suggestive juxtapositions of readily recognizable icons: brief flashes of Garbo, Hepburn, Colette, and Woolf; shorts of a gay pride march in Paris; documentary images of an unspecified locale; outtakes from old narrative films. Profusion, rupture, and heterogeneity are key, with reiterations and contiguities providing sites for the production of meanings.

While these procedures occur throughout the film, they bear directly on its attempt to construct a liberatory discourse that intercuts close observation of the older lesbians' exuberant sexual display with citations from queer history and documentary records of older lesbians socializing, dancing, strolling, and so on. The very speed with which these heterogeneous materials unfold calls forth a reception open to upheavals and accepting of differences. The older women's unabashed sexual display is of a piece with the film's own appetite for images and sounds. Either way, profusion matters.

Still, as a political statement about aging and old lesbians, this plenitude is not without its liabilities. That this segment of *Nitrate Kisses* excludes considerations of race and class, for example, is at once troubling and predictable, for the elision of race and related political questions marks all the documentaries at hand other than *Storme*, whose director and subject are both women of color, and whose silences are personally motivated.[15] Seen thematically, the failure to integrate race and class more incisively into discourses on age and sexuality reflects the current limits of political analysis even within progressive communities. Seen formally, *Nitrate Kisses*' self-referential cinematography also raises questions about the ways it allows spectators to veer toward an intuitively exuberant rather than analytically exacting mode of reception.

The appeal but also the danger of such exuberance is that it can overwhelm the film to the point of reducing its erotic resonance as well as its intelligibility. The conventionally "beautiful" bodies and hip postmodernity (bleached punk haircuts, leather, tattoos, and body piercing) of the three younger couples yield an eloquent choreography of motion and contact that is more familiar and hence more available for desire and identification than the preceding footage of old bodies. The visual pleasure these three couples offer reclaims sex from the unruly domain of hags to the socially sanctioned and therefore reassuring domain of youth-centered sensuality.

Shots of a ravaged landscape intercut into the first sequence further qualify the treatment of the older couple. Starting with compilation footage about Willa Cather's transgendered identity as a transition into a consideration of erasures of lesbian identities, the film intercuts the older lesbians' lovemaking with visual documents and voice-over interview fragments that, together, constitute testimonials to lesbian presence. While this protest against silencing is clearly and forcefully made, the function of the ravaged landscapes is more ambiguous. As a trope, this footage may allude to the damage lesbians have suffered throughout history. This is a thread the second section picks up in its examination of the Third Reich's labeling of lesbians as "asocial." At the same time, however, the juxtaposition of images of old women and devastated landscapes suggests destruction and disaster. While there is considerable humor in parts of *Nitrate Kisses*, in this case there is nothing to prompt an ironic reading.

Ultimately *Nitrate Kisses*' exhibition of the two old women's sexual encounter shares with the preceding films a confidence in self-presentation as a mode of defining identity and a trust in visibility as cinema's contribution to social change.[16] It does so with a difference, though, for its rehabilitating impulse does not skirt the subject of lesbian sexuality as it persists into old age. Especially in relation to the tension *Storme* creates between theatrical display and personal containment, *Nitrate Kisses*' flaunting of decorum is a provocative reminder that lesbians of all ages can relish sex.

Forbidden Love takes a different slant on the tensions between decorum and passion. As a historical inquiry into pulp fiction's role in shaping lesbian fantasies during the 1950s and early 1960s, this film takes as its task recording a particular chapter in the formation of lesbian identities and communities, not advocating for older lesbians. Age appears only in that the film proceeds through interviews with older lesbians, and the impact of these women's presence has mainly to do with their vitality and articulateness as informants who discuss the erotic underpinnings of political identity and action. The interviews anchor collective history in the particularities of each woman's class, occupation, ethnicity, geographic region, gender identification, and sexual practices, and they include invaluable testimonials and documentation concerning coming out, the urban bar and entertainment worlds, dress codes, and butch and femme roles between the late 1940s and the late 1960s. Taken together, these narratives participate in the larger project of retrieving and rewriting queer history.

In contrast to the other documentaries I have discussed, however, *Forbidden Love* creates a reciprocity between fantasy and self-definition, fiction and agency, that uncovers desire and melds it with politics. It does so partly by allowing dramatized chapters of the steamy novel *Forbidden Love* to erupt into the frank interviews. It does so also by setting up a generational continuum among the younger fictional characters, the older documentary informants, and current lesbian viewers, most of whom are likely to be young, given the film's present distribution venues. The documentary segments anchor the fiction in history, while the fictional "chapters" recast the passion and thrill of the original reading experience through the slightly bemused stance of retrospection.

Such dialectics of pleasure and history, invention and documentation, legitimize desire as a dimension of politics. The emphasis here is on "unashamed stories," as the defiant subtitle tells us. Affirming the passionately romantic outlaw world this lesbian fiction created for its original readers, the film delights in velvety, high-contrast, quasi-noir visuals matched with sophisticated jazz and popular tunes. As the documentary's informants stress, pulp lesbian fiction spoke directly to their desires and in many instances facilitated their coming out through narrative codes that cut across demarcations of class and "good taste." The film captures this

Forbidden Love: The Unashamed Stories of Lesbian Lives (Weissman and Fernie 1992). Courtesy Women Make Movies

subversion by pairing each "chapter" with documentation and interviews concerning equivalent real-life experiences: leaving home, finding "the life" in a new city, meeting a new woman.

Though the documentary segments of *Forbidden Love* are formally conventional in their use of talking heads and compilation footage, the fictional segments disseminate a sultry sensuality not to be found in any of the other documentaries I have discussed, including *Nitrate Kisses*. The opening sequence's flirtatious use of sinuous pans, zooms, and lap-dissolves guides the eye across lurid paperback covers and creates a hunger for fantasy that gets reiterated at the start of each dramatized "chapter" when a manicured red-nailed hand turns a new page and a female voice-over resumes the anticipated storytelling. The transitions into documentary occur with the fiction arrested in freeze-frame at the precipice of some new development, the photographic image dissolving back into a lush book-cover illustration. The lap-dissolves remind viewers that fantasy is at once distinct yet inseparable from reality, for as the colors turn lurid and the image gets reduced to crude brush strokes, the actresses's bodies become more curvacious, their hair cascades more abundantly, and their postures adjust to intensify the erotic energy between them. While the novels from which such fictions derive obviously commodified lesbian desires for profit, the film treats their contribution to lesbian self-definition as politically formative during the decades separating World War II and second wave feminism. Like the bar scene and butch-femme roles that Elizabeth Lapovsky Kennedy and Madeline D. Davis show to have defined lesbian identities during the same time period,[17] these novels articulate codes of behavior that hinge on the relation between image and desire and provide models of organizing lesbian community relations.

That the film's informants happen to be exceptionally diverse, articulate, courageous, and charming certainly helps embed longing in action. Their cocky self-acceptance, boundless energy, courage in the face of assaults, and readiness to fight for change are as important to the film's younger viewers as they were to those who lived "the life." As characters, these older lesbians facilitate a critical understanding of the historical, cultural, and political function of lesbian emergence. Yet the collective vision *Forbidden Love* offers is not abstract, for the film shows several of its informants active within politicized communities. We see one woman marching in a demonstration, another officiating in a lesbian and gay church that has suffered several violent attacks, a third analyzing the political implications of her position as an educated Native American on skid row, a fourth battling for recognition as a lesbian West Indian club performer of color, and a fifth discussing the position of women in the military during World War II. Several discuss the power relations and violence that characterized the butch-femme bar scene. Their refreshing irreverence injects feisty realism into the sultry erotica of formula romance. In everyday life, *Forbidden Love* tells us, a dash of swagger can go a long way.

Indeed, for this film's generation of "out" lesbians, and for younger ones too, swagger has proved a crucial life support, born of duress, honed in danger, and buoyed with joy. As a body-centered, working-class male stance—a performative weapon that ensures survival in what Pat Califia

describes as an urban war zone—it signals a strength forged in a masculin-
ized outlaw world of back-alley encounters and bar-room brawls.[18] Evoked
in *Storme*, too, the legacy of this swagger is pride. Central is an undaunted
readiness to fight for the right to be oneself. Associating its participants'
defiant recasting of butch-femme gender roles with street smarts and political savvy, the film acknowledges the scarring but also the resilience that
proved formative in their lives. Most importantly, by joshing us about our
own desires and egging us on to affirm them, it draws us into viewing relations that embed us in a historical and political trajectory continuous with
its original subjects.

Of course *Storme*, *Nitrate Kisses*, and *Forbidden Love* share little by way
of a common subject matter or generic practice, and politically they also
part ways. They may all posit a broadly liberatory political stance, and they
may in their own ways evince faith in visibility as a basis for emancipatory
politics, but they differ radically in the extent to which they redirect our
sights from the private sphere of experience to public arenas of activism.
Still, when they are considered in relation to *Women Like That*, *Women
Like Us*, *West Coast Crones*, and *It's Not Too Late*, these last three films
present something of a united front as pioneering forays within an anti-
ageist queer project. Their efforts to contextualize their documentary testimonials, however indirectly, signal the value of building an informed
materialist base for a queer politics that faces outward, beyond its current
insularity. That *Storme*, *Nitrate Kisses*, and *Forbidden Love* do so with a
certain feisty transgressive swagger endows them with a measure of com-
bative optimism that sets them apart from the more ploddingly didactic
asexuality of the other films. Furthermore, their bringing lesbian desires
out into the open grounds personal experiences in public constraints. Exposing what has always been, they make possible new ways of seeing, identifying, and acting.
    My privileging here of the three films that introduce a measure of
agency and activism should not be mistaken for insensitivity to the real
limitations of old age. In fact, the reluctance to address these limitations directly is a problem in all the films discussed in this essay, with the excep-
tion of *Strangers in Good Company*. As they would have it, physical, material, and psychological disabilities exist only on the remotest periphery of
older peoples' experience, if at all. In this respect these anti-ageist films
inadvertently participate in our society's general practice of ducking painful
truths. Positive images do have their uses as normalizing, optimistic, affectionate interventions in degrading mythologies that occur at the nexus of
sexism, ageism, and homophobia. But as Mary Russo reminds us in her

discussion of the evolution of second wave feminism in the United States, the risk is that we may turn our backs on radical, heterogeneous, unruly, and revolutionary self-definition and accept a more homogenizing reintegration of women (no longer "feminists") into a sedate mainstream.[19] Or, as Amber Hollibaugh and Cherríe Moraga put it, we may drift toward a nonsexual feminism that sees lesbianism as a practice of feminism rather than as a tangle of its own identities, desires, and politics.[20]

From a political point of view, it is mainly the courageous capacity for defiance, experienced in joy and desire as well as in anger, that energizes these last three films. Though *Storme*, *Nitrate Kisses*, and *Forbidden Love* vary greatly in the extent to which they locate personal identities and sexualities within racist and classist as well as homophobic and sexist institutions, they do at least open up a space for considering how desires get formed and performed within diverse political structures. Ironically, what assists them in doing so is the fact that each subsumes age under other considerations. Instead of extracting older lesbians from the flow of life and installing them as a category in timeless stasis, these films honor older lesbians' singularity in history. Taking evident pleasure in these women's agency as they continue to engage in life's ups and downs, these films value their subjects for helping form oppositional queer communities, and for putting forth a liberatory view of a queer old age that affirms desire and treats age as an ordinary dimension of existence.

NOTES

1. This recoil is variously addressed by Vivian Sobchack, "Revenge of the Leech Woman: On the Dread of Aging in a Low-Budget Horror Film," in *Uncontrollable Bodies: Testimonies of Identity and Culture*, ed. Rodney Sappington and Tyler Stallings (Seattle: Bay Press, 1994), 79–91; Barbara McDonald with Cynthia Rich, *Look Me in the Eye: Old Women, Aging, and Ageism* (San Francisco: Spinsters, 1983); and Kathleen Woodward, *Aging and Its Discontents: Freud and Other Fictions* (Bloomington: Indiana University Press, 1991).

2. For further discussion of Dietrich, see Gaylyn Studlar, *In the Realm of Pleasure: Von Sternberg, Dietrich, and the Masochistic Aesthetic* (New York: Columbia University Press, 1988).

3. I take the term *monstre sacré* from Steven Back, *Marlene Dietrich: Life and Legend* (New York: Morrow, 1992).

4. See Jan Rosenberg, *Women's Reflections: The Feminist Film Movement* (Ann Arbor, Mich.: UMI Research Press, 1979), and Julia Lesage, "The Political Aesthetics of the Feminist Documentary Film," in *Issues in Feminist Film Criticism*, ed. Patricia Erens (Bloomington: Indiana University Press, 1990), 222–37.

5. For further discussion of these key questions, see Bill Nichols, *Representing Reality: Issues and Concepts in Documentary* (Bloomington: Indiana University Press, 1991), and the essays in Michael Renov, ed., *Theorizing Documentary* (New York: Routledge, 1993).

6. See Howard Zinn, *A People's History of the United States* (New York: Harper, 1980).

7. Concerning the function of "evidence," see Sonya Michel, "Feminism, Film, and Public History," in *Issues in Feminist Film Criticism*, ed. Patricia Erens (Bloomington: Indiana University Press, 1990), 238–49, and Martha Gever, "What Becomes a Legend Most?" *GLQ: A Journal of Lesbian and Gay Studies* 1.2 (1994): 209–19.

8. See Barbara Halpern Martineau, "Talking about Our Lives and Experiences: Some Thoughts about Feminism, Documentary, and 'Talking Heads,'" in *"Show Us Life": Toward a History and Aesthetics of the Com-*

mitted Documentary, ed. Thomas Waugh (Metuchen, N.J.: Scarecrow, 1984), 252–73.

9. Gever, "What Becomes a Legend Most?" 210.

10. Mary Meigs, *In the Company of Strangers* (Vancouver: Talon, 1991), 16–17.

11. Ibid., 12.

12. Especially telling is Meigs's extended music and dance metaphor, which occurs immediately after she refers to three women's intimate reminiscences about past romances and present desires. The metaphor recasts the heterosexual conversation as a "continuous turnover" of same-sex encounters, thus "queering" it. Ibid., 153.

13. Along similar lines, Jan Zita Grover examines how photographs enhance reality, proposing the ideal as already present and giving it an illusory tangibility that speaks to the photographer's and spectator's desire more than to actuality. Portraits of lesbian couples in the early 1980s, she notes, downplayed sexuality and stressed social respectability, attesting to a longing for recognition and legitimation. See Jan Zita Grover, "Framing the Questions: Positive Imaging and Scarcity in Lesbian Photographs," in *Stolen Glances: Lesbians Take Photographs*, ed. Tessa Boffin and Jean Fraser (London: Pandora, 1991), 184–90.

14. Yvonne Rainer's *Privilege* (1990) contains a "lesbian" character but omits lesbian perspectives on menopause. Rainer's subsequent essay "Working Round the L-Word" describes the elision as bound up in her coming out while she was working on the film. See Yvonne Rainer, "Working Round the L-Word," in *Queer Looks: Perspectives on Lesbian and Gay Film and Video*, ed. Martha Gever, John Greyson, and Pratibha Parmar (New York: Routledge, 1993), 12–20.

15. See Evelynn Hammonds, "Black (W)holes and the Geometry of Black Female Sexuality," *differences* 6.2-3 (Summer-Fall 1994): 126–45. The function of racialized representations in *Nitrate Kisses'* other sections is problematic both because lighting and filming of the interracial gay couple is so "arty" and because other representations of non-whites occur only incidentally, in verité footage that includes a few African-American women. Relevant here is Kobena Mercer's discussion of the relation between ideal types and desire. See Mercer, "Skin Head Sex Thing: Racial Difference and the Homoerotics of the Imaginary," in *How Do I Look? Queer Film and Video*, ed. Bad Object-Choices (Seattle: Bay Press, 1991), 169–222.

16. On the seduction of representations that *hint* at sexual practices, see Judith Mayne, "Primitive Narration," *The Woman at the Keyhole* (Bloomington: Indiana University Press, 1990), 157–83.

17. Elizabeth Lapovsky Kennedy and Madeline D. Davis, *Boots of Leather, Slippers of Gold: The History of a Lesbian Community* (New York: Routledge, 1993).

18. Pat Califia, *Public Sex: The Culture of Radical Sex* (Pittsburgh: Cleis, 1994).

19. Mary Russo, *The Female Grotesque: Risk, Excess, and Modernity* (New York: Routledge, 1994).

20. Amber Hollibaugh and Cherríe Moraga, "What We're Rollin' around in Bed With: Sexual Silences in Feminism: A Conversation towards Ending Them," in *The Persistent Desire: A Femme-Butch Reader*, ed. Joan Nestle (Boston: Alyson, 1992), 243–53.

MARC SIEGEL

[**5**] *Documentary That Dare/Not Speak Its Name: Jack Smith's* Flaming Creatures

No one ever talks about the problems of daily life
and so daily life becomes exotic.
:: Jack Smith[1]

In September 1963, Jonas Mekas and his associates at the Film-Makers'
Coop crashed the annual Flaherty Seminar in Brattleboro, Vermont. That
year the seminar was hosting a cinema verité retrospective featuring work
by documentarists who had previously received Mekas's praise for their
role in inaugurating a new cinematic language. But for Mekas, cinema
verité was no longer capable of grasping the complexities of daily life. He
therefore attempted to intervene in the seminar with Jack Smith's *Flaming
Creatures* and Ken Jacobs's *Blonde Cobra*, "two pieces of the impure,
naughty, and 'uncinematic' cinema that is being made now in New York."[2]
This intervention went largely without notice, and Mekas had to content
himself with a midnight screening and a small, though enthusiastic, audience. He vowed to return another time to disturb those who "slept peace-
fully dream[ing] cinema verité."[3]

    Peaceful dreams lasted only a few months. On New Year's Eve 1964,
Mekas, Barbara Rubin, and P. Adams Sitney stormed the projection booth
at the Third International Experimental Film Exhibition in Knokke-Le
Zoute, Belgium, in order to screen *Flaming Creatures,* which had been excluded from festival consideration. Having hidden the film in the can for
Stan Brakhage's *Dog Star Man,* these three firebrands combated police and
audience alike, at one point even using the face of the Belgian minister of
justice as a screen for Smith's images. Unable to avoid it, the jury eventually did see *Flaming Creatures,* awarded it a special *film maudit* prize, and,
to Mekas's surprise, referred to it as a documentary. "Americans must

really live like that, they thought. A wild image of America we left in Knokke-Le Zoute, I tell you."[4]

Back in New York City, the police were chasing Mekas's screenings of unlicensed underground films from one theater to another. He screened *Flaming Creatures* at the Gramercy Arts Theatre for three consecutive Mondays in early 1964 without incident; then police harassment caused the theater owner to cancel the weekly film showcase. On March 3, at a screening of Smith's film at the New Bowery Theater, the police launched a more aggressive attack. Emerging from the audience after thirty minutes, they halted the screening and seized the film, the projector, and the screen. Mekas, projectionist Ken Jacobs, and the ticket taker found themselves in jail facing charges of obscenity. One of the detectives told the press that *Flaming Creatures* was "hot enough to burn up the screen."[5]

The seizure of *Flaming Creatures* and the critical and political defense of the "naughty and uncinematic cinema," waged predominantly by Mekas in his weekly *Village Voice* columns, brought national attention to underground film. The notoriety resulted in a popular association of the term *underground* with the issue of obscenity. People perceived under-ground films not only as dirty, but also as documents of a perverse sub-culture, or, echoing the Belgian jurists, as evidence that Americans must re-ally live like that. Assertions about the documentary nature of the films irritated Mekas and other critics who valued underground film for its aes-thetic innovation, not for its role in documenting particular (sexual) sub-cultures. Yet by legitimating underground films solely on aesthetic terms, these critics avoided a consideration of how aesthetic innovation can be in-tegrally related to self-representation. While *Flaming Creatures* may have been "impure," too invested in cinematic fantasy to be accepted as a cin-ema verité documentary, it also expressed a "new kind of cinema truth,"[6] one that saw in artifice, in performance the possibility for creating a more fabulous, more livable reality.

Indeed, for present-day queers attempting to reconstruct our histories, the aesthetic value of a film like *Flaming Creatures* cannot be so easily sepa-rated from its role as documentation. Yet much gay historiography has tended to ignore the importance of queer cultural expressions as a kind of documentation, emphasizing instead the organizations and institutions that have been constructed around the articulation of a sexual identity. In an essay in which she questions the very possibility of speaking one's name, in this case the problematic of speaking as a lesbian, Judith Butler observes that "part of what constitutes sexuality is precisely that which does not ap-pear and that which, to some degree, can never appear."[7] How can we be attentive to that excess, to those aspects of sexuality that are excluded by

Flaming Creatures (Jack Smith 1963). Courtesy Anthology Films

the very act of representation? How do we acknowledge those cultural expressions of sexual subcultures that must go unnamed? How then can we discuss documentary that dare not speak its name?

►

Exotic Daily Life

> *How can you not—you know—understand the movements and the gestures?*
> ::   Jack Smith[8]

By 1962, the year Jack Smith began assembling creatures for the parties that became the movie, the existence of urban gay subcultures throughout the United States was widely acknowledged. The publication of the Kinsey Reports (1948, 1951), the birth of *Playboy* magazine (1951), and the frank discussion of sexuality in literary works, particularly among the Beats, attracted mainstream attention to the existence of a diversity of sexual practices. At the same time, specific references to homosexuality in 1950s newspaper reports, mainly in the context of police raids on gay bars or cruising areas, served as a kind of unintentional publicity for the burgeoning urban communities constructed around shared sexual practices. In opposition to widespread social attitudes that equated homosexuality with sin, sickness, and crime, the early homophile organizations attempted to generate an image of homosexuals as respectable members of an oppressed minority group. To this end, most of their efforts were directed at gaining the support of prominent members—doctors, lawyers, educators—of straight society. Despite this orientation toward those who shaped public opinion, the Mattachine Society (founded 1950) and the Daughters of Bilitis (founded 1953) did manage through their publications to create a space where a dialogue among gays and lesbians themselves could occur. This creation of a public gay press, however small its distribution, enabled, according to John D'Emilio, the construction of a community based on "a common vocabulary."[9]

What Mattachine and the Daughters of Bilitis offered gays and lesbians then was a name for themselves, a sexual identity. As with any identity, it was based on a series of exclusions. Both organizations, for instance, cautioned their membership against cross-dressing, cruising, and participation in the bar culture. As D'Emilio points out, because of its accomodationism, the homophile movement actually excluded those people who were most committed to gay and lesbian public life.[10] Mattachine and the Daughters of Bilitis paradoxically distanced themselves from the sexual subculture that had been the site of some of the most significant political activity. For example, as a result of the political and cultural work of José Sarria, a drag queen performer at San Francisco's Black Cat bar in the fifties and early sixties, many men began to recognize their own rights as gay people. Sarria's Sunday-afternoon performances, which incorporated some of the problems of gay daily life into the plots of well-known operas, attracted crowds of over two hundred, more than the combined memberships of the San Francisco branches of the Daughters of Bilitis and the Mattachine Society.[11]

By the early sixties, newpaper reports on homosexuality began to shift from accounts of police harassment to voyeuristic forays into the gay world. On December 17, 1963, the *New York Times* ran a front-page article entitled "Growth of Overt Homosexuality in City Provokes Wide Concern."[12] The story, written in the wake of recent closings of "two more homosexual haunts," contained interviews with psychiatrists, religious leaders, and the police, as well as a leader of the Mattachine Society ("himself an invert"), in an attempt to make sense of "the city's most sensitive open secret— the presence of what is possibly the greatest homosexual population in the world and its increasing openness."[13] That the only gay people given a voice in the article were members of the Mattachine Society testifies to the success of the early homophile movement at gaining a certain degree of visibility. The price of visibility is also evident as the *Times* reserves its greatest scorn for the very same people excluded by the homophiles: "those who are universally regarded as the dregs of the invert world—the male prostitutes—the painted, grossly effeminate 'queens' and those who prey on them."[14]

The closing of "homosexual haunts" was one aspect of a larger campaign to clean up New York City in anticipation of the World's Fair to be held there in the summer of 1964. By April, police had closed all but one of the queer bars, four small theaters for showing unlicensed films (*Flaming Creatures* and Jean Genet's *Chant d'amour*, among others), and coffeehouses that featured nonprofit poetry readings. This was also the time of Lenny Bruce's well-publicized arrest for obscenity. This "horrible cleanup" led the poet Frank O'Hara to wonder "what they think people are *really* coming to NYC for, anyway?"[15]

While it is useful to contextualize the attack on *Flaming Creatures* within a larger offensive against countercultural expression, this acknowledgment of a period of moral panic should not cause us to overlook the specific panic caused by Smith's film, namely, a panic about sexual variety. According to Gayle Rubin, "disputes over sexual behavior often become the vehicles for displacing social anxieties, and discharging their attendant emotional intensity."[16] But Rubin is careful to note that "the realm of sexuality also has its own internal politics, inequities, and modes of oppression." Within a historical period marked by a moral panic, then, "the domain of erotic life is, in effect, renegotiated." Jack Smith's *Flaming Creatures*, the censorial reaction it provoked, and the critical discourse that rose to its defense all testify to such a renegotiation.

The film, shot over eight consecutive weekends in the summer of 1962, depicts the actions of a group of creatures, namely, Smith and his friends, in various drag genres, from Arab harem girls to pseudo-Marilyn Monroe. Almost entirely eschewing dialogue and traditional narrative continuity, *Flaming Creatures* presents a series of tableaux depicted in beautiful washed-out black and white images. The film begins with a lengthy title card sequence in which the creatures parade in front of an elaborately scrawled list of credits. This is followed by a scene of timid flirtation, complete with coy glances from behind fluttering fans; a lipstick commercial; a frantic chase; a rape/orgy; and an earthquake. Finally, after everyone is apparently dead, a vampire emerges from a coffin, nibbles on the necks of a few dead creatures, and ignites a wild celebratory dance that brings the film to a close. The discreteness of each of these events is interrupted by cutaway close-ups of body parts—a quivering female breast, a limp penis, puckered lips—or, in a few breathtaking moments, of *tableaux vivants* in which the creatures' intertwined bodies clutter the entire frame. Most of

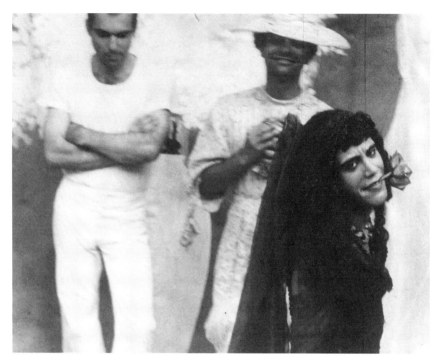

Flaming Creatures (Jack Smith 1963). Courtesy Anthology Films

the sound track is devoted to scratchy recordings of tango, pop music, opera, and rock and roll.

The whispered pronouncements heard during the title card sequence, "Ali Baba comes today," suggest that the flamers' actions are set in "the Orient" or, more appropriately, "Montez-land," the world of Smith's cherished Maria Montez, star of such 1940s cinematic exotica as *Ali Baba and the 40 Thieves* (Arthur Lubin 1944), *Cobra Woman* (Robert Siodmark 1944), and *Arabian Nights* (John Rawlins 1942). Smith's writings, performances, and films abound with references to Montez and her screen personas, particularly "Cobra Woman" and "Scheherazade." As indicated by the title of his 1963 essay "The Perfect Filmic Appositeness of Maria Montez," Smith's interest was not merely in Montez the film star, but in what he called "Montez-land," the fantasy world of her films, the elaborate sets and costumes that were designed to suit "her vision of the world."[17] This vision was suggested not through her convincing performances but through her conviction about her own beauty. "Wretch actress — pathetic as actress, why insist upon her being an actress — why limit her. Don't slander her beautiful womanliness that took joy in her own beauty and all beauty — or whatever in her that turned plaster cornball sets to beauty."[18] Rejecting the category "actress," which could not explain the richness of Montez's performances, Smith argued that we needed to broaden our conception of screen performance. The failure of her acting—that is, failure to allow her humanity to be subsumed beneath a character—resonated with the failure of the sets to achieve any kind of verisimilitude. Montez's performances, which revealed her integrity while reveling in her beauty, thus amounted to a kind of visual truth: "Her image spoke."[19]

Inspired by the suggestive power of the images in Montez's films, Smith attempted in his own work to create a visual reality unencumbered by the fabrications of a story on the sound track. To this end he was also influenced by Josef von Sternberg, whose "movies had to have plots even tho they already had them inherent in the images."[20] *Flaming Creatures*, however, did not have to have a plot since it was not made for Hollywood producers who demanded "explanations." Thus Smith could allow the visuals to "speak" for themselves. His insistence on the expressiveness of a performer's movements and gestures is best explained by reference to the lipstick commercial. While various creatures are shown from different angles putting on lipstick and staring into mirrors, a salesman's voice is heard hawking a new heart-shaped lipstick that "makes outlining your mouth as simple as writing your name." The implication here is that having perfectly outlined lips could replace having a name. Since, as the announcer informs us, "this lipstick is indelible," putting it on represents a serious commitment to speaking through one's makeup. This conviction about the self-designating power of well-applied lipstick is echoed in Boyd McDonald's brief essay on Gloria Grahame's performance in *In a Lonely Place* (Nicholas Ray 1950). According to McDonald, "the badge of [Grahame's] femininity was the fantastically sharp outline of her lips, or, more precisely, her lipstick. . . . Grahame's male costars, no matter how they posed and swaggered, had no weapon to compete with her lipstick; without the slightest effort, simply by standing there with those lips, she stole scenes from everyone else on the screen."[21]

Like Grahame, Smith's creatures spoke for themselves simply by standing there with those lips, not to mention those veils. Smith's insistence on the ability of the visuals to speak for themselves should not, however, be misconstrued as a belief in an aesthetic of objectivity. His aesthetic ideas are undoubtedly in conflict with the direct cinema practitioners' principle of nonintervention. While Richard Leacock, for instance, bemoaned the presence of the camera for its falsifying effects,[22] Smith embraced (cinematic) artifice as a necessary precondition for the acting out of fantasies. He realized that only through artifice—and self-consciously trashy artifice at that—could the reality of his creatures be expressed on film. At one point during the flirtation scene, for instance, Smith literally veils the performers, shooting with a veil hanging directly in front of the camera. Instead of seeking out a preexisting "highly charged atmosphere"[23] in which the camera merely records people being themselves, Smith "help[ed] with the atmosphere"[24] by creating a fantasy space that was integral to his creatures' lives. Donning a veil, or putting on lipstick, did not obscure the flaming creatures; it enabled them.

Smith celebrated the movements of these turbaned, veiled performers without commentary, without explanation, and, most defiantly, without apology. ("We're here! We're queer! And we're going to dress like Scheherazade!") Michael Moon has noted that the flaming creatures' glances, emphasized in Smith's many close-ups, recall the unflinching stare of the vamp, the common screen persona for sexually confident (read: threatening) women.[25] Cops and critics who had read the *Times* on that cold Tuesday in December "knew" as well that a lingering glance also betrayed the homosexual. "Some homosexuals claim infallibility in identifying others of their kind 'by the eyes—there's a look that lingers a fraction of a second too long.'"[26] Like the vamp, the homosexual's sexual desire was suggested by a "lingering look." By returning the stare, the "painted, grossly effeminate 'queens'" on the screen thus implicated the audience in "the exemplary modern urban practice of 'cruising.'"[27]

What finally makes Smith's creatures so threatening is that they are not offered up to knowledge. *Flaming Creatures* is not an insider's view into a subculture. There is no attempt to depict or appeal to a belief in an objective social reality. Instead there is only the suggestive power of the creatures' movements, a complex "visual truth" that elicited laughter from some and violence from others. "A creative event does not grasp, it does not take possession, it is an excursion."[28] Uninterested in containing his creatures within a narrative, within a name, Smith instead releases them into an excursion of beauty. Without a tour guide, or a "voice of God," cops and critics were left to fend for themselves.

That Writing

> *I started making a comedy about everything that I thought was funny. And it was funny. The first audiences were laughing from the beginning all the way through. But then that writing started—and it became a sex thing.*
> :: Jack Smith[29]

In a 1964 *Nation* review that greatly contributed to the film's reception as a "sex thing" for the liberal intellectual set, Susan Sontag attributed Smith's

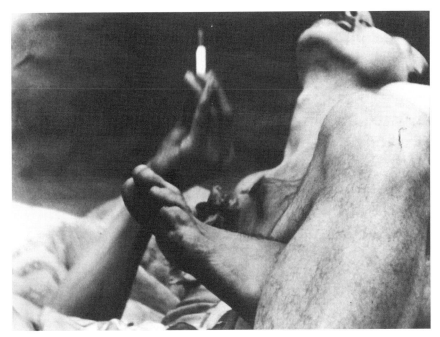

Flaming Creatures (Jack Smith 1963). Courtesy Anthology Films

unapologetic presentation of gender and sexual play to his lack of position on this subject matter. Yet, as I have argued, by not explaining his flaming creatures, by choosing not to offer them up to knowledge at a time when any kind of gender ambiguity was castigated by both mainstream media and homophile organizations, Smith in fact took a very radical position on representations of gender and sexuality. In her liberal defense of obscenity, Sontag, however, did not. Instead, she claimed that "there are some elements of life—above all, sexual pleasure—about which it isn't necessary to have a position."[30] This denial of the very possibility of sexual politics informs much of the early writing on *Flaming Creatures*.

Like many of her contemporaries, Sontag praised *Flaming Creatures* as "that rare modern work of art: it is about joy and innocence."[31] Not appealing to prurient interests, the "images of sex," she claimed, "are alternately childlike and witty."[32] For P. Adams Sitney the film expressed a "myth of recovered innocence."[33] He related it to "romantic mythology [which] frequently centers on the vision of childhood."[34] But what is so innocent about Smith's creatures? And why did these critics align this innocence with childhood? Their appeals to what Parker Tyler has called "the deathless theme of adolescent sex and its pristine discoveries"[35] function both to attribute universalist pretensions to the erotic play in Smith's film and to normalize it. By invoking a mythological innocence in relation to images of Mario Montez in a black veil dancing with a rose in his mouth, or to those of other creatures who reach beneath their skirts to fondle their genitals, these critics neglected the erotics of role playing. For the transvestism among Smith's creatures is not an expression of innocence, but of desire. What Sitney and Sontag's critiques ultimately ignore is the importance of *Flaming Creatures* as an act of self-representation, as a form of documentation.

By confusing adult sexual pleasure with innocence (and innocence with adolescent sexual pleasure), contemporary critics, those "professional attention bandits,"[36] obscured the film's more complicated ramifications within the realm of erotic life. This critical strategy may have been employed to facilitate a connection between misunderstood underground films, made by and for specific communities, and the high art tradition, with its purported universalism. Though it was seized by the police for obscenity, *Flaming Creatures*, it was argued, was not merely obscene. Instead, it evoked the "realms of myths and beauties . . . *through* obscenities."[37] Defenders of the film, for instance, frequently invoked such legitimated chroniclers of deviancy as Milton, Dante, Goya, and Bosch. Jonas Mekas, perhaps the person most concerned with and responsible for the legitimation of underground film, placed Smith's work alongside Ron Rice's *The Queen of Sheba Meets the Atom Man* and Ken Jacobs's *Blonde Cobra* and *Little Stabs at Happiness* in a category he called "Baudelairean Cinema." Invoking the marquis de Sade, Rimbaud, and William Burroughs, Mekas spoke of a "world of flowers of evil, of illuminations, of torn and tortured flesh; a poetry which is at once beautiful and terrible, good and evil, delicate and dirty."[38]

Instead of challenging the validity of these literary and art historical connections, I would like to question the need for them in the first place. Sontag began her article bemoaning "the close-ups of limp penises and bouncing breasts, the shots of masturbation and oral sexuality." Such images, she claimed, "make it hard simply to talk about this remarkable film; one has to *defend* it."[39] Ken Kelman, the author of *Film Culture*'s first article on *Flaming Creatures*, offered similarly tentative praise. Though he relished the film's "beautiful dirtiness," Kelman hesitated to praise perversity itself: "It's beautiful dirty. But it is also redeemed [on] other levels, and high ones."[40] As a defense or redemption of Smith's dirty images, then, both Kelman's and Sontag's critiques ignore what Mekas, for instance, stated quite bluntly: "*Flaming Creatures* will not be shown theatrically because our social-moral-etc. guides are sick."[41] In other words, Kelman and Sontag blamed the film itself for the charges of obscenity leveled against it. By not positing Smith's gender and sexual play as legitimate artistic fare in and of itself, their critiques failed to implicate the truly obscene social forces that constrained such "overt expressions" of perversity.

Though he was a tireless defender of *Flaming Creatures*, Mekas was nevertheless quick to subsume a discussion of the film's alleged obscenity beneath a liberal freedom-of-expression defense. Speaking of his actions at the Belgian festival, he maintained that "we were not fighting for this particular film, but for the principle of free expression."[42] Yet the film under attack was not just any aesthetic expression, but a specific erotic aesthetic expression. As J. Hoberman notes, of the many explicit underground films of the early 1960s, including Kenneth Anger's *Scorpio Rising* and Genet's *Chant d'amour* (both of which were also seized by police for obscenity in early 1964), none has inspired the "rage" and "hostility" that has greeted *Flaming Creatures*.[43] Neither explicitly heterosexual nor "blatantly homo-erotic," Hoberman asserts, "the behavior in *Flaming Creatures* is something else." What unites the most explicit images of genitalia in the film— from the limp penis that dangles over the shoulder of another creature who is seemingly unaware of its presence to the quivering breast that is revealed during the rape scene—is a defiant disregard for the role of the genitals within normative regimes of sexuality. What was under attack then was not simply the documentation of explicit (hetero- or even homo-) sexual acts, but the expression of an eroticism that might go unnamed. It was not solely the realm of art that was under attack, but the possibilities of erotic diversity as well. A defense of the film that would acknowledge the legitimacy of cultural expressions of perversity would thus have to call into question the normalizing effects of the existing organization of erotic life.

▶ ───

The Aesthetic of Failure

> *Juvenile does not equal shameful and trash*
> *is the material of creators.*
> ::   Jack Smith[44]

Though Smith's "comedy" became "a sex issue for the Cocktail world,"[45] it never succeeded in pleasing—that is, arousing—audiences who expected a properly pornographic experience. On one occasion when Mekas screened the film for "a group of upper-class New York writers," he received physical threats. "They would have happily sat through a pornographic movie, which they were expecting to see and which the host had promised them that night—but they could not take the fantasies of Jack Smith."[46] Carel

Rowe encountered a similarly hostile reaction from students when he screened *Flaming Creatures* at "the first (and last) Lurid Film Festival" at Northwestern University in 1972.[47] For the first third of the film the audience enjoyed themselves, laughing raucously, until they suddenly became enraged. Rowe attributed their behavior change to the film's "relentless pansexuality," which countered their erotic expectations. Perhaps it is the film's combination of "pansexuality" and "relentlessness" that so disturbed audiences. In other words, for someone expecting pornography, with its typical narrative of sexual pleasure leading up to penile orgasm, *Flaming Creatures*, with its persistence of flaccidness, was bound to disappoint. In Smith's work and in the work of the Theater of the Ridiculous, the theater company associated with Charles Ludlam in which Smith and most of his performers participated, erotic play was not singled out from other dramatic action. Instead, it was incorporated into an overall performance style that, as Stefan Brecht has noted, emphasized the immediacy and physicality of the moment and not the gradual progression toward a narrative or sexual goal. "All this [was] apt to get *boring* from time to time. Not just because of the failures of talent, skill, or effort but because the action-style of the play and performance so sharpen our awareness of the passage of time and the problem of its use that we become resentful of the foolishness and sterility as wasteful."[48]

Forsaking technical proficiency in every aspect of production, from the outdated film stock and scratchy records to the flaming creatures' "failed" performances, Smith privileged instead the cinematic realization of his and his friends' erotic fantasies.[49] An aesthetic composition was thus not the result of perfection, but the expression of an erotic quest—better yet, the quest for erotic expression:

> After *Flaming Creatures* I realized that that wasn't something I had photographed: Everything really happened. It really happened. I—that those were things I wanted to happen in my life and it wasn't something that we did, we really lived through it; you know what I mean? And it was really real. It just was.[50]

The inextricability of fantasy ("things I wanted to happen") from reality ("we really lived through it") is central to Smith's artistic project. Only after *Flaming Creatures* did he realize that "everything really happened." The "really real" was thus not available to the camera prior to filming. It had to be produced in the process of performing. Though some images, those explicit images of genitalia that so distressed Smith's critics, may seem to offer unmediated access to a prior reality, they could instead be understood as elements within a larger "flow between fact and fiction."[51] Smith's aesthetic is thus not a means of capturing the truth of his erotic life, but of "composing (on) life in living it and making it."[52]

In charting the representation of self in underground film, particularly "the gay underground," Richard Dyer notes an increasing emphasis on aspects of performance in the early 1960s: "The films from the late forties take the film-maker as subject matter, her or his inner life, revealed by dreams, released by ritual, universalized by myth. . . . Films like *Flaming Creatures* [however] show not the film-maker as inner personality, but the performer's outer persona."[53] This shift was from a performance designed to reveal a psychic state to one that expresses a social reality. Mekas also noted this breakdown between the performer and her or his role. Yet, in his assessment, this signaled not the exposure of social processes, but disengagement from the social.[54] Distinguishing Baudelairean cinema from the earlier cinema verité work of such New American Cinema practitioners as Shirley Clarke, Richard Leacock, and the Maysles brothers, Mekas praised the former's "disengagement and new freedom."[55] For him, these films marked an important shift away from a documentary impulse to a cinema of personal revelation. But what are the effects of maintaining this opposition between documentary and personal revelation, between objective and subjective reality, in discussions of *Flaming Creatures?*

The failure of Smith's aesthetic to achieve verisimilitude marked his entire stage and screen oeuvre. As J. Hoberman notes, "virtually every one of his performances was about the impossibility of its own coming into existence."[56] In Smith's later stage work, for instance, the performers, who were often recruited from the audience, would be seen rehearsing their lines with the director (Smith) beside them calling out instructions. Not content with generating a single stage or screen persona over the course of a performance, let alone a career, Smith instead preferred to "'act out' fantasies of his imaginary identities as well as critiques of these fantasies."[57] For Smith and his friends, composing on life became a way of living. Personal revelation was thus linked to a very particular social project, namely, the establishment of what Stefan Brecht has called "*families*, somewhat enduring groups, structured by erotic relations."[58]

The plurality of these destabilized erotic identities confounded those critics who were dependent on the banality of binary systems of gender and sexuality. In the 1970s, Smith's aesthetic exploration of erotic life conflicted with the concept of a unified sexual identity put forward by the early gay liberation movement. "I took my program to a gay theater, and he couldn't understand how it was gay, because he was unable to see it in a context."[59] According to Smith, the gay movement had become "ghettoized" and expected its art simply to "talk about gay things." But Smith's

Flaming Creatures (Jack Smith 1963). Courtesy Anthology Films

work was not directed toward the goal of reaffirming or reconciling oneself to a singular sexual identity or community. Understanding "how it was gay" meant seeing not only art, but also (gay) sexuality in a context. The failure of his aesthetic, the breakdown of a unified representation of erotic life, therefore expressed a flamboyant refusal to be contained within fixed categories of knowledge. Smith's strategic disruption of gender and sexual norms was ultimately an attempt at expressing the possibilities of an eroticism that is always beyond the reach of representation. What he intended to document could not be named. When we look back to queer cultural works like *Flaming Creatures*, when we see both culture and (queer) sexuality in a context, we are continuing Smith's project of "helping the atmosphere." For our quest, like his, is not solely to document that we really do and did live like that, but also to proliferate queer challenges to the normalization of erotic life.

♦──

NOTES

I am grateful to Chon Noriega for his encouragement throughout the process of preparing this essay. Thanks also to Jameel Khaja for some last-minute cross-country help. For careful readings and helpful suggestions, I thank Douglas Crimp and, particularly, Daniel Hendrickson.

1. Quoted in J. Hoberman, "The Theatre of Jack Smith," *Drama Review* 23.1 (March 1979): 12.
2. Jonas Mekas, *Movie Journal: The Rise of a New American Cinema, 1959-1971* (New York: Collier, 1972), 95.
3. Ibid.
4. Ibid., 115. For another account of this episode, see J. Hoberman and Jonathan Rosenbaum, *Midnight Movies* (New York: Harper and Row, 1983), 59.
5. Quoted in Hoberman and Rosenbaum, *Midnight Movies*, 60. See also J. Hoberman, "The Big Heat," *Village Voice*, Nov. 12, 1991, 61, and Calvin Tomkins, "All Pockets Open," *New Yorker*, Jan. 6, 1973, 38–40.
6. David James, *Allegories of Cinema: American Film in the Sixties* (Princeton, N.J.: Princeton University Press, 1989), 111.
7. Judith Butler, "Imitation and Gender Insubordination," in *Inside/Out: Lesbian Theories, Gay Theories*, ed. Diana Fuss (New York: Routledge, 1991), 25.
8. Gerard Malanga, "Interview with Jack Smith," *Film Culture* 45 (1967): 13.
9. John D'Emilio, *Sexual Politics, Sexual Communities: The Making of a Homosexual Minority in the United States, 1940–1970* (Chicago: University of Chicago Press, 1983), 114.
10. Ibid., 125.
11. For more on Sarria, see ibid., 186–89. D'Emilio mentions that Sarria's *Carmen*, for instance, danced her way through the bushes in San Francisco's Union Square, a popular cruising area, in order to escape the vice squad. There are extremely moving personal accounts of Sarria's influence in *Word Is Out* (Mariposa Film Group 1977) and *Before Stonewall* (Schiller and Rosenberg 1984). The statistics on Daughters of Bilitis and Mattachine are from John D'Emilio, "Gay Politics and Community in San Francisco since World War II," in *Hidden from History: Reclaiming the Gay and Lesbian Past*, ed. Martin Duberman, Martha Vicinus, and George Chauncey Jr. (New York: Meridian, 1989), 460.
12. Robert C. Doty, "Growth of Overt Homosexuality in City Provokes Wide Concern," *New York Times*, Dec. 17, 1963, 1. This article is one of the documents collected by Martin Duberman in *About Time: Exploring the Gay Past* (New York: Meridian, 1991), 238–45.
13. Doty, "Growth of Overt Homosexuality," 33.
14. Ibid.
15. Quoted in Brad Gooch, *City Poet: The Life and Times of Frank O'Hara* (New York: Knopf, 1993), 424.
16. Gayle Rubin, "Thinking Sex: Notes for a Radical Theory of the Politics of Sexuality," in *Pleasure and Danger: Exploring Female Sexuality*, ed. Carole S. Vance (New York: HarperCollins, 1992), 267.
17. Jack Smith, "The Perfect Filmic Appositeness of Maria Montez," in *Historical Treasures*, ed. Ira Cohen (Madras and New York: Hanuman, 1990), 68.
18. Ibid., 69.
19. Ibid., 81.
20. Jack Smith, "Belated Appreciation of V. S.," *Film Culture* 31 (Winter 1963–64): 4.
21. Boyd McDonald, *Cruising the Movies: A Sexual Guide to "Oldies'" on TV* (New York: Gay Presses of New York, 1985), 58.
22. Leacock is quoted as saying, "I'd rather not have a camera at all. Just be there." See Brian Winston, "The Documentary Film as Scientific Inscription," in *Theorizing Documentary*, ed. Michael Renov (New York: Routledge, 1993), 44.
23. Ibid., 45.
24. "The people in the theater are supposed to be coming in and helping with the atmosphere." Jack Smith, "Uncle Fishook and the Sacred Baby Poo-poo of Art," *Semiotext(e)* 3.2 (1978): 198.
25. Michael Moon, "Flaming Closets," *October* 51 (Winter 1989): 38–40.
26. Doty, "Growth of Overt Homosexuality," 33. "Most normal persons believe they have a similar facility in spotting deviates. This is true only of the obviously effeminate type—the minority who either openly proclaim their

orientation or who make only perfunctory efforts to disguise it" (one big *sic*).

27. Moon, "Flaming Closets," 40.
28. Trinh T. Minh-ha, "Cotton and Iron," in *When the Moon Waxes Red: Representation, Gender, and Cultural Politics* (New York: Routledge, 1991), 26.
29. Jack Smith, "Uncle Fishook," 192.
30. Susan Sontag, "Jack Smith's *Flaming Creatures*," in *Against Interpretation* (New York: Farrar, Straus and Giroux, 1969), 232. Michael Moon notes that "for every person who actually saw Smith's film, perhaps a hundred know it only from Sontag's description of it." This is a particularly unfortunate irony since Sontag's essay on *Flaming Creatures*, like her article on camp, "depoliticizes the sexual and artistic practices that are its subject" (Moon, "Flaming Closets," 34–36).
31. Sontag, "Jack Smith's *Flaming Creatures*," 232.
32. Ibid., 230.
33. P. Adams Sitney, *Visionary Film: The American Avant-Garde* (New York: Oxford University Press, 1979), 395.
34. Ibid., 396.
35. Parker Tyler, "A Preface to the Problems of the Experimental Film," in *Film Culture Reader*, ed. P. Adams Sitney (New York: Praeger, 1970), 50.
36. Jack Smith, "'Pink Flamingo' Formulas in Focus," *Village Voice*, July 19, 1973, 69.
37. Ken Kelman, "Smith Myth," in *Film Culture Reader*, 282.
38. Mekas, *Movie Journal*, 85.
39. Sontag, "Jack Smith's *Flaming Creatures*," 229.
40. Kelman, "Smith Myth," 282.
41. Mekas, *Movie Journal*, 83.
42. Ibid., 112.
43. Hoberman, "The Big Heat," 72.
44. Smith, "Perfect Filmic Appositeness of Maria Montez," 73.
45. Smith, "'Pink Flamingo' Formulas in Focus," 69.
46. Mekas, *Movie Journal*, 115.
47. Carel Rowe, *The Baudelairian Cinema: A Trend within the American Avant-Garde* (Ann Arbor, Mich.: UMI Research Press, 1982), xi.
48. Stefan Brecht, *Queer Theatre* (Frankfurt: Suhrkamp, 1978), 44–45.
49. Gregory Markopolous noted, for instance, that *Flaming Creatures* offered Joel Markman a chance to fulfill his "insatiable desire" to portray a vampire. See Markopolous, "Innocent Revels," *Film Culture* 33 (Summer 1964): 41.
50. Quoted in Mekas, *Movie Journal*, 95.
51. Trinh T. Minh-ha, "Documentary Is/Not a Name," *October* 52 (Summer 1990): 89. A longer version of this essay appeared as "The Totalizing Quest of Meaning," in Trinh, *When the Moon Waxes Red*, 29–50, and in Renov, *Theorizing Documentary*, 90–107.
52. Ibid., 89.
53. Richard Dyer, *Now You See It: Studies on Lesbian and Gay Film* (New York: Routledge, 1990), 103.
54. Sitney, *Visionary Film*, 382–84.
55. Mekas, *Movie Journal*, 85.
56. J. Hoberman, introduction to Cohen, *Historical Treasures*, 9.
57. Moon, "Flaming Closets," 38. For more on Smith's performances, see Hoberman, "The Theatre of Jack Smith," 3–12; Mekas, "Jack Smith; or, The End of Civilization," in *Movie Journal*, 388–97; and Brecht, *Queer Theatre*, 10-27, 157–77.
58. Brecht, *Queer Theatre*, 30.
59. Smith, "Uncle Fishook," 198.

THOMAS WAUGH

[**6**] *Walking on Tippy Toes: Lesbian and Gay Liberation Documentary of the Post-Stonewall Period 1969–84*

Mother: *It started actually in high school. You were in the plays in high school and did a beautiful job. And that's why I think that speech and drama was a very good start for you . . .*

Father: *Well, all I can say is I think that you get mixed up in the drama, the music, and the arts of that type, I think it's a . . . most people have a tendency toward that type of thing that . . . maybe I'm wrong. I don't know anything about statistics, I've never looked it up but most people who are in arts and drama are walking on tippy toes, a little fluttery, you understand what I mean. When I was a kid, the guys that played the violin, with the long hair, that kind of stuff, they were a little more effeminate than most people, so when you get mixed up with the arty people, that's it. You just join the gang, I guess.*

:: from Tom Joslin's *Blackstar: Autobiography of a Close Friend* (1977)

▶

Introduction: Years of Famine

"The famine is over." Uttering these portentous words in 1980 from my podium as a gay movement film critic, I declared the start of a new era of visibility and productivity in lesbian and gay film.[1] I recently sifted through a decade's worth of my once urgent dissections of the state of gay cinema (c. 1976–85), denunciations of various capitalist-homophobe conspiracies from within and without and overstated celebrations of each new "break-through," and was reminded of how desperate it felt in those days before there were queer film and video festivals in every city and twenty-year-old queers with video cameras at every gathering. *Famine, drought, silence,* and *invisibility* were indeed the words that self-styled cine-pinko-fags like me used to describe the audiovisual environment in the first decade after Stonewall.

Perhaps my frustration was exacerbated because the post-Stonewall famine had coincided, paradoxically, with an age of feasting for the 16 mm social-issue documentary film. From *Harlan County U.S.A.* (Kopple 1976) to *The Battle of Chile* (Guzman 1977), what a thrilling trajectory it was for artists and audiences who wanted to change the world with images of reality! So why, as I started assembling an anthology on "committed documentary" in 1980, could I not include a single gay male documentary in my "radical" corpus, and why did I manage to squeeze in only a single, discreet lesbian-authored short that addressed sexual orientation as part of a spectrum of feminist issues?[2] For my next two attempts to assemble a more inclusive body of lesbian and gay documentary, a 1982 lesbian and gay film and video festival and a 1983 curriculum package, the pickings were still very slim. By then I could draw on the eclectic crop of 16 mm documentary shorts, some uneven work in Super-8 and community video, and ambiguous films by feminists who were not yet willing or ready to claim publicly the L-word label. Why had there been no queer *Harlan County*?

My international working filmography for this essay, about twenty-five pre-1984 documentaries, may now seem too ample to justify the word *famine*. Famine is of course relative (African-American documentarists were then even scarcer than lesbians and gays), but the lesbian and gay corpus of the 1970s is indeed tiny, dispersed, and erratic compared, say, to the sustained wealth of women's movement imagemaking at the same time. A 1978 review of *Gay USA* (Bressan 1977) and *Word Is Out* (Mariposa 1977) by Lee Atwell blamed lingering closets and difficulties in financing for the six-year gap between the promising *Some of Your Best Friends* (Robinson 1971) and *Word Is Out*, but other obvious factors were in play. In the United States, it took some time for Carter-era liberalism to penetrate the blackout in public broadcasting and in the funding bodies. Lesbians and gays remained invisible within the still largely homophobic left and new social movements networks, and it was only in the 1980s that the alternative distribution outfits would take on gay and lesbian titles. Meanwhile, future troupers of 1980s lesbian and gay documentary were tactfully present within leftist and feminist organizations: Richard Schmiechen and Margaret Westcott, for example, were still quietly at work at Chicago's Kartemquin Collective and Montreal's Studio D respectively. It was only on the tenth anniversary of Stonewall at the 1979 Bard College Alternative Cinema Conference that North American lesbian and gay media activists actually came together for the first time and surprised straight leftists with their unified demands.³ The right-wing backlash of the late 1970s fanned the new militancy all the more: Atwell thought that the 1977 Dade County catastrophe (Anita Bryant) had sparked socially conscious filmmakers like artsy pornmaker Artie Bressan to get on the bandwagon, and California's 1978 Briggs Initiative was the catalyst of what would eventually be *The Times of Harvey Milk* (Epstein 1984). Suddenly at the turn of the decade, there did seem to be a few more documentary projects in sight, especially in the United States and Canada, films that would be able to get away with being underfunded, mediocre, local, or single-issue because they were no longer solitary voices in the wilderness.

In 1984, when I came to write an overview article on post-Stonewall documentary (published in 1988), my sampling had swelled to twenty-four documentaries from six countries.⁴ Most were titles from the first half of the eighties, and seven were dated 1977, 1978, or 1979. The only earlier film was *It Is Not the Homosexual Who Is Perverse but the Situation in Which He Lives* (von Praunheim 1971). In addition to discussing particular problems around community accountability and (self-)censorship, I argued that distinctive aesthetic strategies had evolved in response to the ethicopolitical challenges of the identity politics and volatile audience dynamics of a minority steeped in what Jack Babuscio called "the passing experience."⁵ Most importantly, I noticed performance-based techniques for incorporating the input of subjects into the process and for filling in gaps left by conventional documentary methods. Parents of gay filmmakers of the seventies thought that performance had something to do with homosexuality (as we saw in the epigraph), and indeed, the films and videos made by their sons and daughters seemed to bear this out. Their performance-based techniques included particular inflections of standard interviewing, editing, and expert testimony styles, "coming out" variations of consciousness-raising formats borrowed from women's movement documentaries, and expressive elements that were more theatrical than the standard documentary idiom of the day allowed: dramatization, improvisatory role playing and reconstruction, statements and monologues based on preparation and rehearsal, and nonverbal performances of music, dance, gesture, and corporal movement, including those of an erotic and diaristic nature.

What I did not realize in 1984 was that I was summing up the first generation of lesbian and gay documentary. Nor did I realize that by squeezing in the first works of 1984 and 1985 by lesbians and gays of color,⁶ the first few references to AIDS, and *The Times of Harvey Milk* (whose 1985 Oscar symbolized once and for all the real end of famine), I was heralding the next period of what Richard Dyer calls "post-affirmation" cinema,[7] to be marked not only by the Epidemic and postcolonial voices but also by a discursive flux around issues of identity. Looking back in 1995, I am struck by the diversity of this corpus that once seemed so sparse, and by the sense that performance-based aesthetics was both its distinctive contribution and its most important link with the queer nonfiction film and video of the late eighties and the nineties. I would therefore like to devote the rest of this essay to extending my reflection on performance as the crucial idiom of the years of famine.

▶

Performance and Performativity

First I need to define more precisely what performance means as a documentary ingredient. The commonsense, layperson's notion of documentary is that it is a window on an unscripted, undirected, unrehearsed, and unperformed reality. Nevertheless, as I have argued elsewhere, performance and mise-en-scène have been a basic syntax of realist discourse throughout the entire hundred-year documentary tradition: "Performance—the self-expression of documentary subjects for the camera in collaboration with filmmaker/director—was the basic ingredient of the classical documentary."[8] And not only of the classical documentary: throughout the modern phases of documentary as well—if we use Nichols's neat but useful categories, the *observational* impetus of the sixties (Leacock, Wiseman), the *interactive* impetus of the seventies (de Antonio, New Day Films), and the *self-reflexive* impetus of the eighties (Trinh, Marker)—collaborative performance has maintained its centrality in the lexicon of documentary realism.[9] This has been consistently true of that vast majority of documentary productions in which subjects have been aware, actively or passively, of the camera and, by extension, of the spectator.[10]

"Perform" words are very popular in both gender/queer theory and documentary theory these days, and a few overlaps must be sorted out before I proceed. Slippages between the two principal relevant dictionary senses of the word *performance*— "the execution of an action" and "a public presentation or exhibition"[11]—can be as confusing as they are stimulating. The term *performative*, deriving from the first sense and borrowed from speech act linguistics, defines a category of utterance that executes, enacts, or performs the action that is uttered, for example, *I apologize, I sentence, I welcome*, or the *I do* of the marriage ceremony. Hence Judith

Butler's theory that "gender reality is created through sustained social performances," that maleness and femaleness are "performative in the sense that the essence or identity that they otherwise purport to express are fabrications manufactured and sustained through corporeal signs and other discursive means."[12]

Similarly, Bill Nichols posits performative documentary as a dominant of 1990s documentary, reflected in such works as *Sari Red* (Parmar 1988) and *Tongues Untied* (Riggs 1989) that are not only referential (or *constative*, to continue the speech act terminology) but primarily performative. Like an utterance that not only describes but also executes a transformation in the relationship of speaker and listener,

> [performative documentaries] address us . . . with a sense of emphatic engagement that overshadows their reference to the historical world . . . mak[ing] their target an ethics of viewer response more than a politics of group action or an analysis of the ideology of the subject. . . . Performative documentary attempts to reorient us—affectively, subjectively—toward the historical, poetic world it brings into being.[13]

However, as Eve Kosofsky Sedgwick explains with regard to Butler's gender theory, the term *performative* seldom loses the connotation of performance as exhibition and presentation—in short, theater—primarily, Butler argues, as a result of the "apparently unique centrality of drag performance practice as—not just the shaping metaphor—but the very idiom of a tautologically heterosexist gender/sexuality system, and the idiom also of the possibility for its subversion."[14]

Nichols also maintains this connection to theater in the sense that most of his prototype performative films are documentaries that rely on dramatization and self-conscious theatricality (including several by Pratibha Parmar, Isaac Julien, and Marlon Riggs that have become canonical paving stones of the new international queer documentary). Nichols also names as an ancestor "the avant-garde tradition of autobiography that coincides in many aspects with the confessional quality of a number of performative documentaries" and mentions as an example Kenneth Anger (one could add two other performer precursors of queer documentary, Jack Smith and Andy Warhol).

For me as well, the etymological and homonymic overlap of *performative* and *performance* is significant. Thus, although I would like to focus primarily on performance in the sense of collaborative self-expressivity of a theatrical order—which to avoid confusion I will henceforth call "performance," between theatrical quotation marks—I fear that I too shall ultimately end up in "performativity."

Realism and "Performance": From Public to Private

Ain't nothing like the real thing, baby.

::   Song overlaid on climactic montage of anal penetration shots
in *Erotikus* (de Simone 1972)

*This film is about who lesbian mothers and their children
really are.*

::   Prefatory credit, *In the Best Interests of the Children* (Reid,
Stevens, Zheutlin 1977, emphasis added)

*In the field of documentary or cinéma-vérité . . . the index of
reality is somewhat more reliable, and . . . we at least have
the advantage of experiencing not actors impersonating gay
types, but the real thing.*

::   Lee Atwell (1978)[15]

Songwriters, filmmakers, and critics notwithstanding, what I would now
like to show is how, during the post-Stonewall famine years, many lesbian
and gay documentarists did *not* rely on the real thing. To a remarkable extent they eschewed the standard documentary realism of the day, the available documentary repertory of interactive idiom. Like cinematic realisms
of any period, interactive realism, the formulaic mix of interviews and
archival footage joined by the mortar of observational verité and musical
interludes, was basically invisible to the audience of the seventies. Bent
documentarists bent this realism out of shape, developing a wide spectrum
of distinctive "performance" strategies, idioms of subject self-expression—
verbal, dramatic, cinematic, and sexual—that were both an answer to and
an explanation of the invisibility that we felt.[16] Seventies documentary
realism may have seemed adequate for visualizing other fixable identities it
would construct and cement, mix and match—"worker," "visible minority,"
"third world subaltern," and above all "[straight] woman"—but it was
not up to the job for a new political constituency characterized by both an
invisibility of social existence and a fluidity and hybridity of identities.

Instead, lesbian and gay documentarists seemed intuitively to prefer
artificial and hyperbolic "performance" discourses that pushed through
and beyond the realist codes, that "[put] the referential aspect of the message in brackets, under suspension," as Nichols would put it.[17] The extent
to which they did so and the particular "performance" formats they chose
depended on whether the films treated public spaces of political mobilization, the semipublic territory of traditional social networks and sexual
undergrounds, or the private spaces of domesticity, relationships, sexuality,

and fantasy. Many filmmakers would treat two or more of these domains in the same film; hence the tutti-frutti compendium of performance styles that characterizes so many of them.

Public Spaces

The everyday performance discourses of lesbian and gay public life as it emerged after Stonewall (marches, parades, demonstrations, press conferences, zaps,[18] electoral campaigns, concerts, raids, trials) were handily recorded intradiegetically through realist codes. Hence the parade/march genre of which two pioneering 1972 films—Kenneth Robinson's *Some of Your Best Friends* and Jan Oxenberg's *Home Movie*—offer prototypical glimpses. Artie Bressan's jubilant, sunlit *Gay USA* (1977) is the most fully developed example; the angry nighttime demonstrations in Toronto (*Track Two*, Sutherland, Lemon, Keith 1981), Sydney (*Witches and Faggots, Dykes and Poofters*, One in Seven 1980), and San Francisco (*The Times of Harvey Milk*) amount to a contrapuntal negative image. Most of the films of this genre could not seem to get over the novelty of visible queer public life, which had after all had been unthinkable in the sixties.

Before Stonewall (Schiller and Rosenberg 1984), our attempt through the interactive compilation-interview format to retrieve American queer social history of the sixties, came up with only one or two cinematic images documenting public life—most memorably a dignified procession of New York drag queens into a paddy wagon and the lonely shots of the 1965 Mattachine demonstration in front of the White House. Around the same time as *Before Stonewall*, *The Times of Harvey Milk* was such a breakthrough in the homo history genre because of its wealth of audiovisual documentation of newly visible gay public life in the late seventies and early eighties, especially mainstream electoral politics. These shifts from public invisibility to visibility also account for the staggering difference between von Praunheim's two films of this period: *It Is Not the Homosexual* was shot entirely in "performance" modes in 1970 (scripting, sets, dramatization . . . makeup!), while his American *Army of Lovers, Revolt of the Perverts* (1978) was able in the last half of the decade to mix a "performance" shell (agitprop street theater) with strong realist inscriptions of the gay public life that had surged into U.S. streets (observational verité, stock shots, interviews, etc.).

For *radical* politics in the same period, interactive realism was less reliable. Political theater was sometimes captured intradiegetically through observational verité (zoomy and swishy), as in an early zap of a convention

Mark Massi in *Blackstar: Auto-biography of a Close Friend* (Tom Joslin 1977)

of aversion therapists immortalized in *Some of Your Best Friends*. Otherwise, von Praunheim's *Army* is probably typical in that statements by movement radicals are self-consciously static and anemic, leaving the real vigor of radical gay liberation for self-consciously theatrical agitprop skits by the Gay Sweatshop troupe, who camp it up in front of the Meat Rack and undercut the political agenda of "700 leather bars and the right to serve in the army." In *Blackstar*, Joslin likewise turned to "performance," not only for vigor and camp but also for the utopian rhetoric of radical politics, letting his lover Mark declaim a gay lib manifesto, literally from the rooftops, alone in a wintry landscape, a long take long shot at once parodic and straight. In one of Barbara Hammer's few films that deal with public space, *Superdyke*, the artist orchestrates a "performance" of excess, parody, and artifice: Amazon warriors take over urban space and assault its institutional and commercial fortresses (e.g., Macy's) on a rampage of street theater repossession. In short, realism was adequate for mustering ourselves as an electoral minority, but for *real* change (as we used to say), "performance" strategies were preferred.

■————————————————————

Semipublic Spaces

For depicting the traditional semivisible social networks of bars and parties, and the coded male sexual underground of toilets, baths, parks, and street cruising, "performance" techniques were de rigueur—even though observational verité might have been deployed with the day's portable equipment and sensitive color stocks. Though these semipublic sites of community building, socialization, and political resistance are at the center of same-sex histories (as recalled by the nineties genre of lesbian herstory bar films), they are zones fraught with ethical, logistical, and technical tensions. I cannot think of a single bar scene developed through observational verité or interactive realism in the entire corpus, although *We All Have Our Reasons* (Reid, Stevens 1981) does construct a bar scene in well-rehearsed simulated verité, and *Before Stonewall* stages a bar reunion of original participants who intradiegetically "perform" old songs and rituals.

In *It Is Not the Homosexual*, von Praunheim sets up flamboyantly stylized "performance" scenes of parties and bars, only to denounce with his shrill voice-over their undercurrents of self-hatred. The most appealing bar scene in the film, in a neighborhood hangout populated by drag queens, mixed-race couples, leathermen, and other salt of the earth who "don't feel comfortable in piss-elegant bars," is bursting with transvestite yodeling and other "performance" excess. Here the "desperate and lonely" allegorical hero meets his ideological prince, who leads him back home to his anarchist *Wohngemeinschaft*. In this urban commune the hero discovers anarchism and von Praunheim accidentally pastiches women's movement documentary style: a circle discussion of thirtysomething longhaired nude chain smokers lounge on pastel comforters and consciousness-raise about the self-hatred of ghetto and underground. But this realist vision of community is ultimately as "performed" as the garish scenes of alienation.

The underground of parks, toilets, and bathhouses was even more of a challenge to documentarists. Sites of state terrorism and social violence as well as sexual community, they obviously required highly contrived dramatization: *Some of Your Best Friends* reenacted police entrapment in a park, and the victim's resistance became the interactive denouement of the film. A decade later *Track Two* reconstructed the infamous police raids on Toronto bathhouses that triggered the community mobilization that is recorded for the rest of the film in standard realism. But a much shorter film is the real gem of the underground subgenre, abjuring realist imagery in toto: Michael McGarry's *In Black and White* (1979) encapsulated the private space of the public toilet with abstractly visualized closeup carnality, terror, and resistance, laid under a "documentary" montage of conflicting public social voices.

Von Praunheim's stunning toilet queer-bashing scene in *It Is Not the Homosexual* appears in typically theatrical long shot. Toilets, parks, and streets are here the on-location settings for Brechtian agitprop and "the tense choreography of men," all anchored in historical space through his run-on voice-over denunciations. In *Army*, von Praunheim is now a nonjudgmental libertine, acting as on-camera guide to the underworld, as the camera follows him cruising Central Park, the Piers, and the Trucks; inspecting a Manhattan bathhouse (where not surprisingly the Underground has been appropriated and commercialized in the Glory Hole Room); and accompanying John Rechy on a nostalgic, leather-decked verité prowl through some nighttime city, lamenting the subversive undergrounds of yore. The ideological evasions of voice and the complicitous voyeurism of this realist format make *Army* seem more dated than von Praunheim's earlier high artifice.

Jan Oxenberg's *Comedy in Six Unnatural Acts* (1975) matches *It Is Not the Homosexual* and *In Black and White* in its full deployment of "performance" (not a flicker of documentary realism). But Oxenberg was "performing" another kind of border zone between public and private: lesbians' subcultural myths, fantasies, and appropriations of mainstream cultural baggage (from child molester stereotypes to romance). Oxenberg's indulgent and affectionate skits were just as self-consciously theatrical as von Praunheim's, but they effectively engaged communal approval rather than the almost unanimous outrage sparked by *It Is Not the Homosexual's* distancing effects. PBS, however, balked at the intimacy of *Comedy's* "performance"-based subcultural circuitry, pretexting amateurism.[19] In short, "performance" aesthetics may not always have been a reliable means for exploring semipublic space—especially with regard to audiences and broadcasters—but lesbian and gay filmmakers had few other choices in such uncharted waters.

■——

Private Spaces

Consciousness-raising documentaries from the women's movement provided a language used by post-Stonewall lesbian and gay documentarists to deal with private life and the domestic sphere. But not all were as successful as *In the Best Interests of the Children*, which became the best received and most circulated realist lesbian documentary of the period through its instrumentalist focus on the heartstring single issue of custody. Otherwise, trying to express "the personal is political" through realist codes was often a frustrating experience, especially on a low budget. *Word Is Out* scored, thanks to its epic vision of cultural and class diversity, the comprehensiveness of its interviews, and its confessional "coming out" narratives. But by 1980 films of this nature were being disparaged, and not only against ideological checklists that constituted so much movement film criticism of the day. The pioneering lesbian film theorist Caroline Sheldon had already

Pat Bond
in *Word
is Out*
(Mariposa
1977)

challenged "the assumption of film as 'pure' objective recording device"
in 1977 (when as an afterthought she listed five documentaries that constituted a "start" for lesbian political cinema), and Jacquelyn Zita took up
the thread in 1981, lambasting "the pretended truth of objective documentaries," "the operatic confessionals of personal life," and "the 'talking
heads' of political documentary."[20] Quite simply, the antistereotype rhetoric
of positive images, role models, and community enfranchisement did not
always fit realist documentary idioms, whether observational or interactive,
that had evolved in order to communicate the texture of individual experience and were weighted with a liberal heritage of voyeurism and victim
aesthetics. Films deploying collaborative and expressive "performance"
seemed to surmount this problem, especially those dealing with the past or
present private space of personal identities and relationships, with sons,
daughters, and lovers. (The alternative families of *friends* are mostly missing from the period's documentary iconography, especially on the gay male
side; perhaps they did not match preexisting cinematic iconography as
readily as parents and lovers.)

Barbara Hammer's films, known at first only within the women's constituencies to which they were restricted, were exemplary for conveying the
give and take of sexual passion and exchange, relationships and rupture.
They did so not only through the highly stylized editing and image process-
ing she shared with her avant-garde mentors and peers, but also through
corporal and facial acrobatics. *Double Strength* (1978) and *Sync* (1981),
for example, enact erotic vocabularies that are respectively balletic and ges-

tural, based on a collaborative interaction by Hammer and her lover of the moment.

Joslin's *Blackstar* bravely tackles not only connubial intimacy but also familial stress. In contrast to the evasive father and controlling mother of my opening epigraph, the filmmaker's complicitous elder brother offers a jovial verité monologue, but its phony spontaneity is unmasked when the editor includes all three takes. There are more stiff theatricalities and more open wounds in Susana Blaustein's approach to similar territory, *Susana* (1980). The film lines up frontal declarations "performed" by the author-protagonist's sister, ex-lover, and parents; only the tearful pleading sister, the sardonic lover, and brutal Susana ("No, Father . . . you kept telling me to imitate my sister . . .") are actually visualized, while the parents are mercifully provided only in voice-over sound. If "performance" opens wounds in Susana, it heals them in *Michael a Gay Son* (Glawson 1980), which rechannels familial trauma by casting the protagonist's peers as his parents and siblings in role-playing improvisations of rejections and reconciliations.

As Hammer's and Blaustein's films demonstrated fully, lovers are often more cooperative than parents. *Word Is Out*'s realist lovers perform indulgent smiles beside the narrator at the mike. In contrast, Joslin's Mark is bristlingly aware of the inadequacies of cinematic realism for capturing the essence of his relationship with the filmmaker and fills the film with self-reflexive chatter about its uselessness:

> MARK: What about us? I mean this isn't us, and I'm kind of I feeling bad that I'm afraid that we're not going to get us in the film.
> TOM: What is that?
> MARK: It's those seven years that we shared together, the love that held us together—you know the life and things we share.
> TOM: What's missing?
> MARK: This is a construction for a film . . .
> TOM: Yes, no, you keep saying, we keep saying it has to come out in dialogue because there's no way to do it visually. . . . And you keep saying maybe there's nothing between us because we can't find any way of doing it visually and I think that's worth pursuing.
> MARK: OK. Pursue. I'll follow.
> TOM: Tell me, Mark, do you think there's nothing between us?
> MARK: There doesn't seem anything that we can do visually, that's for sure, right?
> TOM: There's nothing visible between us?
> MARK: Maybe.
> TOM: So there's something invisible between us?
> MARK: Christ. Stop it. . . . I wanted just to show what we were like, and that's where we ran into vacancy . . .

The crisis within the realist effort to render a private partnership—"running into vacancy"—is crystallized in this mattress dialogue, in which the partners improvise with a prop, namely a spaghetti-like mass of outtake trims that have literally come "between" them. And when the couple finally agrees on "performance" ("planning something out") as a means of expressing the invisible element of their relationship, what to do? Sex is too highly charged to perform for the camera, except a little discreet cuddling under the sheets, and realist dialogue also went nowhere fast. Thus vaudeville banter and a two-minute disco pas de deux to a Laura Nyro song, climaxing in a presentational pose and kiss for the camera, were chosen to conclude this film. This "performance" scene would be recycled in a similar place fifteen years later in Joslin's posthumous *Silverlake Life: The View from Here* (with Peter Friedman 1993), summing up the relationship once and for all but now in the before-and-after iconographical context of AIDS memorialization—the flashback of an artist who has performed that most private and visual act of all, his own death. In the nineties, it seemed natural for Joslin to choose a hybrid interactive-observational style to tell his last story, but in the seventies, when private gay spaces were still contested, "performance" got the nod.

▶───

Coming Out

> *I'm coming out now, **right?** Here I am on television. Big white face on the screen saying, "Yeah, you know, I'm gay!"*
> ::   Pat Bond in *Word Is Out* (1977)

The Stonewall generation's political ritual of coming out mixed private and public, "outed" the personal, and thereby transgressed the social silence around sexuality and difference. The queen and the butch have played this transgressive role in pre-Stonewall public life as well as in representation (the sixties had been the great decade of queens on documentary, from Warhol to *Portrait of Jason* [Clarke 1967]). However, in the seventies, the transgressive role was to be played not by the queen, who was quickly shuffled offstage by the positive-image agenda of liberation politics (reappearing only in the eighties), but by the assimilationist lesbian/gay who was by definition invisible and therefore required to *speak* his or her transgression.

One might expect that realist modes were more appropriate than theatrical "performance" for capturing this confessional moment because of their premise of spontaneity and inner authenticity, and indeed interactive

Tom Joslin
and Mark
Massi in
*Blackstar:
Auto-
biography
of a Close
Friend* (Tom
Joslin 1977)

realism is often the aesthetic strategy of choice. Yet this ritual is invariably performed and often "performed." I am referring not only to some of the most expressive moments of the coming-out repertory, where interviewees intradiegetically perform gestural amplifications of their narratives—for example, butch Dorothy Hillaire in *Before Stonewall* showing the camera how she literally booted harassers across a bar thirty years earlier. I am referring also to the ritualized, premeditated quality of the coming-out performances, invariably delivered by a preselected (and *prevideotaped* in the case of *Word Is Out*) subject in close collaboration with the filmmakers.

Coming out requires the interactive mode of interview and monologue by its very nature, and its confessional operation also requires the presence of the spectator, mediated through camera and crew. This operation thus posits performance but also performativity in the linguistic sense, *executing* one's identity of outness as well as *describing* it. It is performative also in Nichols's sense, making the viewer who is engaged by the on-camera confession the documentary referent, along with the speaker. This was assumed by Pat Bond's laughing confession in *Word Is Out* and by Bruce White, whose voice on a sixties radio broadcast replayed in *Before Stonewall* says, not laughingly, that not only will his family find out, but "I'm quite certain that I will probably lose my job as a result of the program too. . . . I hope that through this means I can be some use to someone else other than myself." These two speakers of different periods know that they are enacting as well as signifying a relationship—cultural, affective, and political—with the viewer.

Coming out involved transgression of the public-private divide, but even its transgressive power became formulaic. Films such as the staid *Advocate* production *Who Happen to Be Gay* (Beldin, Krenzien 1979), for all their instrumentality in the political context of the 1970s, were also the most complicit in social invisibility and in the rote recapitulation of the interactive recipe (interview/snapshots/observational rock-climbing interlude/interview/workplace interlude/interview). The more these films began to pile up after 1980, the more they deserved Dyer's complaints about "hidden agendas," the erasure of "conflict, contradiction and difficulty," and "the quest for sameness."[21]

Was it to express the essential theatricality of "gay sensibility" or to escape these complicities of realism that there evolved highly theatricalized "performance" variants of the coming-out formula, from Oxenberg's own cryptic juggling act in the "nonmonogamy" sketch in *Comedy* to the explicit self-scripted and self-costumed monologues in *L'Aspect rose de la chose* (Wong 1980), in which each character controlled his own identity "performance"? In any case, the memorable queen who stole this latter film from her fellow collective members with flounces and fabrics was prophetic. For, as the effect of seventies positive images and realism wore off, coming-out "performances" would become all the more prevalent in our nonfiction and would increasingly deploy not rock climbing but more and more of what Sedgwick calls "flaming" lesbian and gay "performative identity vernaculars": "butch abjection, femmitude, leather, pride, SM, drag, musicality, fisting, attitude, zines, histrionicism, asceticism, Snap! culture, diva worship, florid religiosity . . . activism."[22]

Evolving from the very beginning of the seventies was a particular subgenre of "cumming out" films, autobiographical sex "performances" that enhanced the power of coming out both as "performance" and as "performativity." In view of criticism already current during the seventies about the censorship of sexuality by documentaries,[23] it is surprising to rediscover how frequent and brazen the self-erotic imagery of the decade really was. I have written elsewhere of the extraordinary achievement of Curt McDowell's diaristic *Loads* (1980), with its multipartner performance of erotic lifestyle and fantasy.[24] In fact, in *Women I Love* (1976), Hammer had already matched the on-camera authorial orality and one-upped McDowell with a seventies-style lesbian reciprocality ("you-do-me-I-do-you") that his trade partners wouldn't dream of. McDowell and Hammer were far from unique, rivaled in their bravado by von Praunheim's sex acts in *Army of Lovers* (he performs a graphic blow job in a filmmaking workshop he is teaching at the San Francisco Art Institute and has midinterview sex with Fred Halsted, their telephoto encounter framed with flowers and liberation dialogue).

Halsted, author and star in another genre of seventies "documentary," hard-core porn, is sex "performer" in the porn milieu's own attempt at the docuhistory genre, *Erotikus* (1972), where, as on-camera narrator lazily masturbating for the camera, he steers us through the porn industry's selective autobiography. At the same time, soft-core moments seemed equally transgressive. Andrea Weiss writes in *Jump Cut* that the protagonists of *Lavender* (Monahan, Jacobs 1972) "embraced constantly."[25] *Home Movie* and *Susana* went further, the former with Oxenberg's touch-football pileup borrowed from sixties surrogate eroticism, and the latter with its sexy chiaroscuro stills and its dramatized shots of topless cuddling, faces obscured and breasts caressed by long straight seventies hair.

Like all "body" genres, the sex "performance" extrapolations of the coming-out ritual executed a complex, even troubled, performativity. On-camera erotic behavior both described and enacted the utopian confrontational track of identity politics, an in-your-face alternative to the assimilationist politics of invisibility. At the same time, the viewer's arousal was qualified by genre clash; documentary tact was scrambled by erotic exhibition and vice versa. The spectator was engaged, linguistically, politically, and affectively, but also physiologically. Minority politics was not only asserted but also "performed" as sexual exchange.

▶

Shots from a Queer Canon

My conception of seventies documentary is not a monolithic or unitary one. Far from it: famine or no famine, a rich diversity of cultural roots, aesthetic strategies, and ideological negotiations resists efforts to reduce or generalize about this important moment in the history of new social movements in the West and its traces in *the* medium of social change par excellence. One can, however, risk the following generalization: those documentaries closest in organizational links or sensibility to gay and/or lesbian movement agendas are those that remain most anchored to the prescribed realist discourses of seventies documentary and were most visible in community media at the time. In contrast, most of the prophetic "performance" films that stand up well in this retroactive view—autobiographical, experimental, and erotic—had uneven relationships with the lesbian and gay masses who allegedly preferred positive images and realist conventions. Self-indulgent or self-reflexive mannerisms were liabilities in the post-Stonewall political context of simultaneous mobilization and backlash, and much important nonfiction was undervalued or at the very least controversial, never reaching its full potential audience.

Even without these cultural biases, as Nichols explains, performative documentary by definition runs the risk of misunderstanding.[26] Part of the blockage is the way audiences are often disturbed by shifting borders between fiction and nonfiction, and indeed the "performance" films I have privileged in this analysis necessitate a retroactive expansion in the definition of documentary. At the time, who would have called *It Is Not the Homosexual* or Oxenberg's *Comedy* "documentaries"? But now the post-Stonewall generation's documentary image of itself cannot be separated from films that were then marginalized as dramatized, experimental, weird, personal, short, fictional, politically incorrect, amateurish, divisive, pornographic, and inaccessible. In fact, if Nichols is right in identifying performative documentary as the key mode of the nineties, the lesbian and gay "performance" documentaries of the seventies—and earlier (Warhol? Jack Smith?)—must be reclaimed as the key not only to our past but also to the present.

Who says reclamation and redefinition says canon. My post-post-Stonewall queer students of the nineties who watched the seventies documentaries I showed them in stony silence were generational chauvinists (and admittedly the captive audience of a nostalgic and unimaginative teacher). They also saw themselves, I think, as canon busters, queer iconoclasts criticizing the complacent legacy of lesbian and gay baby boomers. They may have been right, but busting a nonexistent canon—fragmented and fragile if it exists at all—may well be misdirected energy. Only a few documentaries from the seventies are available on video, and the critical texts that are constituting our cultural history, such as *The Celluloid Closet*, *Queer Looks*, and *Vampires and Violets*, jump over much of this generation's artistic and political practice. A canon of post-Stonewall documentaries may be exactly what we need. Challenging queer amnesia is not just a question of restoring our cultural history, our performances and our "performances" of the post-Stonewall years, or only a question of preventing young video queers from reinventing the wheel. With the funding crises and political backlash of the nineties, the threat of famine is back, and glimpses of the resourcefulness, courage, energy, and erotic pleasure of our performances during earlier famines may help us tiptoe through the next one.

◆————————————————————————————

NOTES

1. Thomas Waugh, "Lawn Mowers and Harlequins: "Two 'Trigger' Films, *Brad* and *Jenny*," *Body Politic* 63 (May 1980): 32.
2. Thomas Waugh, ed., *"Show Us Life": Toward a History and Aesthetics of the Committed Documentary* (Metuchen, N.J.: Scarecrow, 1984; reprinted 1988). I remember not including the "breakthrough" *Word Is Out* (Mariposa 1977) because I then agreed with ideological criticisms of the film's assimilationist

agenda and its soft-pedaling of activism and transgression. The lesbian-authored short I included was *Heroes* (Barbara Martineau, now Sara Halprin, 1983).

3. Thomas Waugh, "Report on the 1979 Alternative Cinema Conference," *Jump Cut* 21 (1979): 39.

4. Thomas Waugh, "Lesbian and Gay Documentary: Minority Self-Imaging, Oppositional Film Practice, and the Question of Image Ethics," in *Image Ethics, the Moral and Legal Rights of Subjects in Documentary Film and Television*, ed. Larry Gross et al. (New York and London: Oxford University Press, 1988), 248–72.

5. Jack Babuscio, "Camp and the Gay Sensibility," in *Gays and Film*, ed. Richard Dyer (London: BFI, 1977), 40–57.

6. To my knowledge, prior to *Framed Youth* (Lesbian and Gay Youth Video Project 1983) and *Orientations* (Richard Fung, 1984), the only titles in the corpus by directors or codirectors outside of the white Euro-American demographic mainstream were *Word Is Out* (Andrew Brown 1977), *Public* (Arthur Dong 1981), *L'Aspect rose de la chose* (Chi Yan Wong 1980), and *Susana* (Susana Blaustein 1980).

7. Richard Dyer, *Now You See It: Studies on Lesbian and Gay Film* (London: Routledge, 1990), 274ff.

8. Thomas Waugh, "'Acting to Play Oneself': Notes on Performance in Documentary," in *Making Visible the Invisible: An Anthology of Original Essays on Film Acting*, ed. Carole Zucker (Metuchen, N.J.: Scarecrow, 1990), 64–91.

9. Bill Nichols, *Representing Reality* (Bloomington: Indiana University Press, 1991), 32–75.

10. My notion of performance as self-expressive behavior carried out in awareness of the camera, with either explicit or tacit consent and/or in collaboration with the director, needs to be distinguished from what Nichols calls *virtual performance*, the rich repertory of behavioral expression that constitutes the texture of social interaction in real life, recorded by the documentary camera as its unmistakable generic marker since its very beginning. Nichols's concept, apparently derived from sociologist Ervin Goffman's idea of the performance of self in everyday life, is articulated in *Representing Reality*, 122.

11. *Merriam Webster's Collegiate Dictionary*, 10th ed. (Springfield, Mass.: Merriam-Webster, 1993), 863.

12. Judith Butler, *Gender Trouble: Feminism and the Subversion of Identity* (New York: Routledge, 1990), 136, 141.

13. Bill Nichols, "Performing Documentary," in *Blurred Boundaries: Questions of Meaning in Contemporary Culture* (Bloomington: Indiana University Press, 1994), 92-106.

14. Eve Kosofsky Sedgwick, "Queer Performativity: Henry James's *The Art of the Novel*," *GLQ: A Journal of Lesbian and Gay Studies* 1.1 (1993): 1. Although Butler later disavows the "reduction of performativity to performance" and Sedgwick's reading of the centrality of drag as metaphor and paradigm in *Gender Trouble*, Butler seems to leave the options open by using terms like *mime, theatricality of gender, hyperbolic gesture,* and *acting out* (Judith Butler, "Critically Queer," *GLQ* 1.1 [1993]: 17–32).

15. Lee Atwell, "*Word Is Out* and *Gay U.S.A.*," *Film Quarterly* 22.2 (Winter 1978–79): 50–57.

16. Throughout this piece I use the politically incorrect first person plural to evoke the experience I lived as a (colonialized Canadian) member of the heterogeneous (and no doubt hegemonic) discourse community of North American and European lesbian and gay filmmakers, critics, users, and specialized documentary audiences during the seventies, the eighties, and the nineties.

17. Nichols, *Blurred Boundaries*, 96.

18. "Zaps" were a characteristic early-seventies gay lib strategy of public political theater that grafted camp and theatricality onto civil rights tactics like the sit-in. Zaps would be reinvented fifteen years later by ACT UP–style AIDS activists.

19. Edith Becker et al., "The Last Word: WNET Censorship," *Jump Cut* 22 (May 1980): 39–40.

20. Caroline Sheldon, "Lesbians and Film: Some Thoughts," in *Gays and Film*, ed. Richard Dyer (London: BFI, 1977), 5-26; Jacquelyn Zita, "Films of Barbara Hammer: Counter-Currencies of Lesbian Iconography," in "Special Section: Lesbians and Film," *Jump Cut* 24/25 (March 1981): 27.

21. Dyer, *Now You See It*, 245ff.

22. Sedgwick, "Queer Performativity," 13.

23. Ray Olson, "Gay Film Work: Affecting, but Too Evasive," *Jump Cut* 20 (May 1979): 9–12. I echoed this criticism in "Lesbian and Gay Documentary."

24. Thomas Waugh, "Men's Pornography, Gay vs Straight," *Jump Cut* 30 (Spring 1985): 30–36. Reprinted in *Out in Culture: Gay Lesbian and Queer Essays on Popular Culture*, ed. Corey Creekmur and Alexander Doty (Durham, N.C.: Duke University Press, 1995), 307–27.

25. Andrea Weiss, "Filmography of Lesbian Works," *Jump Cut* 24/25 (March 1981): 22.

26. Nichols, *Blurred Boundaries*, 97.

Marriage and Mourning

CHRIS HOLMLUND

[**7**] *When Autobiography Meets Ethnography and Girl Meets Girl: The "Dyke Docs" of Sadie Benning and Su Friedrich*

To what extent can the particular serve as illustration for the general?. . . What generalizations are appropriate? What categories can serve to facilitate understanding and the acceptance of difference rather than diminish our receptivity to the unique in the name of the typical, reducing difference to the measure of otherness . . . ?

I begin with this quote from Bill Nichols's "'Getting to Know You . . .': Power, Knowledge, and the Body"[1] because the questions he raises haunt the terms around which my essay revolves: autobiography, ethnography, and "dyke doc." How are "unique," "typical," "particular," and "general" to be linked to "self"—the basis of autobiography? Or to "subculture" and "culture"—the primary foci of ethnography? What of "lesbian" and the more militant "dyke," especially when they are used as adjectives, as in "lesbian autobiography," "lesbian ethnography," or "dyke documentary"? For me, and also for Nichols, posing such questions has both practical and theoretical implications: as Pierre Bourdieu underlines, aesthetic definition is tightly connected to class distinction, as much a matter of rank as of difference.[2]

To ground my discussion, I ask these questions of three of Sadie Benning's videos and two of Su Friedrich's films. I choose to look at works by these two women primarily for two reasons: because both make creative experimental documentaries that combine autobiographical and ethnographic features and because often, though not always, their work is programmed and distributed as "lesbian."

The better to gauge the impact of Benning's and Friedrich's dyke documentaries *as* dyke documentaries, I first rehearse how autobiography, ethnography, and lesbian have been theorized with respect to self and other, culture and subculture, in literature and film. At the end of this section I argue that Benning's videos and Friedrich's films are often described as "lesbian" autobiographies or ethnographies because they articulate concerns about coming out and kinship shared by many lesbians and gays today.

In the two middle sections of this essay I offer close readings of Benning's *Me and Rubyfruit* (1989), *Jollies* (1990), and *Girl Power* (1992), and Friedrich's *First Comes Love* (1991) and *Rules of the Road* (1992). Since one of my goals is to convey in words something of the ingenious composition and flair for storytelling that characterize their work, I do not at this point restrict my discussions to whether and how autobiography meets ethnography and girls meet girls.

In the conclusion I return to the question of disciplinary boundaries, looking at how critics and audiences variously perceive the "dyke" of these "dyke docs." My desire here is to emphasize how much social context determines textual content in contemporary documentaries—like these by Benning and Friedrich—that marry autobiography to ethnography and "dyke" (or "gay" or "queer") to "doc."

▶

Of Definition and Distinction

The "classic" definition of literary autobiography might well be that proposed by Philippe Lejeune, for whom autobiography is a "retrospective prose narrative that someone writes concerning his own existence, where the focus is his individual life, in particular the story of his personality."[3] In literary autobiographies, author, narrator, and protagonist coincide; the author's signature frequently operates as the guarantee of identity. Defining films and videos as autobiographical is more tricky because, as Elizabeth Bruss cautions, one must distinguish between cinema "eye" (the body behind the camera) and cinema "I" (the body in the film), and differentiate between (usually) single author of a book and (often) collective "auteur" of a film.[4]

Both visual and print autobiographies, however, take the "constitution of identity . . . [to be] the genre's characteristic, even defining, goal."[5] This identity is necessarily fictional, culturally bound, and other-dependent, "grounded in the signs of one's existence that are received from others, as well as from the works of culture by which one is interpreted."[6] Many now argue, therefore, that the "autobiography" label is the result of a "pact" between author and reader or spectator, a pact whose terms are thoroughly mediated by culture.

Ethnography would seem to be a necessary part of studies of why, when, and how literary or cinematic works are categorized as autobiographical. Yet for a long time ethnographers refused to discuss autobiography, in part because they took the "normative subjects of ethnographic inquiry" to be "non-western people doing non-western things."[7] Ethnographic "truth" was held to reside in "raw data" collected in an apparently "authorless" fashion. Ethnographers working in film advocated a "plain" film style composed of long takes, sync sound, whole acts, whole bodies, no scripts, and little editing.[8]

Many contemporary ethnographers, however, find presumptuous the idea that the everyday activities of "non-western people doing non-western things" might somehow contain and even "articulat[e] . . . social meanings,"[9] and preposterous the premise that all cultures can be "understood, on their own terms" or "studied as original wholes."[10] There is, instead, growing *theoretical* agreement—concrete studies are rare—that one must ask how ethnographic films are used, by whom, and general *theoretical* recognition that, as James Clifford says, "there is no single general type of reader [or spectator]."[11] Many agree, moreover, with Judith Okely that "contrary to the expectation that an autobiography which speaks of the personal and specific should thereby elaborate uniqueness, autobiographies may . . . evoke common aspects."[12]

To speak of "lesbian" autobiography or "lesbian" ethnography is, of course, only to complicate further the question of what might be considered unique, typical, particular, or general in autobiography or ethnography. As Biddy Martin says:

> The *lesbian* in front of *autobiography* reinforces conventional assumptions of the transparency of autobiographical writing. And the *autobiography* that follows *lesbian* suggests that sexual identity not only modifies but essentially defines a life, providing it with predictable content and an identity possessing continuity and universality. . . . It is to suggest that there is something coherently different about lesbians' lives vis-a-vis other lives and . . . something coherently the same about all lesbians.[13]

Martin does not mean, of course, that it is impossible or undesirable to write, or to write about, "lesbian autobiography" or, I would add, "lesbian ethnography." But the problems she raises do underline the need for studies that situate themselves geographically and historically with as much precision as possible, while acknowledging that the definitions they proffer are provisional.

At present in the United States, two key concerns emerge from lesbian autobiographies and ethnographies: coming out and kinship.[14] Bonnie

Zimmerman and Martin, for example, both talk about "community," and Martin explicitly discusses "family" and "home" in autobiographical writing by lesbians of color. Both emphasize the roles that coming out plays, agreeing that, while all autobiography restructures the past, "such re-visioning may be particularly essential to the formation of lesbian identity."[15] Anthropologist Kath Weston also conceives of coming out as fundamental, arguing that "at this historical moment, a lesbian or gay identity [is] realized as much in the course of the telling as the feeling or the doing."[16] She contends that coming-out stories restructure the past to accord with the present and reformulate the present as an advancement over the past "to counter the implication that being gay transforms a person into something alien, deviant, or monstrous."[17]

Crucially, Weston situates current debates about gay marriages and families within, rather than on the margins of, broader historical transformations of kinship. She challenges conventional definitions because "to assert that straight people 'naturally' have access to family, while gay people are destined to move toward a future of solitude and loneliness, is not only to tie kinship closely to procreation, but also to treat gay men and lesbians as members of a nonprocreative species set apart from the rest of humanity."[18]

Sadie Benning and Su Friedrich strike similarly self-assured, "uppity" poses in their "dyke docs." Like Weston, Zimmerman, and Martin, both reflect, as "out" lesbians, on marriage and family in their work. Both draw on past experiences, somehow inscribe their voices and bodies, and variously position lesbian and other subcultures in relation to a dominant heterosexual culture. To use Bill Nichols's formulation, both thereby "blur boundaries" between subjectivity and objectivity, autobiography and ethnography, and thus extend how documentary is defined and "queers" are seen.[19]

"Benning on Benning"—and Beyond

Several of Benning's nine videos are overtly presented as coming-out narratives.[20] Though almost half (*New Year, Living Inside, Me and Rubyfruit,* and *If Every Girl Had a Diary*) are recounted primarily in the present, all contain references to Benning's past, and three (*Welcome to Normal, A Place Called Lovely,* and *Girl Power*) even incorporate home movies of baby Sadie. All are narrated, largely in the first person, by Benning herself. All feature close-ups and extreme close-ups of Benning's body, and most are shot in her room, literally enacting what Paul John Eakin calls the "connection between personal space and the concept of self" so important to autobiography.[21]

But Benning also positions her "self" as representative of a larger group, fluidly composed of other young lesbians, alienated teens, riot grrrls. Her expressive, highly personal videos acquire polemical, quasi-ethnographic resonance in consequence. Everywhere, for example, the in-your-face presence of Benning's body challenges the idea that, because lesbians love women, lesbians are somehow men.[22] Throughout her work she insists that she likes being a woman and is *not* a man, though she is quite willing to dress as one: in *Jollies* she shaves her face; in *It Wasn't Love* she acts the part of a bearded gangster; in *Girl Power* she intercuts a picture of herself, with an identical haircut and shirt, between two halves of a Matt Dillon pinup poster. At other moments she adopts stereotypically female roles: in *It Wasn't Love* she becomes a cigarette-smoking vamp in blond wig and heavy makeup; in *Girl Power* she imagines she is Blondie, Joan Jett, and every member of the Go-Gos.

Especially combined with Pixelvision's grainy images, tinny sound, and inescapable box frames, Benning's stress on fantasy and gender performance highlights the constructedness of her autobiographies: though Pixelvision practitioners and theorists often comment on the apparent "infantilism inherent in the form,"[23] Benning's seemingly casual video style is the result of "boiling down . . . hours and hours of tape."[24] All the videos contain intertextual references: clips from old movies and television shows, snatches of songs by famous pop artists or lesser known bands; headlines and photos from pulp magazines and newspapers; drawings, paintings, product labels; Benning's own printed and typed messages. Together these function both as autobiographical extensions of her own voice and as ethnographic reflections on a world where racism and homophobia are ubiquitous, and "private" and "public" have become interpermeable categories.

Benning's third tape, *Me and Rubyfruit*, is the first of her "dyke docs" to signal itself as such, and literally served as her coming-out story.[25] The title assumes viewer familiarity with Rita Mae Brown's comic bildungs-roman about coming out in the South, *Rubyfruit Jungle*. The rest of the video continues the imaginary dialogue of "me *and* Rubyfruit," as Benning and a fictional "girlfriend" exchange comments via intertitles and voice-over monologue. Pirated snatches of hit (heterosexual) songs link teenage lesbian to adult heterosexual love. As Benning paints it, however, hetero-sexual marriage seems dull: "Yeah, I'll get married and wear an apron like my mother. Only my husband will be handsome." Does "husband" here mean girls can be husbands too? The next few lines of dialogue cer-

Jollies (Sadie Benning 1990). Courtesy Video Data Bank

tainly suggest as much: "Why don't you marry me? I'm not handsome, but I'm pretty." In comparison with heterosexual marriage, lesbian love is exciting if—or because—illicit. Though lesbian marriage may be limited to "FANTASY," as Benning proclaims in block letters, it is unquestionably glamorous: "We'll kiss like in the movies, and then we'll be engaged." In a scenario familiar to many lesbians and gays, imagination and, crucially, action "queer" both Hollywood and kinship.

Jollies, Benning's fifth tape, continues her tongue-in-cheek look at her own sexual "history," but in this video marriage is not even mentioned. Benning's deadpan narration begins after a credit sequence performed by naked Barbie dolls. Over extreme close-ups of her eye, ear, nose, and mouth, she says: "It started in 1978 when I was in kindergarten. They were twins and I was a tomboy." She turns toward the camera and, revealing braces on her teeth, continues: "I always thought of real clever things to say like . . . like . . . I love you." A shock cut to Diane Arbus's photo of twin girls, then pans up Benning's hairy leg and over a Mr. Bubbles bottle ironically underscore her youth and the absurd excitement of childhood crushes, especially of a lesbian crush on twins.

Benning mentions two episodes with boys, but describes both in such distanced, even anticlimactic terms that she highlights how unimportant these heterosexual encounters were—and are—to her. The last part of Benning's coming-out story is no less parodic, but reconfigures passion in that, like other coming-out narratives, it paints homosexual identity as an underlying "truth." In direct address Benning tells of exchanging phone numbers with another girl. Then a trumpet blast hails a printed text: "THAT NIGHT I FOUND OUT I WAS AS QUEER AS CAN BE." The final credits, "SPECIAL THANKS TO DEBBIE DAVIS," are accompanied by a woman singing "You give me what I want when I want it." Masks and pans create a strobe-light effect over the words "DEBBIE DAVIS." As in *Me and Rubyfruit*, Hollywood glamour is claimed for lesbians and lesbianism, suggesting that Debbie Davis just might be a star on a par with Bette Davis.

Like many of Benning's earlier tapes, *Girl Power* reflects on unhappy childhood and adolescence. Here, however, Benning consciously portrays herself and her (now visible) girlfriend as "out" young lesbians within a riot grrrl subculture. For Benning, *girl* is "a strong word," especially when it is preceded by the adjective *bad*.[26] Not coincidentally, then, the video begins with "thanks to bad girls girls girls everywhere." Images of "bad girls" of all ages follow, including a home movie of Benning as drooling toddler and new footage of Benning as young adult. "MOM" is tattooed on her lower lip; in the penultimate image "GIRL LOVE" is stenciled on her knuckles. Periodically, written texts flash out warnings like "Violent Youth / Fierce and Furious"; "Ashamed / Ridiculed / Denied / Fucked with / Fuck / You / Man / Hear / Me / or Die."

Clips from documentary films and television shows—an atomic bomb blast, rockets firing, the Rodney King beating, a homophobic diatribe delivered by American Nazi Party leader George Lincoln Rockwell—are intercut with footage shot in Benning's room. In voice-over, Benning says, "In my world, in my head, I was never alone. It was at school, with my father, and in my own culture that I felt most alone." Her juxtaposition of imaginary and "real" spaces subtly critiques and redefines both culture and community.

The final printed texts and credits are accompanied by a Bikini Kill song whose beat, mood, and lyrics echo Benning's images, editing, and narration: "We're Bikini Kill, and we want Revolution! . . . All the doves that fly past my eyes, have a stickiness to their wings. . . . HOW DOES IT FEEL? IT FEELS BLIND. . . . WHAT HAVE YOU TAUGHT ME? NOTHING."[27]

Throughout *Girl Power*, however, Benning's connections of individual girls to girl groups testify to the existence of different community and kinship networks. As the tape ends, Benning cautions us that this is only "the end / for now": "this has been a continuing work in progress / beware be alert / watch out / for / girlpower the movie."

Though nowhere more overtly than in *Girl Power*, in all these "dyke

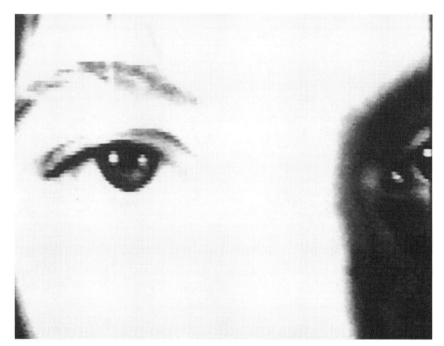

Girl Power (Sadie Benning 1992). Courtesy Video Data Bank

docs" refrains common to contemporary lesbian and gay lives emerge from the intricate rhythms Benning composes using her own life, among them portrayals of coming out as culmination and revelation, protests against injustice, and quests for community and kinship. In these videos, girls love girls, autobiography marries ethnography, and personal expression acquires political resonance.

▶

Su Friedrich's Sidewalk Soliloquies

Where Benning insists in her videos on the formation/revelation of a visible and audible lesbian "self," Friedrich does not usually deal directly with the personal and public ramifications of coming out in her work. Several films, including *First Comes Love* and *Rules of the Road*, instead focus on marriage and families, subtly expanding kinship to include lesbians as well as heterosexuals.[28]

Stylistically, too, Friedrich's films, and especially her latest films, are quite different from Benning's videos. Shot in 16 mm, both *First Comes Love* and *Rules of the Road* make use of the greater depth of focus, clarity of image, and variety of field that film affords. Although both include popular songs, unlike Friedrich's earlier films neither makes extensive use of intertitles or employs excerpts from other films or television shows as a way to distinguish—and link—subcultures and mass culture.

Intriguingly, *First Comes Love* and *Rules of the Road* represent divergent points on the autobiographical-ethnographic continuum. *First Comes Love* is the most clearly "ethnographic" of all Friedrich's films: in it Friedrich studies heterosexual marriage ceremonies from a position literally and figuratively on the sidelines. Thanks to its first-person voice-over narration about personal experience, *Rules of the Road* is, in contrast, Friedrich's most "autobiographical" work to date.

First Comes Love is composed of three elements: (1) intercut black and white footage from four different weddings; (2) fourteen musical selections; and (3) a two-part scrolled text that Friedrich calls "a surprising public service announcement" (the first part lists 120 countries where lesbian and gay marriage is forbidden; the second credits Denmark with being the first country to legalize same-sex ceremonies).[29] In classic ethnographic fashion, Friedrich's camera chronicles each wedding ceremony from "arrival scene" to departure. Less classic, however, is the way she shoots and edits these ceremonies: hers is clearly not the stance of an "objective" scientist. Studied pans, close-ups on accessories rather than faces, and editing that follows gestures rather than bodies make identification of or with an individual bride or groom difficult. The constant intercutting among limousines, flowers, handshakes, back slaps, hugs, and kisses instead emphasizes how much time, money, energy, and enthusiasm are poured into heterosexual wedding celebrations.

In the midst of such widespread approbation, the "PSAs" about the illegality of lesbian and gay marriages stand out starkly. Whip pans, zooms, and rapid editing register a range of emotions toward a ceremony from which lesbians and gays are excluded. The musical selections—all rock, soul, or country hits—also provide nuanced commentary, thanks to Friedrich's juxtaposition of each song against the others, and each song against the images. Though all the lyrics are somehow about love, attraction, or sex, many also convey exclusion, loss, and loneliness. The last song, Willie Nelson's haunting "You Were Always on My Mind," plays as altar boys sweep up rice from the church steps. The juxtaposition prompts questions: Why do people marry? Will these marriages last? At the very end, Nelson's ballad still in the background, Friedrich dedicates her film "for Cathy," adding a personal note to the film's commentary on the exclusion of lesbians and gays from legally sanctioned marriage ceremonies.

In many ways, of course, *First Comes Love* is more *about* heterosexuals than about lesbians. Nevertheless, it is also a documentary *by* and *for* lesbians; as Friedrich jokingly puts it, her film is about "rites and

First Comes Love (Su Friedrich 1991). Courtesy filmmaker

wrongs."[30] By not being visibly or audibly present, she rejects traditional autobiographical subjectivity and at the same time declines the "plain film style" characteristically associated with ethnographic objectivity. In *Me and Rubyfruit*, Benning also refuses to accept that marriage is a heterosexual institution off-limits to lesbians; *First Comes Love*, however, seeks to broaden the meaning of marriage by, as Leslie Kossoff says, "gently yet forcefully asking you to deal with questions of commitment and love and the public announcement of them."[31]

Rules of the Road continues to "queery" kinship, though Friedrich's personal investment is more clearly in evidence since the film is basically about her relationship to, breakup with, and mourning for her lover. The first of Friedrich's films to be shot in color, *Rules* opens with images taken from inside a moving car. Then, in close-up, a woman's hands hold a deck of Greyhound bus playing cards; lay out the film's title, one letter at a time; shuffle the cards; and spell out "by" and "Su Friedrich."

Offscreen, Friedrich tells how her girlfriend celebrated Thanksgiving alone with her brother and his girlfriend one year because she thought her brother would "be uncomfortable if she brought along her own girlfriend." She returns home in "a big old beige station wagon . . . a 1983 Oldsmobile Cutlass Cruiser, a sensible family car," which her brother has helped her to acquire. Suddenly, beige station wagons—parked and moving—appear everywhere. For the rest of the film, Friedrich's camera hunts them out, panning, tracking, and zooming restlessly. These street scenes are intercut with shots of the hands playing solitaire, moments of black, and a few black and white images of a woman rowing. Gradually they make sense as the spaces within which Friedrich searches for, and flees from, the car and lover she has lost.

Descriptions of road trips are illustrated by images shot from a moving car. Some trips are lyrically depicted: "When I was driving, I felt as though I was carrying her in my arms, away from the relentless, claustrophobic city towards an unpredictable and generous expanse of forest or ocean. I wanted to give her that. And I wanted to be with her when she got there." Others involve horrible fights with her lover, fights much like those Friedrich says she witnessed as a child from the backseat of her family's car.

After the breakup, Friedrich imagines what it would be like to turn the corner and see her ex. Quick cuts of different station wagons moving in different directions, followed by blurred, out-of-focus swish pans visually underline her fear that she will not be able to distinguish her lover's car from other station wagons. The constant zooms in to close-ups on license plates are finally explained: in a world full of beige station wagons "ready to surprise me at every turn," Friedrich protects herself from chance—though not entirely undesired—encounters with her former girlfriend by looking at license plates.

Especially at the beginning of the film, the songs heighten the offbeat humor of Friedrich's descriptions and delivery. Subsequent selections briefly translate Friedrich's confidence in her relationship, but the musical selections in the last half of the film are all about anger, loneliness, and bereavement. The last, Randy Travis's "Hard Rock Bottom of Your Heart," plays as the car carrying Friedrich and her camera heads out of New York City. The lyrics convey the ache and emptiness she feels: "I need your love, I miss it. / I can't go on like this / It hurts too much."

Though Friedrich's chosen family has dissolved, and though she has lost her access to the quintessential family car, her lover's station wagon, she *is* leaving town again, together with another woman whose hands we see on the steering wheel. Over the course of the film, moreover, cars, not just queers, have come to seem like family members.[32] While station wagons may temporarily have become metaphors of mourning, they—and every other vehicle—now hold out the promise of a "family" open to all, a family of used car owners:

> The first time I laid eyes on the car, I was disappointed by its homeliness but consoled by the thought that it was unique. . . . Consequently I was surprised to find that there are many thousands of them on the streets of New York. Almost overnight I went from barely noticing their existence to realizing that

Rules of the Road (Su Friedrich 1993). Courtesy filmmaker

> I lived in a world swarming with station wagons. By becoming the owner of one, she seemed to have been initiated into a special clan. And by sharing the car with her, I felt I had become an honorary member of that same family.

The film ends on a hopeful note, with Friedrich making plans to buy her own used car. Retrospectively, we realize that the very first images of the film display the choices she now sees: a pink Vespa, a little red sedan, a dark blue jeep. As *Rules of the Road* closes, "girl" may thus have lost "girl," but Friedrich will soon be back in the driver's seat, following the same "rules of the road" as everyone else. Though *Rules of the Road* is more clearly autobiographical than *First Comes Love*, they share the ethnographic conviction that "self," "love," "kinship," and "culture" should not, cannot be construed as solely, or exclusively, heterosexual.

▶

For Fun and Fantasy

Friedrich and Benning both began making experimental films and videos, respectively, because as women and as lesbians they felt excluded from mainstream movies.[33] Now successful independent artists, both feel keenly the responsibility of representation. Both therefore seek to make their work accessible, but not just to lesbian and gay audiences. Reversing the liberal heterosexual line on queers, Benning says of *Girl Power*: "Most of my friends are straight. We can't, like, shut people out because some girls like men. So what? That's what makes them happy. As long as nobody's being abused or hurt, why exclude anyone?"[34] Friedrich describes *First Comes Love* in terms that are similarly inclusive, yet transformative: "The film doesn't attempt to defend—or discredit—the institution of marriage. Instead, it . . . raises questions about how the double standard regarding marriage affects both gay and straight couples."[35]

But authorial intent does not sufficiently answer the questions of definition and distinction with which I began this essay. How, when, and by whom are the "dykes" of Benning's and Friedrich's "dyke docs" perceived as unique, as typical, as particular, or as general? Who describes their works as autobiographical or ethnographic? Why? Do critics and audiences acknowledge Benning's and Friedrich's openness to others?

Over fifteen years ago, Annette Kuhn signaled the need to take into account "the institutional contexts within which documentaries are produced" in discussing questions of reception and representativeness.[36] Certainly exhibition, marketing, and distribution are key to how lesbian and gay experimental documentaries are seen. Unlike, for example, the gay male experimental documentaries of the 1950s and 1960s, which were usually labeled "experimental" rather than "gay" because they were addressed to and received within art world contexts, Benning's and Friedrich's work is explicitly programmed and billed as "lesbian" at many festivals and in most catalogs, though it is also exhibited and distributed without that label. Not surprisingly, therefore, of the twenty-two reviews of *Me and Rubyfruit*, *Jollies*, *Girl Power*, *First Comes Love*, and *Rules of the Road* indexed as of January 1995, two-thirds are based on screenings at lesbian and gay festivals.[37] Moreover, since Benning and Friedrich refer at length to lesbian issues, include their own bodies or voices or both as markers of lesbian "authenticity" and "identity," and speak openly of and to other lesbians in their work, all twenty-two reviews at some point describe this work as lesbian. In contrast, most critics of Friedrich's earlier films did not usually write about their lesbian content, imagery, and address "except when a veritable constellation of features [were] present, among them: 1) verbal and/or visual representations of lesbian sexual acts, combined with 2) a simultaneous if not necessarily synchronous representation of lesbian issues on both image and sound tracks, for 3) the bulk of narrative time."[38]

Nevertheless, though critics acknowledge the "dykes" of Benning and Friedrich's "dyke docs," *how* they are seen varies a great deal. Most critics as well as most students to whom I have shown these works easily label them autobiographies, diaries, or confessions. Occasionally critics place both women's work in a tradition of personal films, diary films, or psychodramas.[39] Except in the case of *First Comes Love*, however, almost no one discusses these works as ethnographies. In twelve of fifteen interviews and reviews, moreover, no mention is made of Benning's consistent condemnation of homophobia, racism, and sexism, and no recognition is given to her general concern with young people and women. It is as if "autobiography" were understood solely as the inscription of a self-absorbed subjectivity uninvolved with others.[40] Only in the case of *First Comes Love* do critics applaud Friedrich's even-handedness and openness, perhaps because they view the film as "ethnographic" and therefore as "objective."

As my textual analyses show, however, neither Benning nor Friedrich presents lesbian identities as singular, unchanging, or exclusionary. Necessarily, therefore, lesbian and gay spectators are not automatically or as a block "better" spectators of their works. As Benning points out, although lesbian and gay teens devour her work, in part because they recognize in it their own experiences, thoughts, and feelings, "the gay community is just as anti-youth, sexist, and racist as any group; sometimes they're even more scary and conservative, trying even harder than straight people to fit in."[41] That these "dyke docs" are experimental works of course only complicates matters: as Friedrich says, "being a lesbian doesn't automatically make a woman more sophisticated about art, or less desirous of the big-screen-color-love-story-with-a-happy-ending."[42]

When I teach and program these works as autobiographies, ethnographies, or "dyke docs," I worry, I confess. Will describing them as autobiographical induce some viewers to think of the unique solely as singular or exceptional? Will labeling them ethnographic diminish "our receptivity to the unique . . . in the name of the typical?"[43] As a critic and a teacher, I try not to assume that what is said or written afterward equals all that is seen. But because gays are so often excluded from families and so invisible unless they come out, I do insist (especially if no one else does) in post-screening discussions on the impossibility of simple definition or clear-cut distinction where both "dykes" and "docs" are concerned, and I stress the crucial roles production, distribution, and exhibition play in shaping reception.

Because Benning and Friedrich so skillfully mix humor and pathos, imagination and advocacy in their work, however, many audience members become "queer readers," able, willing, even eager to savor erotic desires and acknowledge family resemblances that may or may not be part of their own experiences.[44] For these spectators, fun and fantasy help loosen strict definitions and nuance sharp distinctions. There are times, after all, when lexical precision matters less than shared emotion, as Sadie Benning demonstrates at the end of *It Wasn't Love*:

And yet, in that parking lot, I felt like I had seen the whole world. She had this way of making me feel like I was the goddamn Nile River or something. We didn't need Hollywood. We were Hollywood. . . . It wasn't love, but it was *something*.

◆———

NOTES

Thanks to Chris Cagle, Cindy Fuchs, Su Friedrich, Paul Harrill, Chuck Kleinhans, Chon Noriega, and Paige Travis for comments on earlier drafts.

1. Bill Nichols, "'Getting to Know You . . .': Knowledge, Power, and the Body," in *Theorizing Documentary*, ed. Michael Renov (New York: Routledge, 1993), 176.

2. Bourdieu is not concerned with autobiography or ethnography per se, but is broadly interested in the connections among class, educational background, and aesthetic perception. See Pierre Bourdieu, *Distinction: A Social Critique of the Judgement of Taste*, trans. Richard Nice (Cambridge, Mass.: Harvard University Press, 1984).

3. Philippe Lejeune, "The Autobiographical Pact," in *On Autobiography*, trans. Katherine Leary (Minneapolis: University of Minnesota Press, 1989), 14. The question of time is in many ways crucial to autobiography. Lejeune, for example, maintains that autobiography plays at creating the illusion that producer-work-consumer exist at the same time (126).

4. Bruss goes so far as to claim that "there is no real cinematic equivalent for autobiography." See Elizabeth Bruss, "Eye for I: Making and Unmaking Autobiography in Film," in *Autobiography: Essays Critical and Theoretical*, ed. James Olney (Princeton, N.J.: Princeton University Press, 1980), 296–97. For a critique of Bruss, see Michael Renov, "The Subject in History," *Afterimage* 17.1 (1989): 4.

5. Paul John Eakin, *Touching the World: Reference in Autobiography* (Princeton, N.J.: Princeton University Press, 1992), 67.

6. Janet Varner Gunn, *Autobiography: Toward a Poetics of Experience* (Philadelphia: University of Pennsylvania Press, 1982), 31.

7. Marcus Banks, "Which Films Are the Ethnographic Films?" in *Film as Ethnography*, ed. Peter Ian Crawford and David Turton (Manchester: Manchester University Press, 1992), 120.

8. Other prescriptions include a minimum of voice-over narration, the use of subtitles for indigenous dialogue, the employment of a wide-angle lens, an avoidance of close-ups, and a preference for in-camera editing. See, for example, Banks, "Which Films Are the Ethnographic Films?," 122–24; Peter Ian Crawford, "Film as Discourse: The Invention of Anthropological Realities," in *Film as Ethnography*, 77; and David MacDougall, "Complicities of Style," in *Film as Ethnography*, 93-94.

9. Dai Vaughan, "The Aesthetics of Ambiguity," in *Film as Ethnography*, 107.

10. Asen Balikci, "Anthropologists and Ethnographic Filmmaking," in *Anthropological Filmmaking: Anthropological Perspectives on the Production of Film and Video for General Public Audiences*, ed. Jack R. Rollwagen (Chur: Harwood, 1988), 33.

11. James Clifford, "On Ethnographic Authority," in *The Predicament of Culture: Twentieth-Century Ethnography, Literature, and Art* (Cambridge, Mass.: Harvard University Press, 1988), 37. For a succinct discussion of contemporary debates and silences around ethnographic film, see Bill Nichols, "The Ethnographer's Tale," in *Blurred Boundaries: Questions of Meaning in Contemporary Culture* (Bloomington: Indiana University Press, 1994), 63-91.

12. Judith Okely, "Anthropology and Autobiography: Participatory Experience and Embodied Knowledge," in *Anthropology and Autobiography*, ed. Judith Okely and Helen Callaway (London: Routledge, 1992), 7.

13. Biddy Martin, "Lesbian Identity and Autobiographical Difference[s]," in *Life/Lines: Theorizing Women's Autobiography*, ed. Bella Brodski and Celeste Schenck (Ithaca, N.Y.: Cornell University Press, 1988), 78.

14. Coming out was, of course, also a crucial component of 1960s and 1970s activism. Weston argues that kinship has emerged as a political concern in the 1980s and 1990s as a result of the number of lesbians having children, the rise in gay marriages, and the horrifying percentage of gay men living with and dying of AIDS. See Kath Weston, *Families We Choose: Lesbians, Gays, Kinship* (New York: Columbia University Press, 1991).

15. Bonnie Zimmerman, "The Politics of Transliteration: Lesbian Personal Narratives," *Signs* 9.4 (Summer 1984): 667.

16. Weston, *Families We Choose*, 66.

17. Ibid., 79.

18. Ibid., 22–23. For further discussions of lesbian and gay marriage, see Becky Butler, *Ceremonies of the Heart: Celebrating Lesbian*

Unions (Seattle: Seal Press, 1990), and Suzanne Sherman, ed., *Lesbian and Gay Marriage* (Philadelphia: Temple University Press, 1992).

19. See Nichols, *Blurred Boundaries*, especially 1–16 and 63–91.

20. The expression "Benning on Benning" is taken from Chris Chang, "Up in Sadie's Room," *Film Comment* 29.2 (March/April 1993): 8. Benning began making videos at age sixteen when her father, experimental filmmaker James Benning, gave her a Pixelvision camcorder for Christmas. Titles include *A New Year* (1989), *Living Inside* (1989), *Me and Rubyfruit* (1989), *If Every Girl Had a Diary* (1990), *Jollies* (1990), *Welcome to Normal* (1990), *A Place Called Lovely* (1991), *It Wasn't Love* (1992), and *Girl Power* (1992).

21. Eakin, *Touching the World*, 101.

22. In *Welcome to Normal* Benning admits that when she was younger, "I didn't know I could love women without being a man." She was known by her middle name, Taylor: "I talked like a boy . . ., dressed like a boy, played with the boys. My best friend . . . a boy . . . was paranoid to tell the rest of the neighborhood his best friend was a girl, so he told everybody I was a boy and I just went along with it." Benning's first girlfriend, at age eleven, knew she was a girl. When they broke up, "the whole neighborhood found out I was a girl. I got ridiculed for the next two years, and during high school I was treated so *awful*." Cited in Elise Harris, "Baby Butch Video," *Queer World*, Nov. 15, 1992, 33.

23. Jonathan Romney, "Honey I Shrunk the Kit," *New Statesman and Society* 6.278 (Nov. 12, 1993): 34.

24. Roberta Smith, "A Video Artist Who Talks through a Keyhole," *New York Times*, March 28, 1993, H33.

25. One by one, Benning brought her friends into her room and showed them her tape as a way of declaring her sexual identity to them. See Ellen Spiro, "Shooting Star," *Advocate* 563 (March 26, 1991): 68, and Karl Soehnlein, "Lights, Camera, Lesbian," *Outweek*, Dec. 12, 1990, 49.

26. See Kim Masters, "Auteur of Adolescence," *Washington Post*, Oct. 17, 1992, D7.

27. Thanks to Chris Cagle for Bikini Kill's lyrics.

28. Only *Damned If You Don't* (1987) deals directly with coming out. Friedrich's other work includes *Cool Hands, Warm Heart* (1979), *Gently Down the Stream* (1981), *The Ties that Bind* (1984), *Sink or Swim* (1990), and *Lesbian Avengers Eat Fire Too* (1993, codirected with Janet Baus). *Scar Tissue* (1980) and *But No One* (1982) are not in distribution.

   For a discussion of autobiographical elements in *Gently Down the Stream, The Ties that Bind, Damned If You Don't*, and *Sink or Swim*, see Chris Holmlund, "Fractured Fairytales and Experimental Identities: Looking for Lesbians in and around the Films of Su Friedrich," *Discourse* 17.1 (Fall 1994): 16–46.

29. Publicity blurb written by Friedrich.

30. Ibid.

31. Leslie Kossoff, "History in the Making," *Gay Community News*, Sept. 1–14, 1991, 7.

32. I owe this idea to Paige Travis, who argues: "Both visually and through the narration, Friedrich treats cars like a valuable member of the family. In fact it's possible that the real main character of *Rules of the Road* could be the 1983 Oldsmobile Cutlass Cruiser the narrator comes to love and depend on." Paige Travis, "The Undeniable Connection between Cars and Family in Su Friedrich's *Rules of the Road*," unpublished ms., April 1995.

33. Friedrich says she used to dislike narrative film "partly because I'm a woman (I saw a lot of films about interesting male characters and stupid female characters) and at times because I couldn't identify with the romantic line of the films." Cited in Scott MacDonald, "*Damned If You Don't*: An Interview with Su Friedrich," *Afterimage*, May 1988, 10, and *A Critical Cinema*, vol. 2 (Los Angeles: University of California Press, 1990), 306. Benning describes Hollywood movies as "totally fake and constructed to entertain and oppress at the same time—they're meaningless to women, and not just to gay women." Cited in Smith, "A Video Artist Who Talks through a Keyhole," H33.

34. Masters, "Auteur of Adolescence," D7. Elsewhere, however, Benning does say she makes her videos largely for young lesbian and gay audiences. See, for example, Spiro, "Shooting Star," 68.

35. Publicity blurb written by Friedrich. Friedrich discusses her approach to experimental film in Su Friedrich, "Radical Form/Radical Content," *Millennium Film Journal* 22 (1989–90): 118–23.

36. Annette Kuhn, "The Camera I: Observations on Documentary," *Screen* 19.2 (1978): 81.

37. Indexes consulted include *Film Literature Index*, the *General Periodicals Index*, and the *National Newspaper Index*.

38. Holmlund, "Fractured Fairytales and Experimental Identities," 33.

39. Friedrich's earlier work is sometimes positioned in terms of cinema verité and structuralist materialist film as well. See Simon Field, "State of Things," *Monthly Film Bulletin* 54 (Jan. 1987): 4–6; Lindley Hanlon, "Female Rage: The Films of Su Friedrich," *Millennium Film Journal* 12 (1982-83): 79-86; Bruce Jenkins, "Gently Down the Stream," *Millennium Film Journal* 16-18 (Fall/Winter 1986–87): 195–98; and Scott MacDonald, *Avant-Garde Film: Motion Studies* (Cam-

bridge: Cambridge University Press, 1993), 102-11.

MTV and, more rarely, Benning's father, James, are cited as influences on her work. Benning herself insists that "people on the street, music, everyday images, my mom, how I was raised, way more influence how I work and think than other artists. . . . People I hate influence me a lot; I'm influenced by people that are just total assholes." Cited in Harris, "Baby Butch Video," 63.

40. Reviews of Friedrich's earlier work contained similar oversights. See Holmlund, "Fractured Fairytales and Experimental Identities," 34.

41. Harris, "Baby Butch Video," 63.

42. Su Friedrich, letters to Chris Holmlund, Dec. 10, 1991, and Oct. 4, 1992. Of course many experimental filmmakers also "ghettoize" lesbian work. Benning describes her father's reaction: "My dad said to me, 'You know, I'm really worried that all your work is just going to be on one subject,' and I was like, 'Yeah, my life.' He makes [experimental] films. What are his films about? They're about his life. It just so happens that his sexu-ality isn't something that people are going to label or talk about or say, 'He's the hetero-sexual artist.'" Cited in Harris, "Baby Butch Video," 68. Friedrich says of the experimental film world: "In this old boys' scene there's this assumption that if you're speaking from the point of view of a minority, what you're saying does not have any bearing on their lives, and they can't learn anything from it—which is ridiculous. We spend all our time looking at straight films." Cited in Soehnlein, "Lights, Camera, Lesbian," 48.

43. Nichols, "'Getting to Know You . . . ,'" 180. Such misreadings probably occur, as Kath Weston argues, because "homosexuality in the U.S. is now most commonly understood as an identity that infuses the entire self [and, I would add, that distinguishes homo-sexuals as a group] as opposed to an activity in which any self can participate" (Weston, *Families We Choose*, 24).

44. On "queer readers," see Alexander Doty, *Making Things Perfectly Queer: Interpreting Mass Culture* (Minneapolis: University of Minnesota Press, 1993), especially 1–16.

BEVERLY SECKINGER
JANET JAKOBSEN

[8]   *Love, Death, and Videotape:*
Silverlake Life

The first time I saw *Silverlake Life: The View from Here* was in April 1993 at the Vista theater in Los Angeles (minutes from Silverlake), and I still remember it vividly. It may have been the first time I saw my friend Mark cry. In fact, by the end of the film, everyone in the audience seemed to be wrestling with sniffles and tears, as napkins snatched from the snack bar were passed down the aisles and shared among strangers. When Mark Massi picks up the camcorder moments after his longtime partner Tom Joslin has died, and begins speaking to Tom and to future viewers *through* the camera, then singing to his lover through his tears, it is hard to imagine anyone remaining unmoved. Together in the darkness of the Vista that night, it felt like we had joined Joslin and Massi's community of friends. We had met them, come to know and care about them, and then lost them in less than two hours.

The first time I saw *Silverlake Life* I was alone. It was late at night because the local public television station airs *POV* only after prime time. My lover (the one with the day job) was already asleep. I was so moved by the film, especially the scene where Massi sings "You Are My Sunshine," that the next morning I began singing it to my lover. While I obviously experienced a rare moment of self-appearance based on the "public" appearance of these two gay lovers on U.S. television, I was even more affected by a public broadcast that recognized the pain that we and our friends had experienced in response to the AIDS crisis. While we respond to this grief through participation in AIDS organizing and political struggle, the airing of this film was a dramatic reminder of how rarely the U.S. public allows or recognizes the articulation of this pain.[1] Our initial two viewing experiences took place (perhaps not surprisingly) in the two situations envisioned by editor Peter Friedman—Beverly's in a community theater audience organized around queer and AIDS identifications and Janet's in the public television audience. Our initial interpretations of the film (again not surprisingly) reflect these different viewing sites—Beverly's focusing on the formation and extension of community through the viewing of the film, particularly in relation to her friend Mark, and Janet's focusing on the implications of this film in a broader public arena and possible activist responses to the issues it evokes. We have since seen the film in other settings (in addition to the research for this essay)—Beverly in her "History of Documentary" class and Beverly and Janet in the Tucson "Queer Looks" film and video series. Each of these sites has offered alternative readings from students and spectators who are variously resistant to and moved by the film.

These multiple readings raise a number of questions about contemporary documentary: questions about the relationship between the production and viewing of documentary and the issues and events that it purports to document; and questions about the implications of documentary for the contexts and politics that such films engage. What is the relationship between documentary articulations and "truth" or "reality"? How do the articulations of *Silverlake Life* relate to communities and actions that have formed around queer and AIDS visibility in the United States? In order to explore these questions, it is necessary to consider *Silverlake Life* in the context of the history of documentary filmmaking.

▶ ───

The Making of *Silverlake Life*

Filmmaker Tom Joslin began the video diary *Silverlake Life* when his longtime partner, Mark Massi, developed AIDS in 1989. The focus began to shift when Joslin's own illness accelerated more quickly than Massi's, and Massi increasingly took over the filming duties. Joslin and Massi's primary authorship during the shooting phase was supplemented by the camera work of other friends, especially longtime friend Elaine Mayes, during the final month of Joslin's life. At the end of the wrenching scene described here, Massi promises his dead lover that he and Joslin's friends will complete the "movie" for him.

As Massi's condition continued to deteriorate, Peter Friedman, a former student of Joslin's, inherited thirty-five hours of footage, the fundraising proposal Joslin had developed for the piece, and the responsibility—or at least the opportunity—for completing the work.[2] He shot some additional material with Massi (which eventually was used in the prologue and epilogue sequences), not yet sure if he was going to go through with the project, and finally, after Massi's death in 1991, spent fifteen months editing the film.[3] Joslin's original proposal described a series of six half-hour segments, which would have juxtaposed disparate materials ranging from *Blade Runner* (Ridley Scott 1982) clips to vox pop interviews of Silverlake residents to create more of a neighborhood portrait.[4] Friedman drew on the ideas from this proposal and used the recent diary material, clips from Joslin's 1976 film *Blackstar: Autobiography of a Close Friend* (which explored the personal and political contexts of his own coming out and the early years of his relationship with Massi), some of Joslin's initial voice-over audio recorded for a sample fund-raising reel, and some additional footage he shot of Massi to construct the final ninety-nine-minute version of *Silverlake Life*.[5] The resulting collaborative authorship of the film echoes what Thomas Waugh has argued has been a persistent characteristic of gay documentary since the 1970s.[6] Indeed, the collaboration of Joslin, Massi, and their friends and students in the making of the film invokes a long-standing approach to activist filmmaking as collective struggle.

When Friedman took over the film, he obtained a commitment for broadcast on Channel 4 in England at an early stage of the editing. He realized, he says in interviews, that *Silverlake Life* would thereby become one of the most in-depth portraits to date of what it is like to live with AIDS to be seen by a large, often largely uninformed, audience. At the same time, he wanted the film not to "betray the truth . . . and . . . it had to be true so that people with AIDS and people who knew all about this [would] . . . see it and say, 'Yeah, that's the way it is.'"

But what exactly does Friedman mean by "truth"? What types of "truths" might various audiences take from the film? Although published reviews of the film in both the queer and mainstream press have stressed the film's "emotional honesty," "reality," "candidness," "immediacy," and "gut-level intimacy," reviewers rarely discuss how this film constructs truth, identity, or community.[7] While *Silverlake* and the embedded fragments of Joslin's earlier film *Blackstar* are autobiographical, from the beginning the singularity, assumed by the "auto" in autobiography, is undercut. The opening scenes emphasize that this is a life (and death) story that must be constructed from a box full of tapes. The title, *Silverlake Life: The View from Here*, referring to the community in which Joslin lives (and dies), suggests that this film will express an embodied view that is constructed as much communally as individually. Pursuing this construction process through the medium of (what became a widely viewed) documentary film opens these questions of identity and community out into broader contexts of political struggle.[8] The "truth" of an individual life, in this case Tom Joslin's, is not a whole fabric that must simply be opened to the public to be visible; rather, truths must be stitched together like the various panels of the Names Project quilt, and the process of stitching constitutes the various meanings of community, identity, and documentary.

The self-reflexivity of the film makes it clear that Friedman is not simply seeking to present a direct record of a preexistent reality. Why then do so many of those who view and review the film insist on its "candidness" and "intimacy," echoing claims made by both the direct cinema and the cinema verité movements in the early 1960s?

▶

Direct Cinema and Cinema Verité

To understand what is at stake in such claims of veracity and openness, a brief survey of these movements and subsequent critiques is in order. In the late 1950s and early 1960s, concurrent research undertaken by the Drew Associates in the United States, the National Film Board of Canada, and associates of French ethnographer Jean Rouch resulted in the first lightweight, self-blimped 16 mm sync-sound cameras and portable tape recorders. This new mobile technology in turn facilitated the development of new styles of documentary film production that may be roughly categorized as American direct cinema and French cinema verité. While both of these traditions are rooted in the more direct style of shooting made possible by the new mobile equipment, their epistemological assumptions contrast sharply, working either to efface or to foreground the encounter between filmmaker(s) and subject(s).[9]

The observational documentary tradition known as American direct cinema (major practitioners include Ricky Leacock, Don Pennebaker, Frederick Wiseman, the Maysles brothers, and Alan and Susan Raymond) reflects the positivist notion that seeing is believing. The ideology associated with this style likens the camera to a "fly on the wall," unobtrusively capturing spontaneous, untampered-with "reality" for direct, unmediated presentation to a viewer positioned as an "objective" observer. Observational films eschew the voice-of-God narration of the expository documentary in favor of ambient sync sound and tend to be structured along narrative lines, following the activities of their characters to a climactic crisis and then denouement.

The sense of vitality and present-tense immediacy created by the best examples of direct cinema is undeniable.[10] Critics of the observational mode, however, point to a number of discrepancies between the ideology of unmediated reality espoused by its enthusiasts and the hidden textual operations that produce this impression for viewers.[11] While traces of interaction between filmmaker and subject may be relegated to the outtake bin, the presence of the filmmaker nevertheless inevitably affects the profilmic event that she or he records. The structuring process of editing suppresses some interpretations while it emphasizes—and manufactures—others. Important aspects of a subject's experience or perspective may remain silenced; as Brian Winston puts it, "filming the surface of things reveals the surface of things."[12] Finally, this style of filming exacerbates the potential intrusiveness of the camera "exactly because it allows the filmmaker far greater opportunity to lurk and pry," positioning the viewer with the camera as a voyeur.[13]

By contrast, the cinema verité tradition associated with French anthropologist Jean Rouch uses this same mobile equipment to emphasize catalytic interaction over detached observation.[14] The reflexive cinema verité camera is thus regarded not as a fly on the wall, but as an engaged participant. Producer-subject relations are reconfigured to encourage a shared, mutually participatory process. Such "interactive" films typically foreground the camera, its operator, and the present-tense filming situation.[15] Because the marks of production are revealed, the viewer (according to this ideology) is placed in a more critical relationship to the text. Thus, while both styles capitalize on the mobile equipment's enhanced ability to record unscripted, sync-sound profilmic "reality," they invoke contradictory codes to achieve their realist effects.

While Rouch's cinema verité inspired a generation of French New Wave filmmakers and introduced new possibilities for both the ethnographic film and the documentary, only a handful of his more than one hundred films have been available in the United States. The observational style remained far more influential among American documentary makers during the 1960s, but by the mid-1970s, the initial exuberance about fly-on-the-wall immediacy and truth gave way to critiques of direct cinema. With the growing realization that seeing is not necessarily believing, documentaries from the late 1970s (like Michelle Citron's 1978 *Daughter Rite*) and 1980s to the early 1990s (from Jill Godmilow's 1984 *Far from Poland* to Marlon Riggs's 1989 *Tongues Untied* and Jan Oxenberg's 1990 *Thank You and Goodnight*) became increasingly self-conscious about their own ontological status, mixing genre conventions to disrupt transparent readings of their "content."[16] The intersubjective and reflexive strategies developed by Rouch have become important components of this expanded repertoire.

▶

Transparency and Intentionality in *Silverlake Life*

Silverlake Life similarly draws on both the observational and the catalytic traditions, at times giving an impression of direct observation, at others

Tom Joslin at the pizzeria in *Silverlake Life: The View from Here* (Joslin, Friedman 1993)

focusing on the participation of the camera and its operator in the scene being recorded. Just as the development of the portable 16 mm sync-sound camera rig launched both the direct cinema and cinema verité traditions, the advent of small-format video camcorders has further enhanced the possibility for intimate shooting.[17] The built-in microphones, extreme low-light sensitivity, palm-of-the-hand portability, and do-it-yourself ease of operation of Hi-8 and Super-VHS cameras meant that Joslin and Massi could take their camcorders (relatively) unobtrusively on trips to the doctor, the counselor, the grocery store, the pizzeria, Huntington Gardens, the hospital; capture Tom's late-night reflections in bed by flashlight; and easily pass it from hand to hand as friends pitched in with the shooting.

Despite the small-format camcorder's heightened potential to efface its presence, however, much of the film employs a shooting style that contrasts sharply with the fly-on-the-wall ideal of direct cinema practitioners. This reflexive use of the camera, which does not seek to make itself invisible but rather continually emphasizes the relationship(s) between filmer(s) and filmed and acknowledges, even focuses and comments upon, the camera's presence, more resembles Jean Rouch's notion of the camera as a catalyst that can elicit hitherto unarticulated truths through its interaction with the subject than it does the distanced "objectivity" of observational cinema.[18]

While this strategy in a sense places us *inside* Joslin and Massi's relationship, the sense of intimacy thereby created is also marked as self-conscious and intentional, since we know that their "candid" comments are ultimately intended for public screening.[19] The reflexive elements of the film (the references to the camera and to the box of tapes from which the film is constructed, for example), further suggest the deliberate deployment of all of these strategies for rhetorical effect.

Joslin and Massi's multiple roles in this process, along with their subversion of the traditional singularity of authorship, explain how the film works to counter the frequently unequal relationship between documentary producer and subject. Brian Winston has argued that documentaries historically have tended to focus on "society's victims" and in turn rendered their subjects "the media's 'victim' too," exploiting "deviance" to titillate audiences.[20] This mechanism works by casting the documentary subject as an Other who is passive and clearly separate from either producers or audiences. *Silverlake Life* reconfigures this relationship by collapsing the roles of producer and subject, and emphasizing Tom and Mark's visible role as agents in constructing a document of their lives destined for each other and for a broader public.

The focus on everyday tasks (going shopping, doing laundry, eating pizza, dancing in the living room) also allows the film to eschew an exotic Othering of its subjects, even as it points to the ways in which the preciousness of everyday experience is heightened by the proximity of death. Nevertheless, this sense of quotidian reality is quite self-consciously constructed through a deployment of both a verité shooting style (shaky, hand-held camera, sync sound, lack of narration)[21] and the low-quality image of the camcorder, which by the late 1980s had become a familiar means for signifying "realness."[22]

Beyond its initial purpose of documenting Massi's illness, the camera thus fulfills a number of functions and roles. Shooting footage for the project itself became one of the daily tasks to be completed, like the cooking, cleaning, shopping, laundry, and periodic doctor visits and hospital stays that it recorded: "Elaine said . . . when you were around during that time, whoever was around just helped with whatever there was to be done—help with buying food or help with doing the dishes or help with . . . making the movie."[23] We see the camcorder act as confidant and confessor for each of its producer-subjects in turn, as Joslin quietly ponders his fate in the middle of a restless night or Massi blurts tearfully that he had been ashamed to film for the preceding couple of days, because he had fed Joslin something that had not agreed with him and had made him weaker. Filming also provides an absorbing distraction, a productive joint activity for Joslin and

BEVERLY SECKINGER AND JANET JAKOBSEN

Massi, and a focus of attention that somehow transcends and exists outside of the illness, even as it explores it in unsparing detail.

The camera becomes, increasingly, the medium through which the partners communicate with each other ("You wanted to ask me something on camera?" "Wait till I'm in frame"). Even beyond death, it becomes a sort of magical instrument through which Massi continues to speak with Joslin. Moments after his partner's death, for example, Massi picks up the camera and speaks with and through it to Joslin ("Goodbye, Tom") and then to us ("Isn't he beautiful? He's so beautiful"). Sometime later, when a box bearing Joslin's ashes arrives at the house, Massi has carefully set up the camera on a tripod to film himself unwrapping the package and transferring the ashes into a vase (there is a hole in the bag, and ashes are strewn on the floor as Massi jokes, "You're all over the place, Tom"). Again, the camera acts as a tool that both suggests intimacy and at the same time distances the operator from the immediate situation through the performance of life for the camera.

The final shot of Joslin's body bag functions in much the same way. Massi has recorded the entire transaction with the coroners, and now Joslin's body, wrapped in white plastic, lies in the back of their vehicle, ready to be driven to the morgue. Massi continues to film him through the window, so that his own reflected image is superimposed over Joslin's body. While the camera continues to roll, it seems that their physical connection is somehow prolonged, and Massi keeps shooting, reluctant to let go. When at last the shot cuts to the next scene, Joslin is finally really gone, his absence rendered materially in the moment of the edit.

In the context of the heightened self-consciousness of this current documentary moment, the film's participant-camera shooting style enables simultaneous readings of the transparency *and* the intentionality of its content.[24] The process of constructing reality through the making of the videotape is further complicated by the multiple audiences it addresses. While *Silverlake Life* was clearly intended for eventual public exhibition, it is evident that Joslin and Massi are in some sense the principal viewers of their own personal diary; for example, we see the couple lying in bed/in frame, watching themselves on a monitor as the camera rolls and records their self-observations. The point is thereby made that Joslin and Massi are not simply documenting but are also constituting their own lives through the production and viewing of the videotape.

The editing by Friedman and others combines with the prologue, flashback, and epilogue sequences to foreground further a connection between the construction of documentary and the construction of identity and community. Midway through the film we see material from *Blackstar,*

Tom Joslin and Mark Massi in *Silverlake Life: The View from Here*
(Joslin, Friedman 1993)

which functions within *Silverlake Life* as a kind of flashback. In the
footage from *Blackstar*, Massi reads from *Out of the Closets* as the excla-
mation point to Joslin's descriptions of his own coming out and his interviews with family members who describe their sometimes homophobic
reactions.[25] *Silverlake Life* thus refers to, and reframes, the political project
of *Blackstar*: making gay relationships and everyday lives and struggles
publicly visible, this time within the context of AIDS. As other recent queer
organizing and theory has also recognized, however, a politics premised
on publicity, visibility, and coming out does not provide a direct path to
empowerment any more than direct cinema provided unmediated access
to truth.

The contradictions and dangers faced by *Silverlake Life* in its claims
to make visible both gay life and living with AIDS are many. For the television audience, which Friedman conceptualized as including "a lot of people
who . . . wouldn't know anything about AIDS,"[26] a politics of visibility can
be recuperated into discourses ranging from liberal pluralist "tolerance"
and "sympathy" to more virulent claims that both queers and people living
with AIDS need to be contained. There is thus a possibility that *Silverlake
Life* will be read as reinforcing a homophobic conception that "gay equals
AIDS"—that is, that gay sex is simply a route to infection of both the individual and the social body. Conversely, and quite possibly simultaneously,

the film can be read as "AIDS equals gay," eliding the fact that many communities are affected by the pandemic and dangerously bolstering the idea that the "general" public can contain AIDS by containing gays.

The video does resist these equations to some extent, in part by refusing to accede to the dominant culture's obsession with mode of transmission and number of partners. The refusal to succumb to discourses of blame for viral infection also seems to contribute to a certain absence of sexuality in the film as a whole, however. Despite the film's focus on love between Joslin and Massi, most of the references to sexuality are from the *Blackstar* material. This construction seems to imply that mentioning any form of gay sexuality in relation to AIDS would play into discourses of blame, or that with illness, sexual desires and needs simply cease. This need not have been the case.[27]

The film's public portrayal of living and dying with AIDS, aspects of the pandemic that are generally considered private and intimate, challenges boundaries of "privacy" that allow many to ignore the pain and loss surrounding the disease, and that contribute to public inaction in the United States. The danger in *Silverlake Life*'s assertive violation of the boundaries of the private, however, is that an American public trained to depend on the display of private emotion within the contained boundaries of talk shows and news shows will infer that these images are of individual, but not public, interest. In other words, this film faces the possibility that audiences will recuperate the film's narrative into a story of individual victimization.[28]

A further danger for various audiences, including those constituted by and around queer identities or AIDS activism, is that the story will be taken as *the* story of living and dying with AIDS.[29] Here the film becomes implicated in the politics of production that both constrain and enable public visibility, whether it is queer or AIDS visibility. As Biddy Martin has argued with respect to lesbian autobiographies, the race and class privileges that enabled the telling and publishing of early coming-out stories contributed to the construction of a genre that tends to homogenize stories so as to produce the "lesbian" ending.[30] *Silverlake Life* also depends on Joslin's relatively privileged position as a white, middle-class, established filmmaker, and if it is read as the singular story of AIDS or even of a Silverlake life, it could contribute to a similar homogenization. Most importantly, however, as Douglas Crimp notes, representations that focus on sickness or dying from AIDS should not be the only available portraits of people with AIDS.[31] Each portrait should be considered in light of the conditions of its production and its political effects.

Although the conscious inscription of multiple authorship and reference to joint production within the film resist notions of singularity, no one film can do it all. Key, then, to a politically effective reading of *Silverlake Life* is positioning it within the growing body of AIDS documentaries, including Marlon Riggs's 1989 *Tongues Untied* and 1992 *Non, je ne regrette rien*, Ellen Spiro's 1990 *DiAna's Hair Ego*, ACT UP's 1991 *Voices from the Front*, and Stashu Kybartas's 1987 *Danny*.[32]

The epilogue, following Joslin's death, reminds us finally that for each AIDS death, there are also survivors who must deal with their grief and reconstitute community while they live with the realities of loss. Massi reports experiencing Tom's (spiritual) presence a few times, but when Friedman asks why Joslin doesn't come back more often, Massi concludes, "Because he's dead, and he knows he's dead." Massi's life is shown as more starkly individual after Joslin's death, yet he still depends on communities (of spirit, friends, and AIDS service organizations) to live in and through his loss. He reads to the camera, more than a little cynically, from a book on grieving sent to him by his APLA (AIDS Project, Los Angeles) counselor, while friends at the memorial service struggle with the problems of living in a community that has been forced repeatedly to count its dead.

▶───

Silverlake Life and the New Documentary

In "Mirrors without Memories: Truth, History, and the New Documentary," Linda Williams discusses the changing epistemological assumptions about representations that characterize the current (postmodern) historical moment. Williams points to both a loss of faith in the objectivity of the image and a paradoxical concurrent "hunger for documentary images of the real" (as evidenced, for example, in the recent proliferation of camcorder cop shows and sensationalistic "news" magazines).[33] In this context, some documentary makers have responded by complicating their use of conventional realist strategies such as talking-head interviews and observational footage with scripted, performed, stylized, and overtly manipulated sequences to produce layered, multivalent perspectives on the real. While the resulting "New Documentaries" privilege subjectively experienced and interpreted truths over the assumption of objectivity that frames more traditional documentaries, they retain "a special interest in the relation to the real, the 'truths' which matter in people's lives but which cannot be transparently represented."[34]

Although *Silverlake Life* is not built around sequences as pointedly scripted as the multiple reenactments of Errol Morris's 1987 *The Thin Blue Line*, the poetic, rhythmic structure of *Tongues Untied*, or the whimsical fantasy sequences of *Thank You and Goodnight* (the closest analogue in the film is the lip-synching, choreographed epilogue from *Blackstar*), it nevertheless shares these films' passionately subjective approach to experiential truth. Despite at times employing the observational style of canonical direct cinema, *Silverlake Life* relies more heavily on the participatory method of cinema verité, using the camcorder to fulfill Rouch's prescient predictions of a "shared cinema."[35] This "participant camera" both instigates the performance of life in its midst and foregrounds the personally and politically inflected process of the film's production. As Williams argues, "the truth figured by documentary cannot be a simple unmasking or reflection. It is a careful construction, an intervention in the politics and the semiotics of representation."[36]

The resulting voice of *Silverlake Life* is the product of multiple authors, and it speaks to multiple audiences. The film's disarming, sometimes devastating immediacy is as much the result of skillful and deliberate shooting and editorial choices as of the riveting, all too true story it chronicles. By reconfiguring the relations among producers, subjects, and audiences, the film's multiple creators not only contributed new formal possibilities to the documentary genre, but also provide one more much needed site for examining identity and community formation for people living with AIDS and queer/lesbian/gay/bisexual/transgendered people.

◆──

NOTES

1. The controversy surrounding the PBS airing of Marlon Riggs's *Tongues Untied* (1989), in which he talks about how his own HIV-positive status has affected his life, further demonstrates the active silencing of such public articulations.

2. Joslin taught film at Hampshire College in the 1970s, and Friedman had been his student and protégé, and eventually became a close friend of the couple. Indeed, Joslin taught many students who went on to become prominent documentarians, including Ken Burns (*The Civil War* 1990; *Baseball* 1994) and Rob Epstein (*The Times of Harvey Milk* 1984; *Common Threads: Stories from the Quilt* 1989; *The Celluloid Closet* 1995).

3. Friedman viewed the footage again and again over a period of two months before finally committing to finish the film. See Susan Waugh, "Inside View," *Riverfront Times* (St. Louis), May 12–18, 1993, 32–33.

4. Interview with Peter Friedman by Patricia Leonardi, Peacock Cafe, New York, Oct. 22, 1993. Unpublished transcript.

5. Friedman's restructuring of the footage through editing was perhaps further complicated by the addition of producers Doug Block and Jane Weiner early in the editing process. The final round of editing to prepare the film for the Sundance Festival took place at Weiner's New York City apartment, and she spent many hours with Friedman in the editing room. See Peter Broderick, "Being There," *Filmmaker*, Spring, 1993, 38–39.

6. Thomas Waugh, "Lesbian and Gay Documentary: Minority Self-Imaging, Oppositional Film Practice, and the Question of Image Ethics," in *Image Ethics*, ed. Larry Gross, John Stuart Katz, and Jay Ruby (New York: Oxford University Press, 1988), 248–73.

7. See, for example, Robert Atkins, "Love Story," *Village Voice* 38.24 (June 15, 1993): 45; Peter Broderick, "Being There," *Filmmaker*, Spring 1993, 38–39; David Ehrenstein, "Life and Death in Silverlake," *Advocate*, March 9, 1993, 13–14; Kenneth Turan, "To Be Young, Vital, and Dying of AIDS," *Los Angeles Times*, March 14, 1993.

8. As Thomas Waugh notes, "Ever since Stonewall . . . documentary film has been a primary means by which lesbians and gay men have carried out their liberation struggle" (Waugh, "Lesbian and Gay Documentary," 248).

9. See Stephen Mamber, *Cinéma Vérité in America: Studies in Uncontrolled Documentary* (Cambridge, Mass.: MIT Press, 1974), and Bill Nichols, *Representing Reality* (Bloomington: Indiana University Press, 1991), especially "Documentary Modes of Representation," 32-75. The term *cinema verité* has been used by some critics and viewers to refer to both American direct cinema and French cinema verité. We have chosen to emphasize their distinctions by reserving *cinema verité* for Rouch's catalytic, interactive mode.

10. As Nichols argues, "observational cinema affords the viewer an opportunity to look in on and overhear something of the lived experience of others, to gain some sense of the distinct rhythms of everyday life, to see the colors, shapes, and spatial relationships among people and their possessions, to hear the intonation, inflection, and accents that give a spoken language its 'grain'" (Nichols, *Representing Reality*, 42).

11. See, for example, Brian Winston, "The Tradition of the Victim in Griersonian Documentary," reprinted in *New Challenges for Documentary*, ed. Alan Rosenthal (Berkeley: University of California Press, 1988), 269–88, and Annette Kuhn, "The Camera I: Observations on Documentary," *Screen* 19.2 (1978): 71–84.

12. See Brian Winston, "Direct Cinema: The Third Decade," in *New Challenges for Documentary*, 517–30.

13. Ibid., 528.

14. See Mick Eaton, ed. *Anthropology—Reality—Cinema: The Films of Jean Rouch* (London: British Film Institute, 1979), and Steven Feld, "Themes in the Cinema of Jean Rouch," *Visual Anthropology* 2.3–4 (1989): 223–49.

15. See Nichols, *Representing Reality*, 56.

16. See Linda Williams, "Mirrors without Memories: Truth, History, and the New Documentary," *Film Quarterly* 46.3 (1993): 9–21.

17. While *Silverlake Life* was released to festivals and theaters on film after a series of high-end technical permutations, it was originally shot on Hi-8 and Super-VHS video. See Lorri Shundich, "Peter Friedman, Documentarian: *Silverlake Life: The View from Here*," *Independent* 16.3 (April 1993): 14.

18. See Edgar Morin, "Chronicle of a Film," trans. Steven Feld and A. Ewing, *Studies in Visual Communication* 11.1 (1985): 4–30; Nichols, *Representing Reality*, 44–56; and Eaton, *Anthropology—Reality—Cinema*.

19. Jay Ruby discusses a group of late 1970s films that blend autobiographical subject matter with documentary form, noting the reflexive qualities that resulted from this combination. *Silverlake Life*'s documentary/diary form can be seen as building on this tradition. See Ruby, "The Image Mirrored: Reflexivity and the Documentary Film," reprinted in *New Challenges for Documentary*, 64–78.

20. Brian Winston, "The Tradition of the Victim ," 269–88.

21. Winston coins this rubric for films employing "an easy amalgam of handheld available-light sync shooting" (Winston, "Direct Cinema: The Third Decade," 518).

22. On television commercials and "reality TV" shows like *The Real World* and *Cops*, the camcorder image contrasts with the slick look of big-budget television and betokens unproduced, raw reality. In turn, comedies from *Saturday Night Live* to *Roseanne* have reflexively parodied this aesthetic by simulating the displays (e.g., "REC" and a flashing red light) in camcorder viewfinders. As more and more viewers acquire their own camcorders (the number in the United States totaled 16 million as of May 1994), this contradictory tendency for the camcorder "look" both to signal and to parody direct, untampered-with reality is exacerbated.

23. Leonardi interview.

24. For a reading of form and style in *Silverlake Life* that focuses on the blurring of genre boundaries, see Bill Nichols, *Blurred Boundaries: Questions of Meaning and Style in Contemporary Culture* (Bloomington: Indiana University Press, 1994), 10–11. Nichols asserts in the preface that "inevitably, the distinction between fact and fiction blurs when claims about reality get cast as narratives" (ix).

25. *Out of the Closets: Voices of Gay Liberation*, ed. Karla Jay and Allen Young (New York: New York University Press, 1992 [1972]).

26. Leonardi interview.

27. Both Marlon Riggs's *Non, je ne regrette rien* (1992) and Stashu Kybartas's *Danny* (1987) resist such implications. See Douglas Crimp, "Portraits of People with AIDS," in *Discourses of Sexuality: From Aristotle to AIDS*, ed. Domna Stanton (Ann Arbor: University of Michigan Press, 1992), 362–88; reprinted in *Cultural Studies*, ed. Lawrence Grossberg, Cary Nelson, and Paula Treichler (New York: Routledge, 1992), 117–31.

28. See Winston, "The Tradition of the Victim ," 269–88.

29. Certainly, *Philadelphia* (Jonathan Demme 1993) has been read in this way. The mainstream press coverage did not place it within a broader tradition of films about AIDS, rarely mentioning even previous feature films like *Longtime Companion* (1990), for which director Norman Rene received an Oscar nomination.

30. Biddy Martin, "Lesbian Identity and Autobiographical Difference[s]." In *The Lesbian and Gay Studies Reader*, ed. Henry Abelove, Michèle Aina Barale, and David Halperin (New York: Routledge, 1993), 274–93.

31. Crimp, "Portraits of People with AIDS," 362–88.
32. For further titles, see Alexandra Juhasz, *AIDS TV: Identity, Community, and Alternative Video* (Durham, N.C.: Duke University Press, 1995); Catherine Saalfield, "On the Make: Activist Video Collectives," in *Queer Looks: Lesbian and Gay Film and Video*, ed. Martha Gever, John Greyson, and Pratibha Parmar (New York: Routledge, 1993), 21–37; and catalogs by distributors such as San Francisco's Frameline and Chicago's Video Data Bank.
33. Williams, "Mirrors without Memories," 10.
34. Ibid., 13.
35. "Tomorrow will be the day of the self-regulating color videotape, of automatic video editing, of 'instant replay' of the recorded picture (immediate feedback). The dreams of Vertov and Flaherty will be combined into a mechanical 'cine-eye-ear' which is such a 'participant' camera that it will pass automatically into the hands of those who were, up to now, always in front of it" (Jean Rouch, "The Camera and Man," reprinted in *Anthropology—Reality—Cinema*, 63).
36. Williams, "Mirrors without Memories," 20.

JUSTIN WYATT

[**9**] *Autobiography, Home Movies,*
and Derek Jarman's History Lesson

The points of connection between the documentary film and the home movie are numerous and problematic. While the home movie does "document" a family or social event, it prompts a host of questions that complicate our understanding of the documentary form. Among the many "problem" areas are the unique production and reception situations represented by the home movie (usually made by a family member, often under imperfect technical circumstances, for other members of the family), the degree of mediation and simulation within the home movie (staging events and reactions directly for the camera), and the sociological significance of the form (the cultural and familial indoctrination offered by the home movie). These issues are multiplied by the diversity within the "genre" of home movies: a categorization of home movies must include film "portraits," travel movies, and attempts to recreate filmic narratives within the context of the family and the home.[1] Each of these home movie forms embodies a particular relationship between filmmaker and audience, between "truth" and "fiction."

Although British director Derek Jarman cites pioneers of independent film—Kenneth Anger, Maya Deren, Stan Brakhage, Michael Snow, and Andy Warhol—as influential to his aesthetic and to his goals as a filmmaker, the home movie is also a significant aesthetic influence.[2] Jarman's films do address certain narrational traits associated with the critical pantheon of independent directors; issues of cinematic duration, identification, and sexuality that have been integral to independent cinema also are central to Jarman's work. In terms of Jarman's own position within the world of the independent cinema, however, the integration of personal elements—particularly home movies—within the fictional worlds created in his films represents a significant intervention, both artistically and in terms of identity politics. By referencing his family's and his own past through home movies and published journals and then placing these materials against the elaborate and theatrical worlds within his films, Jarman is able to construct both a personal history and a history of gay life. Using home movies matched to fictional worlds and literary autobiography, Jarman can address issues related to the family, its institutional supports, and gay people. These issues have grown directly from his personal experience—particularly his experience of living with AIDS in a hostile and homophobic society.

While these cinematic "experiments"—mixing the fictional and non-fictional, cinematic and literary autobiography—are ongoing, Jarman develops "a new form of cinema," to use a phrase from the director, in the last decade of his work.[3] "Cinema" is actually a misnomer since Jarman's work crosses media, juxtaposing Super-8 mm, 35 mm film, video, and autobiographical memoirs detailing his experiences and the impetus for each project. Beginning in 1987 with *The Last of England*'s home movie footage, Jarman's films incorporate direct, personal experience—a cinematic diary—as a key structural element. Developing from his own response to the altered social and political climate created by AIDS, Jarman places his films and videos against published journals and his own increasingly visible media presence. The unique, mutually reinforcing structure of Jarman's creative works situates them beyond established media categories.

▶

The Last of England, Home Movies, and the Family

The Last of England is a nonlinear exploration of a barren, desolate urban area, strongly suggesting a postapocalyptic environment. Shot in Super-8 mm and 16 mm, blown up to 35 mm, the film offers images and sequences both disturbing and visually striking: a young punk smashes bottles in an abandoned warehouse, a laconic man in a dunce cap wanders through the sewers, a group of "survivors" is assassinated by a faceless guerrilla, a drunken yuppie gropes one of these guerrillas.[4] These diverse scenes are composed with varying shot lengths: images appear only for an instant or are held for a long time. The cutting augments the dislocation and disorientation created so strongly within this world by Jarman. Apart from these bizarre, theatrical set pieces centered on loss and forms of escape, the film contains footage that echoes a past existence, footage anchored clearly in the "real" world. At first, the appearance of this realistic action seems lost amid the surreal, nightmarish sequences. The real-life material recurs, however, and eventually it is distinct from the remainder of the film. Once it is identified as separate, the action recalls a home movie: a baby plays with a ball on a lawn; two young children pick roses for their mother; a large family gathers for supper as the mother carves the roast; a woman smiles at the camera, modestly hiding her face with her hand; a couple from the 1940s admires a magnificent mountain view in a snowy landscape.

Within the film, these moments are distinguishable as "home movies" in terms of both content and formal composition. As Patricia Erens notes, home movies are identifiable by two major traits: a high degree of self-awareness on the part of the subjects (waving, smiling, mugging) and a vast number of "mistakes" that reveal the amateur status of the filmmaker and the limitations of the equipment.[5] Such "mistakes" include continuity errors, jump cuts, lack of establishing shots, and varying light levels within the shots. On the level of "narrative," home movies are intimately connected, as the term indicates, to the home, the family, and events and actions constructed around both. This association is not accidental. Patricia Zimmermann documents the many connections between amateur filmmaking and the rise of the family in postwar America. With the move to the suburbs in this period, leisure also became decentralized, and the home became the site of leisure-time activity: "Promoting the family as the consummate form of recreational activity, the ideology of togetherness situated amateur filmmaking as 'home movies'—private films for the beatification and celebration of the home."[6] The footage in *The Last of England* adheres to both of these characteristics: action is centered around family events (dinnertime, vacations) and the home (playing in the garden, picking roses behind the house). The footage also betrays its origins through the cast: mother, father, and the children, who age as the footage progresses. These factors, added to the high degree of self-conscious display of the participants, the period settings, and the technical flaws, identify the footage as part of a home movie.

Although there is continuity in the action of the home movies as certain people and places recur, Jarman does not identify the time, place, or participants. Denying the viewer contextual information that would anchor the film, Jarman creates a "generic" home movie. This method contrasts with, for example, Jonas Mekas's adoption of the home movie in films such as *Lost Lost Lost* (1975) and *Paradise Not Yet Lost* (1979). Mekas also constructs family stories—*Paradise Not Yet Lost* charts the growth of his daughter Oona—but he carefully uses intertitles to identify the footage and meticulously follows chronological order.[7] Jarman's creative project depends not only on leaving the footage unidentified, but also on juxtaposing the footage with the hallucinatory sequences of desolation and abandonment. The placement of these sequences shapes the viewer's reception of both modes, the home movie and the experimental footage.[8] Through this structure, Jarman encourages viewers to consider the conventions of each mode.

On the one hand, the postapocalyptic world of terrorists and tattered brides is placed firmly in a time continuum, recalling a culture of fifty years past. The home movies suggest a memory for the various inhabitants of this nightmarish environment—perhaps of a perfect world now gone forever. The home movies also forge a strong point of connection for the viewer based on familiarity with the form of home movies and the generic "characters" who appear in them. Consequently, the theatrical, hallucinatory scenes are invested with a level of emotion as a result of their placement next to the home movie scenes. Without the home footage, the rest of the film could be construed as fantasy. The home movie footage deepens the viewer's emotional attachment to these scenes, offering a past that is immediately recognizable to the viewer as a home movie.

Simultaneously, though, the home movie footage reflects on and is shaped by the avant-garde footage. The effect is subtle, yet most significant. Since the theatrical footage depends so heavily on events varied, fantastic, and alien—a marriage in an abandoned warehouse, a crippled man pouring grain on himself from a bowler hat, two terrorists fucking on the British flag—the viewer forms no firm expectations about the content of future scenes other than that the theme of disintegration and despair will continue. As a result, Jarman creates a world in which the unexpected and the unusual become the norm. Since each episode is so starkly different from the previous one in terms of content, the viewer is receptive to new characters and action. The challenge is to seek the connections between these episodes, to forge a kind of meaning and causation that is not immediately obvious.

This process applies just as much to the home movie footage as to the more experimental material. Since the home movie footage is not identified as such within the film, the viewer initially "reads" the footage as just another episode, only later realizing that the action is aesthetically and thematically separate. In fact, it is part of a home movie. This means that for much of the film, the viewer interprets the home material from the 1920s and 1940s as if it were part of the postapocalyptic world. The result is curious: by "fooling" the viewer through the lack of explicit documentation and identification, Jarman encourages a defamiliarization of the home movie; the familiar is made unfamiliar given its placement with the other material. This feature is central to Jarman's ideological project: the home movies and, more significantly, the participants (the family, the home, the ritualized events associated with both) within these movies are constructed as the experimental world.

Jarman's choice of the home movie as an ideological target is astute. The media form can indoctrinate and educate the young into the family, its past, and acceptance of conventional forms of social interaction. As anthropologist Richard Chalfen writes, "Home movies serve participants as demonstration of cultural membership. Home moviemaking promotes the visual display of proper and expected behavior, of participation in socially approved activities, according to culturally approved value schemes."[9] Through juxtaposition of the two modes, Jarman questions these basic presuppositions, in effect asking what are "proper" and "expected" behaviors, and what are the implications of "cultural membership"? As a result, a home movie scene of a mother carving a roast at first seems macabre and menacing because it follows an array of desperate characters in the previous sequence. Even after the viewer recognizes the footage as "real," it retains an eerie and haunting quality, albeit on a different level. Instead of "reading" the action as part of the theatrical world, the viewer starts to contemplate the dynamics of the family on display in the home movie: Why is the mother grinning so broadly? What is the relationship between the people in this room? When did this scene take place? Where are these people today? The endless questions are inspired less by the footage than by the contrast with the other segments of the film.

The effect is similar to that experienced by filmmaker and theorist Michelle Citron. Reviewing her family's home movies, she found that they confounded her expectations:

> When I asked my father for the home movies, my request was motivated less by sentimental feelings and more by unpleasant memories. I somehow expected the movies to confirm my family's convoluted dynamics. But when I finally viewed them after a ten year hiatus, I was surprised that the smiling family portrayed had no correspondence to the family preserved in my childhood memories.[10]

Citron's expectations are, however, fulfilled through a close examination of the footage that reveals other emotional and psychological dynamics at play: "Under the scrutiny of slow motion, a casual movement of my mother's hand became an agonizingly intrusive and possessive gesture, my funny jostle against my sister was actually hostile."[11] Slow motion here is comparable to Jarman's editing pattern: just as slow motion forces consideration of other meanings within the scene, Jarman's editing provokes a reading of the home movies beyond their most obvious or apparent meaning.

The questioning of the family unit posed by this structure is augmented by a series of episodes in the experimental section centered on rituals involving the family and home life. Following in the tradition of filmmakers such as Kenneth Anger, Andy Warhol, and James Broughton, these sequences evoke the icons of courtship and marriage rituals in a homosexual context.[12] In *The Last of England*, one of the "narrative" strands involves a wedding presided over by bearded male bridesmaids, and a baby wrapped in the *Sun,* a tabloid newspaper. The female bride appears in a later sequence, crying in despair, cutting her wedding dress with scissors. These scenes do not offer parodies of the home movies, but rather another route through which the family and the home are seen as constructed, as exotic, as *not* "natural."

While the family unit may be constructed, the power behind this construction derives from institutional supports and structures that are similarly developed and maintained. These supports have been mobilized against gays and lesbians, most recently under the guise of "family values." As philosopher Richard Mohr writes, "The stereotype of gay men as child molesters, sex-crazed maniacs, and civilization destroyers . . . serves to give the family unit a false sheen of absolute innocence. It keeps the unit from being examined too closely for incest, child abuse, wife battering, and the terrorism of constant threats."[13] The propagation of gay and lesbian stereotypes strengthens the traditional family unit through the "otherness" of homosexuality. Jarman's project depends in part, then, on erasing this equation, on demystifying the family and its relation to persons who are supposedly other.[14] Simultaneously, as another approach to the issue of the family, a considerable literature has addressed the meanings of "family" from gay and lesbian perspectives: either negotiating a role(s) within heterosexual, patriarchal family structures (such as Paul Monette's *Becoming a Man: Half a Life Story* and John Preston's anthology *A Member of the Family*) or establishing a family unit separate from the heterosexual norm (such as Kath Weston's *Families We Choose: Lesbians, Gays, Kinship*).[15]

▶

The Last of England, Extratextual Readings, and Writing History

The ambivalence with which Jarman views the family becomes even more pronounced given the extratextual material supporting the film. More specifically, Jarman has woven the personal and political together in a series of published journals: *Dancing Ledge* (1984), *The Last of England* (1987), *Modern Nature* (1992), and *At Your Own Risk* (1993).[16] These journals recount Jarman's daily experiences as a filmmaker, a Brit, and a gay man; his efforts to raise funds for his films; and the dreams, visions, and motivations behind each of his creative projects. In terms of content, the journals run the gamut from the banal (horticultural hints, weather reports, musings on British politics) to the intensely personal (the day-to-day experiences of living HIV-positive). In particular, Jarman is interested in reconciling the events of his past. For instance, the final volume (*At Your Own Risk*) is

The Last of England (Derek Jarman 1987). Courtesy Museum of Modern Art Film Stills Archive

organized decade by decade, from the 1940s through the 1990s, as a series of reminiscences on his concurrent socialization within and alienation from mainstream society. As Jarman states in the introduction, "My book is a series of introductions to matters and agendas unfinished. Like memory, it has gaps, amnesia, fragments of the past, fractured present. To those who have not lived it, it might appear opaque; those of us who are living it will recognize the map."[17]

By leaving these matters and agendas unfinished, Jarman unveils his family, particularly his ex-RAF father and his creative mother stifled by life in the suburbs. He also reveals the importance of home movies to his family. Indeed, in Jarman's book the footage from *The Last of England* is credited to his grandfather, Harry Puttrock, in the late 1920s and to his father, Lance Jarman, in the 1940s.[18] Derek Jarman seized the family footage after his aunt lost several reels of the earlier footage. As he writes, "I was so unhappy about this, I carried the remaining film with me on one of my visits home, copied what was left onto video, and never returned the originals."[19] The home movies from *The Last of England* become most defiantly his home movies, starring his family, with Derek as baby, toddler, and child. The explicit labeling of the home movies in the journals is significant for several reasons. Most fundamentally, the labeling establishes that history is being constructed, simultaneously Jarman's history (a personal history) and gay history (a political history). This attempt to write history responds to the increased stakes that AIDS has imposed on one part of the gay community, leading to a surge of cultural products that could be described as gay. After more than a decade of adversity imposed by disease and dominant society, addressing AIDS as an issue connects tightly to media representation of gay and lesbian life. Work from the margins has sought to critique the dominant media's representation of AIDS and, by extension, their representation of homosexuality. Jarman tested HIV-positive on December 22, 1986, and his subsequent writings are integral to the reception of his films and videos.[20]

Jarman's media work (film and autobiography) contributes his personal history as one part of a larger gay history that can be pieced together through works on social construction, essential difference, and culture.[21] This goal parallels those of many other films and videos that have attempted to reconsider gay identity through examining the past and addressing the present. Consider, for example, projects that reevaluate the past to comment on the current environment for gay people: Stuart Marshall's presentation of German lesbians and gays living under the Nazi regime in *Bright Eyes* (1986) and *Desire* (1989); Mark Christopher's fantasy of a contemporary student's trip to the (pre-AIDS) 1970s New York gay life in *The Dead Boys' Club* (1992); and John Greyson's imaginary meeting of historical gay artists—Sergei Eisenstein, Langston Hughes, Frida Kahlo, Yukio Mishima—to combat oppressive anti-gay Canadian laws in *Urinal* (1989).[22] Alternately, projects that address contemporary gay and lesbian existence, often under the influence of AIDS, include activist documentaries (*Voices from the Front* [1991], *Stop the Church* [1990], *Laura, Ingrid, and Rebecca* [1990]) and biographies (*Postcards from America* [1994] based on the life and writings of David Wojnarowicz and the film of Ron Vawter's performance piece *Roy Cohn/Jack Smith* [1994]).

Jarman's approach to writing history—contrasting indeterminate time periods and events through his editing—echoes Fredric Jameson's distinction between history and historicism, the latter defined as "the random cannibalization of all styles of the past, the play of random stylistic allusion."[23] This play, in turn, reflects the fragmentation of the subject, undermining both the unity and the uniqueness of the individual style. Jarman's film falls well within the parameters of historicism as defined by Jameson. Indeed, the connection between the theatrical events and the home movies, between "real" time and "imagined" time, and between Jarman's family and the fictional characters constitutes, in Jameson's terms, "a desperate attempt to appropriate a missing past."[24] Jarman's formal and thematic juxtapositions suggest one way to write history in an age of postmodern cultural production.

Considered in conjunction with the film, therefore, literary auto-biographies act as a form of empowerment by addressing the construction of homosexuality through familial and social pressures.[25] Following from such a reading, *The Last of England* could be an extended metaphor for AIDS, in which the postapocalyptic world represents our current social environment dividing those who are "safe" from those who are HIV-positive. In this context, the film becomes less oblique, and the links between oppression and sexuality are explained. Nevertheless, the true difference of Jarman's "new form of cinema" lies in the varying interpretations of the film that depend on familiarity with and appreciation of Jarman's literary journals. For those who have read the journals, the film becomes a doctrine on AIDS informed by personal history and a strong ideological position. For those unfamiliar with Jarman's written work, the film works on a more visceral level, destabilizing our understanding of the home movie, the family, and rigid social roles.

▶

Extending the Project: Jarman's Trilogy

Duncan Petrie suggests that *The Last of England* and Jarman's subsequent films *The Garden* (1990) and *Blue* (1993) form a trilogy, all three stressing Jarman's deepening obsessions both with the past and with the present of living with AIDS.[26] This connection is perhaps overstated, though there are significant formal parallels among the three works.[27] Like *The Last of England*, *The Garden* is composed of disparate episodes, with set pieces varying from a production number of Gershwin's "Think Pink" (against the background of a gay pride parade) to murderous paparazzi attacking a mother and child. The film achieves coherence through the framing device of Jarman at home in Dungeness—tending to his garden, falling asleep at his study, writing in his journal—and through the structuring of the remaining episodes around a biblical theme, the life and death of Jesus. In this context, though, Jesus is replaced by two gay lovers, allowing Jarman to address directly the rise of homophobia in the advent of AIDS. Several sequences are devoted to the persecution of the lovers, most vividly a lengthy police interrogation in which the boys are literally tarred and feathered.

While Jarman does appear in *The Last of England*, apart from childhood shots in the home movie footage his physical presence is limited mainly to shots of him writing, implying that he is "composing" the film. These scenes become significantly more elaborate in *The Garden*. Since this film is centered primarily on Jarman's garden and home and the seaside nearby, more shots of him are laced throughout it; he even, on occasion, places himself within the fantasy framework. Indeed, one of the most visually arresting sequences illustrates a Jarman fantasy or nightmare resulting from his illness. The scene shows the director shivering, naked in a bed placed in the ocean. Circling the bed are "angels" in white robes leading a vigil around the weary and weakened Jarman.

The home movie footage in *The Last of England* is missing in *The Garden*, although Jarman echoes the structure of his previous film by invoking the form of the home movie. For instance, near the beginning of *The Garden*, the two lovers walk along the seaside, eventually lying on the beach for a romantic interlude. The sequence is shot in Super-8, and Jarman allows the noise of the camera recording the scene to dominate the sound track. The faux amateur quality suggests a home movie, as the composition of *The Last of England* does. The home and the family are also central to *The Garden*, which focuses directly on the home, its constitution, and a family consisting of the two male lovers and a young child. While the home movie referencing of *The Last of England* is not repeated throughout *The Garden*, I would argue that a similar method of "reading" is encouraged by Jarman through the alternation of the fantastic set pieces with the placid shots of Jarman at home and through the strong correspondence between the Jarman journals and the home action evidenced in the film.

Both films differ from Jarman's *Blue*, a seventy-five-minute feature of a single blue screen, inspired by the work of French painter Yves Klein. The film extends into the realm of the personal even further through symbolizing Jarman's AIDS-related blindness. On the sound track, Jarman alternates anecdotes from his daily experience of living with AIDS and lyrical meditations on the themes of serenity and loss. Many of these meditations take the color blue as a starting point, seeking the connections between the metaphorical implications of the color and his own memories, feelings, and regrets. These passages evidence Jarman at his most introspective, turning again and again to his past and to his function as an artist. Through these segments, Jarman becomes empowered, physically and intellectually, by exploring the connections among imagination, memory, and artistic creation. The structure of the piece and the movement between the meditations and medical details respond to a question that Jarman poses in *Blue*: "If I lose my sight will my vision be halved?" Blue demonstrates that his "vision" was not impaired in the slightest.

As AIDS became an increasing threat to Jarman's physical well-being, the personal elements, such as the home movie structures and references to his family in *The Last of England* and *The Garden*, transform into a focus on Jarman himself. Following from this shift, AIDS is no longer alluded to indirectly, but instead constitutes the primary focus of *Blue*. Jarman's changing relation to AIDS is evident through interviews with the media, from a certain wry detachment ("I've conquered HIV, so why not make a film about that") to acceptance of his own mortality ("I shall not win the battle against the virus, in spite of slogans like, 'Living With AIDS'—symptomatic of a society that cannot come to terms with death").[28]

Like *The Last of England*, *Blue* extends our understanding of documentary cinema, principally through the linking of the sound track to a static screen. Jeffrey Ruoff writes in "Conventions of Sound in Documentary" that recent documentaries, such as *Roger & Me* (1989) and *Lightning over Braddock* (1988), "have rediscovered the possibilities of voice-over narration, using personal, ironic, and interpretive commentary to counterpoint the synchronous images and sounds."[29] With *Blue*, the voice-over narration is even more significant than in other documentaries since the "narrative" is driven entirely by the audio track rather than by a match of audio to visuals. Jarman and sound designer Simon Fisher Turner expand the possibilities for the sound track of Jarman's "documentary" by varying the relationship between Jarman's voice-over narration and a secondary audio track of sound effects.

The challenge to the viewer/listener is announced immediately. *Blue* opens with a series of notes, each one minutely different from the last. The notes form a series that is then repeated. The effect is twofold: the subtle differences between the notes suggest that the viewer must listen with care (in a heightened state of reception, as Jarman is forced to), and the series itself implies that, while the notes are separate, each is linked to the next. A continuity is established. Following the structure suggested by this opening, *Blue* is composed of a series of incidents, anecdotes, and reminiscences, largely addressing the experience of living with AIDS. Each episode is distinct, yet they are all related to Jarman's experience of living with AIDS. While they are separate, the episodes also achieve power through accumulation. As well as delineating the structure, the opening series suggests a hearing test, referring to the medical discourse on AIDS within the film. The scale uncovers the diverse ways through which Jarman and Turner construct the sound track. Jarman manipulates the sound track, at times using sound effects to reinforce the voice-over narration, at other times replacing the voice-over narration altogether (offering the "aural" equivalent of the virus). Most distinctively, Jarman foregrounds his own control and manipulation of the sound track. For instance, describing a visual test, Jarman states that the doctor tells him to "look up, look down"; another voice (the doctor) repeats the instructions. Jarman controls all he hears, structuring the sound track according to his memory, imagination, and dreams. As his visual sense diminishes, the aural gains precedence.

While *Blue*'s experiential uniqueness for the viewer separates it from the other films, Jarman's uncompromising political stance nevertheless connects it to his previous work. On the most fundamental level, the physical limitation imposed on Jarman—his loss of vision—is suggested to the viewer by the single, unchanging blue screen. The analogy is imperfect, of course, since the viewer can choose to turn away from the screen at any time. While Jarman argues for the hope implicit in the blue screen, a monochromatic screen also restricts the viewer's visual pleasure.[30] In this manner, the film is much more challenging for the viewer than those invoking the specter of AIDS through commercially acceptable, recuperable narratives. Jarman's meditation on AIDS traced throughout all three films, via the home movie format and the monochromatic film, continues the tradition of gay and lesbian filmmakers who feel that they cannot express themselves within conventional narrative terms.

Of course, Jarman is not alone in responding via film, video, and literature to AIDS and the toll the phenomenon has exacted on gays and lesbians. Certainly some of the most formally experimental work of the past several years—Marlon Riggs's *Tongues Untied* (1989) and *No Regret (Non, je ne regrette rien)* (1992), Todd Haynes's *Poison* (1991), Gregg Bordowitz's *Fast Trip, Long Drop* (1993), along with Jarman's works—evidences the range and diversity to which narrative and stylistic codes can be manipulated in video and film.[31] The deviation of these codes from conventional and commercial storytelling allows the filmmakers to address issues far "beyond" the arena of Hollywood filmmaking. Jarman's specific intervention, both within this set of creative work and within the larger framework of gay and lesbian cinema, is based first and foremost on how he has responded to AIDS through his creative projects—particularly the integration in his films of his political activism with direct personal experience. The starting point for this new phase was offered by the artist's return to the home movies central to *The Last of England*. Each subsequent work refines the model instituted by Jarman in this film by placing his personal experience with AIDS against a symbolic, often surreal environment.[32] All three engage viewers at different levels depending on their knowledge of Jarman's writings and published journals. Of the three, though, *The Last of England*, reliant on the generic home movie as a structuring device, may function most potently as a text about personal development, (homo)sexuality, and AIDS, since Jarman refuses to limit the possible meanings associated with the film. The marginalization, exclusion, and persecution experienced by the survivors in the film appeals to viewers' personal experience(s) of discrimination. Of course, viewers' own encounters with discrimination may not pertain to sexuality, as is the case in so many of Jarman's films.

Regardless of viewers' particular connection with discrimination, the film elicits a range of responses, most centered on the individual's empathy with the survivors in the film.

Although gays and lesbians may be more likely to read Jarman's journals, the suggestion of different readings dependent on familiarity with extratextual material does not collapse simply into a gay (or queer) versus straight interpretation of the film.[33] Alexander Doty warns of the dangers of this model: to view gay texts only in relation to dominant society is "to perpetuate our [queer] status as subcultural, parasitic, self-oppressive hangers-on."[34] Since *The Last of England* is so open in its narrative and aesthetic strategies, it is entirely unclear how one would position either a dominant or an oppositional reading of the text. Therefore, the utility of specifying straight (dominant) and queer (oppositional) readings is extremely limited in this case. Rather, as I have suggested, the reception of the film can be shaped by the viewer's familiarity with Jarman's writings and other creative projects.

Even for the uninitiated, the film operates as a significant lesson on the AIDS epidemic. Through establishing a link between the family (in the home movies) and the totalitarian society, Jarman makes viewers question established social roles and the structures that support them. Such a line of inquiry could be applied productively to the AIDS epidemic to unharness the social structures that stigmatize those who are affected and hamper the development of funding for treatment, care, and research. Jarman's work falls between media boundaries, with interpretation varying according to the viewer's familiarity with the context of production. Consequently, his projects cannot be dismissed by mainstream society in the same way that cultural products confronting AIDS more explicitly are. Nevertheless, labeling in other ways—audiences categorizing his projects as experimental or alternative media—could still set boundaries for Jarman's work.

In conclusion, consider another adoption of Jarman's home movies, in Annie Lennox's video "Ev'ry Time We Say Goodbye" for the AIDS research and relief video/music project *Red, Hot & Blue*, a coalition of musical artists covering Cole Porter songs to raise money for AIDS.[35] Set in a space suggesting a den or a family room, the video appropriates Jarman's home movie images (the children playing in the garden with their mother, the family at the beach) projected either onto Lennox's body or on a stark white wall. While the video is moving, specifically in the context of an AIDS artistic project, the piece lacks the power, the complexity, and the ideological project inherent in Jarman's mass media work.[36] In part this is due to the video forcing a single reaction from the viewer: the song's melancholy lyrics, the nostalgic imagery, the tear running down Lennox's cheek, and the context of the video within the AIDS education project are mutually reinforcing. *The Last of England*, on the other hand, multiplies the possible meanings of the home footage, with interpretations destabilizing social roles, stigmatization, and the family. While Lennox's borrowing of the home footage causes a temporary sadness, soon forgotten, Jarman's own appropriation argues fervently for gay culture, politics, and humanity in the face of AIDS. The permanence of this intervention is constituted not just by the formal experimentation, but more prominently by the manner in which Jarman's work clarifies and extends an appreciation of creativity amid courage, pain, and a collective political battle.

NOTES

I wish to thank Chris Lippard and the editors for comments on an earlier version of this manuscript.

1. Fred Camper, "Some Notes on the Home Movie," *Journal of Film and Video* 38.3–4 (Summer/Fall 1986): 10.
2. Dennis Cooper, "The Queer King: Derek Jarman and the New Gay Film," *LA Weekly*, April 10, 1992, 22.
3. Jarman died in 1994 at the age of 52.
4. For an analysis of the economic determinants of Jarman's technological choices, see Duncan Petrie, *Creativity and Constraint in the British Film Industry* (London: Macmillan, 1991), 200–202. Petrie discusses the collaborative nature of Jarman's work and the fact that this aspect meant "the collection of material was often freer than is usually the case on a production tightly controlled by the strictures of schedule and budget" (202).
5. Patricia Erens, "The Galler Home Movies: A Case Study," *Journal of Film and Video* 38.3–4 (Summer/Fall 1986): 17.
6. Patricia Zimmermann, "Hollywood, Home Movies, and Common Sense: Amateur Film as Aesthetic Dissemination and Social Control, 1950–1962," *Cinema Journal* 27.4 (Summer 1988): 25.
7. Jeffrey Ruoff describes the stylistic and contextual features that serve to anchor Mekas's home movies in "Home Movies of the Avant-Garde: Jonas Mekas and the New York Art World," *Cinema Journal* 30.3 (Spring 1991): 6–28.
8. I am referring to the fantastic, constructed footage as alternately avant-garde and experimental. Each term has a specific historical definition, although, as Jonas Mekas notes, after 1960 various descriptors — avant-garde, experimental, personal, individual film, independent film — were used synonymously. See Mekas's "Independence for Independents," *American Film*, September 1978, 38–40.
9. Richard Chalfen, "The Home Movie in a World of Reports: An Anthropological Appreciation," *Journal of Film and Video* 38.3–4 (Summer/Fall 1986): 106.
10. Michelle Citron, "Concerning *Daughter Rite*," *Journal of Film and Video* 38.3–4 (Summer/Fall 1986): 93.
11. Ibid., 94.
12. In this realm, Jarman's film most strongly echoes James Broughton and Joel Singer's *Devotions* (1983). Against the anarchic background of bearded nuns, culinary leathermen, and penile rock gardens, Broughton and Singer replay courtship clichés and scenes of domestic routine in a gay context. Unlike Jarman, though, they create an effect of normalcy, calm, and order through these familiar scenes transposed to gay life.
13. Richard Mohr, *Gay Ideas: Outing and Other Controversies* (Boston: Beacon, 1992), 255.
14. Larry Kramer's play *The Destiny of Me* (New York: Plume, 1993), the sequel to his seminal *The Normal Heart*, explores similar territory. Activist Ned Weeks, undergoing experimental AIDS treatments, interacts with his family from three decades earlier. Weeks must be reconciled to the patriarchal abuses against his teenage self in order to accept medical treatment and continue his activist battle.
15. Paul Monette, *Becoming a Man: Half a Life Story* (New York: Harcourt Brace Jovanovich, 1992); John Preston, ed., *A Member of the Family: Gay Men Write about Their Families* (New York: Dutton, 1992); Kath Weston, *Families We Choose: Lesbians, Gays, Kinship* (New York: Columbia University Press, 1991).
16. *Dancing Ledge* (London: Quartet, 1984); *The Last of England* (London: Constable, 1987);

Modern Nature (London: Vintage, 1991); *At Your Own Risk* (London: Vintage, 1993).

17. Jarman, *At Your Own Risk*, 5.

18. Jarman, *The Last of England*, 176.

19. Ibid., 176.

20. Jarman, *At Your Own Risk*, 95. Jarman explicitly places his own work within the creative production of artists writing and producing art works dealing with AIDS. He even reprints announcements and anecdotes from these other writers in his published journals. The appendix to *At Your Own Risk* begins, for example, "While I was writing this book, I was in touch with friends who are involved in the struggle for civil rights. Many of them sent me information and the best way to include it was to publish what they had written" (135).

21. Thomas Piontek addresses this body of gay cultural criticism in "Unsafe Representations: Cultural Criticism in the Age of AIDS," *Discourse* 15.1 (Fall 1992): 128–53.

22. Other examples of recent films and videos centered on gay and lesbian history, although not on AIDS, are *Before Stonewall* (Schiller, Rosenberg 1984), *When There Was Silence* (Stephen Bourne 1988), *Strip Jack Naked* (Ron Peck 1991), and *Last Call at Maud's* (Paris Poirier 1993).

23. Fredric Jameson, "Postmodernism, or The Cultural Logic of Late Capitalism," in *Postmodernism*, ed. Thomas Docherty (New York: Columbia University Press, 1993), 74.

24. Ibid., 75.

25. For an explanation of the basic presuppositions of this theory, see Mildred Dickemann's "Reproductive Strategies and Gender Construction: An Evolutionary View of Homosexualities," *Journal of Homosexuality* 24.3 (1993): 55–71. Dickemann rejects a genetic basis for homosexuality in favor of social, and particularly familial, factors. As Dickemann comments, "All sexuality is in part situational—the product of the interaction of familial and social pressures, social opportunities, and individual temperament and experience" (65).

26. Duncan Petrie, quoted in *Blue* press release, Zeitgeist Films, 247 Centre Street, New York, NY 10013.

27. *Aria*, a feature-length collection of opera "shorts" made in 1987, contains a drama by Jarman inspired by Charpentier's aria "Depuis le jour." Jarman's story concerns an aged woman recalling an affair from many years ago. Using Super-8 footage to evoke time past, the piece contains many strong parallels with *The Last of England*, made in the same year. For a discussion of Jarman's contribution to the work, see Guy Phelps,

"Omnibus or What's Opera, Don?" *Sight & Sound* 56.2 (Spring 1987): 192.

28. Cooper, "The Queer King," 22, and Paul Burston, "Blue Yonder," *Time Out*, August 18, 1993, 21.

29. Jeffrey Ruoff, "Conventions of Sound in Documentary," in *Sound Theory Sound Practice*, ed. Rick Altman (New York: Routledge, 1992), 222.

30. As Jarman explains regarding his choice of blue as a basis for the film, "Where are you when all you have in front of you is blue? You are before infinity" (Ken Shulman, "When Creation Fills a Deathly Silence," *New York Times*, Oct. 3, 1993, H13).

31. An examination of this topic, covering films and videos through 1993, is offered in my article "College Course Film: AIDS, the Mass Media, and Cultural Politics," *Journal of Film and Video* 45.2–3 (Summer/Fall 1993): 91–105.

32. *Glitterbug*, completed in early 1994 by David Lewis, editor Andy Crabb, and Jarman, as the nominal director, offers the counterpart to *Blue*: a barrage of images from Jarman's home movies shot between 1970 and 1985, with the sound track free of voice-over narration. Brian Eno provides a musical score for the film. Originally shown on the BBC, *Glitterbug* has not received distribution within North America. Interestingly, *Variety*'s review contrasts two versions of the film, one without titles placing the time, place, and people within the home movies, and one with titles added by the BBC. Critic David Rooney comments that "the definitive version, however, contains no commentary apart from Eno's music" (*Variety*, May 4, 1994, 10).

33. The difference between gay, lesbian, bisexual, and queer readings, a very thorny issue, is addressed by Alexander Doty in "There's Something Queer Here" in his book *Making Things Perfectly Queer: Interpreting Mass Culture* (Minneapolis: University of Minnesota Press, 1993). Doty suggests that "queer" readings are open to all—gays, lesbians, straights—as a particular kind of mass culture reception practice. Doty uses the term *queer* to mark a flexible space for the expression of all aspects of non- (anti-, contra-) straight cultural production and reception" (3).

34. Doty, *Making Things Perfectly Queer*, 104.

35. Derek Jarman, *Queer Edward II* (London: British Film Institute, 1991), 62.

36. Jarman would later appropriate both Lennox and the song for a key sequence in *Edward II* (1992) in which the fourteenth-century British monarch Edward II and his lover Gaveston dance before Gaveston is banished from England.

Mirrors

LYNDA GOLDSTEIN

[10] *Getting into Lesbian Shorts:*
White Spectators and Performative
Documentaries by Makers of Color

▶

Getting into Lesbian Shorts

> *Border crossings are always trouble. First of all, who's in*
> *control? Second of all, is it dangerous? And finally, do you*
> *have the courage to go across?*[1]

A friend wrote after the San Francisco International Lesbian and Gay Film
Festival in 1994 that she simply "couldn't get into these damn lesbian
shorts." I laughed aloud at her annoyance with the programming, which
simultaneously evoked Jesse Helms's calling Roberta Achtenberg a "damn
lesbian,"[2] frustrated sexual desire, and unavailable tickets to sold-out programs, however unintended these meanings might have been. What she
had meant was that her ability to "get into" the shorts was thwarted by the
low production values, murky visual and audio quality, and amateur performances—no matter how aesthetically justified and financially motivated.
Combined with loopy, antinarrative structures and cut-and-splice mixing
of fiction and documentary, these formal characteristics can limit access for
audience members invested in narrative logic or the referential reality effect
of traditional documentary. But the reading process of "getting into" lesbian shorts also indicates the convoluted cultural territory mapped out between spectators and performative documentary film and video shorts.
How, especially, might white lesbian spectators "get into" the contentious
gender and sexual identity politics and articulations of sexual desire gener-
ated by lesbian documentary film and video makers of color?[3]

Watching documentaries by lesbians of color, white lesbian viewers
must traverse culturally coded racial and ethnic differences, most often
within the context of queer film and video festivals that are at once cultural,

social, and political occasions.[4] One result is that whiteness, too, is constructed as a raced and queer experience. In what follows, I concentrate on four short works, Dawn Suggs's *I Never Danced the Way Girls Were Supposed To* (1992), Yvonne Welbon's *Sisters in the Life* (1993), Cheryl Dunye's *Greetings from Africa* (1994), and Mari Keiko Gonzalez's *Love Thang Trilogy* (1994). Combining fictional and autobiographical narratives of adolescent love, passing, racism, homophobia, interracial/ethnic desire, steamy sex, and coming out to parents, these texts navigate the frequently troublesome territory of erotic and political affinities between women (as daughters, friends, lovers, and "sisters"). Addressing their audiences with humor, wit, and irony, these works facilitate access into specifically raced/ethnic lesbian identities and desires.[5]

▶
_____

Performative Violations

Our identities are sources of pleasure as well as oppression.[6]

Performative documentary films and videos, Bill Nichols writes, use techniques more typically associated with lyrical film and video making: layered voice-overs, reconstructed and visibly staged "memories," and claustrophobic or jerky camera work. They document the emotional reality of a particular subject's experiences while simultaneously making connections to the social, cultural, and political world in which that subject is historically situated. This means that the film or video maker can document the experience and identity of a subject with marked racial, gender, and sexual differences in ways different from those of conventional documentary, which is less concerned with subjective realities. Viewers, then, can come to an affective and critical understanding of both a particular subject and themselves in the moment of viewing.

According to Nichols, the perpetual reinvention of "real," embodied, particular subjects in such works speaks to the viewer (often through direct address, dream sequences, and so on) in ways that "make the viewer rather than the historical world a primary referent."[7] Importantly, this referencing of the viewer is accomplished within a larger sense of shared social or political purpose. Yet this primary referencing of the spectator frequently also functions as a troublesome incursion upon that viewer's sense of self. Trinh T. Minh-ha insists that "[a] subject who points to him or herself as subject-in-process, [or] a work that displays its own formal properties or its own constitution as work, is bound to upset one's sense of identity."[8]

Performative documentary not only makes visible the instability of the textual subject but also inevitably produces reconfigurations of the viewer's sense of self. Racial/ethnic border crossings in particular complicate a viewer's affinities with the subject, as Nichols would agree. However, his analysis of performative documentary is focused on textual performances with little exploration of *contextual* performances. Surely, border violations in and around "raced" or "ethnic" subjects can be celebratory as well as troubling, especially when they occur at queer film and video festivals that privilege the immediacy of an imagined community. Indeed, the makers discussed here predicate any knowledge about the represented subject on an affective relationship with an imagined lesbian viewer, even though that "real" viewer may not articulate his or her identity as "lesbian." They in/directly appeal to viewers' experiences *as* lesbians within particular and historically situated hip, urban, multicultural women's communities, forming affinities between the textual subject(s) and viewers along lines of erotic and political sensibilities, and shared senses of style and humor.

By extending Nichols's analysis to white lesbian readings of lesbian shorts by women of color within the context of film and video festivals, I am not arguing for some simple simpatico relationship between white audience members and the lesbians of color represented by the texts. Rather, I am arguing that white lesbians who "get into" these shorts do so within a viewing community founded on a deeply entwined relationship between (inter)racial erotics and politics. Pleasurably implicating white lesbian viewers in this relationship while highlighting their whiteness (often by exclusion), the texts construct a sort of troubling yet celebratory borderland in which race and queerness are simultaneously eroticized and politicized. And they do this not as individual texts but as performative players in a specific context.

▶───────────────────────────────────────

Contexts of Reception

> We very rarely ever belong exclusively to one homogeneous and monolithic community, and . . . for most of us, everyday life is a matter of passing through, traveling between, and negotiating a plurality of different spaces.[9]

Often grouped with other shorts at popular international queer film and video events, performative documentaries are read by and within a community bearing witness to itself: as Martha Gever writes, "our identities are constituted as much in the event as in the images we watch."[10] Indeed, many festivals in larger cities such as Berlin, Toronto, New York, Chicago,

Washington, D.C., and San Francisco have become tourist destinations for mostly white and middle-class vacationing queers seeking ready-made communities in which to spend their leisure time. These imagined communities are constructed along fairly specific borderlines of gender, sexuality, and race in terms of audience composition (a matter of economic and cultural access favoring whites, gay men, urban dwellers, middle-class consumers, and media literates). To "vacation" at a queer film and video festival is necessarily to be positioned as queer within its dominant cultural event-ness. But it is also a markedly temporary and contingent positioning, sure to shift when one's "vacation" ends.

The specific borderlines of the festival community are usually formed by the theme- and gender-specific programming of features and shorts. In fact, sexual identity is constructed *as* theme so that most lesbian shorts, like their gay male counterparts, are grouped with others under obvious (or not so obvious) programming titles such as "Wicked Women" or "Girls Night Out."[11] Such titles help audiences more readily identify the thematic content of the queer video packages they are about to watch/consume.[12] Even when the titles themselves do not promise a gender-specific package, dykes can be seen filing in at 9 P.M. for "Fluttering Objects," as gay boys leave the 7 P.M. program of "Bodies and Body Doubles."[13]

Programming, of course, is also often race/ethnic-specific, designed to appeal to an audience of color or at least one concerned with the intersections of race and queer/lesbian sexuality.[14] During the 1980s, however, programming more often effaced racial/ethnic identities by constituting "lesbian programming" primarily in terms of a "vanilla" sexual identity, producing a lesbian subject that was effectively constructed as unmarked, as "white"—even when works by lesbians of color were included in a general package—and as nonsexual. Commenting on the ubiquity of lesbian representations as "vanilla" throughout the 1980s, filmmaker Cheryl Dunye explains in *Vanilla Sex* (1992) that she was initially puzzled when she heard white lesbians use the term "vanilla sex" to describe erotic play without toys. Lesbians of color she knows who speak of "vanilla sex" are less interested in categorizing specific sexual practices than in referring to sex with white women.

▶

Thinking through Race

> Precisely because of our lived experiences of discrimination
> in and exclusion from the white gay and lesbian community,
> and of discrimination in and exclusions from the black

> community, we locate ourselves in the spaces between
> different communities.[15]

Certainly, a direct, in-your-face infusion of sexual identity politics in works by lesbians of color has served as a corrective to erasures of race/ethnicity and sexuality.[16] Representing themselves in films and videos, and calling attention to eroticism and a wider variety of sexual practices, these makers indicate the extent to which whiteness itself has operated as a visibly (un)marked and unremarked upon category for white lesbian film and video makers and audiences.[17] When these works are programmed together with other shorts raising similar questions, it becomes impossible for white tourists, in particular, to overlook the gender and racial borderlines along which queer "community" is constructed and celebrated at these festivals.[18] Thus, while Bill Nichols may lament an "absence of a specifically political frame within which performative documentary might be received,"[19] I would argue that queer film and video festivals serve, at least in part, as such a political frame in which to read and become "queer."

Indeed, recent changes in programming formats at New York's Mix 94, for example, grouped film and video shorts by both men and women under "multiculti" thematic titles such as "Circuit Breakers" and "Polysex-oflagellick," playing to audiences across gender, sexuality, and race/ethnic lines.[20] This crossover and defamiliarization of the standard "lesbian" or "gay" programming mix has everything to do with an infusion of queer politics into production and programming, so that the determination of what is meant by "lesbian," "gay," or "queer" has itself been remapped along more fluid lines.[21] For our purposes, then, we need to keep in mind that determinations of "lesbian" as a gendered sexual identity and programming designation will shift in relation to changing conceptualizations of identity politics. As individual films and videos are included (or not included) and curated in fluctuating juxtapositions to other shorts at a variety of festivals, the ways in which they produce meanings of "lesbian" will fluctuate. Also, their meanings will shift with the composition of the audience and in terms of individual and collective responses (spontaneous jeers or applause erupting throughout a theater). Further, and perhaps more importantly, as these festivals gain in popularity, the demographics of lesbian/gay/queer audiences may change.[22]

But the politics of inclusion and of erotics in programming mixes under the rubric of "queer" at film and video festivals still requires the kind of critique posed by Yau Ching's Mix 94 curated program "Roseanne: Not Queer Enough." Questioning "the conventions of queer media programming—what has been missed, and whose privileges are being perpetuated,"

Ching argues that too often, work by queers of color or with feminist politics has been rejected by festivals as "not queer enough" because it does not represent a market-specific, queer identity.[23] To the extent the audience itself reflects this queer homogenized identity (the "Absolut Queer" as commodified, consumerist, depoliticized, and deracinated),[24] Ching's critique suggests further questions about the discursive identities that increasingly homogenized queer tourists are visiting and perhaps "buying into" at festivals.

Borderland Confessions

> *A borderland is a vague and undetermined place created by the emotional residue of an unnatural boundary.*[25]

All of the subjects in these shorts address their lesbian audiences as confidants to whom they confess the joys and tribulations of being a dyke of color in erotic and loving relationships with other women. Both Cheryl Dunye in *Greetings from Africa* and Mari Keiko Gonzalez in *Love Thang Trilogy* directly address their viewers, though Dunye does so by playing a scripted role as "Cheryl," and Gonzalez is heard only in voice-over narration with Desiree Veerasawmy and Sikay Tang (in "Just a Love Thang" and "Sky Dyking") and Desi del Valle (in "Eating Mango") acting as "her" or "her" lovers. Yvonne Welbon and Dawn Suggs indirectly address their audiences. Welbon combines talking-head interviews with Donna Rose and Maggie Montejano (who directly address Welbon offscreen) with black and white sequences of recreated memories in *Sisters in the Life*, while Suggs uses disembodied voice-over narrators (who shift from homophobic to dyke-grooving) in *I Never Danced the Way Girls Were Supposed To* to comment on the "real" domestic life of black lesbians.

Most audience members derive complex pleasures in being privy to these pseudoautobiographical confessions, for they invite participation in gossipy dyke dramas of love, longing, and loss. When they are told with ironic humor, they are virtually irresistible. For instance, after a compliment on her breasts from L, the white woman she lusts for in *Greetings from Africa*, Cheryl chatters nonstop about the occasions on which she does and does not need to wear a bra. When L slides naked and uninvited into the bathtub with her, Cheryl flashes an embarrassed and toothy smile. In *Sisters in the Life*, partners Rose and Maggie giggle together at their arrogance in maintaining cranky, middle-aged lists of minimal requirements for a potential lover: "employed, registered to vote, civic-minded, relatively

Greetings from Africa (Cheryl Dunye 1994). Courtesy Women Make Movies

sane. Not going through a serious therapeutic thing. No 12-steppers." "I was more specific. I wasn't even looking for a Latina. I wanted her to be Mexican."

For many white lesbian spectators, familiar with the ambiguities of flirtation and getting the joke about lesbians in perpetual twelve-step therapy, these moments allude to experiences of specific, embodied lesbians much like themselves and those they know. They may, therefore, read these moments as part and parcel of those experiences that constitute their own communities, regardless of how racially homogenized or integrated their experiences may be. Affinities of experience and humor, then, are integral components of a dialectic between the texts and their spectators that is further enabled by the queer film and video festival. For within the context of these imagined lesbian communities, those lesbians who might not get into these same shorts were they to watch them on home video or in some other context may find themselves in affinity by virtue of their communal viewing.

More importantly, perhaps, the wry performances invite viewers to share in an embarrassed or ludicrous moment of erotic desire while ironically highlighting split subjectivity. In *Greetings*, Cheryl the filmmaker, Cheryl the rueful narrator, and Cheryl the flustered bather are all "present." In *Sisters*, a split occurs between the remembered list-making Donna and Maggie and the presently happily partnered Donna and Maggie (neither matching the ethnic/racial identity the other had wanted). The performativity of these moments specifically opens up dialectical spaces with viewers who can then engage with the texts—through the "characters"—on a number of levels, often simultaneously. Yet for some spectators, viewing the whiteness of L's body as it slips into the tub with Cheryl's dark one or hearing Maggie speak her desire for a Mexican lover and Donna for an Afro-centric woman may be puzzling or troubling because it is outside their actual experiences or acknowledged desires. Indeed, insofar as spectators are cognizant of their position as *white* tourists in the documented realities of lesbians of color, they may be discomfited by their implicit alliance with L's bold gesture of interracial desire or by their explicit exclusion from Maggie's and Donna's articulated desires.

▶
_____

Racing Desire

> The question is not am I—or are you—a lesbian but, rather, what kinds of lesbian connections, what kinds of lesbian machine, we invest our time, energy, and bodies in, what kinds of sexuality we invest ourselves in, with what other kinds of bodies, with what bodies of our own, and with what effects?[26]

Cheryl Dunye frames *Greetings from Africa* as a narrative about being single and dating in the nineties (after participating in all that eighties "serial monogamy"), a situation familiar to many. But the film is not a typical "Greetings from the Dating Scene" story. Indeed, it may be viscerally troubling for white lesbian spectators because it so obviously traverses the borderlines of erotics and politics in the land of "vanilla sex" within an urban, woman-identified, racially mixed community by exploring the ways in which black and white women can be sexual tourists in one another's lives.

Whiteness is represented in *Greetings* as a fickle object of desire in the character of "the mysterious L," a woman who fetishizes all things African-descended: jazz, apartment decor, African-American studies departments, Peace Corps assignments, and, of course, women. Blackness, in the character of Cheryl, is represented as beguiled by whiteness yet complicit in the seduction: "Reel me in, L." While it is clearly the exotic, "African" object of L's attention, Cheryl's persona, reprised from Dunye's earlier video work,[27] is so endearingly gawky that she seduces the audience, which further implicates viewers in the complexities of interracial desire.

The film juxtaposes Cheryl's direct-address, black and white confessional moments with full color, reenacted memory sequences of her flirtation with L. Filmed in full frontal close-up in the confessional moments, Cheryl is disarmingly available to us, bare-shouldered in her overalls, with round glasses and nearly shaved head. She seems to expose her soul to us, at once goofy and ironic as she guilelessly recounts her narrative of falling for L, whose "mysteriousness" is partly a matter of her already having a girlfriend, though L describes her partner to Cheryl as a former roommate. Cheryl ruefully reenacts the scene in which she learns the "truth" about L toward the end of the film. When Cheryl remarks to another African-American woman at a party that she "has a hard-on for L," reaction shots clue us in before the other woman speaks that *she* is L's present girlfriend.

Charmed by Cheryl's ironic delivery and direct-address confessions (which allow a certain midframe stability and comfort for audiences), the white viewer may well find herself complicit in the dynamics of interracial desire as they unfold. She may, as the following example illustrates, learn that her coy viewing of the film is a raced experience from the perspective of the African-American subjects in the film. At one point during a reenacted memory sequence, Cheryl's friend Dee asks her about the status of her relationship with L, who is rumored to frequent African-American studies departments. Cheryl struggles to articulate precisely where they are in relationship land, leading Dee to conclude that theirs "must be a white girl thing." Dee means, of course, that the relationship is predicated on interracial attraction, but also indicates that this is a "thing" white girls, not black women, determine.

This essential white girl "thing" is defined as a longing for a hip African identity through an eroticized attachment to black women, which is explicitly marked as a white "tourist" gesture by the "Greetings from Africa" postcard L sends to Cheryl during her Peace Corps stint. That L's "Greetings" initiate Cheryl's *Greetings* may prompt some white lesbian viewers to reevaluate their own eroticization of black women, especially insofar as they are hooked by the affinities of style, politics, and ironic humor directly addressed to them by this film. Thus, watching *Greetings* within the tourist context of a queer film and video festival may be both celebratory and troubling for white spectators, even as they possess a certain racial cognizance. Ruth Frankenberg argues that "white women become much more conscious of the racial ordering of society" when they are in primary relationships with people of color, though they often find themselves "in changed positions in the racial order, albeit on contingent and provisional terms."[28] To the extent that white viewers enter into an eroticized relationship to Cheryl, they in turn are "reeled in," made complicit in the fuzzy dynamics of interracial desire. This is not to say that they explicitly "identify" with L (who seems rather oblivious to the hold she has over Cheryl), but that they may assume shifting affinities and affections with Cheryl that can generate a critical consciousness of the mutual and cyclical seductions across racial lines, producing an eroticized politics of interracial desire.

B. Ruby Rich has argued that "queers have the potential for a different *relationship* to race, and to racism, because of the very nature of same-sex desires and sexual practices."[29] Race may replace gender as an eroticized difference between two same-sex lovers. But as *Greetings* suggests, such a substitution between white women and women of color is often fraught with inequities and misrepresentations. Relationships between women of color may be formulated along differently determined lines of politicized and eroticized affinities, but for white viewers they are also fraught with the race relations peculiar to the United States, as illustrated by Donna Rose and Maggie Montejano in Welbon's *Sisters*, Mari Keiko Gonzalez's *Love Thang Trilogy*, and Dawn Suggs's *I Never Danced*. Works like these may be structured as "real life" experiences of a "raced" life. For example, in *Sisters*, Welbon establishes that her interviewees are "real" women in their late thirties telling their stories of first and current love, "real" women whose stories may evoke affective responses in viewers who have experienced their own awkward adolescent love relationships. This "real-ness" is buttressed by black and white reenactments of fourteen-year-old Donna Rose's simultaneous love for a girl named Karen and a boy named Felton, and by the jointly told tale of the relationship between Maggie and Donna, both of them women for whom a woman of color is essential as a partner.

Works featuring relationships among women of color may also be structured as fictionalized documentations of desire and struggle. Gonzalez uses a voice-over narrator in her tripartite *Love Thang*, a diary-like video compilation of encounters with objects of desire, anti-Asian violence projects, and distant mothers to address her audience. By not embodying the segments' narrator persona, she establishes more oblique relationships to the video's subjects than did Dunye and allows for less certainly defined dialectical spaces in which viewers may participate. For instance, the first encounter, "Just a Love Thang," is matched to images of two young Asian lovers making out. Mina (the narrator) tells the audience she spends every Wednesday and Saturday eating awful frozen yogurt at Tastee Delight until Sachito finally asks her name (matched to an overly lit close-up of Sachito's strapped-on dildo) and they begin seeing one another.

As the two women kiss and strip, the voice-over of Mina's character speculates about Sachito, the frozen yogurt slinger: "I knew there was so much more to her. Maybe a poet, a drummer, a filmmaker or an architect, a dancer, a carpenter . . . a dyke." The musings on Sachito's career potential humorously suggest the sexy allure of professional dyke-ness, matched by an image of Sachito in a James Dean pose, in leather cap and denim vest, with a defiant smirk at the camera. There is a certain playfulness here in the fluidity of fantasized professional identities.

During the initial make-out scenes, the images of the two women are insecurely attached to the characters of "Mina" and "Sachito." Because viewers can only speculate that Sachito, an urban guerrilla against Asian bashing, is the more Japanese-appearing actor (played by Tang) who poses as "a dyke," audience efforts to ascribe a specific racial/ethnic identity to the "Asian" lesbians in this short are complicated. While this can make for flexible lines of affinity among Asian women viewers, white viewers may experience more troubling instabilities. This is, of course, part of the point of the video: destabilizing notions of "race" and erotics through dialectical exchanges. In the second and third parts of *Love Thang*, Gonzalez reiterates conversations with disembodied maternal interlocutors who are simultaneously positioned within and outside the video text. In "Sky-dyking," her Asian Indian character (played by Veerasawmy) writes letters to her mother who has been living for years in Ireland, but these letters fail to mention her erotic life. In "Eating Mango," her long-suffering Filipina character owns up to her erotic life as a dyke but must patiently explain to mom that she does not have a "Puerto Rican fetish." To the extent that audience members identify with the performative affinities constructed by Gonzalez, they too are invited to consider the slipperiness of "race" and desire.

Whiteness does not have a subject/object position in this trilogy, but is evoked through the bright, overlit visual image of a dildo, or through verbal references to sheep and sky-written language in "Sky-dyking." Positioned outside the text, white spectators may enjoy Gonzalez's concluding promise of the pleasures of eating mango "til the sun goes down in your Puerto Rico" in "Eating Mango," but not as a promise extended specifically to them as subjects. The handheld video camera may position viewers behind the camera and its disembodied voice, which so seductively suggests that viewers embody it, but this narrator specifies her Filipina identity. Throughout the three pieces, Gonzalez thereby performatively documents desire among women of color—Asian, Pacific Rim, and Latina—yielding new ways of thinking about the slippages of Asian lesbian identities outside the hegemony of white lesbian communities.

These slippages—among makers and characters, texts and viewers, and subjects in the text—form some of the pleasures of getting into perfor-

"Skydyking." Courtesy Frameline

mative documentaries. A pastiche of anthropological examinations of "other" cultures, Dawn Suggs's *I Never Danced the Way Girls Were Supposed To* plies the line between the realism of *Sisters* and the fiction of *Love Thang*. The video begins with a voice-over dialogue between two narrators slipping from authoritative knowledge to incredulity at strange customs to stereotypical misinformation about the exoticism of lesbian sexuality. The segments switch from color to low-image black and white with a third voice-over narrator who describes a ritual of "girls find girls." Here, Suggs is playing with a couple of visual registers, each struggling to more authentically document the "real" story of black lesbian life. Which is it? The romance of meeting in black and white or the color sequence of domestic bliss with Felice polishing her "mannish" shoes and "pretty" Jackie eating cheese sandwiches, then spurning Felice's sexual advances on their couch?

But Suggs is also suggesting through her send-up of classical voice-over that the sexual "other" may not behave in essentially exotic ways when observers are *not* around. When viewers are invited to look into Jackie's refrigerator for clues about "where people come from," the voices finally identify themselves as queer: "sometimes I don't know what goes through straight people's minds. Maybe they think we prefer fruit." The "we" here aligns the narrators with queer spectators regardless of their raced identities. Later, as Suggs cuts from the interrupted kiss between Jackie and Felice to the triple-take eye contact of "girl meets girl," the lyrics of

Chaka Khan's "I'm Every Woman" cue up. The linkage of song and image imply that every woman is a black lesbian, a proposition that may trouble some white lesbian viewers while it grants temporary passage to coolness for others. "Oooh, she is fierce." "Slammin'." Finally, as Suggs reprises the opening shot of Jackie and Felice walking along a New York City sidewalk, the intrepid narrators speculate on whether they might be tempted to "get it on with another woman." In revising the voice-over dialogue of the initial visual sequence from "that one looks like a man" to "slammin'," Suggs shifts from homophobic to queer-friendly discourse. For some white spectators, identifying this shift as positive and lesbian-affirming may also occasion another shift: from undervaluing or exoticizing black lesbians' attractions to appreciating black lesbian sexuality in a vernacular ("slammin'" and "I'm Every Woman") that allows a temporary and limited border crossing into the lives of Jackie and Felice one Saturday afternoon.

Color Lines

Initiating dialectical exchanges with their "lesbian" audiences along color lines, these performative documentaries construct ways for their audiences to discover linkages and affinities with women of color and, especially for white spectators, to become race-cognizant of their own positions within lesbian communities in ways that are eminently productive. As sexy and politically engaged texts, they demand readings that "walk the walk" in the border zones of desire along lines that mark all of us as "raced." The challenge to tourists, of course, is not only to "walk the walk" of understanding and complicity for raced and queered subjects between self and text, as Nichols would have it. Nor is it sufficient to do so within the context of celebratory and imagined communities of festivals. The challenge is to do so outside these reading spaces and in the real communities in which we live.

NOTES

My thanks to Miranda Joseph for her stimulating comment, though it was unrelated to the videos and questions of reception across color lines discussed here. Fond gratitude to Lisa Henderson for her engaged reading and to Virginia Smith for all else.

1. Marusia Bociurkiw, "Bodies in Trouble," in *Queer Looks: Perspectives on Lesbian and Gay Film and Video*, ed. Martha Gever, John Greyson, Pratibha Parmar (New York: Routledge, 1993), 137.

2. Achtenberg was confirmed as assistant secretary of fair housing and equal opportunity at the Department of Housing and Urban Development in 1993 despite Senator Helms's condemnation.

3. For the purposes of this essay, I mean by "lesbian" those women who specify visible and eroticized relations to other women

(usually but not necessarily to the exclusion of men). By "women of color" I mean those women for whom a cultural, social, political, and aesthetic identity is today articulated by and self-consciously derived from an alliance with socially constructed categories of race or ethnicity marked by "color." "White" designates those who derive their (often unarticulated) self-identity from an alliance with dominant, European-descended culture. I do not, however, mean to suggest that any of these categories are monolithic; all are crossed by other differences, of class, politics, generation, and so on. I focus throughout on North American audiences and makers.

4. My use of "queer" is premised on in-your-face visibility politics and theory but also marks a convenient inclusion of dissident sexual identities, though some have argued it excludes lesbians. How differently gendered/raced/sexed queer viewers might read these shorts is suggested by, but is outside the scope of, this paper.

5. White documentarians also deploy their racial/ethnic selves in their work, but more frequently in ways that reinforce whiteness as the cultural norm so that it operates as a "given" in the text.

6. Richard Fung, "The Trouble with 'Asians,'" in *Negotiating Lesbian and Gay Subjects*, ed. Monica Dorenkamp and Richard Henke (New York: Routledge, 1995), 128.

7. Bill Nichols, *Blurred Boundaries: Questions of Meaning in Contemporary Culture* (Bloomington: Indiana University Press, 1994), 94.

8. Trinh T. Minh-ha, "Documentary Is/Not a Name," *October* 52 (Spring 1990): 95.

9. Kobena Mercer, "Dark and Lovely Too: Black Gay Men in Independent Film," in *Queer Looks*, 240.

10. Martha Gever, "The Names We Give Ourselves," in *Out There: Marginalization and Contemporary Cultures*, ed. Russell Ferguson et al. (Cambridge, Mass.: MIT Press, 1990), 200–201.

11. The first program title is taken from the program guide for the third annual Inside Out Lesbian and Gay Film and Video Festival of Toronto, May 6–16, 1993; the second from the Philadelphia International Gay and Lesbian Film Festival, July 6–16, 1995.

12. Prior to the acceptance of video into the Fifth New York Lesbian and Gay Experimental Film Festival in 1991, Super-8 and 16 mm were the cheap film stock choices. Yet film requires access to expensive developing and editing equipment that for a number of reasons limits access to filmmaking for lesbians of color, who consequently turn to video. While most programming segregates video shorts from feature films, thereby restricting audiences, at least it ensures exhibition space for work by lesbians of color.

13. Toronto, 1993.

14. For example, one program at the 1994 New York Lesbian and Gay Film Festival (in conjunction with the Gay Games Cultural Festival) included *Carmelita Tropicana: Your Kunst Is Your Waffen* (Ela Troyano), *Coconut/Cane & Cutlass* (Michelle Molabeer), *Khush* (Pratibha Parmar), and *Storme* (Michelle Parkerson). The only connection among these very different kinds of work is that all are directed by and concern women of color.

15. Mercer, "Dark and Lovely Too," 239.

16. A number of documentaries specifically make visible the experiences of lesbians of color using talking-head interviews and straightforward narratives. See, for example, *(In)Visible Women* (Marina Alvarez and Ellen Spiro 1991) and *Among Good Christian Peoples* (Jacqueline Woodson and Catherine Saalfield 1991).

17. Of course there have been notable exceptions. See *What's the Difference between a Yam and a Sweet Potato?* (Adriene Jenik and J. Evan Dunlap 1992) and *Ritual and White Lies* (Christine Minor and Elspeth Kydd 1991).

18. "Girls Night Out: A Program of Lesbian Themed Shorts" at Philadelphia's 1995 festival, curated by Cheryl Dunye, is one such program. Shorts included *Cruel* (Desi del Valle 1994), *Central Park* (Sande Zeig 1994), *Ife* (H. Len Keller 1993), *Maya* (Catherine Benedek 1992), *Souvenir* (Lisa Cholodenko 1994), *Le Poisson d'amour* (Paula Gauthier 1994), *Sister Louise's Discovery* (Margaret Hetherman 1994), and *Carmelita Tropicana: Your Kunst Is Your Waffen* (Ela Troyano 1993).

19. Nichols, *Blurred Boundaries*, 106.

20. A precedent for this programming format can be found in "Fire!" a collection of video work (and one film) by gay and lesbian artists of the African diaspora, curated by Cheryl Dunye and Thomas Allen Harris for the Sixth New York Lesbian and Gay Experimental Film Festival, 1992.

21. Consider, for instance, that the Chicago Gay and Lesbian Film Festival was initiated by a queer-friendly straight-identified woman (Brenda Webb) and that Cuban-American videomaker Ela Troyano is the straight sister of dyke performance artist Alina Troyano (Carmelita Tropicana).

22. Holly Hughes ironically notes this kind of fluid insta-lesbian construction in her play *World without End*: "I think I feel okay about saying this because we're all women here tonight, right? Okay. We're not all women. But we're all lesbians. I mean anyone can be a lesbian, gender is no obstacle" (Holly Hughes, *World without End*, in *Out from Under: Texts by Women Performance Artists*, ed. Lenora Champagne [New York: Theatre Communications Group, 1990], 24).

23. The politics of race and postcolonial identi-

ties are perhaps the most obvious "other" issues for Ching, but one could easily include the politics of beauty, breast cancer, aging, or family life here. Some examples of documentary work by queers that may not be "queer enough" are *The Displaced View* (Midi Onodera 1988), *Warrior Marks* (Pratibha Parmar 1993), and *Complaints of a Dutiful Daughter* (Deborah Hoffmann 1994).

24. Absolut Vodka's support of queer film and video festivals through sponsorships and advertising inevitably helps to construct a queer identity associated with hipness and consumerism.

25. Gloria Anzaldúa, *Borderlands/La Frontera* (San Francisco: Spinsters/Aunt Lute, 1987), 3.

26. Elizabeth Grosz, "Refiguring Lesbian Desire," in *The Lesbian Postmodern*, ed. Laura Doan (New York: Columbia University Press, 1994), 81.

27. Earlier titles include *Janine* (1990), *She Don't Fade* (1991), *Vanilla Sex* (1992), and *The Potluck and the Passion* (1993).

28. Ruth Frankenberg, *White Women, Race Matters : The Social Construction of Whiteness* (Minneapolis: University of Minnesota Press, 1993), 135.

29. B. Ruby Rich, "When Difference Is (More Than) Skin Deep," in *Queer Looks*, 319; emphasis in the original.

CYNTHIA FUCHS

[**11**] *"Hard to Believe": Reality Anxieties in Without You I'm Nothing, Paris Is Burning, and "Dunyementaries"*

Reality is more fabulous, more maddening, more strangely manipulative than fiction. To understand this, is to recognize the naivety of a development of cinematic technology that promotes increasing unmediated "access" to reality.
::   Trinh T. Minh-ha, *When the Moon Waxes Red*[1]

I've been looking so long at these pictures of you,
That I almost believe that they're real.
::   The Cure, "Pictures of You"[2]

I'm not trying to look real.
::   Dorian Corey, *New York Times* interview[3]

"You Know"

The film version of *Without You I'm Nothing* (John Boskovich 1990) opens on Sandra Bernhard, alone and focused on her own reflection. Staring into a dressing table mirror, she twists individual strands of her hair, snipping precisely at stray hairs with her scissors. The camera circles her, pauses on her profile. She waits a beat, then looks away from the mirror and into the camera. Slowly, she speaks: "You know, I have one of those really hard to believe faces. It's sensual. It's sexual. At times, it's just downright hard to believe."

The simplicity of this introduction is deceptive in several ways. While Bernhard's monologue establishes a fixed opposition between "you" and "I"—audience and performer—her turn from the mirror to the camera also blurs this distinction, underlining their interdependent relation, in that her unwaveringly intense gaze locates "you" along a continuum of observation, as yet another mirror. In addition, her performance is simultaneously familiar and aloof, complicating her self-assessment: the paradoxical point is that you do believe what she says; her face is "hard to believe." At once claiming and resisting conventional structures of visibility and (access to) knowledge, Bernhard's ironic performance insists that what "you know" and what she may be ("nothing") are ineluctably linked. The reality of each is conditioned by that of the other.

Without You I'm Nothing is concerned with such relational realities; a faux documentary, the film questions the very basis of documentary, a reality that exists "out there," available for capture on celluloid. As it represents scenes from Bernhard's "real" off-Broadway show (also titled *Without You I'm Nothing*), interviews with "Sandra"'s associates, and some obviously dramatized offstage events, the film takes up the process of this representation as its central problematic. Aligning its viewers with a mostly black, frankly bored diegetic audience in a Los Angeles nightclub, the movie offers their and your discomfort in contradistinction to Bernhard's seemingly reckless appropriations of a variety of identities that are not "hers." Certainly she resists easy categorization, embodying a series of characters: a gay man and Jewish, black, and WASPish women, sixties idealism and nineties cynicism, New York cool and West Coast glam, Nina Simone and Patti Smith.

Refusing to secure any of these identities as "real" or "original," least of all that of a person named Sandra Bernhard, the movie charts a series of dynamic ambiguities and continual movements across differences of race, sexuality, gender, generation, and class. Moreover, and more troublingly, the film will not offer a single, coherent alternative to the epistemological conventions of reality and identity that it critiques. Instead, it repeatedly displays Bernhard's isolated, ostensibly uncomprehending, and highly visible body, to the point that she appears nearly naked (dancing awkwardly in pasties and a G-string for an all but empty room) during the closing moments. As it is repeatedly exposed and dislocated, this spectacular body presses audiences to be aware of their own interpretive participation in the film's effects, namely, their visceral responses to and assumptions about Bernhard's performance.

Insisting on such effects and interrogating structures of representation and reception, *Without You I'm Nothing* challenges the notion of fixed, visible, documentable reality. This challenge is premised on two assumptions, that identity and experience necessarily shift in relation to audiences, reading practices, and representational apparatuses, and that a practical political strategy must engage these instabilities. This engagement in turn constitutes a "queering" of documentary possibilities, acknowledging the reality of what is conventionally unseen or unreadable, what is "closeted," what is "hard to believe." In what follows, I will trace three such engagements, in Bernhard's movie, in Jennie Livingston's *Paris Is Burning* (1990), and in two of Cheryl Dunye's videos, *Janine* (1990) and *She Don't Fade* (1991). As a group, these works articulate a shifting and complex understanding of identity, affirming the entanglements of invisible and visible realities. As separate texts, they offer diverse examples of what Donna Haraway has termed "situated knowledges," self-conscious and critical images of living in "meanings and bodies that have a chance for the future."[4] The questions they raise are productively linked and different: *Paris Is Burning* looks at a particular group of transvestites and transsexuals in order to question cultural orders of "realness"; Dunye's videos mix autobiography and (what could be) fiction to rethink relations among character, actor, and viewer, particularly among black and white, straight and queer women; and *Without You* stages Bernhard's elusive characterizations to emphasize the dilemma of identity in and as representation, with a particular focus on bisexuality as it challenges a relentlessly monosexual system of coding and representation.

Situating identity as a function of diverse styles and effects, these texts represent it as a process rather than a stable position, specifically a process involving and implicating multiple audiences and performers. At stake in each is the difficult relation of visibility to reality and identity, especially as this relation is complicated by evolving queer politics and documentary possibilities. If it is out of sight (as bisexuality remains, despite or because of coverage in *Newsweek*), is identity unknowable or unclaimable? If, as Trinh observes, "every spectator mediates a text to his or her own reality," is documentary formally or effectively different from fiction?[5] Does documentary have a particular relation to reality? Does queerness have a particular relation to representation? Each film and video answers these questions with more questions, mapping a constellation of anxieties about queer expression, verification, and representation by complicating traditional links between visibility and identity (those links that produce closetedness) and, in particular, by insisting that race, gender, and class are inextricable from sexuality in any conception of identity or reality.

Flow

Trinh writes that "there is no such thing as documentary."[6] Her declaration reads metaphorically and ironically, not as a dismissal of the genre or a denial of its styles and conventions, but as a challenge to documentary's investment in visibility as a direct conduit to reality. "A documentary aware of its own artifice," she continues, "is one that remains sensitive to the flow between fact and fiction."[7] Such self-reflexivity challenges what she calls conventional documentary's "totalizing quest of meaning," one that is conducted, presumably, both by and in pursuit of the thing called "meaning," but one that is always unfinished. Seeking order, conformity, and confirmation, such a quest classifies deviance (so that it is reincorporated into the "normalizing," meaningful system), rewrites subjects as objects "of study," and insists on a system of binary difference that obscures complexities and incongruities of lived relations.

Paris Is Burning resists such totalizing gestures, offering instead an ambivalent "flow between fact and fiction." The film presents a series of 1980s New York City competitions among black and Hispanic drag queens, carefully translating the balls' different categories, such as "Executive Realness" and "Banjee Girl," as labels over images of the ballwalkers. These labels underline the balls' unreadableness to outsiders, even as they are so elaborately visible, situating viewers as lacking knowledge, as outsiders looking in. The labels also construct the ballwalkers across multiple positions, as knowledgeable within their own community (as when they argue over ball rules and who is breaking them) and as unknown outside of that community. At issue is the status of knowledge as it is constituted through visibility. "The performance at these balls," Peggy Phelan writes, "represents that which cannot be seen precisely by underlining that which is seen."[8] Granting visibility to gay men of color as they act out "the power connoted by whiteness," Phelan argues, the film locates that power precisely in its status as "unmarked."[9]

The subversive potential of such visibility, however, is surely limited, even if exposure within the film's representational system appears to have very practical and immediate effects. In a *New York Times* article on the death of Angie Xtravaganza, Jesse Green writes, "Once mainstream America started copying a subculture that was copying it, the subculture itself was no longer of interest to a wider audience, and whatever new opportunities existed for the principals dried up."[10] The cycle of appropriation and commercialization that Green describes here speaks to the film's own representational scheme and ideological investigation, its calculated recontextualization of ethnographic documentary's concern with authentic images of an "other" culture as a necessarily reflexive enterprise.[11] Such images reveal as much about the dominant culture's need for conformity through corroboration as they do about the subculture's desire to "pass" into that conformity.

The film's interview subjects delineate the consensual reality, the conformity, that shapes the ball subculture. Corey, for example, defines "shade" and "reading." "Shade," he explains, is a refined form of "reading" (the "art of insults"), in which "I don't tell you that you're ugly, but I don't have to tell you . . . because you *know* that you're ugly." This particular knowledge comprises assumptions about identities and experiences: "If we're all the same thing . . . if I'm a black queen and you're a black queen, we can't call each other black queens, that's not a read, that's just a fact," he says. But this "fact" can be less than transparent to outsiders (hence Corey's instruction). As a relation between individuals and within a community, this fact is perpetually (re)produced in processes of reading and representation. While scenes of the sensational balls enact a standard documentary appeal to reality in their handheld camera work and shots of emotional dialogues among participants, these are framed by images of the queens' extensive, self-conscious preparation: the competitors are shown making or mopping (stealing) costumes, applying makeup, establishing the detailed rules for various categories. Such self-consciousness frames the film itself: its status *as* representation is variously foregrounded and linked to the interrogation of realness constituted by the balls.

For instance, *Paris Is Burning* contests the "real" referents for the ballwalkers' performances when it cuts from the "Executive Realness" contest to shots of white businesspeople on the street; introduced ironically under Cheryl Lynn's "To Be Real," their claim and right to "realness" are expressly thrown into question. Though bell hooks contends that the film, whose white lesbian maker remains off screen, "in no way interrogates whiteness,"[12] this juxtaposition of the differently performing (and differently rewarded) white and black "executives" italicizes that visibly raced identities inflect class, gender, age, and sexuality. While *Paris Is Burning* leaves the power imbalance between the ball subculture and dominant culture intact (and how could it not?), it engages a complex critique of the prescriptive codes of reality and identity, specifically through its visual organization.

"To be real," observes one interviewee, means "to be able to blend." The film demonstrates that blending works in multiple, incongruous ways, granting invisibility along with visibility. For instance, Octavia St. Laurent sits on a stool in her sparsely furnished apartment, pointing out the many "moods" of her idol, white supermodel Paulina Porizkova, visible in a series of makeup advertisements that Octavia has tacked to the smudgy wall behind her. This image—black Octavia framed by many Paulinas and other white models—makes clear that her desire is both conditioned and limited by racist norms: Octavia is not going to be "the next Paulina." But she could be someone else (though the field is hardly exploding with black,

Latina, or Asian superstars, Naomi Campbell being the most visible, singular example). When Octavia attends a models' convention, unnoticed among the mixed-race crowd of young women hoping to land agency contracts, it is conceivable that whether or not she is a genetic woman is the least of her (or their) concerns.[13] As the film celebrates Octavia's intervention into this grandly hallucinatory environment, Phelan sees it as unable to come to terms with the "figure of the (white) woman as the cipher for that distance" between "symbolic identification and identity itself."[14] But the movie, I think, questions this very opposition between "symbolic identification and identity itself." Octavia's pass suggests that investment in "identity itself," while it pays well to those who are in historically privileged positions, is not necessarily an investment in reality, or rather in "realness." Demonstrating that its subjects' desires are premised on prevailing (racist, heterosexist) codes of performance as a means to white, straight identity, the film also critiques the notion of "identity itself," especially as it shapes viewers' desires (what you want to be or possess, and their inevitable connections). At issue here is the viability not of a particular community, queer ballwalkers or straight executives, but of the belief system that sustains class, race, gender, and sexuality as visible, continually self-authenticating categories.

The film's reassessment of "identity itself" has as its corollary a deconstruction of traditional documentary practices and aims. Jackie Goldsby writes that it displays a previously unseen world and that "the documentary is probably the only genre that will acknowledge this world as it is: colored and queer."[15] True enough. But the text, I think, takes on this problematic assumption that being visible is the same thing as being acknowledged, or that documentary presents anything "as it is," in its focus on the balls as potent and volatile sites of performative "realness." As Judith Butler argues, "*Paris Is Burning* documents neither an efficacious insurrection nor painful subordination, but an unstable coexistence of both."[16] Its juxtapositions of balls and domestic life, grand artifice and diurnal acts maintain that illusion "is," rejecting the conventional notion that being "real" has a meaning apart from or superior to that of illusion. More importantly, illusion, performance, desire, and being are shown to be interrelated. The film's audiences and actors constitute shifting dynamics, not fixed positions. What once seemed unchanging, authentic, even essential properties—whiteness or femaleness, for instance—are now recognizably in flux, contingent and yet still real.

In other words, this documentary takes the problematic of reality per se as its focus. For all its attention to the extravagances of old-fashioned male-to-female drag (rendered in images of Corey and Pepper LaBeija at makeup tables and in full diva regalia), *Paris Is Burning* also contemplates what might be redundantly termed the unremarkable pass, the 24-7 existences of Octavia, Venus Xtravaganza, and others who identify as pre- or post-op transsexuals and who live as women, invisible except when they are picked out by the camera. Butler argues that the invisible is precisely what is meaningful, since it lets "that which cannot fully appear in any performance persist in its disruptive promise."[17] Passing as women-as-images, Octavia and Venus embody—or, more exactly, gesture toward—that "disruptive promise," resisting the "totalizing" meaning of racial or sexual identity as it would be assigned to them.[18] At the end of the film, we learn that Venus has been killed; she appears in snapshots and footage, some repeated from earlier in the film and now endowed with a different meaning, as Angie talks tearfully about her dead daughter. Now invisible in another sense—as a statistic, another murdered gay male prostitute—Venus serves also as a nostalgic gesture toward meaning and identity. If passing reconfirms visible boundaries, between male and female, white and Latino, gay and straight, death and life, it only does so by reconfirming them as fictions, for according to *Paris Is Burning*, no performance is authentic and authenticity is performative: what is visible is what remains unreadable, and what remains unseen—Venus's corpse—means too much and not enough.

▶━━━━━━━━━━━━━━━━━━━━━━━━━━━━━━━━━━━━━━━

Fictions of Identity

The interrogation of performance as a means to identity and identification is reframed in the autobiographical format of Cheryl Dunye's short videos. Like *Paris Is Burning*, *Janine* asserts the relational realities that underlie what Diana Fuss has termed "fictions of identity," those malleable stories of self-affirmation that constitute membership in and across communities and difference between individuals.[19] *Janine* combines coming out as confession, using the familiar documentary device of direct address to the camera to claim a queer desire and identity. In *She Don't Fade*, such performative relations are redoubled, as the narrator, named "Cheryl," not only frames the story of a fictional character named "Shae," but also reframes it with her own experience of making the video called *She Don't Fade*. While both videos trace the development of an autobiographical persona— "Cheryl"—they use different representational strategies, the first focused on naming her desire as an affirmation of identity (coming out), the second on complicating her desire (its multiplicities, her attractions to various

Shae is "torn between two lovers" in *She Don't Fade* (Cheryl Dunye 1991). Courtesy Video Data Bank

women), enacting her identity as process. Each video reconsiders the constitution of knowledge as it shapes reality.

Janine problematizes Dunye's assertion and embodiment of a specifically black lesbian identity in relation to an audience, but disallows that identity's completion and fixity: coming out is a perpetual process. Her direct address creates a triad of subjects: you, me, and Janine, the titular subject who is repositioned as object in Dunye's high school snapshots and memories. Dunye's performance of uncertainty—her halting, awkward, and repetitive speech, her shrugs and sighs—situates Janine, a white woman she "had feelings for," both as an emblem of social and sexual repression and as the occasion for Dunye's coming out. Represented as a process, Cheryl's coming out also means becoming "Cheryl," the central character in what the maker has termed her "Dunyementaries."[20] This character is a vehicle for an ongoing, conventionally autobiographical plot (Dunye's first-person recollections of her experiences over the course of several videos)[21] as well as for restructuring and calling into question the subjective realities of that plot.

She Don't Fade (Cheryl Dunye 1991). Courtesy Video Data Bank

The video opens with Cheryl seated before the camera in a medium shot, her look and monologue apparently unmediated as she introduces herself and explains her reasons for making this document of her relationship with Janine. A series of snapshots of Janine—whom Cheryl calls "the epitome of whiteness"—with Cheryl and other classmates in uniforms emphasizes the pressure to conform as Dunye recalls it; these pictures are intercut with Dunye's direct address and brief, stop-motion images of Cheryl attempting to blow out candles, a "birthday" ritual that alludes to her developing self-consciousness of the ritual and the moment it marks. Cheryl's desire to both be and have Janine shapes her memory of their relationship: "I was always trying to be more like her and her world and get more into it." As the video progresses, it becomes clear that Dunye was never able to "get into" Janine's anything. While more snapshots emphasize Dunye's extremely visible difference from her classmates (hers being the only black face in photo after photo), she recalls her efforts to fit in, to be part of Janine's "world."

Her memory of coming out to Janine is at once explicit and cryptic. Janine is upset, and "the next thing was a phone call I get and it was her mom and she said, you know Cheryl, I know that you can't afford a doctor, but I'll really pay for you to go to a doctor to talk to someone about your problems." At this point the camera cuts from Cheryl's talking head to a typewritten emphasis: "About MY PROBLEMS!!!!" This shift in representational strategy and tone, from acquiescent to exasperated, indicates that the character "Cheryl" is quite aware—and is making us aware—of the other meaning of Mrs. Serrelli's offer. "And ever since then," Cheryl says, again on camera, "I kinda, y'know, fuck that, fuck that whole situation."

Clearly, Cheryl's anger is directed both specifically (at Janine and her mother) and more broadly ("that whole situation," meaning the Serrelli situation and culturally condoned homophobia). The video investigates evolving codes of knowledge as they shape the girls' relationship: coming out is a function of Cheryl's developing self-knowledge and sharing this knowledge with others. Ironically, Janine (via Cheryl's recounting) and Cheryl both repeat the phrase "you know," as if they both mean (and know) the same thing, but they plainly do not. Eventually, as Cheryl tells it, she must reject Janine's assumptions in order to stake out her own reality, again through a phone conversation:

> She was all, Wasn't it so fun then, Cheryl? Weren't we good friends then, Cheryl? And y'know, personally, it wasn't a great time for me, because I felt so in the closet then, and so upset that I blocked a lot of that. And I was like, No, I don't remember that. I wasn't into it, you know?

In resisting Janine's efforts to rewrite their past, Cheryl calls on her audience for confirmation. Her last, carefully articulated "you know?" after a series of quickly rhythmic "y'knows" throughout her speech projects a shared experience (or at least recognition) of homophobia, racism, and classism. But this "you know?"—posed as a question—is also addressed to Janine, within and beyond the recollected conversation, emphasizing that the relationship between speaker ("Cheryl") and listener ("you") necessarily remains uncertain.

The tension between resolution and doubt implied by Cheryl's questions, recollections, and misstatements throughout the tape continues to its end. As she declares, "I think that I'm over the whole Janine Serrelli thing, and that's about it," the video shows Cheryl blowing out her candles at last, depicting a kind of closure. But a final gesture leads to the possibility of further movement, beyond the tape's diegetic confines: the image cuts to black as the sound track offers more, the noise of Cheryl leaving the set, chair scuffing as she rises and walks. Such irresolution is to the point of Dunye's developing project, as she structures her "self," on the edge of fiction and autobiography, as a site of perpetual construction and interrogation, approximating what Trinh describes as the "subject who points to him/her/itself as a subject-in-progress, a work that displays its own formal properties or its own constitution as work."[22] *Janine*'s confessional structure situates Dunye's black lesbian identity as it is self-expressive and trans-parent. But its complex intersections of sound and video tracks also contend that this "self" is continually shaped and reshaped, named and renamed, by the same oppressive Philadelphia-mainline whiteness that informed her early self-image as good girl, as "class clown," as necessarily—because no other options were visible—straight. Rather than establishing a fixed identity, then, this confession underlines the perpetual movements of relationships and realities. The question of what "you know," paralleled by the question of where Cheryl goes after she leaves the set, remains unanswered.

She Don't Fade further problematizes Dunye's relation to the audience in that she appears as two "characters." Again the video opens as she faces the camera, introducing herself as Cheryl, who will be playing "Shae," a woman intent on taking a "new approach" to relationships. The text alternates between Shae's narrative and Cheryl's, the diegesis in which Shae meets and becomes interested in two black women, Margo and Niki, and Cheryl's decisions about narrative structure made during the video's production. Together, the stories elide but also sustain the distinctions between character and maker, text and experience, outlining their contingent relations while reiterating what appear to be their differences. In its focus on Dunye as a split subject—actor, maker, and character—She Don't Fade would appear to redress the problem that Phelan finds at the center of Paris Is Burning's ethnographic project—"once the subject is turned into the Subject-who-is-supposed-to-know, the subject is misrecognized"[23]—by offering a subject who emphasizes her performance as not "knowing" and as being "misrecognized."

She Don't Fade is simultaneously faux ethnographic (at the beginning, Shae decides to make a video about "women," one of whom she attempts unsuccessfully to interview on the street) and faux autobiographical (Cheryl and her best friend, Paula, who plays "Paula," discuss their relationship, and it is never clear whether this is a relationship between Shae and Paula or Cheryl and Paula).[24] The video's invitation to its audience to participate in the symbiotic narratives of Cheryl's and Shae's fantasies and uncertainties becomes especially acute when Shae's relationship with Margo turns to sex. They tentatively look through a book while they are seated on a bed, and they quietly and carefully begin to kiss. The camera cuts to their naked bodies in bed, still tentative, even awkward. Suddenly, offscreen (male and female) voices interrupt their close encounter with laughter and instructions to the performers to punch up the action. As they resume the scene, the video shifts to still frames and freeze-motion imagery, with the sound of an orchestra "warming up" in the background: the scene offers multiple beginnings and no climax. This break in the narrative further confuses the roles Dunye is playing, as they collide in one moment, no longer differentiated by Cheryl explaining her situation and Shae acting it out. The collapse intensifies the video's analysis of relational realities, its restructuring of roles and identities as interconnected, shifting, and productive.

Resisting audience (mis)recognition at the same time that she assumes it, Cheryl/Shae invites viewers to rethink their relations to her own declarations of knowledge by making it impossible to situate her absolutely—to know her—as one or the other (or even someone else). She cautions her viewers that though they may think she's "into Margo," such is not the case: within minutes she has spotted Niki on a stairway and is fantasizing about a new relationship with her. This fantasy mirrors the sex scene with Margo, opening on the women seated on a bed with a book, then cutting to their embrace. That Shae does not "actually" meet Niki until later reorganizes the entire narrative into a kind of temporal loop, which remains by definition unfinished, looking forward to the introduction again, which situates what has happened in the "past": they are finally introduced to one another at a party, and as they walk off screen (as Dunye did in *Janine*), a white woman at the party takes up a microphone and announces that "the rest is history, or should I say herstory." The narrative breaks down in order to continue. Her stories unfolding in an ever-present, Dunye continues to perform the complications of relational realities.

▶ _____

"Like a Fuckin' Documentary"

The intersections of racial, class, and sexual identities that shape *Janine*'s recollection of coming out and *She Don't Fade*'s investigation of shifting desires come into sharp and disturbing focus in *Without You I'm Nothing*. Like Dunye's "Dunyementaries," *Without You* critiques documentary convention and expands it by parodying the confessional form. But if Dunye's work articulates the difficulties of narrative and identificatory resolution, the Bernhard movie discounts resolution out of hand. Instead, it presents serial, unending, reciprocal "fictions of identity," each of which traverses the borders of truth and illusion differently. Included are interviews with her ostensible manager (a prototypical "mannish lesbian" played by Lu Leonard) and her friend Steve Antin (as himself and identified only as "Actor"), and appearances by a decidedly prosaic Madonna clone named Shoshana (Denise Vlasis) and a silent black woman (named "Roxanne" only in the closing credits [Cynthia Bailey]). Each of these characters interrupts and perpetuates the film's ambiguous status—real and not real, confessional and fictional, bounded and transgressive—by commenting on the action as it happens, recalling past events, or variously inserting "themselves" into the text. Antin's story about his experience with Jodie Foster, with whom he appeared in *The Accused* (1988), goes to this point of categorical ambiguity. Impressed with her performance in the film, he says, "It was like a fuckin' documentary, she was so *real* in it!"

Designated "actor" Antin's appreciation for an effectively rendered reality ironically highlights *Without You I'm Nothing*'s simultaneous emulation and interrogation of documentary—as a set of conventions. Pretending to capture Bernhard's experiences on stage in front of an increasingly ill at ease black nightclub audience, the film sets up an oppositional relationship between a "you" and an "I" that conspicuously "races" both subjects; as Elspeth Probyn observes, Bernhard "positions herself as inescapably white."[25] The question that occurs to me, however, has to do with the extent (and effect) of the "self" that Bernhard looks to "be." For the film is "nothing" (as its title suggests) if not a sustained challenge to regimes of reality and identity that are premised on this notion of "self" as individual and social agent.

Probyn, in fact, makes a similar point in her discussion of the film, titled "'Without *Her* I'm Nothing': Feminisms with Attitude," as she argues that the film's pronounced "silences" regarding "Sandra"'s lesbian desire (here, for Roxanne) leave readers with nowhere to turn but their own imaginations, where, Probyn suggests, they might "remember what the film forgets."[26] I would argue, however, that the process of forgetting is precisely what this provocative film "remembers"; it insists that you recall, that "you know," your own situated relationship to each identity it represents. Bernhard's manifestly appropriative performances—she sings "Four Women" and "Me and Mrs. Jones" as the patrons shift in their seats and sigh with annoyance—indict the peculiar forgetting that grounds white, heterosexual cultures. Repeated images of the club's nonplussed, repulsed viewers make it difficult for the film's viewers to respond otherwise to Bernhard's act: she is so smug and oblivious to her audience's reaction that you can't help but resent her. The film extends this construction of your displeasure through the "interviewees," who share their own disparate responses to "Sandra" (she is alternately "too grand" and "pretty geeky") and gossip about her "boyfriend," a black male hairdresser named Joe.

But if this narrative (and in particular a scene showing the couple engaged in sex, shot from a dispassionate overhead angle: it seems more out of place than a part of the movie's various recollections) would seem to signal Bernhard's heterosexuality, the film's more complex and compelling relationship is between Bernhard and Roxanne, constituting what Jean

Walton refers to as "the 'dykey' undertone of that ostensibly hetero narrative."[27] Roxanne's appearances tend to follow Bernhard's stage monologues; and where Bernhard remains in the club, Roxanne traverses downtown Los Angeles: she walks past the Watts Towers, studies in lab coat and glasses, reads *The Kabbalah and Criticism* outside a kosher meat shop, showers with other women (or, more precisely, runs through the shower area clutching her towel), and listens to N.W.A. (while snipping her hair in a way that specifically refers to the movie's first scene, with Bernhard at her dressing table, and denotes a cycle of effects and relations: Who is copying whom? Who is imagining whom? Who is "you" and who is "I"?).

Always outside the theater where Bernhard is enclosed, Roxanne's literal movement reframes Bernhard's metaphorical movement across identities.[28] Each type of movement (differently) figures an understanding of relational realities and "situated knowledges." Bernhard's whiteness grounds the film's critique of racism (which is mediated through Roxanne), as it is, along with her gender, her most visible "identity." Beyond this, however, lies another dilemma that the movie never quite articulates: how is it possible to represent an "invisible" identity, one that is assessed by desire rather than appearance and, moreover, one that rejects singular desire? Rather than looking for *Without You*'s "lesbian" imagery, allusions, and affirmations, I find myself more intrigued by its perpetual breakdown of exactly this kind of categorization and construction. If I was concerned with labeling this representation of Bernhard (as a real "self," as an emblem of some identity), I would consider using the term *bisexual,* because she has used the term (if pressed),[29] but more because it remains elusive, beyond explicit, always recognized, and fixed imaging. It is in this sense, then, in its retreat from representation, that bisexuality becomes a useful focus for my discussion of *Without You.*

So, while almost any scene in the film might demonstrate its insistence on and deconstruction of identity fictions, I will look here at the final one, in which Bernhard dances awkwardly in her G-string, her exposed body, both naked and elaborately staged, under excruciatingly slow and uncomfortably framed close-ups, to Prince's "Little Red Corvette." That she introduces her routine by first stumbling over her own words (addressing her audience, she says, "Without me, I'm . . .," then correcting herself) and then by acknowledging the "Little Paisley God" himself (the only time that she does refer to any "original" performer) gestures toward the radical racial ambiguity and gender/sex fluidity that her performance imagines.[30] Then she sings the song once herself, standing stock-still, wrapped in a U.S. flag,[31] backed by a set of atavistic sylvan dancers. When she is done singing, she drops her flag/robe and starts to dance; it is not until the end of this performance that the camera cuts back to the audience (unlike previous acts, where shots of upset spectators cued reactions). Everyone has left the building, except Roxanne. On the white tablecloth before her, she has written in red lipstick "Fuck Sandra Bernhard."

This stunning moment marks a collapse of narrative systems and realities, in that the two figures who have seemed to have no material relation now face and reflect each other in the same space. As it punctuates the film's investigation of relational realities, the scene makes only one point clear: "you" and "I" function as a system and in process. But assigning one position or another to Bernhard, "Sandra," or Roxanne becomes impossible. Roxanne's silence throughout the film is here underlined and undone, yet her written declaration allows multiple readings (does *fuck* designate lust or derision or both?) and leaves Bernhard, after all her previous chatter, with nothing to say. Roxanne seems to reject Bernhard's clumsy acts of confession, appropriation, and artifice while also reframing them, so that they are pulled into another process of reading, where Bernhard is positioned as the audience for Roxanne's exit from the film frame, out the "theater" door into blinding whiteness.

It is Roxanne's climactic movement that seems to leave *Without You I'm Nothing* without definition, exacerbates its unresolved tensions between the real and the represented, object and subject. As her departure leads and calls attention to the whiteness that is nothing without its diverse "others," it also invokes what Trinh calls the "reflexive interval," where, she writes,

> the play within the textual frame is a play on this very frame, hence on the borderlines of the textual and extra-textual, where the positioning within constantly incurs the risk of de-positioning, and where the work, never freed from historical and socio-political contexts nor entirely subjected to them, can only be itself by constantly risking being no-thing.[32]

Without You claims this risk in its titular allusion to the interdependence of audience-camera and performer-subject. Bernhard, Roxanne, and their multiple audiences shape one another, are continually "subjected to" each other.

That this identity may be read as bisexual is perhaps the film's most profound "risk," for the identity yet remains elusive, different, invisible and unknowable. This is a reading that will not give itself up to everyone; it obliges readers to acknowledge their situatedness and the "intervals" they inhabit. While bisexuality has been denounced as "noncommitment," as a politically suspect "phase," Elisabeth Daumer argues alternatively that bisexuality is "a sign of transgression, ambiguity, and mutability" that chal-

lenges "all notions of fixed, immutable identities" and "articulat[es] a plurality of differences among us in the hope of forging new bonds and allegiances."[33] In other words, bisexuality extends queer possibilities for identity, visibility, and reality. *Without You* understands plurality as political
"work-in-progress," makes visible the contexts and categories of knowledge, and embraces reflexive ironies and relational realities.

NOTES

*Thanks to Chris Holmlund for her careful
reading and constant inspiration.*

1. Trinh T. Minh-ha, "The Totalizing Quest of
   Meaning," *When the Moon Waxes Red: Rep-
   resentation, Gender, and Cultural Politics*
   (New York: Routledge, 1991), 39–40.
2. The Cure, "Pictures of You," *Disintegration*
   (Electra 1989).
3. Jesse Green, "Paris Has Burned," *New York
   Times*, April 18, 1993, 9:11.
4. Donna Haraway, "Situated Knowledges:
   The Science Question in Feminism and the
   Privilege of Partial Perspective," in *Simians,
   Cyborgs, and Women: The Reinvention of
   Nature* (London: Routledge, 1991), 187.
5. Trinh, "All-Owning Spectatorship," *When the
   Moon Waxes Red*, 93.
6. Trinh, "The Totalizing Quest of Meaning," 29.
7. Ibid., 41.
8. Peggy Phelan, *Unmarked: The Politics of
   Performance* (London: Routledge, 1993), 96.
9. Ibid., 94.
10. Green, "Paris Has Burned," 9:11.
11. As Ann Cvetkovich suggests, "the internal
    differences among the speakers make it dif-
    ficult to ascribe a single position or politics
    to the subculture" (Ann Cvetkovich, "The
    Powers of Seeing and Being Seen: *Truth or
    Dare* and *Paris Is Burning*," in *Film Theory
    Goes to the Movies*, ed. Jim Collins, Hilary
    Radner, and Ava Preacher Collins [New York:
    Routledge, 1993], 168).
12. Hooks argues that the film takes its subjects'
    veneration of whiteness at face value: "What
    could be more reassuring to a white public
    fearful that marginalized disenfranchised
    black folks might rise any day now and make
    revolutionary black liberation struggle a re-
    ality than a documentary affirming that colo-
    nized, victimized, exploited, black folks are
    all too willing to be complicit in perpetuating
    the fantasy that white ruling-class culture is
    the quintessential site of unrestricted joy,
    freedom, power, and pleasure" (bell hooks,
    "Is Paris Burning?" in *Black Looks: Race and
    Representation* [Boston: South End Press,
    1992], 149). Judith Butler argues in response
    that the film is "ambivalent" about "racist,

misogynist, and homophobic norms of oppression" (Judith Butler, "Gender Is Burning,"
in *Bodies That Matter: On the Discursive
Limits of "Sex"* [New York: Routledge, 1993],
127, 128).
13. In other words, Octavia's status as genetic
    male or surgically reassigned female (should
    she get the operation she wants) is less im-
    portant in a business based so extremely on
    appearances than whether those appear-
    ances sell products.
14. Phelan, *Unmarked*, 104.
15. Jackie Goldsby, "Queens of Language: *Paris
    Is Burning*," *Afterimage* 8.10 (May 10, 1991);
    reprinted in *Queer Looks: Perspectives on
    Lesbian and Gay Film and Video*, ed. Martha
    Gever, John Greyson, and Pratibha Parmar
    (New York: Routledge, 1993), 114.
16. Butler, "Gender Is Burning," 137.
17. Butler, "Imitation and Gender Insubordina-
    tion," *Inside/Out: Lesbian Theories, Gay The-
    ories*, ed. Diana Fuss (New York: Routledge,
    1991), 29.
18. Marjorie Garber writes that "transsexuals
    and transvestites are *more* concerned with
    maleness and femaleness than persons who
    are neither transvestite or transsexual" (Mar-
    jorie Garber, "Spare Parts: The Surgical Con-
    struction of Gender," in *The Lesbian and Gay
    Studies Reader*, ed. Henry Abelove, Michele
    Aina Barale, and David M. Halperin [New
    York: Routledge, 1993], 334). While there are
    readers and readings of *Paris Is Burning* to
    support this generalization, the film, I think,
    complicates such assumptions in its represen-
    tations of various queens and cross-dressers,
    some of whom, most memorably Pepper
    LaBeija, seem invested in living through the
    distinctions between "maleness and female-
    ness." On transsexualism and the cultural
    and political constructions of gender, see also
    Judith Shapiro, "Transsexualism: Reflections
    on the Persistence of Gender and the Erotics
    of Cultural Appropriation," and Sandy Stone,
    "The *Empire* Strikes Back: A Posttranssexual
    Manifesto," both in *Body Guards: The Cul-
    tural Politics of Gender Ambiguity*, ed. Julia
    Epstein and Kristina Straub (New York: Rout-
    ledge, 1991), 248–79 and 280–304.

19. Diana Fuss, *Essentially Speaking: Feminism, Nature, & Difference* (New York: Routledge, 1989), 104.
20. Dunye coined the term to emphasize her work's focus on herself, as both character and "real" person (Jeannine DeLombard, "Creative Difference," *Philadelphia City Paper*, May 13–20, 1993, 5).
21. These videos include *Janine*, *She Don't Fade*, *The Potluck and the Passion* (1993), *Vanilla Sex* (1992), and *Greetings from Africa* (1994). The "Cheryl" saga continues in her feature film, *The Watermelon Woman* (1996).
22. Trinh, "The Totalizing Quest of Meaning," 48.
23. Phelan, *Unmarked*, 106.
24. That Paula is white adds another twist to the possible ways that viewers may position themselves, though the video, unlike *Janine*, doesn't take racial and cultural difference as its thematic focus.
25. Elspeth Probyn, *Sexing the Self: Gendered Positions in Cultural Studies* (London: Routledge, 1993), 159.
26. Ibid., 162.
27. Jean Walton, "Sandra Bernhard: Lesbian Postmodern or Modern Postlesbian?" in *The Lesbian Postmodern*, ed. Laura Doan (New York: Columbia University Press, 1994), 254. For another reading of the lesbian narrative in *Without You I'm Nothing*, see bell hooks's condemnation of Bernhard's appropriation of black culture as embodied by Roxanne: "Is she the fantasy Other Bernhard desires to become? Is she the fantasy Other Bernhard desires? The last scene of the film seems to confirm that black womanhood is the yardstick which Bernhard uses to measure herself" (bell hooks, *Black Looks*, 38).
28. Bernhard's "movement" culls from stand-up comedy, tour de force acting, and, of course, camp, that most subversive *and* conventional mode of performance, an act that assumes both artistic intention and inside knowledge of that intention on the part of its audience.
29. Bernhard has said, "I've had long-term relationships with both men and women. If that classifies me as bisexual, then I'm bisexual" (Lily Burana, "Sandra Bernhard: Acting Lesbian [Interview with Sandra Bernhard]," *Advocate* 618, [December 15, 1992]: 70).
30. For a discussion of the race, gender, class, and sexual ambiguities performed by The Artist Formerly Known as Prince, see Cynthia Fuchs, "'I wanna be your fantasy': Sex, Death, and the Artist Formerly Known as Prince," in *Women and Performance: Queer Acts*, ed. José Esteban Muñoz and Amanda Barrett (1996), 16.
31. For a discussion of this use of the flag in relation to queer nationality, see Lauren Berlant and Elizabeth Freeman, "Queer Nationality," in *Fear of a Queer Planet: Queer Politics and Social Theory*, ed. Michael Warner (Minneapolis: University of Minnesota Press, 1993), 193–229.
32. Trinh, "The Totalizing Quest of Meaning," 48.
33. Elisabeth D. Daumer, "Queer Ethics; or, The Challenge of Bisexuality to Lesbian Ethics," *Hypatia* 7.4 (Fall 1992): 103.

CHRIS STRAAYER

[**12**] *Transgender Mirrors:*
Queering Sexual Difference

Since the invention of homosexuality more than a century ago, professional
and lay "audiences" alike have situated gender as its primary marker—as
both what marks it and what it marks. From Weimar Germany's "third
sex" to second-wave feminism's "lesbian-woman," gay men and lesbians
have been measured in terms of their femininity and masculinity, which
then have laid claims on their femaleness and maleness. Although gender
displaced sexual orientation in these crude schemes, it also provided a primary visual semiotics through which queers communicated their sexualities. The present essay also reverses the signifying chain: rather than an
en-gendering look at queerness, I take a queering look at gender.[1]

While they are often characterized as distinct traits, gender and sexual
orientation are not entities that can be plucked from or implanted in a person. Outside the social event known as "self," they do not exist. Neither
are they uniform from self to self. Gender and sexual orientation come into
"being" within individual-cultural complexes that variably form and incorporate them. (The concepts of transgender and homosexual identities, born
from oppression as well as resistance, always remain most suitable to the
oppressors' dehumanizing mode of thought.) Transgendered people and gays
and lesbians are fighting and delighting on multiple fronts simultaneously.

In this essay, I will discuss two independent video documentaries: *Juggling Gender* (Tami Gold 1992), which profiles Jennifer Miller, a bearded
lesbian; and *OUTLAW* (Alisa Lebow 1994) which profiles Leslie Feinberg,
a transgendered lesbian. These works dispute binary sex and the sex-gender
matrix. Because feminism has enacted the most intensive investigation of
gender, it offers an appropriate starting point for discussion. While I understand that feminism is not a static and impermeably bounded discipline,
I nevertheless find its paradigm of sexual difference inadequate to certain
questions about identity raised by *Juggling Gender* and *OUTLAW*.

In writing about independent documentary, I am less concerned with the distinction between representation and reality (the issue of document) than with the competition between different representations to define "reality" (the issue of independence). I take as a given that the documentaries I discuss are instances of discourse rather than windows on reality. Nevertheless, I also assume that the producers and subjects enacting such discourse are communicating with real purpose. Although both mainstream and independent documentaries are mediated, they are differently mediated at the institutional level. Independent productions avoid much of the gatekeeping and censorship of corporate financing entities and exhibition venues.

As I see it, the problem of mistaking representation for reality is now most salient not at the level of the viewership, but in the claim made by dominant ideology on representation itself. I focus on *independent* media production because it dearticulates the "insider" perspective that too often imbues mainstream media as well as contemporary theory. These video profiles in particular represent "outsider" experiences by foregrounding otherwise marginalized voices. Acknowledging the existence of such voices exposes the self-serving conflation of center with all, mainstream with society. I am not suggesting that independent media's sanctioned charge should be to accurately represent reality or even potential reality. Rather, I am looking at these specific videos as counterdominant discourses that *produce* countermeanings. I value them not only for their difference from mainstream representations but also for the important contributions they offer to theorizations of subjectivity. Again and again, "outsider" representations reveal the inadequacy of dominant ideology—sometimes through wrenching testimony.

Juggling Gender is a portrait of Jennifer Miller, a woman in her early thirties who began to develop a beard in late adolescence. Although beards do not uniformly occupy a sex-defining position across different races and cultures, they do in Miller's family and culture.[2] As her beard thickened, Miller became increasingly estranged from her family. Her grandmother urged her to undergo electrolysis, but Miller experienced the process as an extremely painful mutilation; further, having come out in the lesbian-feminist era and then undergoing electrolysis made Miller feel like a traitor to herself and her cause. If lesbian feminism's aesthetic of natural womanness encouraged letting one's leg and underarm hair grow, why not facial hair too? In lesbian bars and other women-only spaces, however, many women have resented the confusion Miller's appearance can cause. They never expected to mistake a "natural" woman for a man. Ironically, it was cultural feminism's endorsement of essential womanhood that enabled Miller to challenge the codification of sexual difference.

Jennifer Miller in
Juggling Gender
(Tami Gold 1992)

Miller describes how having a full beard has altered her gender, which is formed not only from who she is and how she behaves but also by her interactions with society. She would like the term *woman* to include her; however, after years of also being treated like a man, she thinks of herself as not just woman. Her experiences on the street have widened her construction to incorporate sometimes being man.[3]

Against earlier plans for college and professional life, Miller helped create a feminist circus where her "freak" status is acceptable. In the circus, she juggles, bearded and bare-breasted, foregrounding her sexual discontinuity. She eats fire, lies on a bed of nails, and performs other circus acts to make explicit society's ostracizing gaze at her. Performing as a Coney Island sideshow, she reminds the audience that many women have beards, that nonbearded femininity is constructed via shaving and electrolysis. "Women have the potential to have beards," she challenges them, "if only they would reach out." Unlike the women in the audience, however, Miller *is* the bearded lady, constructed as such by their look *at* her.

At the end of *Juggling Gender*, Miller is shown at a lesbian and gay pride march performing "faggot" drag. As she notes, there are as yet no codes for performing a bearded lesbian gender. Faggot behavior, she explains, is a response to being looked at, a situation to which she relates. Suddenly the camera pans back and forth between Miller and a drag queen sticking out their tongues to mime each other.

Miller's life as a bearded lesbian combines two discourses that elsewhere have produced altercation—cultural feminism and gay male drag. Many feminists, including many lesbian feminists, have read gay male drag as misogynous, even as they criticize the trappings of femininity for women. The fact that gay drag was read as a criticism of women themselves (rather than a parody of the masquerade)[4] illustrates the lasting power of reactionary codes even as they are deconstructed. In the present semiotic system, it *is* difficult to undo the collapse of woman with feminine masquerade. But Jennifer Miller's decision to let her beard grow exposes the *complicity* of many women in *maintaining* a system in which a beard is an essential definer of sex. Although under severe ideological pressure that would naturalize and thus strongly determine it, most women *consciously* choose electrolysis. If women are essentially different from men, this difference is certainly not attributable to a lack of facial hair. An essentialist position that also claims the accoutrements of masquerade or relies on the reconstruction of bodies is questionable. On the other hand, if one is constructed in the meaning that one's signs have to others, is not the presence or absence of accoutrements and facial hair an important producer of gender?

Miller's performance demonstrates how essentialist and constructionist discourses can lead into each other. Allowing her beard to grow is a direct extension of her cultural feminist training; but in so doing Miller belies the essentialism on which cultural feminism is based. In taking cultural feminism's tenet of "naturalness" to its logical conclusion, Miller risks exclusion from that very community, because to that community, as to mainstream society, she risks appearing to "be" a man.

Jennifer Miller is not the only character in *Juggling Gender,* for videomaking is also a means of performing. Offscreen but verbally present, the videomaker Tami Gold narrates her experience of making the tape. Gold initially explores her identity as a feminist, but her contact with Miller causes her to question gender itself. "What is a woman?" she asks. By including herself in the video as a thinking and learning presence, Gold suggests a responsible viewing mode for us. Our similarity to and difference from Coney Island audiences become clearer as Gold situates us to hear and consider what Miller is saying. Like Gold herself, we stare at Miller's image, but the tape infuses this voyeurism with a keen awareness of Jennifer

Miller's subjectivity. Rather than hiding Miller's body and shying away from her "freakish" self-presentations, Gold contextualizes such images with Miller's testimony. Gold not only constructs Miller's image but also constructs herself as our surrogate. As such she encourages self-critical, intellectually engaged, and informed looking.

Endocrinology, psychoanalysis, and object relations are among the dominant discourses that define gender identity. Although many factors distinguish these theories, they all understand gender as basically fixed. Recent endocrinology research looks to the fetal environment for the determination of a core gender identity; psychoanalysis looks to the oedipal stage up to approximately age five and only secondarily to adolescence; object relations theory looks to the preoedipal mother-child relation in very early childhood. Many feminist theorists who assert the construction of gender follow object relations to understand sex attribution as the primary determinant of gender. I agree that sex attribution is influential, but, taking Jennifer Miller's gender juggling as a case in point, I neither locate it exclusively in early childhood nor understand it as fixed. Gender formation is constantly in process; rather than being a root of oneself, it continues throughout life via interactions with others. Not only one's mother is a gender mirror, but also everyone else one meets in life. The process of sex attribution (that is, gendering) does not stop at birth. For most people, complicity with binary gender semiotics (sex role stereotypes, conventional clothing, and so on) allows social interaction to reinforce birthtime sex attribution and thus gender. For others, voluntary or involuntary nonconformity causes radical disruptions and contradictions.

Wearing a beard, Jennifer Miller crosses the semiotic boundary between female and male and thus alters the basis upon which others construct her gender. This circular, interactive formation raises complex issues about "self." Obviously, had Miller concealed her beard, as other women have, her gender identity today would be different than it is—not because gender resides in biology (which can be controlled), but because of (a different) cultural production. A person, then, is simultaneously the producer of a persona and the product of the way(s) others read (and project into) that persona (and its failings).

Although Jennifer Miller is "out" as a lesbian in *Juggling Gender*, the tape produces meaning for the most part via its feminist voice.[5] Gold underlines the tape's feminist parameters by replacing the disembodied male authority of voice-of-God documentaries with cinema verité segments, performance, interviews, and attributable, subjective voice-overs by Miller and herself. She identifies herself as a continuing feminist even as her (particular) feminist perspective and assumptions are challenged by Miller.

Miller also identifies as a feminist even though some feminists reject her. More importantly, Miller is portrayed as neither hero nor outlaw, for both positions would support an all-or-nothing mode of thinking. Instead she is cast as a noncomplicit survivor, which is why she impresses many audiences as a role model.[6] As such, she variously identifies as a woman and passes as a man.

Miller expresses "contradictory" positions throughout *Juggling Gender:* at times she asserts that she *is* still a woman (despite mistaken interpretations by strangers), but she also clearly insists that her gender is no longer reducible to *woman*. In my analysis here, I do not claim direct access to Jennifer Miller, Tami Gold, or *Juggling Gender*. Instead, I am elaborating on *my reading* of the tape. My own theorization of gender dismisses any prediscursive nature/body that would fix gender. I understand both gender and sex as "knowable" and negotiable only through convention. Like Gold and Miller, who are feminists challenging feminism, *Juggling Gender* pressures feminism rather than attacks it.

In 1970, at the Second Congress to Unite Women, the "lavender menace" disrupted scheduled events with a staged coming out that confronted straight feminists with their heterosexism and homophobia. Ironically, while denaturalizing the gathering's assumed unity, the action ultimately functioned to unite heterosexual women and lesbians via a circulated position paper from the Radicalesbians entitled "The Woman Identified Woman." In this short paper, the authors concisely argued that straight feminists should, like lesbians, channel their nurturance toward other women. In this way, they posited lesbianism as a feminist practice and feminism as the defining characteristic of lesbianism. The paper began, "What is a lesbian? A lesbian is the rage of all women condensed to the point of explosion." The Radicalesbians suggested that the straight versus lesbian split in the women's movement was attributable to patriarchal oppression on two counts: first, lesbianism, as distinct from heterosexuality, was the result of women's struggle for self-growth; and second, accusations of lesbianism were used by men to keep straight women in subservient roles. The paper called for straight women to lose their defensiveness by refusing to consider lesbianism as negative and to replace their internalized sexism with a commitment to women:

> It must be understood that what is crucial is that women begin disengaging from male-defined response patterns. In the privacy of our own psyches, we must cut those cords to the core. For irrespective of where our love and sexual energies flow, if we are male identified in our heads, we cannot realize our autonomy as human beings. . . .
>
> Only women can give each other a new sense of self. That identity we have

to develop with reference to ourselves and not in relation to men. This consciousness is the revolutionary force from which all else will follow, for ours is an organic revolution. For this we must be available and supportive to one another, give our commitment and our love, give the emotional support necessary to sustain this movement. Our energies must flow toward our sisters, not backward toward our oppressors.[7]

Terralee Bensinger has argued that this document sacrificed lesbian sexuality to the politics of sexual difference.[8] One can readily see its contribution to a lesbian continuum where feminist mutuality (aka sisterhood) rather than sexuality defines the term *lesbian*. From a different perspective, Eve Kosofsky Sedgwick has described the document as "a stunningly efficacious coup of feminist redefinition" that provided a rare shift in the understanding of lesbianism, from a model of gender inversion to one of gender separatism.[9] I would like to briefly highlight what I see to be a related and equally important negotiation in the document, between two modes of identity.

Cultural feminism seems an essentialist discourse par excellence. Inverting the sexual hierarchy without disturbing sexual binarism, it valorizes female over male characteristics. Cultural feminism appropriates men's association of women with nature as the model for a better world. Extrapolated from women's birthing capacity, nurturance becomes a gender-defining principle.[10] In "The Woman Identified Woman," the Radicalesbians were able to turn the accusation of male-identification (previously directed at lesbians, who, because of their attraction to women, were assumed to be like men—that is, not real women) back on straight feminists by asserting the source of identity to be relational rather than integral. Directed at lesbians, the accusation of male identification posits a condition of self (virilization); directed at straight women, it posits a condition of (nonfeminist) allegiance. Viewed through this lesbian-feminist lens that understands identity through relations, personal relations with men jeopardize straight women's gender identity, while lesbians' female gender is secured by their romantic relationships. In this sense, sexual practice is not totally absent from the document's scene. In fact, object choice now determines gender via a schematic directly opposed to the assumption of heterogender that previously cast lesbians as "wannabe" men. Rather than basing *feminist* identity on what one is, the privileged ethic of nurturance was deployed to relocate such identity in how and toward whom one directs one's energy. This is a significant shift in terms. Unlike the gender essentialism on which female identity is based, feminist identity (the woman identified woman) is based on relational behavior. Further, such behavior ironically is attributed to natural womanness.

Although situated somewhat differently, Jennifer Miller's gender identity is also relations-based. Treated like a man, she becomes manlike. It is not her beard but rather people's reactions to its mark that have altered her gender. Those who see her as a man (as well as those who see her as a woman, or as a bearded woman) help mold her gender. Their gaze is her gender mirror. Like their gaze, her gender is both multifaceted and culturally specific; thus it disrupts unified concepts of gender. Unlike both cultural feminists and the Radicalesbians, Miller wants the category of women to expand to include her "virilization."

Elizabeth Grosz's book *Volatile Bodies* is a project against the dualism of mind versus body. Describing the body as a sociohistorical product that functions interactively,[11] Grosz implants corporeality in the theorization of subjectivity. The material textures of bodies, rather than being blank pages waiting for cultural inscription, participate in and affect such inscriptions. This would seem to support Jennifer Miller's account of her gender formation.

In her final chapter, "Sexed Bodies," Grosz uses the work of Mary Douglas, Julia Kristeva, Luce Irigaray, and Iris Young to scrutinize how, in Western culture, bodily fluids that "attest to the permeability of the body"[12] are assigned to the feminine. Orifices and leakage threaten a masculine order that relies on a notion of self as closed entity. A production of otherness thus underlies man's projection of the body itself onto woman, which seeks to eliminate his own pervious status and claim for him alone the supposedly more neutral, less situated mind. "Women, insofar as they are human, have the same degree of solidity, occupy the same genus, as men, yet insofar as they are women, they are represented and live themselves as seepage, liquidity."[13] Patriarchal discourse does not describe subject formation as relational but rather as the ascension to a bounded, phallic self.

While Grosz challenges the mind-body dualism and presses that challenge against the "mechanics of solids" that inscribes and supports male subjectivity,[14] she generally preserves the dualism of sexual difference. She deontologizes sex, but culturally produced sexual difference remains essential to her argument. Although she alludes to hermaphroditic bodies and more than two sexes, she ultimately posits "the irreducible specificity of women's bodies."[15] One instance of specificity is menstruation, notable for its difference from the excretory functions mastered during toilet training. Appearing during female adolescence, it is the reemergence of the out of control body, the dirty. Menstruation thus is seen as *significantly* different from the flows shared by male and female bodies. In a footnote Grosz writes: "I am not advocating a naturalist or even a universalist attribute. Nonetheless, it is also true that all women, whatever the details of their physiology and fertility, are culturally understood in terms of these bodily flows [menstruation and lactation]."[16] Although it is conventionally marked, sexual difference remains salient.

This may be so, but it is disappointing that Grosz does not more aggressively apply her theorization of corporeal experience to affirm and explore more varied subjectivities arising from further elaborated bodily specificities. In a discussion about gay men's sexual practices, she does suggest embraced permeability as a possible component of male sensibility. Nevertheless, she ultimately remains primarily concerned with the generalities of two sexes:

> There will always remain a kind of outsideness or alienness of the experiences and lived reality of each sex for the other. Men, contrary to the fantasy of the transsexual, can never, even with surgical intervention, feel or experience what it is like to be, to live, as women. At best the transsexual can live out his fantasy of femininity—a fantasy that in itself is usually disappointed with the rather crude transformations effected by surgical and chemical intervention. The transsexual may look like a woman but can never feel like or be a woman.[17]

But if a transsexual looks like a woman, will she not also be culturally understood/treated/formed in terms of menstrual flow (despite its absence)? Grosz does not extend her discussion toward the question of how a transsexual's changed corporeality and appearance *do* affect subjectivity. The strength of Grosz's work is that it asserts that the experience of one's body (including one's relation to cultural meanings of one's sex) contributes to the formation of subjectivity. From this she rightly concludes that one's previously sexed life experience and subjectivity do not simply drop away with a sex change. However, does the influence of bodily and relational experiences suddenly halt with a sex change? What might Grosz's investigation of corporeal experience throughout her book offer to understanding how subject formation continues as bodily changes occur, whether via sex change or menopause? My pointing to an interplay of representation, perception, and experience with regard to subject formation allows that the (changing) body can influence subjectivity without discounting contrary gender identifications. To my mind, Grosz stops short of the potential her own work suggests.

We might ask, Is sexual difference not only productive for but necessary to feminism? Does "this gulf, this irremediable distance" between the sexes, as Grosz puts it,[18] prevent a fluidity of sex? Is feminism itself dependent on a "mechanics of solids" to postulate subjectivity?

Jennifer Miller's beard arrived on her with discursive valence. After all, it is a secondary sex characteristic. As such, it was supposed to (but did not) support an already sexed subjectivity, a sexual identity. A beard is supposed to be a reward at the end of horrifying *male* adolescence, a solidification after that messy stage of bodily transformations. Secondary sex characteristics are conceptualized as the final confirmations, not complications, of one's sex. They are *supposed* to offer relief after prolonged worries about whether our childish bodies will deliver the "appropriate" sexes or ultimately expose us as "freaks."

We patrol gender expressly because our claim to normality (that is, conventional humanness) has been made to rely on it. Not to be one's true sex is a crime against the law of pure difference. Mary Douglas's definition of dirt as that which is (culturally determined to be) out of place describes Jennifer Miller's beard. Hair is a waste product of our bodies, like urine, menstrual blood, and toenails. A man's beard, evidence of "masculine" flow, is best kept shaved or trimmed into a sculpture. A bearded woman, evidence of flow across sexual difference, is cultural feminism's abject.

In *Bodies That Matter*, Judith Butler analyzes how "properly" gendered bodies are materialized through heterosexual norms and how such formation of heterosexual subjects relies on foreclosures that produce homosexuality and gender inversion as abject: "The abject designates here precisely those 'unlivable' and 'uninhabitable' zones of social life which are nevertheless densely populated by those who do not enjoy the status of subject, but whose living under the sign of 'unlivable' is required to circumscribe the domain of the subject."[19] Constraints generate both sanctioned and unsanctioned positions but uphold the former via a logic that repudiates the latter. Such a normative scheme would understand Jennifer Miller as having failed to materialize as a (human) subject. Instead, her deformation serves as the constitutive "outside" by which normality is constituted and regulatory norms are fortified.[20] Her abject status locates her outside subjecthood. She is alive but not fully human.

The underlying problems in this operation, which affect all gay and lesbian and transgendered "subjects," are an Althusserian-influenced totalizing of ideology[21] and an overwillingness in Lacanian psychoanalysis to relegate irregular subjects to the "unrepresentable," a zone lacking symbolization and hence subjects. This is to mistake dominant ideology for all symbolization and to assume that what is unrepresented is unrepresentable. By contrast, Jennifer Miller does not experience herself as abject, and she obviously claims subjecthood. She has not undergone a "psychotic dissolution" simply because she is no longer one-sex-identified. Nor does *she* see herself as the "living prospect of death."[22]

Despite her valuable identification of regulatory regimes that construct abjection, Butler details this operation *rhetorically* from an "inside" perspective. This limits the "imagination" of her theorization and contributes to the naturalization of a particular standpoint, which is then allowed to define abjection. Certainly, it can be argued that no person can exist totally outside dominant ideology, and therefore that the dominant ideology's abject is uninhabitable. However, given the coexistence of "other" discourses that rearticulate dominant terms from "other" positions (that dominant ideology would assign to the abject), a particular subject materialization may be considerably more complex than such a regulating discourse would suggest. Part of what dominant ideology expels via assignment to *its* abject is, in fact, *formative* counterdiscourse.[23]

Butler opposes (theoretically speaking) any claim to coherent identity.[24] Following Laplanche and Pontalis's theorization of fantasy as the staging and dispersion of the subject, in which the subject cannot be assigned to any one position, Butler asserts that the normative subject is produced not by the refusal to identify with the other, but rather through *identification with* an abject other:[25]

> A radical refusal to identify with a given position suggests that on some level an identification has already taken place, an identification that is made and disavowed, a disavowed identification whose symptomatic appearance is the insistence on, the overdetermination of, the identification by which gay and lesbian subjects come to signify in public discourse.[26]

Likewise, Butler is careful to qualify the subversive potential of gender performativity. One cannot simply take on gender like one chooses clothing; this would imply a subject prior to gender. Rather, it is repetition in gender that forms the subject. Butler credits subversive rearticulation of the symbolic to the return of figures once repudiated (to the imaginary); this establishes a process of resignification rather than opposition and attributes contestation to the process of signification that inadvertently enables what it attempts to restrict.[27] Although Butler allows for inexact repetitions, she is opposed to attributing any amendments to personal choice or deliberation:

> The practice by which gendering occurs, the embodying of norms, is a compulsory practice, a forcible production, but not for that reason fully determining. To the extent that gender is an assignment, it is an assignment which is never quite carried out according to expectation, whose addressee never quite inhabits the ideal s/he is compelled to approximate. Moreover, this embodying is a repeated process. And one might construe repetition as precisely that which *undermines* the conceit of voluntarist mastery designated by the subject in language."[28]

Butler's work is outstanding for its deconstructions of identity and "natural" gender. However, her elucidation here seems more useful for understanding women's attempts to live up to an ideal—that is, their complicity with the maintenance of sexual difference—than for understanding feminist rejections of the ideal. For example, it better accounts for electrolysis as gender performativity ("the tacit cruelties that sustain coherent identity, cruelties that include self-cruelty")[29] than for Miller's refusal of electrolysis. It better explicates women's assumption of dominant norms for purposes of self-hatred than Miller's unconventional strength. Jennifer Miller's gendering cannot be explained simply as a failure to repeat. Certainly, the development of a beard on her body misses its conventional assignment; however, is not her decision to let the beard grow a choice (even if it is derived from a feminist ideology), and the subsequent (re)gendering (via the responses of others to her body) a result of her deliberate action (or inaction)? Does not Miller's bodily utterance alter the language of gender to some extent? Does not Gold's videotape reveal the boundary between symbolization and the "unrepresentable" real to be always in practice a fiction produced from a particular (dominant yet limited) point of view?

What I am suggesting by my discussion of Jennifer Miller in *Juggling Gender* is a salient temporality in subject formation. If indeed the subject is always a subject-in-process, then at any one point she is formed, being formed, and forming. Does not her formedness grant some subjectivity (however provisional), which she exercises even as cultural norms continue to interpellate her? My insistence on taking up marginal rather than (exclusively) dominant perspectives in theorizing subjectivity opens the way for *appreciating* a difference between a *failure* to repeat and a *refusal* to repeat.

In *OUTLAW* Leslie Feinberg, a transgender lesbian, describes her life as an everyday struggle. Feinberg is interviewed in a variety of meaningful settings. At the Pyramid Club, she refers to the female impersonators as sisters. At Liberty State Park in New Jersey, she criticizes people who assume the right to stare. At the Hudson piers, a Manhattan site notorious for transgenderist (and gay) gatherings and bashings, she explains that any place where transgenderists go becomes dangerous (for them). In her backyard, she explains that, to her, *butch* means butch on the street, an act of courage that earns one the right to engage in whatever acts she wants to in bed. At the gym, surrounded by workout machines and mirrors, she describes her self-image as a combination of how she sees herself and how the world sees her. In choosing the gym as an interview setting, Feinberg contributed to her media construction in a way transgenderists seldom are al-

Leslie Feinberg in *OUTLAW* (Alisa Lebow 1994)

lowed to do. Rather than simply exposing the transgendered body for spectacle, Feinberg retains her subject position in an environment symbolic of self-empowerment.

Feinberg's testimony is solemn throughout *OUTLAW*. Only at rare moments does her enjoyment of life break through: in her exquisite "men's" suits, in scenes with her lover repotting plants and watching a home movie. When clips from *The Rocky Horror Picture Show* suggest a reprieve from her testimony of constant oppression, Feinberg reminds us that a mere movie is not going to liberate Eighth Street (in New York City, where the film was then playing midnights) from transgender bashing. Elsewhere, when Feinberg speaks of transgenderists reclaiming their histories, her smile is undercut by an edit to helicopters flying overhead in formation.

The pleasure in viewing *OUTLAW* derives from the complex collaboration of Feinberg's discourse and Alisa Lebow's disquisition. Using music (Danny Galton's "Funky Momma," for example), intertitles ("Suit and Tie Optional," for example), and extradiegetic imagery (a woman bodybuilder, for example), Lebow both underlines and adds ambiguity to Feinberg's analysis of transgender oppression. At one point Feinberg expresses disapproval and impatience with people who compare their childhood gender crossings with her lived experience. Such linkages erase the actual repression she risks when, for instance, she uses a public washroom. Lebow's inclusion of footage from the film *Yentl* at this point in the tape both demonstrates how transgenderism is often trivialized and also implies a continuum from feminist cross-dressing to transgenderism, which offers a conduit for viewer identification.

Lebow's videomaking is most aggressive when she re-presents a scene of Feinberg appearing on the *Joan Rivers Show*, where Feinberg proclaims the need for transgenderists to name and speak for themselves. Through skillful editing, Lebow becomes Feinberg's co-conspirator. "I'm so sick of being psychologized. I'm so sick of being studied like a butterfly pinned to the wall," says Feinberg in voice-over as the face of a token authority figure, clinical sexologist Roger E. Peo, Ph.D., appears on the screen. Then Lebow audiocuts to sync sound as Peo begins, "I'm not in a position to judge and say this person should do this thing or that thing. What I try to do is . . ." On the original broadcast, the authority no doubt went on to state his opinion, but in the Lebow/Feinberg version his appraisal is excised. Smoothly but decisively, Lebow interrupts him with an audiovisual cut to Feinberg, who continues, now in sync sound: "All our lives, we've always seen ourselves refracted through other people's prisms. We're always hearing people analyze us, describe what our feelings are, what our thoughts are. How about talking about why Jesse Helms needs some therapy?"

OUTLAW begins with a discussion of Joan of Arc and ends with a dedication to Brandon Teena and Marsha P. Johnson. Brandon Teena (born Teena Brandon but living as a male) was raped by two young men on Christmas Eve 1993 in Nebraska. Although Teena's face was injured and a hospital test confirmed recent vaginal penetration, his attackers were released after questioning. No arrests were made. One week later, on New Year's Eve, the same young men allegedly killed Teena. Martha Johnson, a drag queen veteran of the Stonewall rebellion, was found dead in the Hudson River (off the piers) after the 1992 New York City gay pride march. Although there were signs of resistance, Johnson's death was declared a suicide after a perfunctory police investigation. In addition to the outsider status guaranteed by their transgenderism, Teena and Johnson were working-class people. Like Feinberg, they lacked the protection of class privilege experienced by more acclaimed historical cross-dressers such as Radclyffe Hall, George Sand, and Gertrude Stein. It is significant to Feinberg that the powerful and persecuted Joan of Arc, who not only sported men's clothes but also passed as a man, was a peasant. That Feinberg could not know this as a child is a culpable suppression of (transgender) evidence. Gender and class are inseparable in all of these people and their expressions; we cannot know the meanings of their different transgenders without also knowing their class situations.

While claiming both transgenderism and homosexuality, Feinberg is careful to distinguish between them. During her interview at the Pyramid Club, she draws two intersecting circles on a blackboard and indicates her own position: within the intersection. *OUTLAW* reminds us that much of the violence enacted against gays and lesbians actually is directed at transgenderism.[30] Of course, as I remarked at the beginning of this essay, gender and sexual orientation have been intertwined historically by sexological discourse and homosexual appropriation of such discourse for self-coding. Transgenderism is attacked partly because it reads as homosexuality and vice versa. It is therefore important neither to collapse homosexuality and transgenderism nor to overlook their specific imbrications.

Eve Kosofsky Sedgwick argues in "How to Bring Your Kids Up Gay" that neither an essentialist nor a constructionist position guarantees safety for homosexual subjectivity. She locates a shift during the 1970s and 1980s from pathologizing adult homosexuality to pathologizing childhood gender crossing. The 1980 edition of the American Psychiatric Association's *Diagnostic and Statistical Manual* was both the first not to contain an entry for "Homosexuality" and the first to contain the entry "Gender Identity Disorder of Childhood." To Sedgwick, this *preventive* measure expresses the rage of parents, professionals, society at large, and even gays and lesbians at sissy boys and, to a lesser extent, butch girls. Ironically, she points out, the new psychoanalytic move to pathologize gender disorder while depathologizing sexual orientation is based on the recent theoretical move to distinguish gender and sex orientation (for example, the gender constructionist approaches of John Money and Robert Stoller).[31] This makes it clear that the attempt by some homosexuals to pry apart gender and sexual orientation not only is inadequate but can fuel a reactionary discourse against those among us who cross gender. Therefore, any rejection of masculinity in lesbians or metaphoric feminization of the term *lesbian* warrants extreme caution.

Juggling Gender and *OUTLAW* re-present voices that contest the borders generally assumed to dominate symbolization and subject formation and problematize theory that situates its rhetorical point of view strictly within those borders. I understand gender and gender formation to be more flexible than the paradigm sexual binarism produces and to be continually influenced by social experience. By focusing on independent media, I call attention to alternative representations as well as alternative subjects.

NOTES

1. This essay draws on two excerpts from my book *Deviant Eyes, Deviant Bodies: Sexual Re-Orientations in Film and Video* (New York: Columbia University Press, 1996). The videos discussed, *Juggling Gender* and *OUTLAW,* are distributed by Women Make Movies, 462 Broadway, Suite 500D, New York, NY 10013; telephone 212-925-0606; fax 212-925-2052; E-mail distdept@wmm.com.

2. For a wide-ranging discussion of differently sexed and gendered cultures, see Gilbert Herdt, ed., *Third Sex, Third Gender* (New York: Zone, 1994).

3. In *Juggling Gender,* gender often refers also to sex. Because of Miller's being perceived as one of the male sex, her constructed gender-sex expands beyond womanness.

4. Mary Ann Doane, drawing on Joan Riviere, has argued that womanliness *is* the masquerade of femininity ("Film and the Masquerade: Theorizing the Female Spectator," in *Femmes Fatales: Feminism, Film Theory, Psychoanalysis* [New York: Routledge, 1991], 17–32). I complicate this in chapter 5 of *Deviant Eyes, Deviant Bodies*.

5. The video foregrounds feminism over lesbianism. The extent to which the absence of lesbian sexuality is a by-product of the tape's focus, necessary for its feminist efficacy, and/or a self-conscious avoidance of the dangerous terrain of gender inversion explanations of homosexuality is difficult to determine.

6. The function of role model is important here because, as Judith Butler argues, the performative utterance has no valence unless it is repeated (*Bodies That Matter: On the Discursive Limits of "Sex"* [New York: Routledge, 1993], 107). Ultimately, Miller's rearticulation "exposes the norm itself as a privileged interpretation" (*Bodies,* 108) and serves as a model for *not* citing, *not* repeating assumed symbolic categories. In this way, I question the precision and efficacy of using the term *citation* (or *repetition*) to refer to both complicit and subversive acts.

7. Radicalesbians, "The Woman Identified Woman," in *Radical Feminism,* ed. Anne Koedt, Ellen Levine, and Anita Rapone (New York: Quandrangle, 1973), 166.

8. Terralee Bensinger, "Lesbian Pornography: The Re/Making of (a) Community," *Discourse* 15.1 (1992): 74.

9. Eve Kosofsky Sedgwick, *Epistemology of the Closet* (Berkeley: University of California Press, 1990), 84, 88.

10. See Alice Echols, *Daring to Be Bad: Radical Feminism in America 1967-1975* (Minneapolis: University of Minnesota Press, 1989);

Alison M. Jagger, *Feminist Politics and Human Nature* (Totowa, N.J.: Rowman and Allanheld, 1983); and my discussion of motherhood in chapter 5 of *Deviant Eyes, Deviant Bodies*.

11. Elizabeth Grosz, *Volatile Bodies: Toward a Corporeal Feminism* (Bloomington: Indiana University Press, 1994), x, xi.

12. Ibid., 193.

13. Ibid., 203.

14. Ibid., 204.

15. Ibid., 207.

16. Ibid., 228 n17.

17. Ibid., 207.

18. Ibid., 208.

19. Butler, *Bodies,* 3.

20. Ibid., 16.

21. The continued deployment of the repressive state apparatus should remind us that the ideological state apparatus is not as totalizing as it would have us believe.

22. See Butler, *Bodies,* 98: "The breaking of certain taboos brings on the spectre of psychosis, but to what extent can we understand 'psychosis' as relative to the very prohibitions that guard against it? In other words, what precise cultural possibilities threaten the subject with a psychotic dissolution, marking the boundaries of livable being? To what extent is the fantasy of psychotic dissolution itself the effect of a certain prohibition against those sexual possibilities which abrogate the heterosexual contract? Under what conditions and under the sway of what regulatory schemes does homosexuality itself appear as the living prospect of death?"

23. For clarification, I want to stress that I am not taking up an imagined "other" position with respect to Butler. I am not promoting a humanist view of free will and individuality. I agree with Butler that language constrains subject formation. Nevertheless, I think that theoretical investigation should include the choice and responsibility within these limitations. To think of culture as *all* determining is neither accurate nor productive. Butler *asks:* "Does not the refusal to concur with the abjection of homosexuality necessitate a critical rethinking of the psychoanalytic economy of sex?" (*Bodies,* 97). Butler's focus here is sexual orientation, but I think she produces the same question regarding gender.

24. This includes those claims from the homosexual abject, whether gay, lesbian, sissy, butch, or femme (Butler, *Bodies,* 113). As she states, "Heterosexuality does not have a monopoly on exclusionary logics" (*Bodies,* 112).

25. Butler, *Bodies*, 267, 112.

26. Ibid., 113.

27. Ibid., 109.

28. Ibid., 231; emphasis in the original.

29. Ibid., 115.

30. Such violence is also directed at transgender-ism among heterosexuals.

31. Eve Kosofsky Sedgwick, *Tendencies* (Durham, N.C.: Duke University Press, 1993), 154–64.

KATHLEEN McHUGH

[13] *Irony and Dissembling:*
Queer Tactics for
Experimental Documentary

Appearances deceive. "Queer" cultural identity and the problematics of
contemporary documentary converge on this (platonic) point.[1] The phenomenon of heterosexual presumption (one is straight until proven otherwise) frequently places queer subjects in a position that mimics and inverts
the structure of dramatic irony. Presumed straight, the queer subject becomes an actor in a scene staged by another, by another's cultural imaginary. Yet in this scene, the actor knows more, is more than her or his audience, more than his or her culture imagines. A knowledge effect, which
undermines the assumed coherence of identity as such, arises from the dynamics of this staging: of who the subject is not.

This effect accrues to the queer subject, producing a necessarily ironized
or metasubjectivity; consciousness of a self at odds with the self culturally
perceived and sanctioned is a consciousness that exceeds and therefore
knows the limits and inadequacies of the social contract, knows intimately
its failure to represent all its subjects. Thus, queer subjectivity is in some
sense founded upon the ruse of appearances, on structural misrecognitions.
Gay theorists note a "gay sensibility," associated with camp, "which
stresses the absolute importance of mastering appearances and assuming
identities in a gay life where passing for straight . . . is so critical."[2] In this
sensibility, knowledge effect often becomes ironic affect (a symptomatic
transformation when knowledge is divorced from power?). Richard Dyer
writes that "the ability to hold together intense devotion to something with
a simultaneous irony or even derision towards it is characteristic of much
gay culture."[3] The queer film and video makers I will discuss work back
from affect to effect, using the incongruities of queer cultural identity to
fashion visual texts that question the incongruities of perception, representation, and identity for everyone.

A similar irony also concerned with authenticity and representation informs the problematics of contemporary documentary film and video. Sergei Eisenstein presciently outlined the terms of this problematic in his condemnation of the nonfiction film. The cinema's astonishing capacity to record appearances was precisely the attribute that rendered documentary films the most capable of dangerous mystification. The reality in front of the camera must be subjected to stylistic and conceptual interventions before the film could convey the historical truth that existed beyond appearances. Subsequent critiques of realism and of the presumptions of cinema verité have led to complex reassessments of documentary stylistics.[4] The task of the film or video maker who accepts these critiques is to structure the text such that its knowledge effects emerge from the ironic structure of the text's assertions; in documenting the dissembling of appearances, the "not" of any assertion is staged.

In lesbian and gay experimental documentary, these ironies—subjective, affective, and representational—converge. Queer filmmakers perhaps have an edge in experimental, reflexive nonfiction because of their experience living in reflexive and rhetorical subjectivities.[5] Thus this work presents a particularly rich field for investigating effective tactics in experimental nonfiction film and video production in general, because it interrogates representation both in relation to the medium and in relation to the subjects of the work. In this essay, I would like to examine the films and videos of three artists—John Goss, Joyan Saunders, and Bill Jones—for the very diverse ways they approach and fabricate a "queer" nonfiction. Rather than defining what queer identity *is* and offering evidence for the incontrovertible historical reality of a monolithic, unilateral queerness, they are more true to their subject. They respect the representational and subjective "nots" that subtend queer experience and identity. Each artist presents the extreme complexities and contradictions involved in any construction of identity; taken together, they indicate the myriad possibilities of representational tactics available to apprehend, while not crudely defining or limiting, very elusive subjectivities.

Insofar as each deals with queer/gay iconography or subject material and eschews an unambiguous realism in presenting that material, the work of Goss, Saunders, and Jones loosely falls within the lineage of queer experimental documentary inaugurated by pioneers Kenneth Anger, George Kuchar, and Jack Smith. However, the connection would not be evident in the appearance of their videos and films; the very diverse and complex trajectory of experimental documentary and the disparate influences on each of these artists distinguish them both from the originators of the genre and from each other. While actively using and subverting the codes of an array of other documentary traditions (which I will discuss specifically later),

Saunders and Goss weave biography, created biography, and autobiography into formats derived from postmodern art tapes, conceptual art, and experimental documentary (see Chris Marker's work as an example of these genres). Goss's career as a Los Angeles performance artist and an AIDS activist inflects his work both aesthetically and affectively, while Saunders's work in photography influences her treatment of video images. The work of Bill Jones emerges from diary films of the sixties and seventies, feminist experimental filmmakers, and work with poetic documentary, home movies, and deconstructed camp (Jonas Mekas, Robert Frank, the punk Super-8 movement of the seventies and early eighties).

Goss, Saunders, and Jones all, in very different ways, cleverly misdirect the audience's trust in the image, soliciting the emotions that would attend the telling of a true story, while pointedly subverting the conventions of its telling. Rather than using the concreteness and immediacy of the filmic image to present an argument or thesis, their work employs tactics to deconstruct the truth value of various modes of documentary representation. Thus theoretical and ethical issues standard to documentary film criticism, such as those concerning evidence and proof of a discernable thesis, no longer hold. The standard these artists establish and by which they should be measured is a paradoxical (an ironic?) one. It involves a process whereby meaning effects are produced, but always in a context where their veracity is simultaneously called into question. These tactics serve an array of approaches to queerness, gay and lesbian sexuality, and identity. My essay will investigate the permutations of this interaction between deconstructive tactics and queer subjects in John Goss's *Wild Life* and *He's Like*, Joyan Saunders's *Here in the Southwest* and *Brains on Toast*, and Bill Jones's *Massillon*.

In John Goss's work, the performance artist's informed, sophisticated attention to representational media and reflexive rhetoric blends neatly with the activist's dedication and sensitivity to social issues, ultimately to the benefit of both. The work of Goss's that I will discuss refuses the straightforward, realist format of much activist work while also insisting that queer life, youth, and icons be given visibility, albeit a nuanced and complex one.[6] Goss's *Wild Life* (1985), for example, employs tactics drawn from conventional documentary—the interview format, an observational camera that discreetly tracks its subjects—to fashion a pseudo ethnography/biography of its subjects, two queer Latino youth, Cesar and Carlos. Early sequences of the film alternate between fragments of interviews Goss conducts individually with each adolescent. Goss, off-camera, directs questions—name, how old are you, how long have you been in Los Angeles, where do you go to high school, what are you studying—to each boy, seated at an angle to, but facing, the camera. Both are fifteen and both have been in the United States less than ten years. In the first sequence, Cesar interrupts Goss's questions by telling him he is a Gemini. Following Cesar's lead, Goss asks what this means. Cesar explains, becomes embarrassed, laughs, and the tape cuts to the interview with Carlos. Goss goes back and forth between footage from the two interviews several times, his questions to Carlos picking up where Cesar left off and vice versa. The two discuss their future plans (Carlos is thinking about the air force; if Carlos goes, Cesar says, he will go with him), being gay, how they knew they were gay (Cesar threw up the first time he kissed a girl), and what being gay means.

Goss complicates the conventional format of the interview in the relay editing that structures this opening section and in his framing of the two adolescents (both sit in medium shot, Cesar facing screen right, Carlos screen left). Both the framing and the editing cues suggest that the boys are talking to and facing each other, as well as talking to Goss. This tactic formally undercuts the conventional ethnographic binary of interviewer/interviewee by staging the interaction as a threeway (the tape is edited such that Carlos's responses to Goss shape the questions that Goss asks Cesar, and so on). Goss also structures his initially staid, informant-profile questions in such a way that Carlos's and Cesar's responses exceed or undercut them, frivolously or ideologically. Cesar obviously feels that to know him, a person should know his sun sign. And their answers to "How long have you been in L.A.?" indicate that the ethnically sensitive question might have been "How long have you been in the United States?" In this way, Goss's interview performs the ethnographic filmmaker's (structural?) inability to address appropriate questions to members of a community that she or he does not belong to. (Goss is gay, but not Hispanic and not a teenager.) These tactics also reflexively undercut the hierarchy between interviewer and interviewee that characterizes the "interactional mode of documentary representation" that Goss uses and subverts in this and other sections throughout the tape.[7]

Throughout *Wild Life*, Goss emphasizes Carlos and Cesar's knowledge in contradistinction to his own. In the next sequence of the video, as well as at its end, Goss identifies the two as his collaborators; their desires shape the film. On camera, they tell him they want the video to be about their "wild life [the term is theirs], what we encounter, how we take the life." Goss follows their directive. Yet in the sequences that follow, aspects of that life—talking on the phone, meeting at a bus stop, Carlos changing into his wild clothes on the street because his mother doesn't approve of them ("too feminine"), walking in Griffith Park, the two having an argument—are rendered in such a way that the promise of the ethnographic film, to know and experience the life and community of another, is actively and aggressively foreclosed. Goss consistently employs tactics that emphasize both the filmmaker's and the viewer's inability to penetrate, to actually be *in* Carlos and Cesar's wild life.

To begin with, Goss makes use of contradictory styles, frequently to represent the same event or action. He shifts back and forth from pointedly artificial simulations of actions—Cesar and Carlos, standing or sitting side by side on a sparse set, enact a phone call with toy phones or simulate an argument—to highly realistic on-location sequences that chronicle Carlos waiting for Cesar at a bus stop, Carlos changing into his wild clothes in the doorway of a building, the two walking in Griffith Park, and so on. But even in the on-location sequences, Goss cleverly sabotages this staple of cinema verité/observational documentary in several ways. He never employs sync sound in them, opting instead for nondiegetic sound mixes of music, silence, and voice-overs provided by Carlos and Cesar that describe what we are seeing. We must rely on these voice-overs, because the cinematography consistently hampers what we are seeing. It either frames the boys in long shot (we watch Carlos wait at the bus stop and change his clothes from across the street, and both the distance of the shot and passing cars continually limit or obstruct our view) or it captures them, more often than not, with their backs to the camera.

Two sequences are particularly effective in this regard. In Griffith Park, a favored meeting place for this community of minors, the camera, in medium long or long shot, follows Cesar and Carlos as they walk around, greet and mingle with their friends, laugh and joke. We are not privy to what they are saying; from our vantage point, we can look at this community, literally over the shoulders of Carlos and Cesar, but we are definitely not included in it. In another sequence that makes a similar point about Carlos and Cesar's relationship, Goss cuts back and forth between the two performing an argument on the set and performing what looks like a much more realistic conflict as they walk along railroad tracks. In the first instance, we can hear and see them, but they are clearly playing. In the second, they *act* much more physically and realistically, but we cannot hear them, their backs are to us, and the point is made that even if we could see or hear them, it is still only a representation, not the life, nor their relationship itself. The embrace that ends the sequence, rendered in long shot with the boys' backs to us, emphatically excludes us.

As I hope my description has indicated, *Wild Life* alters an array of documentary styles not as an empty formal exercise, but in the paradoxical but necessary interests of giving voice and visibility to two Latino queer adolescents while also indicating what will fail in that encounter. Goss enhances this effect with the interview material that features Carlos and Cesar engaged in self-representation, and by how he arranges their disclosures. Most viewers will conclude (as I did), after hearing that Cesar will join the air force if Carlos does, that the two are lovers. In fact, they are not. They are best friends and they make it clear that even though they both have lovers, their primary relationship is with each other. This false assumption highlights the fact that there are many axes of difference that separate Carlos and Cesar from the filmmaker and from any number of the film's spectators. One, very important to Goss, is that they are teenagers and their devotion to each other instead of to a romantic partner derives from this difference, rather than from their ethnicity or sexual preference.

Similarly, Goss includes interview material from Cesar that is very contradictory. Having recounted his first nauseous kiss with a girl, Cesar later tells Goss, in response to his question about the girls' names on his notebook, that they are his girlfriends. He quickly explains that he has only been with twelve girls and that when he is with them, he is not pleasing himself, but pleasing them. Later, he asserts that he is completely gay. Spectators may take this material in a variety of ways, but I saw it, in the context of the rest of the video, as a caution to any ethnographic or theoretical endeavor that would value neat generalizations and unambiguous categories over the paradoxes and contradictions endemic to sexuality and self-representation.

Finally, the video's visual evasions and circumspections factor in the spectator's life experiences as a salient and crucial feature of its reception, thus positioning queer Los Angeles Latino youth, the video's subjects, as its most privileged spectators. Because these youth experience the "life," the video's ethnographic critique will not obstruct their viewing and identification with its scene. Other spectators, however, will see a film about two compelling queer Latino youth that is humorous, engaging, yet oddly distanced and perhaps not completely satisfying. They will grasp aspects of Carlos and Cesar's wild life without being able to fully empathize or identify with them and their lives. And these nots, these inabilities, are precisely Goss's point.

Goss's later film *He's Like* (1986) relays its message about queer identity and representation through a focused visual conundrum or joke. *He's Like* presents alternating interview footage from four informants who all seem to be answering a question put to them by an interviewer we never see or hear—"What's he like?" The only information we get about the "he" of the title comes from the four men, who are initially framed in medium close-ups that obscure much of their location. In the alternating interview sequences, the men convey anecdotal material about friendship, homophobia, queer sexuality and love, events humorous, weird, or profound that involve "him." As the sequences progress, the shot distances get longer, or the camera angles become more revealing; we get the sense that we are learning more about each interviewee from our increasing visual access to his location. But instead, new visual information continually changes what we think we know about the informants. Underscoring (literally and figuratively) this witty play with visual knowledge, the testimonies of the informants about what "he's" like become sufficiently contradictory that we understand that the four are not talking about the same person. Goss's subtle and complex understanding informs the film's basic representational joke: we learn more about the informants than about their subject(s) in talking-heads documentary. But he deconstructs his own punch line, such that each progressive shot of the informants changes our understanding of them, too. Goss's tricks with representation wittily remind us how "tricky" visual documentation and assignations of subjectivity can be.

Video artist and photographer Joyan Saunders similarly deconstructs visual situations where documentation and constructions of subjectivity intersect, but the modes that she "takes on" (in the dual and contradictory sense of mimicking and undermining) are autobiographical and science documentaries. In *Here in the Southwest* (1986) and *Brains on Toast* (1992), a collaboration with Liss Platt, Saunders ironizes the diverse tactics and truth claims of both modes by fashioning a hybrid from them and bringing it to bear on gender and sexuality. In juxtaposing the personal or subjective authority that grounds autobiographical documentary with the objective authority structured in scientific documentaries, Saunders undermines the efficacy of both. Her videos challenge both the affective, testimonial truth of experience and the analytic, objective facts of biological determinism, two argumentative modes often mobilized to render the "true" nature of normative gender roles and sexual preferences. In so doing, she also implicates the documentary cinematic conventions used to ground and convey these different modes of authority.

Here in the Southwest, for example, begins in a kitchen, in a location coded as personal, a place for women's private gossip and conversation. The camera frames a woman's hands washing dishes as a nondiegetic female voice says, "Listen to *this*!" Yet the salacious news we hear mocks (again in both senses of the word) the usual fare of the coffee klatch. The voice recounts the existence and scientific study of "whiptail lizards," a species comprised entirely of females who reproduce by parthenogenesis, as the camera pans to frame another woman, sitting at the kitchen table and reading from a science journal. We see her lips, slightly out of sync with the voice-over, mouthing the same words. The camera travels back

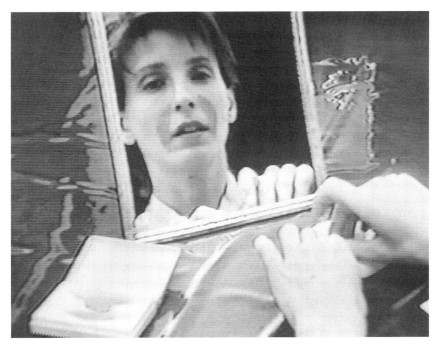

Here in the Southwest (Joyan Saunders 1984)

and forth between the two women as their voices blend with other, non-diegetic women's voices to debate the significance of the lizards to theories about the genetic merit of men and the possibility of lesbian separatism. Finally, the woman at the sink says, "But this is a long way from a lesbian feminist utopia."

This brief sequence demonstrates how Saunders's use of hybridity challenges the differing truth claims of scientific facts and personal testimony and experience by using their representational tropes in conjunction with each other. The mise-en-scène (kitchen) and situation (two women, visually coded as lesbians, having a conversation) "watched" by the camera invite us to identify with the cinema's immediacy and voyeuristic power, responsible in both fiction and documentary films for opening up private life for our scrutiny. Yet Saunders instantly undercuts this visual impression by counteracting it on the sound track: the dialogue, the dry, ironic affect of the actors, and the layering of voices all preclude any emotional identification with the actors or with an "intimate" situation. The echoing diegetic and nondiegetic voices, each touting separatist lesbian myths verified by the existence of the whiptailed lizards, perform a certain representational relation often constructed between biological "facts" and the naturalization of "straight" gender roles and lifestyles. This sequence indicates that biological facts can be marshaled to naturalize any gender arrangement or sexual preference. The sequence concurrently deconstructs the customary authority afforded the voice-over in expository documentary. This voice, typically male, articulates and explicates the generalized truth the audience should derive from the particularized evidence contained in the documentary image. Saunders challenges the inductive, hierarchical relation usually posited between these two voices or sources of knowledge by simply having them *say the same thing*. By changing the way the voice-over reiterates the evidence manifested in the diegesis (echoing it rather than abstracting it to a generalized statement), Saunders at once points to the selective and nonobjective echoing in all processes of abstraction (the relation between the particular and the general always involves selection of details appropriate to a given generalization), and reveals one way the authority of objectivity and abstraction is specifically constructed in expository documentary. As her example of the whiptail lizards makes clear, such generalizations always embody a biased, self-interested position derived from limited experience. Where audiences are inclined to accept biological determinism when it speaks in the voice of dominant ideologies about sexuality and gender (where it mirrors condoned social experience), its rhetorical flaws are quickly revealed when it is put in the service of alternative views. Saunders thus generalizes and *typifies* a certain historical moment in the discursive evolution of lesbian feminism (these myths and their rhetoric) while exposing the representational and rhetorical processes whereby such generalizations are validated.

Saunders invokes autobiography and personal testimony more directly in other moments in the video to refashion the relationship between experiential knowledge and its connection to much more broad cultural generalizations about sex and sexual interaction. She appears in all of her pieces and frequently delivers what appear to be personal anecdotes that ground the video's issues. These autobiographical conventions may prompt the viewer to assume that the piece is about Saunders, its credibility both guaranteed and limited by her experience and perceptions. Yet Saunders confounds these expectations in a variety of ways: she belatedly identifies herself as a fictional character in the last sequence of *Here in the Southwest*; when she delivers revealing personal information, she consistently does so in an absolutely flat, disaffected tone of voice (as do her other actors), and she often frames herself in odd ways or situations; and, finally, she frequently constructs her screen persona with contradictory significations, suggesting alternately (by references to lovers, dialogue about photographs, and so on) that that persona is heterosexual and lesbian.

Saunders derives multiple effects from these autobiographical deconstructions. Her techniques preclude viewer identification and empathy and instead focus attention on how Saunders's character is presented and what she says and does. Similarly, she often accomplishes the depersonalization of the autobiographical voice by using facts about gender in alienating ways. In *Here in the Southwest*, during a picnic sequence, Saunders responds to another woman's comment that she has never had sex in the desert by saying in a monotone, "Neither have I, but I have on the beach. I imagine it's probably the same . . . sand in all your mucous membranes." Her comment pointedly alludes to female anatomy to utterly deflate the romantic cliché of having sex on the beach (the *From Here to Eternity*, Calvin Klein ads myth); it also completely undermines what would otherwise be a titillating personal revelation. At the same time that Saunders depersonalizes what may or may not be *actual* autobiographical information, she also points to the conventional connections between personal and social discourses about sex (the romantic cliché, for example) by defying them. Her defiance indicates the ways scientific and personal information about sex and gender are usually representationally segregated. Her clinical reference to mucous membranes elicits the other woman's wry response: "Somehow I pictured it differently." Saunders consistently uses personal information to initiate not emotional, identificatory effects, but rather sociological, political, or theoretical ruminations about cultural constructions of sexuality.

In another sequence in *Here in the Southwest*, Saunders uses an anecdote to reorganize visual signifiers, slang, and clichés often associated with women into a powerful allegory about the entrapments and enigmas of sexual difference. The camera focuses on, then pans slowly away from an empty birdcage with an open door. It comes upon what appears to be a framed photo of Saunders, yet as the camera centers the photo, Saunders's image begins to speak. It is a mirror. Her face remaining caught there in the mirror, she recounts several stories about birds — one about a bird that flies out the window and disappears, one about exotic birds at a show, and one about a bird who bites her. At the exotic show, the birds are not caged, yet they do not fly away. Their owner explains that "once caged, they lose their desire to fly" and besides, their feathers are trimmed. The matrix of clichés brought together by the imagery and stories — women as birds, as caged birds, the vexed relation of women and mirrors, the mirror as women's cage — is transformed by the final story Joyan tells. Applying a product called Wings (feather-shaped green appliqués that supposedly get rid of crow's-feet) to her mirrored face, she discusses an incident involving a cockatoo that, a shop owner informs her, hates women and loves men. After an old man, who has been petting the bird, leaves, the cockatoo becomes wildly upset. Joyan goes to feed the bird to comfort it and it bites her savagely.

In the sequence that follows, a group of women, including Saunders, sit around a picnic table and try to make sense of the incident. How does the bird know the difference between men and women? How did it acquire a bias against women? The sequence cleverly exploits the enigma of the bird's behavior to rehearse all the explanations we use to try to decipher sexual difference. What are the signs? What is their source (cultural, biological)? How do we (mis)interpret them? Saunders builds *Here in the Southwest* around gender enigmas demonstrated by lizards, someone's cat, and various birds and around the discourses her characters use to make sense of these enigmas. The video underscores our culture's relentless reliance on science to explicate and normalize sexuality; the lesbian feminists' seeking a precedence for their sexuality in the authority of lizards wittily recalls the "birds and the bees" euphemism for sexual knowledge. At the same time that Saunders pokes fun at such facile recourse to animal behavior, she also indicates, by the examples she chooses, the arbitrary and exclusionary character of most scientific interpretation. Saunders insistently links the critique of biological determinism to the conventions of both science documentaries and those of autobiography by refusing to use voice-over, talking-head interviews, the recording of personal life, or the representational conventions of supporting statistics and documentation in ways that are generically appropriate.

In her later work *Brains on Toast: The Inexact Science of Gender* Saunders, together with collaborator Liss Platt, continues to investigate the documentation of gender and sexuality, focusing much more specifically on the formal, representational conventions of "friendly" television science documentaries. Incorporating interviews with people on the street, expert testimony, lab footage delimiting the results of pertinent experiments, and an organization that neatly encapsulates and explicates its subject, *Brains on Toast* hilariously demolishes the myth of scientific objectivity and visual documentation, simply by assuming the various tropes of its televisual, documentary rhetoric in the interests of many usually repressed subjects.

Saunders begins this work with a convention adopted from nature documentaries. This genre uses expository voice-over and the trope of personification to relate to the audience the emotions of the mother and father lion as they nurture their young, hunt for food, fight other lions, and so on. The popularity of these nature programs lies in their ability to solicit audience identification with the lions (zebras, giraffes, hyenas, cougars, bears, seals) and their travails by having the empathetic voice-over speak the animal's experience in the framework of Ozzie and Harriet. Thus, the video begins in the San Diego Zoo, the camera watching a baboon climb down a rope and a monkey swing from tree to tree to a raucous rendition of the song "I Enjoy Being a Girl." Having enacted the personification fallacy, Saunders follows it with a series of impromptu interviews of male passersby in front of the cage. Platt and Saunders construct a witty visual irony or conceit here, using the animal cage as backdrop for the men's responses to the question "Would you get pregnant if you could?" The interviewees, framed so the audience can see the caged baboons behind them, assert in various responses "Don't mess with nature—that's my motto." Along with the obvious indictment of our contradictory relations with "nature," the sequence also demonstrates that the most spontaneous interview is always already "staged," locations often having as much to say as any "man on the street."

An early sequence set in a classroom lays out the didactic agenda of the piece. The professor, attired in a red dress, comes in and announces to her class that they will be studying science's role in gender construction. An intertitle that reads "Subject: Science and Gender; Are there significant differences between the genders?" comes on the screen. A second follows with "Where to look: A) Brains B) Hormones C) Reproduction D) Private parts." The "Brains" section begins in a mock laboratory where the professor and her assistant, garbed in white coats, are weighing brains. The professor explains to her assistant that in the 1850s, craniologists decided that men were smarter than women because their brains were bigger. "Bigger was better even then," she observes wryly. The assistant protests that that kind of reasoning would mean that elephants were smarter than men. "Yes, that was known as the elephant problem," the professor remarks. She continues, "They then came up with a formula that looked at brain size in proportion to body weight. It was discovered that men were indeed smarter than elephants, but this formula had to be jettisoned when they found that, according to it, women were smarter than elephants and men." She sticks a sign reading "male" in the heavier mass on the scale, one reading "female" on the lighter one. Because of the preceding sequence and its information (is it "true?" parody? what does brain size mean, proportional or not, anyway?), this data or measurement is unreadable, indecipherable. The sequence indicates humorously yet emphatically the importance of context and interpretative bias in comprehending scientific facts.

In the next several sequences, different theories about brains and gender are aired in an array of settings: women at a dinner (where "brains" are cooked and served) discuss gender and brain lateralization; in another lab setting a woman explains, as an egg boils over a Bunsen burner, the Victorian theory that women's reproductive functions depleted their capacity to think, and vice versa; while a graphic crawl recounts men's decreasing fertility over the past several decades, a woman discounts the Victorian theory of atrophied eggs and asks, "What's wrong with this picture?" The coda to this section consists of a child's ditty about three fishes accompanying footage of sperm surrounding and penetrating an ovum, and then of a zygote dividing after fertilization. The irreconcilable incongruity of scientific discourses that open and close this section—anatomical versus cellular biology—underscores the gross and shifting physical logics that have organized scientific theorizing about gender: for brains, "bigger is better"; for Victorian women, the "up" or "down" options—the female brain is only nurtured at the expense of reproductive organs; for fertility, "atrophied" eggs (quality) or sperm counts (quantity). The final shots (of ovum and sperm) testify to the highly variable information that scientific data can give us, relative to their context (the sperm wriggle to the beat of the music), while also indicating the limits of scientific explanation. Visually and conceptually, the cellular drama of fertilization bears no evident relationship to the size and gender of brains. This sequence performs the lack of any relationship simply by accepting and trying to represent science's assumption of such a relation.

Saunders and Platt continue in this vein throughout their program. In the section about hormones, scientific research that denies links between aggression and testosterone is relayed over shots of a bullfight. The reproduction section concludes, from information derived from the zoo interviews, with an assertive question: "Pregnancy is women's work?" Finally, in the private parts section—subtitled "Seeing Is Believing"—commentators recount instances of hermaphroditism and the heinous surgical practices used to "correct" these abnormalities while engaging in sexual foreplay or while reading scientific manuals in their bedrooms. As it concludes, *Brains on Toast* appears to be a clever parody of the misguided conventions and foibles of sex education documentaries, laced with stunning visual ironies and very "creative" research protocols throughout. Yet in the credit sequence, Platt and Saunders deliver their final, scintillating twist, an irony that encompasses the entire video. Inverting the very structure of parody on itself, they reveal that all the research findings and studies cited were derived from "legitimate" scientific sources. Calling the very concept of legitimacy into question, this revelation nevertheless puts a different spin on all the information that has preceded it. As in Saunders's earlier work, obscure, repressed, marginal knowledge is put forth in texts that rigorously refuse any serious or univocal authority. Throughout, the rhetorical fallacies addressed in the text always involve the representational fallacies that present that text to an audience. Saunders consistently critiques the identificatory and objective structures of visual documentary—visual determinism—as she also questions the limited perspectives of both experience and science in telling the truth of sexual difference.

Of the three artists I discuss here, Bill Jones addresses the question of queer identity most directly and least ironically. In ways very different from Saunders's, he takes on and depersonalizes the genre of autobiography in his film *Massillon* (1991). Jones wants to reframe the inception of a queer identity; to do so, he divides his film into three sections, each of which addresses different aspects of that identity formation. The first section, titled "Ohio," recounts the narrator's personal experiences and dawning awareness of his sexuality as a child and adolescent. The second, entitled "The Law," neatly encapsulates the first, by recounting the history, evolution, and current status of sodomy laws in the United States. The third, "California," uses images of planned communities to explore issues pertaining to heritage, tradition, history, memory, and, finally, justice and the limitations of the social contract. *Massillon* begins at the level of the personal, but the film's perspective telescopes out, placing its personal narrative in legal, religious, and historical contexts that illustrate their adverse effects of these on individual subjects.

Jones has said that his primary interest as an artist and filmmaker is in ideas, and the paradox of his work is that he works in a medium ill suited for conceptual expression. He wants to visually represent what cannot be depicted or shown. *Massillon*, an essay in images, approaches the paradox that motivates it in several ways. Jones emphasizes the semantic importance of the sound track, inverting the traditional hierarchy of image over sound in film. There are no people depicted in *Massillon*, save for a few isolated figures in long shot, captured in the home movies that the narrator/ Jones watched as a child and that he uses here to commence and end his film. This tactic effectively generalizes the import of specific images, as Saunders's very different strategies do, but Jones is less interested in undercutting or deconstructing the voice of his film than he is in working with conceptual generalities about queer identity and the forces involved in its construction and containment. Finally, the documentation that Jones performs eschews the veracity of images altogether. He tells us what the images do not or cannot show. The words are the thing.

Massillon begins with a black screen and Jones's voice telling us about his early memories of family vacations. His father took home movies of the places they traveled—Washington, D.C., and Niagara Falls—and Jones reflects that his memories of these places are memories of home movies. The sound track falls silent as the home movies play on the screen: images of Niagara Falls and then shots from an array of historic locations in D.C. The significations attached to Niagara Falls—honeymoons, romance, sexu-

Massillon (William E. Jones 1991)

ality, marriage, conception—together with the legal, political, and historical significance of the U.S. capital articulate a visual coupling that subtly but concisely invokes the conceptual coupling that Jones will address in his film: the state, government, and the laws and their interaction with sexuality, "nature," sanctioned romance, and procreative bias. As the home movies give way to contemporary shots of Massillon, the silent sound track faintly registers the sound of church bells, of a truck going over a bridge. Jones's voice intones, "I grew up in Massillon, Ohio."

The film's first section is filled with visually lush sequences that contemplate landscapes and landmarks in Jones's hometown and its environs. Jones's camera does not move, but rather holds images, in long takes, sometimes in complete silence. We hear him recount anecdotes from his childhood and adolescence that slowly become more and more focused on a sexual identity at odds with the pastoral images and small-town values that shape his existence there. The stunning beauty of the images provides an increasingly ironic backdrop for the tales that Jones tells. A boyhood friend discreetly but firmly distances himself after Jones tentatively reveals his growing awareness of his sexual preference. A wrestling match at school becomes sexually and emotionally charged for Jones and a wrestling partner, who whispers to Jones, "I'm going to fucking kill you" as he tries to pin him. Jones, never succumbing to melodrama, succeeds both in capturing the obscurity and confusion of the emotions and desires that shape these situations and in documenting the repressive forces that render them potentially destructive or dangerous, and certainly discriminatory and unjust. The final anecdotes in the "Ohio" section graphically recount Jones's first experience with anal sex , then tell of his inability to find any news account in Massillon of the Supreme Court's *Bowers v. Hardwick* decision affirming the constitutionality of antisodomy laws.

Camera movement signals the transition from this section to the next. Visually recording cars and landscape passing by on a highway, this sequence contains an entire broadcast of a religious fundamentalist radio show that reveals chilling facts about President Reagan's reorganization of the judicial system ("Reagan has appointed half of all 575 federal judges and 168 appeals court judges"). The speaker links this reorganization to the religious right's agenda to criminalize abortion and all alternative sexualities.

In parts two and three of the film — "The Law" and "California" — Jones uses an array of theoretical and historical sources to recontextualize the "Ohio" section. "The Law" describes the nuances of sodomy laws in various states, as we see images of each state's capitol building. Jones points out the peculiarities and biases of language that haunt these laws and continues, in "California," to analyze the historical movements that have linked church and state, then the state and the medical establishment, in defining and regulating sexuality. His complex argument unearths a wealth of material that indicates how arbitrary our idea of "normative" sexuality is. We hear this argument as we look at examples of planned communities in California. The state, the domicile, tradition, memory, history *and* exclusion, repression and discrimination. Jones's film ends as it begins, with footage from home movies. We cannot watch it in the same way, nor can we ignore the links he has insisted upon between the state and sexuality. The representational "nots" that Jones makes manifest are precisely these links. A quote from Diderot follows the credits, to the effect that the connections between church and state are "one more thread that binds us hand and foot."

As I hope my descriptions have indicated, the three video artists and filmmakers I have discussed here do not fit into a clearly defined school or movement; they are more alike for what they do not do than what they do. All refuse the certainty of visual documentation while working within a mode of filmmaking that once defined its truth as "documentary." In each filmmaker's work, the self-reflexive critique of the visual field is wedded to ethnographic, autobiographical, and scientific investigations of or meditations concerning queer subjectivity and sexuality. Yet again, these investigations and meditations distinguish themselves by what they cannot or will not say, and by how that failure or inability is demonstrated within these videos. By linking visual documentation with rhetorical fallacies, appearance with deception, visibility with demonstrations of what we do not or cannot know about the subjects depicted, all these filmmakers register a profound and crucial lesson about queer identity and documentary. The only truths that can be told about identity and truth are limited, and the truest statements, the most veracious documentation, can only document those limitations. Working with/in all these nots, all these impossibilities, these filmmakers gesture at what has been left out, not recounted, not seen, a very elusive and queer subject.

NOTES

1. Bill Nichols, in his *Representing Reality: Issues and Concepts in Documentary*, indicates the fundamental significance of this problematic by opening his text with the question "Can we love the cinema and Plato, too?" (Bloomington: Indiana University Press, 1991), 3.

2. Richard Dyer, *Now You See It: Studies on Lesbian and Gay Film* (London: Routledge, 1990), 118. Dyer is paraphrasing Jack Babuscio's "Camp and the Gay Sensibility" in *Gays and Film*, ed. Richard Dyer (London: British Film Institute, 1980), 40–58.

3. Ibid., 125. Peggy Phelan notes this affective complexity in her observations of the competitive drag balls documented in Jennie Livingston's *Paris Is Burning* (1990): "The layers here are thick: ironic, ambivalent, and earnest. " See "The Golden Apple" in her book *Unmarked: The Politics of Performance* (New York: Routledge, 1993), 93–111.

4. Bill Nichols identifies four documentary modes of representation: "expository (classic voice-of-God commentaries, for example); observational (which minimizes the filmmaker's presence); interactive (where the filmmaker and social actors acknowledge one another overtly in conversation, participatory actions, or interviews), and reflexive (where the filmmaker draws the viewer's attention to the form of the work itself)" (xiv). He argues that though these four forms arose in dialectical progression, each form "aris[ing] from the limitations and constraints of previous forms," they all persist, and are sometimes "combined and altered within individual films" (*Representing Reality*, 32–33).

5. All subjectivities could be said to be rhetorical. The experience of queers, many of whom "pass" precisely because of the phenomenon of heterosexual presumption, gives them a more immediate access to the mystifying figuration of the "unified" subject. This edge or "in" sight would not be limited to queers, of course. Anyone who experiences "passing"—identity disjunctions wherein the nefarious connections between social distinctions, identity, and appearance are revealed, by definition, to the "passing" subject—would have access to such an edge. For an incisive consideration of this phenomenon and its relation to all identity construction, see Carole-Anne Tyler's article "Passing: Narcissism, Identity and Difference" in *differences* 6.2 (1995).

6. Not all of Goss's work falls in this vein. His *Wrecked for Life: The Trip and Magic of the Trocadero Transfer* (1993), constructed around a series of interviews, documents an oral history of the famous queer disco club in San Francisco. In this piece, Goss is much more interested in recording the memories of all the staff, artists, and patrons he could find than in rigorously reflexive stylistics.

7. The term and the ethical/ideological concerns are outlined in Bill Nichols's *Representing Reality*, 44–56.

LYNDA McAFEE

Film and Videography

This anthology is committed to questioning the boundaries of what might be considered documentary, queer, lesbian, or gay, yet filmographies and bibliographies tend to do quite the opposite. Through a series of inclusions and exclusions, these lists can create and fix the very parameters one seeks to interrogate. For example, what does one do with the works of Bruce Weber, Barbara Hammer, Derek Jarman, Midi Onodera, or Sadie Benning? Do you include all their work, some of it, none of it? Which works do you call documentaries? Which ones do you call queer, lesbian, or gay? Do right-wing, anti-gay pieces, such as *The Gay Agenda*, belong in a queer documentary film and videography? What about educational films on homosexuality intended for schoolchildren? That each video or film considered brings with it a series of difficult questions with inconclusive answers indicates how complex and unstable the categories queer and documentary are.

The two questions—What is queer? What is documentary?—acted as a sort of litmus test for each selection. Subject matter, more than filmmaker or videomaker, became a key determinant. Films and videos that address issues considered central to queer, lesbian, and gay sexualities are included. Thus, right-wing documentaries and educational films and videos are mixed in with films and videos by out queer, lesbian, and gay filmmakers and videographers. What others say about us can be as revealing as what we say about ourselves and each other. The criteria used to decide what constitutes a documentary were equally broad in an attempt to call into question the characteristics generally associated with this label. Works that utilize traditional conventions (talking-head interviews, archival footage, voice-over narrators, "cinema verité" shooting styles) were deliberately juxtaposed with more experimental works that challenge such conventions.

To ensure that the films and videos listed are accessible, distribution became a third major criteria. Works in this film and videography are limited to documentaries currently in U.S. distribution for rental or purchase. Distributors are indicated by code for each entry. Addresses are listed at the end. Unfortunately, this last criterion of distribution excludes many historical queer documentaries that have fallen out of distribution, international documentaries that do not have a U.S. distributor, and documentaries and home movies that were never picked up for distribution. These harder-to-find documentaries may be found at libraries, archives, public and private film collections, community and art house screenings, and film and video festivals.

Will everyone agree with the inclusions and exclusions? Absolutely not. In questioning the selection process, however, you become engaged in the very questions integral to this anthology.

Each entry contains: Title (Country, year of production) Director (unless noted otherwise). Running time. [Code for Distributor(s)] Brief description. Whenever possible, information was taken directly from film/video credits. In some cases, distributor catalogs or other published sources were used.

Absolutely Positive (USA, 1991) Peter Adair. 87 mins. [F] Testing positive for HIV provided the impetus for director Peter Adair to make this film. Eleven people, ages seventeen to fifty-five, discuss their HIV-positive lives.

Acting Up for Prisoners (USA, 1992) Eric Slade and Mic Sweeney. 27 mins. [F] Documents ACT UP's successful campaign to bring adequate health care and human rights to women prisoners with HIV at Frontera, the California Institution for Women.

Actions Speak Louder Than Words (GB, 1992) Richard Kwietniowski. 22 mins. [F] Offers staged pieces by six deaf performers based on their experiences of being gay and deaf in Great Britain.

The ADS Epidemic (Canada, 1987) John Greyson. 5 mins. [VDB] Tongue-in-cheek safe-sex music video about the ADS (acquired dread of sex) epidemic.

Adventures in the Gender Trade (USA, 1993) Susan Marenco. 40 mins. [FLib]

Writer and performer Kate Bornstein recounts her transition from boy child to transsexual lesbian.

Affirmations (USA, 1990) Marlon Riggs. 10 mins. [F] Explores black gay desires and dreams beginning with an affectionate, humorous confessional and moving on to a wish for empowerment.

Age 12—Love with a Little L (USA, 1990) Jennifer Montgomery. 22 mins. [WMM] Uses adolescent memories and staged scenes to explore the construction of lesbian identity based on forbidden desire and transgression.

AIDS in the Barrio (USA, 1989) Peter Biella and Frances Negrón. 29 mins. [CG] Examines the impact of AIDS in Hispanic-American communities, focusing on the specific economic, social, and cultural factors that influence perception of the AIDS crisis.

American Fabulous (USA, 1991) Reno Dakota. 105 mins. [FR/I] Features Jeffrey Strouth spinning wild and raunchy gay tales from the backseat of a 1957 Cadillac.

Among Good Christian Peoples (USA, 1991) Catherine Saalfield and Jacqueline Woodson. 30 mins. [F, TWN] Presents Jacqueline Woodson's story of growing up as a black lesbian Jehovah's Witness.

Andy the Furniture Maker (GB, 1987) Paul Oremland. 40 mins. [F] Details the sexual and artistic accomplishments of an outspoken young gay artist who has moved to London from the country.

The Angelic Conversation (GB, 1985) Derek Jarman. 82 mins. [Mystic] Celebrates homoerotic love using Shakespeare's sonnets as a basis.

Anthem (USA, 1991) Marlon Riggs. 9 mins. [F] Edited in a music video style. Provocative juxtaposition of Afrocentric and queer symbols that politicizes and celebrates the homoeroticism of African-American men.

Audience: San Francisco (USA, 1983) Barbara Hammer. 10 mins. [Canyon] Hammer records audience thoughts and reactions to a screening of her works at San Francisco's Roxy Theatre.

Backyard Movie (USA, 1991) Bruce Weber. 9 mins. [Z] Overlays old home movies, footage of frolicking dogs, and naked men on trampolines with text describing Weber's youthful obsessions and his parents' attempts to teach him the facts of life.

Ballot Measure 9 (USA, 1994) Heather MacDonald. 72 mins. [Z] Records the 1992 battle over Oregon's anti-gay ballot initiative. Exposes the strategies of the religious right and documents the struggles and eventual success of lesbians, gays, and their allies.

Because This Is about Love: A Portrait of Gay and Lesbian Marriage (USA, 1992) Shulee Ong. 28 mins. [FLib] Profiles five lesbian and gay couples who have made lifelong commitments to each other by participating in a marriage ceremony.

Before Stonewall: The Making of a Gay and Lesbian Community (USA, 1984) Greta Schiller and Robert Rosenberg. 87 mins. [CG, F] Chronicles the strategies of resistance employed by gays and lesbians in the United States prior to the Stonewall rebellion through a mix of archival footage and contemporary interviews.

Beyond Imagining: Margaret Anderson and the Little Review (USA, 1991) Wendy Weinberg. 30 mins. [WMM] Profiles Margaret Anderson, who in 1914 founded the *Little Review,* an influential literary journal. Includes Anderson's personal life and the women she loved.

Black Body (USA, 1992) Thomas Harris. 7 mins. [TWN] Uses text, special effects, and a bound male nude to emphasize the humanity underlying the more complex and diverse definitions of black identity and sexuality.

Black Is . . . Black Ain't (USA, 1995) Marlon Riggs. 86 mins. [CN] Riggs's final film mixes personal stories and performance to examine the definition of "blackness" and challenge African-Americans to accept multiple identities in constructing community.

The Blank Point: What Is Transsexualism? (USA, 1991) Xiao-Yen Wang. 58 mins. [CG] Interviews one female-to-male and two male-to-female transsexuals in an effort to understand why some individuals decide to undergo sex reassignment surgery.

Blue (GB, 1993) Derek Jarman. 76 mins. [Z] In Jarman's final film, the only image is a solid blue screen. The autobiographical narration considers Jarman's life, his struggle with AIDS, and his encroaching blindness.

Bodies in Trouble (Corps Trouble) (Canada, 1991) Marusia Bociurkiw. 15 mins. [F] Melds narrative and agitprop elements in a video about the lesbian body under siege. Produced as a call to action against the threats of the new conservative right.

Bondage see *Female Misbehavior.*

Both (USA, 1993) Vic De La Rosa. 8 mins. [F] Captures a day in the life of HIV-positive lovers Jeff and Gary in San Francisco.

Bright Eyes (GB, 1986) Stuart Marshall. 85 mins. [F, VDB] Three-part documentary made for Great Britain's Channel Four. Uses dramatic reenactments and tabloid representation to examine the historical and social context of AIDS.

The Broadcast Tapes of Dr. Peter (Canada, 1992) David Paperny. 45 mins. [Direct] Condenses the video diaries of Dr. Peter Jepson-Young, who chronicled his life with AIDS for the Canadian Broadcasting Corporation (CBC). See also *The Dr. Peter Diaries.*

Bust (USA, 1991) Richard Morrison and David Wojnarowicz. 15 mins. [Drift] Artist Wojnarowicz speaks of the altered consciousness of the terminally ill and his own imminent death from AIDS.

Cancer in Two Voices (USA, 1994) Lucy Massie Phenix. 43 mins. [WMM] Documents the final three years of Barbara Rosenblum's life with her partner Sandra Butler after Rosenblum learns she has advanced breast cancer.

Chance of a Lifetime (USA, 1986) John Lewis. 42 mins. [GMHC] Produced by Gay Men's Health Crisis and designed for use by gay and bisexual men and health educators. Sexually explicit tape comprised of three vignettes focusing on safer-sex negotiations between partners.

The Changer: A Record of Our Times (USA, 1991) Frances Reid and Judy Dlugacz. 60 mins. [F, Wolfe] Documents the making of Chris Williamson's 1975 album *The Changer.* Intercuts clips and stills of the 1970s and 1980s women's music scene, contemporary interviews, and footage from a 1990 Williamson concert.

Changing Our Minds (USA, 1991) Richard Schmiechen. 75 mins. [F] Tribute to psychologist Dr. Evelyn Hooker, who, based on her studies of gay men, advocated the removal of homosexuality from the American Psychiatric Association's list of disorders.

Chasing the Moon (USA, 1991) Dawn Suggs. 4 mins. [TWN] Meditations of a black lesbian grappling with the memory of an attack that makes her wary about being out on the street.

Chinese Characters (Canada, 1985) Richard Fung. 22 mins. [VDB] Addresses the history of homoerotic representation of Asian men and how Asian men relate to pornography.

Choosing Children (USA, 1984) Debra Chasnoff and Kim Klausner. 45 mins. [Cambridge, F] Visits with six families headed by lesbians of various ethnic and racial backgrounds. Shows a variety of family structures.

Chuck Solomon: Coming of Age (USA, 1986) Marc Huestis. 57 mins. [CG] Documents the life and contributions of gay artist Chuck Solomon, a mainstay of San Francisco's theatrical community, who was diagnosed with AIDS in 1985.

Coconut/Cane and Cutlass (Canada, 1994) Michelle Mohabeer. 30 mins. [WMM] Poetic rumination on exile, displacement, and national identity from the perspective of a young Indo-Caribbean lesbian who has migrated to Canada.

Coming Out Under Fire (USA, 1994) Arthur Dong. 71 mins. [Z] Combines archival footage with contemporary interviews of gay and lesbian military veterans in order to construct a history of their service during World War II. Framed by the 1993 Senate hearings on the military's ban against homosexuals.

Common Threads: Stories from the Quilt (USA, 1989) Robert Epstein and Jeffrey Friedman. 79 min. [Direct, Wolfe] Uses interviews, photographs, and home movies to commemorate the lives of five people who have died from AIDS. Surviving friends, family, and lovers have memorialized them by creating panels for the AIDS quilt.

Complaints of a Dutiful Daughter (USA, 1994) Deborah Hoffman. 44 mins. [WMM] Hoffman chronicles the degenerative stages of her mother's Alzheimer's disease and her own evolving acceptance of her mother's illness.

Comrades in Arms (GB, 1990) Stuart Marshall. 52 mins. [FLib] Intercuts interviews, archival footage, and period reenactments to tell the stories of the secret lives of gays and lesbians serving in the British armed forces during World War II.

Culture Wars (USA, 1995) Tina DiFeliciantonio and Jane Wagner. 60 mins. [KQED] Examines the backlash against gay and lesbian visibility since the AIDS epidemic. Focuses on the murder of Julio Rivera, the controversy over Marlon Riggs's *Tongues Untied,* and Oregon's anti-gay ballot measure. See also *The Question of Equality.*

Daddy and the Muscle Academy (Finland, 1991) Ilpo Pohjola. 55 mins. In English and Finnish with English subtitles. [Z] Combines interviews and hundreds of hypermasculine erotic drawings by well-known artist Tom of Finland. Creates both a portrait of the artist and a look at the gay leather scene.

Danny (USA, 1987) Stashu Kybartas. 20 mins. [VDB] A personal documentary of a young man's death from AIDS. Explores the difficulties of Danny's return home and his attempts to reconcile with family members.

The Darker Side of Black (GB, 1993) Isaac Julien. 55 mins. [Noon] Considers homophobia and sexism in rap music and Jamaican reggae. Interviews with Ice-T, Shabba Ranks, and Cornel West.

Daughters of Dykes (USA, 1994) Amilca Palmer. 14 mins. [WMM] A group of teenage girls speak about being raised by lesbian mothers, their own "coming out" process as daughters of lesbians, and their feelings about sexual orientation.

DHPG, Mon Amour (USA, 1989) Carl M. George. 13 mins. [Drift] Home-movie footage of Joe Walsh and David Conover. Focuses on the couple's hopes that the experimental AIDS drug DHPG will help prolong David's life.

DiAna's Hair Ego (USA, 1990) Ellen Spiro. 29 mins. [VDB] Features cosmetologist DiAna DiAna and her partner, Dr. Bambi Sumpter, who together created the South Carolina AIDS Education Network.

The Displaced View (Canada, 1988) Midi Onodera. 52 mins. [WMM] Weaves experimental, narrative, and documentary forms in a compassionate love letter to the women of Onodera's family. Shows Onodera's own search for identity within the suppressed history of the Japanese in North America.

Double Strength (USA, 1978) Barbara Hammer. 20 mins. [WMM] Study of a lesbian relationship between two trapeze artists.

Double the Trouble, Twice the Fun (GB, 1992) Pratibha Parmar. 25 mins. [WMM] Blends documentary and narrative elements in an examination of disability and its effect on gay men and lesbians.

Dr. Paglia see *Female Misbehavior*.

The Dr. Peter Diaries (Canada, 1992) David Paperny. 285 mins. [Direct] Complete video diaries of Dr. Peter Jepson-Young, who chronicled his life with AIDS for the Canadian Broadcasting Corporation (CBC). Compiled in the order that the two-minute diaries originally aired. See also *The Broadcast Tapes of Dr. Peter*.

Dream Girls (GB, 1993) Kim Longinotto and Jano Williams. 50 mins. [WMM] Behind-the-scenes look at the women in Japan's Takarazuka Revue, where the females who play the romantic male roles are objects of desire for Japanese women and teenage girls.

Dry Kisses Only (USA, 1990) Jane Cottis and Kaucyila Brooke. 75 mins. [VDB, WMM] Humorous look at lesbian readings of popular culture. Uses manipulated film clips and short vignettes to consider lesbian subtexts in classical Hollywood films.

Dykeotomy (USA, 1992) Deborah Fort. 19 mins. [WMM] Uses autobiographical stories, video art, and archival footage to examine the videomaker's positioning in society as a lesbian and as a woman who has trouble following rules.

Dyketactics (USA, 1974) Barbara Hammer. 4 mins. [WMM] A classic, avant-garde filmic celebration of lesbian sensuality and sexuality.

Educate Your Attitude (Canada, 1992) Teresa Marshall and Craig Berggold. 30 mins. [F] From the four-part Canadian series *Fresh Talk: Youth and Sexuality*. Features young men and women, ages fifteen to twenty-four, who speak about love, gay identity, interracial relationships, masturbation, sexuality, and AIDS.

Exposure (Canada, 1990) Michelle Mohabeer. 8 mins. [WMM] Dialogue between two lesbians—a Japanese-Canadian writer and an Afro-Caribbean poet—that reveals the intertwining of sexual and ethnic identity and the women's common experiences of racism and homophobia.

Eye to Eye (USA, 1989) Isabel Hegner. 18 mins. [FR/I] The life of late photographer Robert Mapplethorpe, as recounted by Jack Walls, his longtime lover and model.

FaerieFilm (USA, 1993) Eugene Salandra. 7 mins. [Ospkn, Saland] Animated celebration of the Radical Faeries and their pagan rituals.

Fast Trip, Long Drop (USA, 1993) Gregg Bordowitz. 54 mins. [Noon] Autobiographical look at the videomaker's coming out as a Jewish gay male, his AIDS activism, and his own HIV-positive status.

Fated to Be Queer (USA, 1992) Pablo Bautista. 25 mins. [C] Interviews with four Filipino gay men about their concerns as gay people of color in the San Francisco Bay Area.

Fear of Disclosure (USA, 1989) Phil Zwickler and David Wojnarowicz. 5 mins. [F, VDB] Explores through music video format the implications of revealing to a potential lover that one is HIV positive.

Female Misbehavior (Germany/USA, 1983–92) Monika Treut. 80 mins. [FR/I]

Four film portraits released as a package. *Dr. Paglia* features the infamous author of *Sexual Personae*. *Bondage* looks at S/M. *Annie* focuses on performance artist Annie Sprinkle. *Max* presents a female-to-male transsexual.

Fighting Chance (USA, 1990) Richard Fung. 31 mins. [VDB] A sequel to *Orientations*. Considers the effects of the AIDS epidemic on Asian-Canadian gays.

Fighting for Our Lives (USA, 1987) Ellen Seidler and Patrick DuNah. 28 mins. [WMM] Focuses on how women of color are taking action in their own communities to reduce the spread of AIDS among women.

Fighting in Southwest Louisiana (USA, 1991) Peter Friedman and Jean-Francois Brunet. 27 mins. [FLib] Portrait of Danny Cooper, an openly gay mailman in a small Louisiana town. Cooper recalls his battles to overcome homophobia and assert his rights in rural America. Also discusses his struggle against AIDS, the loss of his longtime lover, and the growth of a new relationship.

First Comes Love (USA, 1991) Su Friedrich. 22 mins. [Drift, WMM] Juxtaposes footage of four wedding ceremonies to an amusing medley of popular love songs, and a startling statement to consider the emotional ambiguities of this ritual for many gay men and lesbians.

Flesh and Paper (GB, 1990) Pratibha Parmar. 26 mins. [WMM] Portrait of Indian lesbian poet and writer Suniti Namjoshi, born into an Indian royal family, now living in England.

Flowing Hearts: Thailand Fighting AIDS (USA, 1992) John Goss. 28 mins. [VDB] Documents grassroots AIDS education in Thailand.

Forbidden Love: The Unashamed Stories of Lesbian Lives (Canada, 1992) Aerlyn Weissman and Lynne Fernie. 85 mins. [WMM, Wolfe] Interviews nine lesbians who were out in the Canadian beer parlors and clubs during the 1950s and 1960s. Weaves in a melodramatic dramatization of a lesbian pulp romance.

Framed Youth; or, Revolt of the Teenage Perverts (GB, 1983) Produced by Lesbian and Gay Youth Project. 50 mins. [F] Young gay men and lesbians take to London's streets with cameras and microphones to confront heterosexual views on homosexuality.

Framing Lesbian Fashion (USA, 1992) Karen Everett. 60 mins. [F, Wolfe] Archival photos, personal stories, and a fashion runway tell the history of lesbian fashion and reflect on changing lesbian identities.

Frankie and Jocie (USA, 1994) Jocelyn Taylor. 20 mins. [TWN] Explores a black lesbian's complex relationship with her straight brother.

Free to Be Me (USA, 1991) David Murdock. 23 mins. [EVC] Concerned about the discrimination experienced by their gay and lesbian friends, a group of Educational Video Center (EVC) students worked for a semester to create this tape, which is intended to dispel homophobia.

From a Secret Place (USA, 1993) Produced by Karin Heller, MSW, and Bill Domonkos. 40 mins. [Fnlght] Six teens speak about the process of coming out. Also interviewed are several supportive parents and a psychotherapist who specializes in counseling gay and lesbian adolescents.

The Funny Tape (USA, 1993) Produced by John Scagliotti. 60 mins. [CG, Wolfe] A selection of comedy highlights from the historic first year of broadcasts of

In The Life, PBS's first lesbian and gay series.

The Gay Agenda (USA, 1992) Produced by The Report. 20 mins. [Report] The producer, a media organization of the religious right, seeks to counter what is described as the "powerful, well-funded homosexual lobby." Free copies sent to members of Congress and circulated throughout the Pentagon.

Gay and Lesbian Teens (USA, 1985) Produced by WGBY-TV. 30 mins. [PBS] Part of the *Soapbox with Tom Cottle* series. Clinical psychologist Dr. Tom Cottle talks with teens about their sexuality. A group of gay and lesbian teens share their personal stories.

Gay USA (USA, 1977) Arthur Bressan Jr. 78 mins. [F] Footage from the June 1977 gay pride parades and marches in six cities (San Francisco, San Diego, New York, Chicago, Houston, and Los Angeles) intercut to construct an image of a national gay community.

A Gay View/Male (USA, 1975) Laird Sutton. 17 mins. [MFI] Produced by the National Sex Forum as an educational video. Three gay men share personal feelings about being gay.

Gay Women Speak (USA, 1979) Laird Sutton. 15 mins. [MFI] Produced by the National Sex Forum as an educational video. Intimate discussion among three professional women active in the lesbian and gay community.

Gay Youth (USA, 1992) Pam Walton. 40 mins. [FLib, Wolfe] Contrasts the stories of two gay young people as a way to break the silence surrounding adolescent homosexuality. Addresses issue of gay teens and suicide.

Generation Q (USA, 1995) Robert Byrd. 60 mins. [KQED] Focuses on gay and lesbian youth. See also *The Question of Equality.*

Gently Down the Stream (USA, 1983) Su Friedrich. 14 mins. [Drift, WMM] Scratched onto the film is the text of fourteen of the filmmaker's dreams, selected from eight years of her journals.

Girl Power (Part 1) (USA, 1992) Sadie Benning. 15 mins. [VDB] Informed by the underground "riot grrrl" movement and set in part to music by Bikini Kill. Presents a raucous vision of what it means to be a radical girl in the 1990s.

God, Gays and the Gospel (USA, 1984) Mary Anne McEwen. 58 mins. [CG] Archival footage, photos, and interviews are combined to trace the history of the Metropolitan Community Church, a Christian church with a special outreach to gays and lesbians.

Green on Thursdays (USA, 1993) Dean Bushala and Deirdre Heaslip. 77 mins. [FR/I] A look at Chicago's lesbian and gay antiviolence movement. Includes interviews with survivors of anti-gay violence and a street patrol walk with Chicago's Pink Angels.

Greetings from Africa (USA, 1994) Cheryl Dunye. 12 mins [WMM]. Dunye's development as an artist and character continue in this story about "Cheryl's" interest in the mysterious "L."

Greetings from Out Here (USA, 1993) Ellen Spiro. 58 mins. [VDB] A tour of gay Dixie, capturing the places, politics, and quirky roadside characters of the South.

Greetings from Washington, D.C. (USA, 1981) Lucy Winer. 28 mins. [WMM] Documents the first gay and lesbian rights march on Washington.

A Hard Reign's Gonna Fall (USA, 1989) Dean Lance. 7 mins. [VDB] A series of thought-provoking illustrations cut to Bob Dylan's lyrics show the videomaker's perspective on the AIDS epidemic.

Heaven Earth & Hell (USA, 1993) Thomas Allen Harris. 25 mins. [EAI, TWN] Harris reflects on the "trickster" figure in African and African-American culture while recounting the story of his first love.

Her Giveaway: A Spiritual Journey with AIDS (USA, 1988) Mona Smith. 21 mins. [WMM] Portrait of lesbian Carole Lafavor, a member of the Ojibwe tribe. Lafavor relates how she has used her traditional Native American beliefs and healing practices in living with AIDS.

The Hidden Epidemic (USA, 1991) Produced by Gay and Lesbian Community Action Council, Minneapolis. 30 mins. [MFI] Considers how homophobia affects HIV risk reduction efforts.

The History of the World According to a Lesbian (USA, 1988) Barbara Hammer. 22 mins. [F] Traces visible evidence and uncovers suppressed references to women who love women from prehistory to contemporary times. Accompanied by the sarcastic sounds of the 1950s lesbian quartet the Sluts from Hell.

Hollow Liberty (USA, 1995) Robyn Hutt. 60 mins. [KQED] Analyzes anti-gay legislation and court rulings such as the military ban against homosexuals and the U.S. Supreme Court's ruling upholding state sodomy laws. See also *The Question of Equality.*

Home Movie (USA, 1972) Jan Oxenberg. 12 mins. [F] Combines fast-edited, found family footage with an added voice-over that comments wryly on the schoolgirl images and the filmmaker's feelings of difference.

Homosexuality and Lesbianism (USA, 1976) Produced by Document Associates. 26 mins. [CG] Psychologists, psychiatrists, and gay people respond to teens' questions, concerns, and fears regarding homosexuality.

Homoteens (USA, 1993) Joan Jubela. 60 mins. [F] Presents autobiographical portraits produced by five gay and lesbian youths in New York City.

Honored by the Moon (USA, 1990) Mona Smith. 15 mins. [WMM] Probes the historical and spiritual roles played by Native American lesbians and gays through interviews taped at a conference for Native American gays, lesbians, friends, and supporters.

I Am My Own Woman (*Ich Bin Meine Eigene Frau*) (Germany, 1992) Rosa von Praunheim. 91 mins. In German with English subtitles. [Milest] Chronicles the life of transvestite Charlotte von Mahlsdorf through interviews and staged scenes. Recounts her life in Germany, including growing up under the Nazi regime and her leadership in Germany's gay liberation movement.

I Never Danced the Way Girls Were Supposed To (USA, 1992) Dawn Suggs. 7 mins. [TWN] A satirical look at misconceptions regarding black lesbian life.

If Every Girl Had a Diary (USA, 1990) Sadie Benning. 6 mins. [VDB, WMM] Training her Pixelvision camera on herself and her bedroom, a teenage Benning searches for identity and respect as both a female and a lesbian.

If She Grows Up Gay (USA, 1983) Karen Sloe Goodman. 23 mins. [F] Interviews a young African-American working-class mother who talks about her pregnancy and raising her daughter with her lesbian lover in New York.

If They'd Asked for a Lion Tamer (GB, 1987) Paul Oremland. 40 mins. [F] A tongue-in-cheek tribute to British drag performer David Dale.

I'm Not One of 'Em (USA, 1974) Jan Oxenberg. 3 mins. [F] A female spectator at a Roller Derby talks about her unique experiences with lesbianism.

I'm You, You're Me (USA, 1993) Catherine Saalfield and Debra Levine. 26 mins. [WMM] Looks at HIV-positive women making the transition from prison to independent living.

Improper Conduct (France, 1983) Nestor Almendros and Orlando Jimenez-Leal. 115 mins. In French and Spanish with English subtitles. [NY] Indictment of Castro's Cuba centering on its systemic persecution of writers, intellectuals, dissidents, and homosexuals.

In the Best Interests of the Children (USA, 1977) Frances Reid, Elizabeth Stevens, and Cathy Zheutlin. 53 mins. [WMM] Portrays the diversity of experience among eight lesbian mothers and their children with particular attention given to the issue of child custody.

Intro to Cultural Skit-Zo-Frenia (USA, 1993) Jamika Ajalon. 10 mins. [TWN] Explores black identity and challenges homophobia and sexism among African-Americans.

It Is What It Is . . . (USA, 1992) Gregg Bordowitz. 60 mins. [GMHC] A multi-ethnic cast of young people use dramatic vignettes and "on the street" interviews to uncover and dispel stereotypical thinking regarding homosexuality. Offers solidarity to young gay viewers, considers the effects of the AIDS crisis, and suggests a variety of safer sex practices.

It Wasn't Love (USA, 1992) Sadie Benning. 20 mins. [VDB] A lustful encounter with a "bad girl" illustrated through the gender posturing of Hollywood stereotypes.

James Baldwin: The Price of the Ticket (USA, 1989) Karen Thorsen. 87 mins. [CN] Uses archival footage and Baldwin's own words to examine his literary contributions, his homosexuality, his life in France and Turkey, his participation in the American civil rights movement, and his death from cancer in 1987.

Janine (USA, 1990) Cheryl Dunye. 10 mins. [TWN] Uses direct address and visual metaphor to examine class, race, and sexual difference. Examines a black lesbian's relationship with a white, upper-middle-class girl from high school.

Jareena: Portrait of a Hijda (USA, 1990) Prem Kalliat. 24 mins. [TWN] Explores through Jareena, a transsexual living in the city of Bangalore, the lifestyle, attitudes, and history of the Hijda, a society of eunuchs who have thrived in the Indian sex trade for centuries.

Joey Goes to Wigstock (USA, 1992–93) Leonard Freed. 10 mins. [FR/I] Follows drag performer Joey Arias to restaurants and clubs around New York City, culminating at the Wigstock festival.

Jollies (USA, 1990) Sadie Benning. 11 mins. [VDB, WMM] Lesbian teenager Benning uses her Pixelvision camera to give a chronology of her crushes and kisses, tracing the development of her emerging sexuality.

Juggling Gender (USA, 1992) Tami Gold. 27 mins. [WMM] A portrait of performance artist Jennifer Miller. Miller, a woman who refuses to shave her full beard, offers insight into issues of femininity and sexuality as she describes her life as a "bearded lady."

Just Because of Who We Are (USA, 1986) Heramedia Collective. 28 mins. [WMM] Combines contemporary interviews and archival footage to focus on physical and psychological violence against lesbians.

Keep Your Laws off My Body (USA, 1990) Catherine Saalfield and Zoe Leonard. 13 mins. [WMM] Juxtaposes intimate images of a lesbian couple at home with jarring footage of police descending on an ACT UP/New York demonstration.

Khush (GB, 1991) Pratibha Parmar. 24 mins. [WMM] Looks at recent attempts to create solidarity among South Asian gays, lesbians, and bisexuals living in Great Britain, North America, and India.

Khush Refugees (USA, 1991) Nidhi Singh. 32 mins. [C] Two exiles, Rahul, an immigrant from India, and Dante, an ex-marine from suburban Ohio, attempt to assimilate into San Francisco's gay community.

Kiev Blue (USA, 1992) Heather Mac-Donald. 28 mins. [FLib] Nine gay men and lesbians speak about their lives in Kiev under Article 121, which criminalizes homosexuality.

Kim (USA, 1988) Arlyn Gajilan. 27 mins. [F] Life of a young Puerto Rican lesbian coming out and coming of age in New York City.

L Is for the Way You Look (USA, 1991) Jean Carlomusto. 24 mins. [WMM] Considers the women who have served as role models and objects of desire for young lesbians. Playfully analyzes how media images affect the construction of identity.

Labor More Than Once (USA, 1983) Liz Mersky. 52 mins. [WMM] Charts arduous legal battles undertaken by lesbian Marianne MacQueen to retain legal right to visit her son and, later, to maintain her status as mother.

Last Call at Maud's (USA, 1993) Paris Poirier. 77 mins. [F] Combines vintage photos, historical footage, and contemporary interviews in a look at the lesbian bar scene from the 1940s to the 1980s. Particular focus on the 1989 closing of Maud's, a landmark San Francisco lesbian bar.

The Last of England (GB, 1987) Derek Jarman. 87 mins. [Mystic] Indictment of the British establishment, whose lost empire becomes an allegory for humanity's loss of soul.

The Last Time I Saw Ron (USA, 1994) Leslie Thornton. 12 mins. [Drift] Video meditation on life, death, AIDS, and art. Includes footage from *Philoktetes Variations,* a theatrical treatise on the betrayal and death of Philoktetes by his friend Odysseus. Stars gay performer Ron Vawter, who died shortly after the play began production.

Laura, Ingrid, and Rebecca (USA, 1990) Philippe Roques. 7 mins. [F] Three activists speak of their efforts to get the men in ACT UP to acknowledge women's health issues.

Lesbian Avengers Eat Fire Too (USA, 1993) Janet Baus and Su Friedrich. 55 mins. [Ladysl] Documents the first year in New York of the Lesbian Avengers, a direct action group. Group members swallow fire in remembrance and defiance of the deaths by arson of a gay man and a lesbian in Oregon.

A Lesbian in the Pulpit (Canada, 1990) Produced by the Canadian Broadcasting Corporation. 28 mins. [FLib] Part of the CBC's *Man Alive* series. Portrait of a lesbian minister in the United Church of Canada.

The Life and Times of Allen Ginsberg (USA, 1993) Jerry Aronson. 82 mins. [FR/I] Presents the Beat Generation through the eyes of poet Allen Ginsberg. Interviews with Williams Burroughs, Ken Kesey, Jack Kerouac, Abbie Hoffman, and Timothy Leary.

Lifetime Commitment: A Portrait of Karen Thompson (USA, 1988) Kiki Zeldes. 30 mins. [WMM, Wolfe] After Sharon Kowalski's disabling auto accident in 1983, her lover, Karen Thompson, launched a landmark, and ultimately successful, legal battle against Kowalski's family and the state of Minnesota.

A Litany for Survival (USA, 1994) Ada Gay Griffin and Michelle Parkerson. 90 mins. [TWN] Uses interviews, poetry, and archival and verité footage to document the life and work of Audre Lord, an award-winning writer and cultural theorist.

Living and Dying (Ich Lebe Gern, Ich Sterbe Gern) (Switzerland, 1990) Claudia Acklin. 72 mins. [F] Examines the life of Swiss television interviewer Andre Ratti, who shocked his countrymen when, at the age of fifty, he came out as a homosexual who had AIDS.

Living Inside (USA, 1989) Sadie Benning. 4 mins. [VDB, WMM] When she was sixteen, Benning stopped going to high school for three weeks and stayed inside with her Fisher-Price camera, her TV set, and a pile of dirty laundry.

Living Proof: HIV and the Pursuit of Happiness (USA, 1993) Kermit Cole. 72 mins. [FR/I] Introduces the HIV-positive subjects of Carolyn Jones's 1992 photo exhibit of the same title.

Looking for a Space: Lesbians and Gay Men in Cuba (USA, 1993) Kelly Anderson. 38 mins. [FLib] Looks at the history of persecution of gays and lesbians during the early years of the Cuban revolution as well as the situation of lesbians and gay men in Cuba today.

Looking for Langston (GB, 1989) Isaac Julien. 47 mins. [TWN] Meshes archival footage, photographs, poetry, and reenactments to evoke the atmosphere and homoerotics of the Harlem Renaissance and writer Langston Hughes.

London (GB, 1994) Patrick Keiller. 84 mins. [Z] Witty contemplation of the city's history, people, politics, art, architecture, scandals, and guardsmen's uniforms by two former lovers.

Long Time Comin' (Canada, 1993) Dionne Brand. 52 mins. [WMM] Profiles two African-Canadian lesbian artists, painter Grace Channer and singer/songwriter Faith Nolan.

Love Makes a Family: Gay Parents in the 90's (USA, 1991) Produced by Remco Kobus, Marla Leech, and Daniel Veltri. 16 mins. [Fnlght] Introduces three families headed by gay parents who discuss the issues they have faced in forming families and raising children.

Love Thang Trilogy (USA, 1994) Mari Keiko Gonzalez. 12 mins. [C, F] Three sensual vignettes portraying aspects of Asian-Pacific lesbian lifestyles and concerns.

March in April (USA, 1994) Stephen Kinsella. 60 mins. [FR/I] A personal record of the 1993 March on Washington for Lesbian, Gay and Bi Equal Rights and Liberation.

The March on Washington (USA, 1993) Produced by John Scagliotti. 30 mins. [CG] Episode of the public TV series *In the Life*. Chronicles the April 1993 March on Washington for Lesbian, Gay and Bi Equal Rights and Liberation.

The March on Washington (USA, 1993) Produced by The Report. 15 mins. [Report] The religious right attempts to expose the liberal bias of the mainstream media by countering the local and national news coverage of the 1993 march on Washington with their own coverage of the event.

Massillon (USA, 1991) William Jones. 70 mins. [Drift] Recounts growing up gay in a small Ohio town through juxtaposition of autobiographical narration with lyrical shots of empty Midwestern landscapes.

Me and Rubyfruit (USA, 1989) Sadie Benning. 4 mins. [VDB, WMM] Chronicles the enchantment of teenage lesbian love and considers the taboo prospect of a female-to-female marriage.

Memory Pictures (GB, 1989) Pratibha Parmar. 24 mins. [F, WMM] Addresses racism and sexual identity through the story of gay Indian photographer Sunil Gupta, whose family migrated from Asia to Canada.

Metamorphosis: Man into Woman (USA, 1990) Lisa Leeman. 58 mins. [FLib] Documents the male-to-female transition of Gary into Gabi through sex-reassignment surgery. Raises questions regarding gender stereotypes and expectations.

Minoru & Me (GB, 1992) Toichi Nakata. 45 mins. In English and Japanese with English subtitles. [F] Self-reflexive real-life drama about the filmmaker and his houseguest Minoru. Nakata obsesses about portraying Minoru's cerebral palsy, while Minoru struggles with coming out.

A Moffie Called Simon (Canada, 1987) John Greyson. 15 mins. [F] Through dramatization, Greyson examines the events leading up to the jail term of black gay activist and South African student leader Simon Nkodi.

Moscow Does Not Believe in Queers (Canada, 1986) John Greyson. 27 mins. [VDB] Diary of ten days at the 1985 Moscow youth festival as an out-of-the-closet gay delegate.

A New Year (USA, 1989) Sadie Benning. 4 mins. [VDB, WMM] In a version of the "teenage diary," Benning places her feelings of confusion and depression alongside grisly tabloid headlines.

Nitrate Kisses (USA, 1992) Barbara Hammer. 67 mins. [F] Interrogates the erasure of lesbian and gay history. Uses explicit sexual scenes in exploring sexualities often marginalized within the gay and lesbian community — older lesbians, interracial couples, and S/M dykes.

No Need to Repent: The Ballad of Rev. Jan Griesinger (USA, 1989) Ann Alter. 27 mins. [WMM] Portrait of Jan Griesinger, an ordained minister in the United Church of Christ who came out as a lesbian at age thirty-five.

No Porque Lo Digas Fidel Castro (Not because Fidel Castro Says So) (USA/Cuba, 1988) Graciela I. Sanchez. 10 mins. In Spanish with English subtitles. [F] Insider's look at the situation for Cuban sexual minorities.

Non, je ne regrette rien (No regret) (USA, 1992) Marlon Riggs. 38 mins. [F, VDB] Intimate disclosures of five HIV-positive African-American gay men are intertwined with music and poetry to illuminate the difficulties they face in coping with the AIDS epidemic.

Not All Parents Are Straight (USA, 1986) Kevin White and Annamarie Faro. 58 mins. [CG] Examines the dynamics of the parent-child relationship within several households where children are being raised by gay and lesbian parents.

Not Just Passing Through (USA, 1994) Jean Carlomusto, Dolores Perez, Catherine Saalfield, and Polly Thistlethwaite. 54 mins. [WMM] Four-part document of lesbian history. Photographs and oral histories memorialize African-American lesbian Mabel Hampton, who was central to the founding of the Lesbian Herstory Archives. Part two records the story of the Lesbian Herstory Archives' rescue of Marge McDonald's diaries of lesbian life in the Midwest during the 1950s. The organization Asian Lesbians of the East Coast is the focus of the third section. The final part is a behind the scenes look at New York's WOW Cafe, a site for lesbian theater.

One Adventure (USA, 1972) Pat Rocco. 98 mins. [Ospkn] Eight members of the gay organization One, Inc. visit gay organizations in six European countries.

One Nation under God (USA, 1993) Teodoro Maniaci and Francine Rzeznik. 83 mins. [FR/I] A journey into the world of ex-gay ministries and conversion therapies. Features two former leaders of one of the biggest ex-gay ministries who renounce their homosexuality but then fall in love.

Orientations (Canada, 1984) Richard Fung. 56 mins. [TWN, VDB] More than a dozen Asian men and women speak about how being Asian and gay has shaped their lives.

Other Families (USA, 1993) Produced by Dorothy Chvatal. 49 mins. [Fnlght] Focuses on seven adults, ages eighteen to forty, who were raised by lesbian mothers.

Our House: Gays and Lesbians in the 'Hood (USA, 1992) Cyrille Phipps and Donna Golden. 30 mins. [TWN] Produced by Black Planet Productions as part of the Not Channel Zero television series. Examines homosexuality and sexual discrimination as they affect African-Americans.

Out in Silence (USA, 1994) Christine Choy. 30 mins. [FLib] Portrait of Vince,

a gay Asian-American who is HIV-positive. He performs with a gay theater group and lectures in an effort to educate Asian-Americans about AIDS.

Out in Suburbia (USA, 1989) Pam Walton. 28 mins. [FLib] Eleven lesbians discuss their daily lives and demonstrate that they lead "conventional" suburban lives.

Out in the Garden (USA, 1990) Vincent Grenier. 15 mins. [FCoop] Depicts the struggle of a gay man who tries to come to terms with the news that he is HIV-positive.

Out: Stories of Lesbian and Gay Youth (Canada, 1994) David Adkin. 43 mins. [FLib] Records the personal stories of gay and lesbian youth who come from diverse cultural and racial backgrounds.

"Out" Takes (USA, 1989) John Goss. 13 mins. [VDB] Juxtaposes scenes from *Pee Wee's Playhouse* and a popular Japanese children's show in a look at gay sensibility, homophobia, and gender roles on broadcast television.

Outcasts (Netherlands, 1991) Leigh B. Grode. 25 mins. [F] Integrates recreations of pre-Nazi lesbian nightlife, images of Nazi concentration camps, and portraits of lesbians of that era in an effort to tell the history of lesbians and gays under Germany's Third Reich.

OUTLAW (USA, 1994) Alisa Lebow. 26 mins. [WMM] Features Leslie Feinberg, a self-identified "gender outlaw" who confronts society's assumptions regarding gender. Feinberg, a lesbian who passes for a man, argues for the needs and rights of the transgendered community.

Outrage '69 (USA, 1995) Arthur Dong. 60 mins. [KQED] Examines the early history of the gay liberation movement, including looks at the Stonewall riots and Anita Bryant's 1977 anti-gay Save

Our Children campaign. See also *The Question of Equality*.

Paris Is Burning (USA, 1990) Jennie Livingston. 78 mins. [FInc] Focuses on voguing and the drag balls of Harlem. Deals with issues of race, class, gender, and sexuality through its look at black and Latino gay men who both emulate and parody high fashion.

Passion of Remembrance (GB, 1986) Maureen Blackwood and Isaac Julien. 80 mins. [TWN, WMM] Multilayered commentary on racism, sexism, homophobia, police brutality, and the decline of industrial society in Margaret Thatcher's England.

Pedagogue (GB, 1988) Stuart Marshall. 11 mins. [F, VDB] Parodies a documentary interview by subjecting a closeted British schoolteacher to intense questioning and camera voyeurism. Made in response to anti-gay legislation prohibiting public funding for the "promotion of homosexuality."

Pink Triangles (USA, 1982) Triangle Film Collective. 35 mins. [Cmbrdg] Chronicles the historical persecution of homosexuals from the Nazi and McCarthy eras to contemporary denouncements by the religious right.

A Place Called Lovely (USA, 1991) Sadie Benning. 14 mins. [VDB] References the types of violence individuals find in life by collecting images from a variety of sources including movies, tabloids, and children's games.

A Plague on You (GB, 1987) Produced by Lesbian and Gay Media Group. 58 mins. [F] Attacks the British government's first AIDS awareness advertisements.

P(l)ain Truth (Finland, 1993) Ilpo Pohjola. 15 mins. [Z] Portrays the feelings, memories, and thoughts of a female-to-male transsexual.

Positive (Germany/USA, 1990) Rosa von Praunheim. 80 mins. [FR/I] The second part of von Praunheim's AIDS trilogy chronicles the activism of New York's gay community in its fight against the epidemic. Special attention is given to the efforts of journalist/filmmaker Phil Zwickler, writer Larry Kramer, and singer/songwriter Michael Callen.

The Potluck and the Passion (USA, 1993) Cheryl Dunye. 30 mins. [F, TWN, VDB] Humorous "pseudodocumentary" that explores racial, sexual, and social politics through a look at a lesbian potluck dinner.

Privilege (USA, 1990) Yvonne Rainer. 103 mins. [Z] Tackles the taboo subject of menopause and female sexuality.

Queer Son (USA, 1993) Vickie Seitchik. 48 mins. [F] Portrait of parents coping with their children's gay or lesbian sexual orientation. Made by the mother of a gay man.

The Question of Equality (USA, 1995) Produced by David Meieran. 240 mins. [KQED] Four-part TV series exploring the efforts of lesbians and gay men to secure equal rights protections and live openly without fear of violence or discrimination. See also *Culture Wars, Generation Q, Hollow Liberty*, and *Outrage '69*.

Rage & Desire (GB, 1992) Rupert Gabriel. 17 mins. [F] Traces the life and work of black gay photographer Rotimi Fani-Koyode.

Rapture (USA, 1992) Sara Whiteley. 8 mins. [F] Portrays urban performers who hang weighted balls from temporary piercings in the skin and dance in ecstasy in an effort to cross the line between the physical and the spiritual realms.

Reframing AIDS (GB, 1988) Pratibha Parmar. 36 mins. [F] Examines the social and political problems that the AIDS epidemic has created for a multiracial range of lesbians and gay men.

Remembrance (USA, 1990) Jerry Tartaglia. 5 mins. [F] Mixes scenes from *All About Eve* with home movies to investigate the relationship between life and art.

Rules of the Road (USA, 1993) Su Friedrich. 31 mins. [WMM] Relates the demise of a lesbian relationship by focusing on one of the primary objects shared by the couple, a beige station wagon with fake wood paneling.

Running Gay (UK, 1991) Maya Chowdhry. 20 mins. [CG] A look at lesbian and gay athletes and the homophobia they face in the mainstream sports world. Documents the 1990 International Gay Games in Vancouver as an example of how lesbian and gay athletes are coping with discrimination.

Sacred Lies, Civil Truths (USA, 1993) Cyrille Phipps and Catherine Saalfield. 60 mins. [Grant] Produced in response to the 1992 anti-gay referenda in Oregon and Colorado. The first half studies the tactics used by the religious right. The second is an effort to counter homophobic propaganda by presenting a gay perspective on such issues as family values, religion, and gay youth.

The Salt Mines (USA, 1990) Susana Aikin and Carlos Aparicio. 47 mins. [TWN] Profiles the marginalized lives of Latino gay men and transvestites who live in the abandoned trucks of a New York Department of Sanitation depot.

Samuel and Samantha on "The Emancipation of All" (El Salvador, 1993) Jorge Lozano and Samuel Lopez. 23 mins. [TWN] Experiences of a Latino gay man, Samuel/Samantha, a Salvadoran college student and drag queen living in Toronto.

Sandra's Garden (Canada, 1991) Bonnie Dickie. 34 mins. [WMM] Story of Sandra, a lesbian who was sexually abused by her father and who has struggled to cope with the trauma of incest with the help and support of the women in her community.

Sandy and Madeleine's Family (USA, 1974) Sharrie Farrell, John Gordon Hill, and Peter M. Bruce. 30 mins. [MFI] Documents the 1972 court case in which lesbians Sandra Schuster and Madeleine Isaacson were sued by their husbands for child custody. The women were granted custody, but they were required to establish separate households.

School's Out: Lesbian and Gay Youth (USA, 1993) Ron Spalding. 30 mins. [CG] Examines the difficulties facing gay and lesbian teenagers and the emergence of new educational programs, such as New York City's Harvey Milk School, designed for them.

Seams (Brazil/USA, 1993) Karim Ainouz. 30 mins. In Portuguese with English subtitles. [F] Account of Brazil's social and sexual constraints for women and gay men, as seen through the eyes of the filmmaker's five elderly Brazilian great-aunts.

Seth's Aunts (USA, 1991) Nina Dabek. 3 mins. [F] Views a queer family from a child's point of view.

17 Rooms; or, What Do Lesbians Do in Bed? (GB, 1985) Caroline Sheldon. 9 mins. [WMM] Humorous short that addresses the befuddlement about lesbian sex.

Sex and Money (Holland, 1991) Produced by the Humanist League, Amsterdam. 50 mins. [FLib] Dr. John Money shares his ideas on gender identity in this look at transsexuality and sex-reassignment surgery.

Sex and the Sandinistas (GB, 1991) Lucinda Broadbent. 25 mins. In Spanish with English subtitles. [WMM] Nicaraguan gays and lesbians speak about their experiences as gay men and lesbians in Managua and their life after the insurrection.

Sex Is (USA, 1992) Marc Huestis and Lawrence Helman. 80 mins. [Osider] Combines interviews with explicit sex scenes to explore gay male sexuality.

She Don't Fade (USA, 1991) Cheryl Dunye. 24 mins. [TWN, VDB] Through a mix of documentary and fiction, this "Dunyementary" takes a self-reflexive look at the sexuality of a young black lesbian looking for love.

She Even Chewed Tobacco (USA, 1983) Liz Stevens and Estelle Freedman. 40 mins. [WMM] Originally a slide show, this video documents some of the extraordinary women of nineteenth-century California. Features historical portraits of women passing as men.

Sick (USA, 1986) Cecilia Dougherty. 5 mins. [F] Autobiographical monologue about chronic illness.

Silence = Death (West Germany/USA, 1990) Rosa von Praunheim. 60 mins. [FR/I] The art community's call to arms in the battle against AIDS and homophobia opens with a provocative performance piece by Emilio Cubiero and includes David Wojnarowicz, Keith Haring, and Allen Ginsberg.

Silent Pioneers (USA, 1984) Lucy Winer. 42 mins. [FLib] Recounts the lives of eight elderly gay men and lesbians who battled for survival over many decades and paved the way for younger generations of gays and lesbians.

Silverlake Life: The View from Here (USA, 1993) Tom Joslin and Peter Friedman. 99 mins. [Z] Powerful video diary records in graphic detail the daily struggles of Joslin and his companion, Mark Massi, in living with AIDS.

Sink or Swim (USA, 1990) Su Friedrich. 48 mins. [Drift, WMM] Autobiographical account of the highly charged relationship between father and daughter. Comprised of twenty-six short stories in which a girl remembers her father.

Sisters in the Life: First Love (USA, 1993) Yvonne Welbon. 30 mins. [TWN] A thirtysomething black lesbian recollects falling for her best friend in junior high school.

Snow Job: The Media Hysteria of AIDS (USA, 1986) Barbara Hammer. 10 mins. [F] Deconstructs the misrepresentation of AIDS in the popular press, where distortion amounts to a "snow job" promoting increased homophobia.

Spin Cycle (USA, 1991) Aarin Burch. 5 mins. [WMM] Autobiographical work in which a young African-American lesbian filmmaker ruminates about her craft and her relationships.

Splash (USA, 1991) Thomas Harris. 10 mins. [TWN, VDB] Explores the interplay between identity, fantasy, and the homosexual desire of preadolescence within the construction of black masculinity.

Sticks, Stones and Stereotypes (USA, 1988) Cindy Marshall. 31 mins. [Select] Addresses violence, racism, and homophobia in schools by intercutting theatrical skits and interviews with young people.

Stigmata: The Transfigured Body (USA, 1991) Leslie Asako Gladsjo. 27 mins. [WMM] Explores concepts of beauty, stereotypes of femininity, and female sexuality through a look at women engaged in body modification such as tat-tooing, cutting, piercing, and branding.

Stonewall: Twenty-Five Years of Deception (USA, 1994) Produced by The Report. 27 mins. [Report] An organizing tool of the religious right. Looks at the history of gay activism to uncover the "inner workings of homosexual organizations."

Stop the Church (USA, 1990) Robert Hilferty. 24 mins. [F] Hilferty's self-proclaimed indictment of the Catholic Church. Includes ACT UP's controversial 1989 demonstration against Cardinal John O'Connor at St. Patrick's Cathedral in New York City.

Storme: The Lady of the Jewel Box (USA, 1987) Michelle Parkerson. 21 mins. [WMM] A portrait of Storme De-Larverie, former master of ceremonies and male impersonator with the legendary Jewel Box Revue, America's first integrated female impersonation show.

Strip Jack Naked (GB, 1991) Ron Peck. 90 mins. [F] Starts as an account of the making of Peck's 1980 film *Nighthawks* and ends as a look back at growing up gay in London.

Superstar: The Life and Times of Andy Warhol (USA, 1991) Chuck Workman. 87 mins. [NY] A look at the life and art of Warhol, including speculations on his ambiguous sexuality.

Susana (USA/Argentina, 1980) Susana Blaustein. 25 mins. [WMM] Autobiographical portrait of Susana, who leaves her native Argentina to live as a lesbian outside the strictures of Latin American culture and family pressures.

Sync Touch (USA, 1981) Barbara Hammer. 12 mins. [WMM] Juxtaposes lesbian images with common clichés in a humorous inquiry into the nature of the lesbian aesthetic.

Teenage Homosexuality (USA, 1980) Produced by CBS News for *30 Minutes*. 11 mins. [Crsl] Five Houston teenagers discuss the difficulties of living closeted lives and of coming to terms with their sexuality.

Ten Cents a Dance (Parallax) (Canada, 1986) Midi Onodera. 30 mins. [WMM] Addresses sex, sexual identity, and the difficulties of communication. Features three couples (two women, two men, one man and one woman); each couple divided by a split screen.

Testing the Limits (USA, 1987) Produced by the Testing the Limits Collective. 30 mins. [TWN, VDB] Details the ways in which community activists, health care workers, drug rehabilitation counselors, and local political figures have waged war against AIDS.

Thank God I'm a Lesbian (Canada, 1992) Laurie Colbert and Dominique Cardona. 55 mins. [WMM] Uses interviews to explore the diversity of lesbian identities, examining issues such as coming out, racism, bisexuality, S/M, and outing.

Thank You and Goodnight (USA, 1990) Jan Oxenberg. 77 mins. [Gold, Wolfe] Dubbed a "docufantasy" by Oxenberg. Combines documentary footage and "fictional" scenes in a candid and moving account of the illness and death of Oxenberg's grandmother.

They Are Lost to Vision Altogether (USA, 1989) Tom Kalin. 10 mins. [Drift, VDB] An attempt to reclaim eroticism via sensual imagery in defiance of the Helms Amendment's refusal to fund explicit AIDS prevention information.

This Is Dedicated (GB, 1993) Produced by Alleycat Productions. 24 mins. [FLib] Portrait of three people who have lost a lesbian or gay partner to death.

This Is My Garden (USA, 1991) Alex Benedict. 26 mins. [FLib] Uses interviews and photographs to describe the emotional impact of AIDS on the lives of five men who recently lost their partners to the disease.

This Is Not an AIDS Advertisement (GB, 1988) Isaac Julien. 10 mins. [F] Shot on Super-8 in Venice and London, Julien's two-part meditation on the AIDS crisis reacts against homophobic and racist safe-sex ads while conveying this message: "Feel no shame in your desire."

The Ties That Bind (USA, 1984) Su Friedrich. 55 mins. [Drift, WMM] Friedrich presents her mother's life in Nazi Germany by juxtaposing images of her mother's daily activities with her voice-over narration of the stories of her past.

The Times of Harvey Milk (USA, 1984) Robert Epstein. 87 mins. [Oct] Charts the rising career and tragic murder of Harvey Milk, supervisor for the city of San Francisco and one of the nation's first openly gay elected officials.

Tiny and Ruby: Hell-Divin' Women (USA, 1988) Greta Schiller and Andrea Weiss. 30 mins. [CG, F] Portrait of an all-woman jazz band of the 1940s focusing on two band veterans, drummer Ruby Lucas and her longtime lover, jazz trumpeter Tiny Davis.

To My Women Friends (Russia/Germany, 1993) Natasha Sharandak. 64 mins. [F] Interviews six Russian lesbians about being a lesbian in the former Soviet Union under Article 121, which criminalizes homosexuality.

Toc Storee (USA, 1992) Ming-Yuen S. Ma. 22 mins. [C, TWN] Addresses issues of sexuality, subjectivity, tradition, and identity in Asian gay contexts.

Tongues Untied (USA, 1989) Marlon Riggs. 55 mins. [F] Through poetry, performance, and song, this video articulates the difficult position of African-American gay men silenced by the homophobia of black straight communities and made invisible by the racism of white gay communities.

Turnabout (USA, 1993) Dan Bessie. 58 mins. [FLib] Portrait of three men who mixed live cabaret with marionette shows in the Turnabout Theatre. Shows Harry Burnett, Forman Brown, and Roddy Brandon, who quietly cohabited, coming out in their eighties.

Two-Spirit People (USA, 1991) Lori Levy, Gretchen Vogel, and Michel Beauchemin. 20 mins. [F] Overview of historical and contemporary Native American concepts of gender, sexuality, and sexual orientation.

Until the Cure, I Offer the Care (USA, 1992) John Outcalt. 10 mins. [FLib] Portrait of Ron Mule, a gay Vietnam veteran, who works as a private-duty nurse for those with AIDS.

Urinal (Canada, 1989) John Greyson. 100 mins. [F] Mix of news and comic invention in which Eisenstein, Mishima, and others investigate the policing of public toilets in Ontario.

Variations on a Theme (USA, 1986) Dominic Cappello. 20 mins. [MFI] Produced by the National Sex Forum. Men and women discuss the social, psychological, and political ramifications of growing up gay and lesbian.

Video Album #5/The Thursday People (USA, 1987) George Kuchar. 60 mins. [VDB] Documents the daily life of the late underground filmmaker Curt McDowell.

Vital Signs (USA, 1991) Barbara Hammer. 10 mins. [F] Takes stock of humanity in the age of AIDS, as well as the filmmaker's own mortality.

Viva Eu! (Brazil, 1989) Tania Cypriano. 18 mins. [TWN] Tribute to artist Wilton Braga, one of the first people in Brazil to be diagnosed with AIDS.

Voguing: The Message (USA, 1989) David Bronstein, Dorothy Low, and Jack Walworth. 13 mins. [F] Traces the roots of voguing as a black and Latino gay dance form that appropriates and plays with poses and images from mainstream fashion.

Voices from the Front (USA, 1991) Sandra Elgear, Robyn Hutt, and David Meieran. 90 mins. [F] Produced by Testing the Limits collective. Documents AIDS activism of direct action groups such as ACT UP.

War on Lesbians (USA, 1992) Jane Cottis. 32 mins. [WMM] Critiques the invisibility of positive images of lesbians by intercutting a satirical look at supposed experts on sexuality with documentary interviews with lesbians.

We Are Family (USA, 1986) Dasal Banks. 57 mins. [FLib] Three families are profiled in this look at gay and lesbian parenting.

We Are Hablando (*Tenemos La Palabra*) (USA, 1990) Raul Ferrera-Balanquet. 15 mins. [LMVC] Experimental documentary offers a multilayered examination of personal, artistic, and global censorship.

Welcome to Normal (USA, 1989) Sadie Benning. 19 mins. [VDB, WMM] Reflects on being a tomboy and asks "What's the sense in life if you can't be who you are?"

West Coast Crones (USA, 1991) Madeline Muir. 28 mins. [F, Wolfe] Nine older lesbians, ages sixty-one to seventy-six, speak about their lives, their sexuality, internalized and external ageism, and the process of growing old.

Where Are We? (USA, 1992) Robert Epstein and Jeffrey Friedman. 73 mins. [TP] Two gay filmmakers record their travels through the rural South. Includes gay marines at Camp Lejeune.

Where There Was Silence (GB, 1988) Stephen Bourne. 20 mins. [F] Examines audience reaction to the 1961 British thriller *Victim*, a film dealing with homosexuality and blackmail.

Which Is Scary (USA, 1991) Paula Gauthier. 15 mins. [F] Seven individuals tell of their experiences encountering homophobia.

Who Happen to Be Gay (USA, 1979) Dale Beldin and Mark Krenzien. 23 mins. [Direct] Interviews with three lesbians and three gay men are combined with verité footage showing them at their jobs in this ABC-TV documentary.

Whoever Says the Truth Shall Die (Netherlands, 1981) Philo Bregstein. 60 mins. [Kino] Examines the life of director Pier Paolo Pasolini. Considers the possibility that Pasolini's death was politically motivated.

Witches and Faggots, Dykes and Poofters (Australia, 1980) One in Seven. 45 mins. [WMM] Documents the history of social and political oppression of lesbians and gay men in Australia.

Without You I'm Nothing (USA, 1990) John Boskovich. 90 mins. [Wolfe] Adapted from Sandra Bernhard's off-Broadway show. A comedy cabaret featuring singing, dancing, and jokes.

A Woman in My Platoon (Canada, 1989) Marilyn Burgess. 20 mins. [WMM] Looks at the experience of lesbians in the Canadian armed forces during World War II. Includes footage of a 1986 debate in the Canadian Parliament regarding discrimination against homosexuals.

Women I Love (USA, 1976) Barbara Hammer. 27 mins. [WMM] Combines footage shot over a five-year period in a collective portrayal of four of the filmmaker's lovers.

Women Like That (GB, 1991) Suzanne Neild. 25 mins. [WMM] A sequel to *Women Like Us* in which eight participants discuss their changed lives since the tape's popular broadcast in Great Britain.

Women Like Us (GB, 1989) Suzanne Neild. 49 mins. [WMM] Sixteen lesbians, ages fifty to eightysomething, tell about their lives from the 1920s to the present.

Women of Gold (USA, 1990) Eileen Lee and Marilyn Abbink. 30 mins. [WMM] Eight Asian-Pacific lesbians who participated in the 1990 Gay Games express their passion for women and sports and share their impressions of growing up female and gay in Asian-American families.

Word Is Out (USA, 1977) Mariposa Film Group (Peter Adair, Nancy Adair, Andrew Brown, Robert Epstein, Lucy Massie Phenix, and Veronica Selver). 130 mins. [NY] In a collage of interviews, gay men and lesbians of varied ages, class identities, professions, and lifestyles speak openly of their childhoods, their first loves, and their often painful road to self-acceptance.

The World Is Sick (sic) (Canada, 1989) John Greyson. 38 mins. [VDB] Documents the events of the 1989 International AIDS Conference in Montreal.

World of Light: A Portrait of May Sarton (USA, 1979) Marita Simpson and Martha Wheelock. 30 mins. [Wolfe] Biography of lesbian poet and writer May Sarton. Includes footage of Sarton reading from her poetry and novels.

▶

Distributors

[C] CrossCurrent Media
346 Ninth Street, 2nd Floor
San Francisco, CA 94103
(415) 552-9550

[Canyon] Canyon Cinema
2325 Third Street, Suite 338
San Francisco, CA 94107
(415) 626-2255

[CG] The Cinema Guild
1697 Broadway, Suite 506
New York, NY 10019-5904
(212) 246-5522

[Cmbrdg] Cambridge Documentary Films
P.O. Box 385
Cambridge, MA 02139
(617) 354-3677

[CN] California Newsreel
149 Ninth Street, Suite 420
San Francisco, CA 94103
(415) 621-6196

[Crsl] Carousel Films
260 Fifth Avenue, Room 705
New York, NY 10001
(212) 683-1660

[Direct] Direct Cinema Limited
P.O. Box 10003
Santa Monica, CA 90410
(800) 525-0000

[Drift] Drift Production and Distribution
709 Carroll Street, #3R
Brooklyn, NY 11215
(718) 857-4885

[EAI] Electronic Arts Intermix
536 Broadway, 9th Floor
New York, NY 10012
(212) 966-4605

[EVC] Educational Video Center
60 East 13th Street, 4th Floor
New York, NY 10003
(212) 254-2848

[F] Frameline
346 Ninth Street
San Francisco, CA 94103
(415) 703-8654

[FCoop] Filmmakers Cooperative
175 Lexington Avenue
New York, NY 10016
(212) 889-3820

[FInc] Films Incorporated
5547 North Ravenswood Avenue
Chicago, IL 60640-1199
(800) 323-4222

[FLib] Filmakers Library
124 East 40th Street, Suite 901
New York, NY 10016
(212) 808-4980

[Fnlght] Fanlight Productions
47 Halifax Street
Boston, MA 02130
(617) 524-0980

[FR/I] First Run/Icarus Films
153 Waverly Place, 6th Floor
New York, NY 10014
(212) 727-1711

[GMHC] GMHC
129 West 20th Street
New York, NY 10011
(212) 337-1950

[Gold] The Samuel Goldwyn Company
10203 Santa Monica Boulevard
Los Angeles, CA 90067
(310) 284-9278

[Grant] Maria Elena Grant
c/o Lavender Light Gospel Choir
70-A Greenwich Avenue, #315
New York, NY 10011

[Kino] Kino International
333 West 39th Street, Suite 503
New York, NY 10018
(212) 629-6880

[KQED] KQED, San Francisco
(800) 358-3000

[Ladysl] Ladyslipper
613 Vickers Avenue
Durham, NC 27701
(800) 634-6044

[LMVC] Latino Midwest Video
Collective
P.O. Box 47343
Chicago, IL 60647
(312) 342-6047

[MFI] Multi-Focus, Inc.
1525 Franklin Street
San Francisco, CA 94109-4592
(800) 821-0514

[Milest] Milestone Film & Video
275 West 96th Street, Suite 28-C
New York, NY 10025
(212) 855-7449

[Mystic] Mystic Fire Video
P.O. Box 422
Prince Street Station
New York, NY 10012
(800) 999-1319

[Noon] Noon Pictures
611 Broadway, Room 742
New York, NY 10012
(212) 254-4118

[NY] New Yorker Films
16 West 61st Street
New York, NY 10023
(212) 247-6110

[Oct] October Films
630 Fifth Avenue, 30th Floor
New York, NY 10111
(800) 628-6237

[Osider] Outsider Productions
2940 16th Street, Suite 200-1
San Francisco, CA 94103
(415) 863-0611

[Ospkn] Outspoken Productions
1725 West Catalpa Avenue, 3rd Floor
Chicago, IL 60640
(312) 878-9282

[PBS] PBS Video
1320 Braddock Place
Alexandria, VA 22314-1698
(800) 344-3337

[Report] The Report
42640 10th Street West
Lancaster, CA 93534
(800) 462-4700

[Saland] Eugene Salandra
(212) 260-0738

[Select] Select Media
225 Lafayette, Suite 1102
New York, NY 10012
(212) 431-8923

[TP] Telling Pictures
347 Dolores Street, #307
San Francisco, CA 94110
(415) 864-6714

[TWN] Third World Newsreel
335 West 38th Street, 5th Floor
New York, NY 10018
(212) 947-9277

[VDB] Video Data Bank
37 South Wabash Avenue
Chicago, IL 60603
(312) 899-5172

[WMM] Women Make Movies
462 Broadway, Suite 500-C
New York, NY 10013
(212) 925-0606

[Wolfe] Wolfe Video
P.O. Box 64
New Almaden, CA 95042
(800) 642-5247

[Z] Zeitgeist Films
247 Centre Street, 2nd Floor
New York, NY 10013
(212) 274-1989

Contributors

CHRIS CAGLE is a graduate student in English at Brown University working in film studies and queer theory. He also has contributed to a forthcoming anthology of bisexual theory entitled *RePresenting Bisexualities*.

LINDA DITTMAR is a professor of English at the University of Massachusetts at Boston, where she teaches film through the English department, women's studies, and American studies. She is coeditor of two anthologies, *From Hanoi to Hollywood: The Vietnam War in American Film* (1990) and *Multiple Voices in Feminist Film Criticism* (1994), and has published numerous essays in the areas of film, literature, and pedagogy in a variety of anthologies and journals, including *Wide Angle, Iris, boundary 2, Mosaic, Novel,* and *Radical Teacher*.

CYNTHIA FUCHS is an associate professor of English and Film & Media Studies at George Mason University in Virginia. She has recently published articles on Michael Jackson, cyborgs in U.S. popular culture, and The Artist Formerly Known as Prince.

LYNDA GOLDSTEIN teaches in the English department and the Women's studies program in the Commonwealth College of Penn State University. She writes on the politics of identity and representation in popular culture.

RONALD GREGG is a film historian who was an activist against anti-gay campaigns in Oregon and Missouri. Now living in Chicago, he has a Ph.D. from the University of Oregon and is writing a book on the influence of the gay male subculture on film content, star construction, and censorship in 1930s Hollywood.

CHRIS HOLMLUND is an associate professor at the University of Tennessee at Knoxville, where she teaches film, women's studies, French literature, and critical theory. Her essays on mainstream, independent, and experimental film and video and French feminist theory have appeared in a number of anthologies and journals, including *Screen, Cinema Journal, Feminist Studies, Camera Obscura, New Formations, Jump Cut,* and *Discourse.*

JANET JAKOBSEN is an assistant professor of women's studies and religious studies, a founding member of the Committee for Lesbian, Gay, and Bisexual Studies, and cofounder of the "Lesbian Looks" and "Queer Looks" film and video series at the University of Arizona. She has worked as a policy analyst, lobbyist, and organizer in Washington, D.C. Her recent publications include articles in journals such as *Hypatia: Journal of Feminist Philosophy* and the *Journal of Feminist Studies in Religion,* as well as in the anthology edited by Annette Kuhn, *Queen of the Bs: Ida Lupino behind the Camera.* Her book *Working Alliances: Diversity and Complexity in Feminist Ethics* is forthcoming.

LYNDA McAFEE is the former film/video historian at the Donnell Media Center of the New York Public Library, where she programmed film and video and participated in collection development. She has a degree in film studies from the University of California, Santa Barbara, and has done graduate work in the cinema studies department at New York University. She is currently completing a master's degree in library and information science.

KATHLEEN McHUGH is an assistant professor of comparative literature in the Department of Literatures and Languages at the University of California at Riverside. She serves as chair of the Film and Visual Culture Program, which she helped to found. She has published articles on film and feminist theory in journals including *Screen, Jump Cut,* and *Semiotica.* She is currently completing a manuscript entitled *Swept Away: The Uses and Abuses of Domesticity* on images of the home and modern constructions of femininity.

BEVERLY SECKINGER is assistant professor in the Department of Media Arts at the University of Arizona, where she also directs the Lesbian Looks Film and Video Series. Her videotapes include *Alice Unplugged* (1996, codirected with Joyan Saunders), a pair of provocative infomercials on lesbian life in the nineties; *Bottoms Up* (1996, codirected with Joyan Saunders), an experimental narrative comedy about a TV sex therapist and a riot grrrl ingenue with a camcorder; *Planet in My Pocket* (1995), a mixed-genre satire of consumer multiculturalism; and *Letter from Morocco* (1991), a personal documentary about neocolonial relations. Her work has been screened at the Big Muddy Film Festival, the Athens International Film and Video Festival, the W.O.W. Cafe and the Knitting Factory in New York City, the Minnesota Film and Video Expo, and the Center on Contemporary Art in Seattle. She is currently completing *Mommie Queerest,* a comic video about mother-daughter conflicts over gender socialization.

MARC SIEGEL is a graduate student in critical studies at UCLA's School of Theater, Film, and Television.

CHRIS STRAAYER is an associate professor of cinema studies at New York University and the author of *Deviant Eyes, Deviant Bodies: Sexual Re-Orientations in Film and Video* (1996).

ERIKA SUDERBURG is a multimedia artist and critic who works in photography, film, video, and installation. Her work has been exhibited internationally at various institutions including Capp Street Projects in San Francisco, the American Film Institute, the Museum of Modern Art in New York, Pacific Film Archives in Berkeley, Millennium Film Workshop in New York, the Kitchen in New York, Kunstlerhaus in Stuttgart, and Grazer Kunstverein in Austria. She has been on the faculty of the California Institute of the Arts, Art Center College of Design in Pasadena, and Otis College of Art in Los Angeles. She is currently associate professor of art at the University of California, Riverside. Suderburg is coeditor, with Michael Renov, of *Resolutions: Contemporary Video Practices* (Minnesota, 1996).

THOMAS WAUGH is a professor of cinema at Concordia University in Montreal, where he has taught film studies since 1976. In the past decade he has also taught interdisciplinary courses based on sexual representation, lesbian and gay cinema, and AIDS. In addition to publishing many articles in periodicals ranging from *The Body Politic* to *Jump Cut* and *Cineaction!*, he edited *"Show Us Life": Toward a History and Aesthetics of the Committed Documentary* (1984) and is the author of *Hard to Imagine: Gay Male Eroticism in Photography and Film from their Beginnings to Stonewall* (1996).

JUSTIN WYATT is an associate professor of radio, television, and film at the University of North Texas. He is the author of *High Concept: Movies and Marketing in Hollywood* (1994) and a contributing editor of *Detour* magazine. He is currently completing a manuscript on the aesthetics and reception of Todd Haynes's *Poison.*

Index